SEAN O'CASEY

THE MAN AND HIS WORK

DAVID KRAUSE

Sean O'Casey

THE MAN AND HIS WORK

AN ENLARGED EDITION

MACMILLAN PUBLISHING CO., INC.
NEW YORK
COLLIER MACMILLAN PUBLISHERS
LONDON

Macmillan Publishing Co., Inc.
866 Third Avenue, New York, N.Y. 10022
Collier-Macmillan Canada Ltd.

Library of Congress Cataloging in
Publication Data

Krause, David
  Sean O'Casey: the man and his work.

  Includes bibliographical references.
  1. O'Casey, Sean, 1880-1964.
PR6029.C33Z68   1975   822'.9'12   74-11129
ISBN 0-02-566640-1

First Printing 1975
Printed in the United States of America

To My Mother and Father

CONTENTS

PREFACE

THE record of Sean O'Casey's life and work is made up of a series of notable battles. Out of these struggles he has emerged as a controversial and alienated figure, yet in the fighting he invariably raised some of the crucial issues of our time. On what terms must a man live? On what terms must an artist write? O'Casey has been defining and defending his terms all his life, following his own vision of the truth with the tenacious integrity of a man totally committed to the art of life and the life of art.

In writing this book I set out to recreate and evaluate those events and battles which shaped his life and inspired his dramatic genius; and in analysing his plays it has been my purpose to discover what he was aiming at and what methods he used to achieve his ends. Each chapter is organized around a central theme. The first chapter is rooted in O'Casey's Dublin, its economic, political, and religious tensions. The following chapters move on to a consideration of: the genre of tragi-comedy and the first three plays; the Abbey Theatre's controversial rejection of *The Silver Tassie* and the function of 'ideas' in the drama; the 'prophetic' plays in relation to morality and entertainment; the comic fantasies as a criticism and a celebration of life; the sources and poetic values of the O'Casey language; the Autobiography as a work of art and a revelation of the artist, with a conclusion on the aesthetic and ethical impulses that have dominated his life and work. As an aid to the reader who wishes to make a further investigation into these subjects, I have included background material and bibliographical references in the extensive Notes. I have not attempted to write a biography, for O'Casey, though now in his eightieth year, is still writing and still fighting.

This book could not have been written without the generous help of two grants from the Howard Foundation and the American Philosophical Society, which gave me the opportunity to gather material and do the actual writing during a year and a summer in Dublin. Part of the third chapter, 'The Playwright's Not For Burning,' appeared in *The Virginia Quarterly*, Winter 1958, and I am grateful to the editor for permitting me to use it here in a

revised and expanded version. I should like to make acknowledge-
ments also to Messrs Macmillan & Co. for their generous per-
mission to quote from the Plays and Autobiography of Sean
O'Casey; to the same publishing house and to Messrs A. P. Watt
& Son for several quotations from works by W. B. Yeats. The
Society of Authors kindly allowed me to include passages from the
work of G. B. Shaw and I am grateful to Messrs Faber & Faber
Ltd. for permission to make quotations from the writings of
T. S. Eliot, O.M.

I am also deeply indebted to Mr and Mrs James Plunkett for
their invaluable comments and friendship; Professor David H.
Greene for his wise counsel through the years and for suggesting
significant improvements in the manuscript; Professor Edwin
Honig for reading the manuscript and suggesting a number of
important revisions; Mr Timothy O'Keeffe for his editorial work
and wisdom, and his faith in the book; Dr H. A. Pogorzelski for
his valuable editorial advice and help in preparing the Index; Dr
Emmet Larkin for his extremely useful suggestions and for allow-
ing me to read part of the manuscript of his forthcoming book on
Jim Larkin; Dr Richard J. Hayes, Director of the National
Library, Dublin, and his very co-operative staff, particularly Mr
Alf MacLochlainn, Mr Thomas O'Neill, and Mr Michael Breen;
Mr George Byrne, Librarian of the Pearse Street Public Library,
Dublin; Mr and Mrs Sean O'Casey for their friendly help and
encouragement. It would be impossible to list all the people who
have aided me in my work and given me various kinds of informa-
tion about O'Casey and Dublin, but I would like to express my
gratitude to the following: Mr and Mrs John Edward Beaver, Mr
Ernest Blythe, Mr Frank Cahill, Mr and Mrs Jack Carney, Mr
Barney Conway, Mrs Kathleen Corcoran, Mr Fergus Corcoran,
Mr and Mrs Cyril Cusack, Mr Gabriel Fallon, Mr Eric Gorman,
Mr Jack Hanratty, Mrs Katie Kenna, Mr James Larkin Jr., Mr
Francis MacManus, Miss Ria Mooney, Mr Angus O'Daly, Mr
Michael O hAodha, Mr Joseph O'Rourke, Dr Lennox Robinson,
Mr and Mrs Alan Simpson, Mr Seamus Scully.

I must finally point out that while all these people have kindly
helped me in my work, they are not responsible for the views I
have expressed.

D. K.

August 1959
Dublin

PREFACE TO THE SECOND EDITION

◄◄◆►►◄◆◆►►◄◆◆►►◄◆◆►►◄◆◆►►◄◆◆►►◄◆◆►►◄◆◆►►◄◆◆►►◄◆◆►►◄◆◆►►

In 1958 when I was on my way to Ireland to write this book, I stopped in to see O'Casey at his home in Devon, as I had done each summer since 1954 when we first met, and I asked him if he could give me any special aid or advice. 'Only some nonadvice,' he said, 'that you go off and write your own bloody book. Don't listen to the criticonians, and for God's sake don't listen to me on O'Casey, just say what you have to say and stand by it.'

I thanked him and said I planned to find a quiet cottage in the Wicklow mountains where I could think and write. He laughed. 'Maybe you do need one bit of advice from the old crow,' he said. 'You won't get to know me or my plays sitting silent on a mountain in Wicklow. Is it the song of Synge or the caw of O'Casey you're looking for? No, you'll have to go down into the clatter of Dublin town for the rough and ready likes of me. Dublin's your only man.'

So I went off and wrote the book in Dublin, on the clattering northside of the city, O'Casey's rough and ready Dublin. Now, fifteen years later, I like to believe that I wrote my own bloody book, that in spite of the 'criticonians' I said what I wanted to say and I'll stand by it. But if I were writing it at the present time, I think I would try to organize the book around O'Casey's comic genius, the sources and strategies of laughter in his work, because I believe they reflect his greatest gift. Even his tragi-comic vision, which I had previously identified as his finest achievement, is controlled by the comic not the tragic impulse in his art. I would have to grant that his noncomic and lyrical achievements are also impressive, but I suspect that his failures are more likely to occur when he upstages his low comic muse. The rough and ready comic caw of the Green Crow is his only man.

Above all it is the knockabout comedy of O'Casey that interests me now: the comic fall or redemptive pratfall of man, the comic profanation of what has become too sacred, the comic *non serviam*, the varieties of antic laughter that reveal him at the peak of his dramatic power. This belief has prompted me to add a new chapter for this edition, 'A Final Knock at O'Casey's Door.' The chapter is loosely controlled by the metaphor of a comic knock, and it is divided into two parts—one on his life as I knew it: 'Sean O'Casey, 1880–1964: The Man Remembered'; the other a reassessment of his plays: 'Master of Knockabout: The Work Revisited.'

When O'Casey died in 1964, the editors of the *Massachusetts Review* asked me to write a memorial essay, which appeared in the Winter–Spring 1965 issue of the magazine, and I am grateful to the editors for allowing me to use that essay here as the first part of my new chapter. It represents a summing up of all my personal memories of the man as I had known him over the last ten years of his life, from 1954 to 1964. The second part of this chapter contains my most recent thoughts about Casey's unique contribution to the tradition of antic comedy in modern drama, my knock of recognition, and I'll have to stand by it.

D. K.

May 1974
Providence

SEAN O'CASEY

THE MAN AND HIS WORK

CHAPTER I

Prometheus of Dublin

Damn braces. Bless relaxes.
Blake's 'Marriage of Heaven and Hell'

Go, traveller,
And imitate, if you can,
One who played a man's part
In defence of Liberty.
Swift's 'Epitaph'

Neither to change, nor falter, nor repent;
This, like thy glory, Titan, is to be
Good, great and joyous, beautiful and free.
Shelley's 'Prometheus Unbound'

I. THE INFERNO OF HIS DISCONTENT

SEAN O'CASEY was born in Dublin on 30 March 1880,[1] at 85 Upper Dorset Street, a short distance from the house on Lower Dorset Street where the dramatist Sheridan had been born, and just around the corner from 7 Eccles Street where Joyce's Leopold Bloom had lived. He was christened John and his surname was Casey, but in his twenties when he learned the Irish language and turned his interests to the cause of Irish freedom he gaelicized his name to Sean O'Cathasaigh, later anglicizing the surname to O'Casey when the Abbey Theatre accepted his first play. John Casey was the last of thirteen children, eight of whom had already died in infancy, mostly of the croup, a type of diphtheria prevalent in the poorer families, born to Michael and Susan Casey. The mother and father were both in their forties when John arrived to join three brothers and a sister as the only children who were to grow to adulthood.

The Caseys were Protestants in predominantly Catholic Dublin,

1

although Michael, originally from Limerick, was the son of a
mixed marriage, a Catholic father and Protestant mother. When
his father, a farmer, died at an early age, Michael's mother reared
him, her last-born and favourite child, in her own Protestant
faith, while the rest of the children remained devout Catholics.
But the religious tensions in the family regularly led to violent
quarrels, and when his mother died Michael, outnumbered and
out of sympathy with the others, turned his back on them and
Limerick and went to live in Dublin. John inherited his father's
independent traits, and later in life also developed his father's
antagonism toward pietistic Catholicism. Like his father he eventually turned his back on the city of his birth, to a large degree but
not entirely due to his reaction against religious cant. Actually, the
religion into which O'Casey was born was in itself an alienating
factor, when one considers what it meant to be poor and Protestant in 1880 in a city of 250,000 people where eighty per cent of
the population was Roman Catholic and predominantly poor, and
most of the Protestant minority was prosperous or titled Anglo-
Irish.

In Dublin the vigorously Protestant Michael Casey fell in love
with a devout and gentle young Protestant girl from Wicklow
named Susan Archer, and in 1863 they were married. Michael
earned his living as a commercial clerk, and for some years he
worked for the Irish Church Mission, a proselytizing Protestant
organization which would only have employed men who were
dedicated to the unenviable cause of 'Souperism'—as it was called
by the Catholics who had been offered free soup and Protestant
salvation during the Great Potato Famine of 1845–7. Thus,
Michael's strong religious convictions led him to work for the
I.C.M. at a much lower salary then he could have earned in the commercial world. With his modest salary he just managed to get by,
raising a large family and living in the poorer section of the city.
But he died suddenly of a spinal injury at the age of forty-nine, and
thereafter his wife and her five surviving children were gradually
reduced to the poverty and hardship of tenement life. And for the
youngest child, who was six years old when his father died, the
squalor of the tenements was to become the crucial experience of
his life. For children especially, the Dublin slums too often turned
out to be a graveyard.

Infectious diseases and malnutrition were the chief causes of the abnormally high infant mortality-rate in Dublin in the late nineteenth century—higher than in the Moscow of the Tsars or the Calcutta of plagues and cholera—and the sickly little Johnny had contracted a chronic eye disease which plunged him into a frightening world of pain and semi-darkness. A filmy membrane had formed over his weak and infected eyes, and the left eye was damaged by an ulcerated cornea. This meant endless trips to the hospital for drops, ointments, bandages, and hot and cold water soakings; and it meant that the half-blind boy, forced to avoid the sun and all forms of strong light, spent much of his time hiding and moaning in dark corners, not too difficult to find among the dirty tenements and alleyways of north Dublin.

Those early years of pain and isolation left deep scars on the mind and body of the young O'Casey, but they were only a prelude to the years of deprivation and bitterness that awaited him in young manhood. Those tragic years were in large measure a part of the tragedy of Irish history. For Ireland at the turn of the century was an impoverished agrarian country, reduced to economic and political impotence by seven hundred years of British misrule, and by the accident of geography which gave her a rough island climate of heavy mists and rains. It was a time of great political as well as economic unrest, and there was not much relief forthcoming from the parliamentary struggle for Home Rule or from the internal feuds and 'betrayals' of Irishmen by Irishmen. O'Casey was only eleven years old when Ireland's 'Uncrowned King', the martyred Parnell, was 'betrayed and hounded' into an early grave by his own countrymen—although Gladstone and the English Non-Conformists were as determined to renounce him after the disclosure of his relationship with Mrs O'Shea as were the Roman Catholic Bishops in Ireland. But young as he was, the tragic image of the alienated and fallen Chief was to become for him, as it was for so many Irishmen, a symbol of his own frustrations in the country which he loved and eventually left in self-exile. Like the young Stephen Dedalus, listening to the bitter quarrels over Parnell at the Christmas dinner, the young O'Casey would always remember the anguished laments for 'Poor Parnell! My dead King!'

There was, however, another controversial Chief who played a dominant role in modern Irish history and had an even stronger influence on O'Casey early in the twentieth century—and he was the labour leader Jim Larkin, the 'Uncrowned King' of the Dublin working people. The revolutionary Larkin, enraged by the miseries of the exploited poor, fierce in his principles and herculean in his street-corner oratory, came to the suffering city to launch a fight for improved living standards by preaching what he called 'the divine mission of discontent'—a phrase that was to become significant for O'Casey's own career.

It is not too difficult to trace the major causes of this discontent in Dublin. *The Medical Press*, an objective and even conservative journal of medicine, often ran editorials and leading articles protesting against the abnormally high mortality-rate, which it directly attributed to the fact that the chief victims, the working people, lived a near-starvation existence in disease-ridden, overcrowded slum tenements. Early in 1880, the year of O'Casey's birth, the death-rate in Dublin was 44·8 in every 1000 of the population, in comparison with 27·1 in London, and *The Medical Press* commented: 'Upon comparison with English, European, and Asiatic cities it appears that Dublin out-strips the world in its unhealthiness—calculating upon this week, which is by no means exceptionally bad. Excepting Plymouth, the worst record of the week in England is that of Liverpool, 36·0, while that of Dublin is 44·8. Calcutta shows for 37·0 and Alexandria 40·0; but no other city—no matter where situated—approaches Dublin in unhealthiness.'[2] In order to gain some perspective of what these appalling figures meant, they should be contrasted with the death-rate in Dublin City for the first quarter of 1958 which was 12·5 per 1000 of the population. When one considers this terrifying situation, it may be apparent why eight of O'Casey's brothers and sisters born before 1880 had died of infant diseases. The wonder is that, sickly as he was, he himself managed to survive at all.

In January 1890 the death-rate was 44·2, largely due to the high incidence of respiratory diseases in children. And when in January 1900 it rose to 46·0, *The Medical Press* came out with a blasting editorial which it titled, 'The Dublin Holocaust'. It identified tenement conditions as the main cause of tragic 'holocaust':

The mortality-rate of Dublin City has reached the awful proportion of 46·0 per 1000, while in English cities it is 18·0 or 19·0 . . . The 'tenement' house has been marked down by two Commissions of Inquiry and by common consent of every critic as the *fons et origo mali*. These

habitations of the Dublin poor are, in the majority of cases, the dilapi-
dated wrecks of the mansions of nobility and gentry, and their aristocratic dependents, who kept state and squandered their patrimonies in
Dublin in the time of the Georges, and these mansions, for the past
hundred years, since the Union, have been abandoned and crumbling
to ruin. The remaining shells of houses are bought for a nominal sum
by speculators and let out to the poor at a profit before which the
income of the mines of Golconda or the dividend on Guinness's
brewery are as nothing. [3]

But this scathing indictment had no effect on the city officials or
the Irish landlords, and nothing was done about these death-trap
tenements until Jim Larkin came to Dublin in 1908. It was not
until after the 1913 General Strike and Lock-Out, which was a result of Larkin's attempt to organize the working class of Dublin in
a battle for improved living conditions, that the first step toward
direct action was taken. The strike led to the establishment of a
Government Housing Commission in November 1913, and in the
following year the Commission published the findings of its extensive inquiry in a 433-page report of minutes of evidence, charts,
appendices, and 51 photographs of typical tenement and street
scenes. This massive document revealed that 25,822 families of
87,305 people, or almost one-third of the population of Dublin,
lived in 5,322 tenement houses, the majority of which were declared to be unfit for human habitation. And 20,118 of these
families, or seventy eight per cent of the people in the tenements,
lived in one-room dwellings.

All the functions of life from birth to death were carried on in
one room. Many tenements with seven or eight rooms, which when
the houses were built in the eighteenth century had accommodated
a single family, now had a large family in each room with an
average of over 50 people in a house; there were also instances of
houses bulging with as many as 73, 74, and 98 people. And yet
there were many people who could not even afford to live in these
hovels, for over 30,000 of the 305,000 population of the city were
being evicted yearly because they were unable to pay the rent.
Generally the only water supply for a house was furnished by a
single water tap in the yard. The water closet, usually in a state of
disrepair, was also in the yard, or where there was no yard, in a
dark and rat-infested basement. The Commissioners not only

heard evidence but made many personal investigations, and here is one characteristic example of their discoveries: 'Having visited a large number of these houses in all parts of the city, we have no hesitation in saying that it is no uncommon thing to find halls and landings, yards and closets of the houses in a filthy condition, and in nearly every case human excreta is to be found scattered about the yards and on the floors of the closets and in some cases even in the passages of the house itself'.[4] Many years later O'Casey recalled his life in the tenements and described a similar scene:

Then, where we lived, with thousands of others, the garbage of the ashpit with the filth from the jakes was tumbled into big wicker baskets that were carried on the backs of men whose clothing had been soaked in the filth from a hundred homes; carried out from the tiny back yards, through the kitchen living-room, out by the hall, dumped in a horrid heap on the street outside, and left there, streaming out stench and venom, for a day, for two days, maybe for three, till open carts, sodden as the men who led the sodden horses, came to take the steaming mass away, leaving an odour in the narrow street that lingered till the wind and the rain carried trace and memory far into outer space or into the heaving sea. Hardly a one is left living now to remember how this was done, or the work remaining behind for the women to purify hall and kitchen so that the feet felt no crunching of the filth beneath them, and the sour and suffocating smell no longer blenched the nostrils.[5]

All this testimony indicates that these miserable hovels bred little beyond foul stenches, rats the size of large kittens, and an alarming rate of fatal typhoid, enteric fever, and tuberculosis in children. There were innumerable cases of food adulteration and poisoning, and in one instance a dairy was situated next to a cellar polluted with human excreta and huge rats.

Working conditions were no better than the housing. More than half of the population of the city, 169,736 out of 305,000, had been classified under the heading of 'Indefinite and unproductive class'. In the 'Unskilled labour class' there were 45,159 people, or about one-seventh of the population. The average wage for men was 14 shillings for a week of 70 hours; and women worked in some cases as many as 90 hours for anywhere between 5 and 10 shillings a week. Steady employment in the city was to be found in prostitution, a thriving and wide-open tourist industry that was in evidence on most of the main streets. The lower class Dubliners had little to look forward to beyond disease, drunkenness, and death. Commenting on the 'putrid slums of Dublin' before a Board of Trade inquiry into the cause of the 1913 strike, Jim Larkin testified: 'Why, in Mountjoy Prison there was better accommodation. He had the honour of being there a few times (laughter), and by the way, it was the criminals who were outside, men who carry on a system of brutality and despotism—Christian gentlemen, so-called; and there were the men who denied the right of the working men to combine for the protection of their interests; men and women were brutally murdered under the capitalist system. Such things were happening in Dublin—the greatest Church-going city, he believed, in the world.'[6]

And all this is but a fraction of the overwhelming evidence, a very short view of the state of Dublin at the turn of the century. About the same time that the British Government commissioned its Housing inquiry, late in 1913, the Federated Employers of Dublin commissioned an Englishman named Arnold Wright to present the employers' side of the strike. The resulting book, *Disturbed Dublin*, is mainly an apologia and a calculated attack on 'Larkinism', but even Mr Wright had to acknowledge the brutal facts of lower-class life in the city, and at one point he observed: 'The Dublin slum is a thing apart in the inferno of social degradation. Nowhere can there be found concentrated so many of the evils which are associated with the underworld of our modern civilization. To say that the men and women live like beasts of the field is the merest truth.'[7]

This was O'Casey's Dublin. This was the inferno of his discontent. It was a city in which nearly one-third of the people lived in outrageous conditions of filth, slavery, fear, and ignorance. These conditions left deep scars on the body and mind of the young O'Casey which he was never to forget. Dublin at the turn of the twentieth century must have been for him something like the London that Blake saw at the turn of the nineteenth century:

> *I wander thro' each charter'd street*
> *Near where the charter'd Thames does flow,*
> *And mark in every face I meet*
> *Marks of weakness, marks of woe.*

In every cry of every Man,
In every Infant's cry of fear,
In every voice, in every ban,
The mind-forg'd manacles I hear.

O'Casey's Dublin was not unlike the oppressed Dublin to which Swift had come in 1713 as Dean of St. Patrick's Cathedral; it was not unlike the Dublin to which Shelley had come in 1812 to hand out copies of his revolutionary *Address to the Irish People* on street corners. After two centuries life was still an inferno for the wretched Dublin masses. Swift might well have been passing his 'savage indignation' on to men like Larkin and O'Casey when, after thirty-two years of observing and writing about the hopelessly destitute and enslaved Dubliners of his time, he wrote the bitter and challenging Epitaph for his tomb in St. Patrick's Cathedral:

Here lies the Body of
Jonathan Swift, s.t.d.
For thirty years Dean
Of this Cathedral.
Where savage indignation
Can no longer gnaw his Heart.
Go, traveller, and imitate, if you can,
One who played a man's part
In defence of Liberty.

Jim Larkin played his part when he organized the unskilled labourers of Dublin in his newly formed Irish Transport and General Workers' Union in 1909 and brought a militant spirit of hope to the city. The young O'Casey, although he was still to write his plays in defence of Liberty, played his part by becoming an active member in Larkin's union and serving as one of the Chief's assistants during the 1913 strike. Having wandered from job to job with long periods of unemployment by the time he was thirty, O'Casey—stock-boy, sweeper, handyman, hod-carrier, docker, pick and shovel navvy on the roads and railroads—was well qualified to join the unskilled ranks of Larkin's union.

Technically, the 1913 strike was a failure for the union, and yet the employers could hardly be called the victors. For though the men went back to work without any material gains after being locked out for eight tragic months, the employers had been defeated in their principal aim, which was to destroy Larkinism and the trade union movement in Ireland. Morally, therefore, Larkin and the strikers had won the first important battle in the history of the Irish labour movement; they had paved the way for the recognition of the union as a force equal to management. There were still many hard battles ahead for the Dublin labouring classes, but Jim Larkin had brought unity and a sense of purpose to their growing ranks. He put courage into the Irish people when he told them, 'An injury to one is the concern of all'; and he put fear into the Irish employers when he warned them, 'You'll crucify Christ no longer in this town.'[8]

Larkin, then, was the crucial figure and personal hero of O'Casey's early manhood. Both men had lived through years of great hardship and they were inspired by a common cause. Larkin was born in 1876 in Liverpool of a Northern Irish family, and at the age of nine he was working forty hours a week in a dairy and a butcher shop, earning 2s. 6d. plus a penny currant bun, and a glass of milk on Saturday night. As a young man he became a sailor, then a docker at Liverpool, where he became active in the dockers' union. Before he came to Dublin in 1907, his attempts to organize workers in Belfast and Cork had led to strikes, and the news of his rousing oratory and militant union principles preceded him. Rumours were spread about the city that he was the anti-Christ, and that he wore his familiar wide-brimmed black hat in order to cover the third eye he had in the centre of his forehead. But Larkin who, as he said, 'feared God but no man', soon convinced the wretched slum-dwellers that they had no choice but to organize and fight. Addressing them in Liberty Hall, the union headquarters, or at street meetings in Beresford Place, he defined their cause and whipped up their courage; he sang songs, quoted passages from the Bible, Shakespeare, and Shelley.

But he could also be an enraged titan on the platform when he was hurling thunderbolts at those who battened on or condoned the evils of the Dublin slums. It is difficult to recreate the full image and impact of the man from the printed record of his speeches, for he seldom spoke from a prepared text, and his personal dynamism had to be heard and seen when he was in action in front of an audience. When he went to London in 1913 to gain support for the Dublin strikers, he addressed a huge labour rally in the

Albert Hall, and the novelist David Garnett, then a university student, saw him give one of his characteristic performances. Twenty-five years later Garnett still remembered the incident vividly enough to write the following description of Larkin:

He was incomparably the finest orator I have ever heard, just as Chaliapin was the finest singer—and for the same physical reasons. Larkin was, I believe, actually taller than Chaliapin and could have outroared the Russian. There was no fat on him. He was absolutely unself-conscious and seemed to care nothing whatever for his audience. I cannot remember any appeal to reason, or anything constructive in his speech, which was a recital of wrongs and an assault on persons. He was deadly in earnest and, walking up and down like an infuriated tiger, he roared out his message of defiance to the capitalist system and the death of Murphy. There, striding about the platform one beheld the whole of the sweated, starved, exploited working class suddenly incarnate in the shape of a gigantic Tarzan of all the slum jungles of the West. [9]

Although he became known as the great strike-leader, it was his aim to organize unions, not strikes, and it was the absolute refusal of the employers even to enter into open negotiations that invariably led to the strikes which Larkin himself deplored and accepted only as labour's last resort. But he was a marked man in Dublin, feared by the capitalists he had come to scourge, and even assailed by the Catholic clergy who at that time had little sympathy with the trade union movement. In spite of the fact that he was denounced by many priests and by the Catholic press, Larkin boldly insisted that he was a Catholic *and* a Socialist at a time when the *Irish Catholic* was frantically warning the people that Socialism was tantamount to Satanism. Shortly after the union was forced to strike in late August 1913, that newspaper came out with a leader called 'Satanism and Socialism', warning the strikers to listen to their priests and go back to work, to renounce Larkin who was referred to as 'that Moloch of iniquity'. [10] The editorial also introduced a political note when it stated that Larkinism or Socialism was the enemy of Ireland's national ideals as well as Christianity: 'From beginning to end Socialism is anti-Christian and unpatriotic. There is scarcely a single national ideal long cherished by our people of which the Socialism now daily and nightly preached at Beresford Place is not the negation.' [11]

Three years earlier James Connolly, who was Larkin's second in command at the union and was soon to become one of the martyrs of the 1916 Rising, had discussed the role of the clergy in Irish history, specifically in politics and labour, in his book, *Labour, Nationality and Religion*. He had written the book in reply to a Father Kane, s.j., who had denounced Socialism in a series of Lenten Discourses delivered in Dublin in 1910. Connolly, like Larkin a Catholic and a Socialist, insisted that the two beliefs were not incompatible:

The Socialist doctrine teaches that all men are brothers, that the same red blood of a common humanity flows in the veins of all races, creeds, colours and nations, that the interests of labour are everywhere identical, and that wars are an abomination. Is not this also good Catholic doctrine —the doctrine of a Church which prides itself upon being universal or Catholic? How, then, can that doctrine which is high and holy in theory on the lips of a Catholic become a hissing and a blasphemy when practised by the Socialist? . . . After all (Father Kane's) long discourse, after again and again admitting the tyranny, the extortions, the frauds, the injustices perpetrated in our midst every day by those who control and own our means of existence, he has no remedy to offer but pity! After all his brave appeal to individuality, to national honour, to the heroic spirit in poor men and women, he shrinks from appealing to that individuality, to that national honour, to that heroic spirit in the poor and asking them so to manifest themselves as to rescue their lives from the control of the forces of mammon. Professing to denounce mammon, he yet shrinks from leading the forces of righteousness against it, and by so shrinking shows that all his professed solicitude for justice, all his vaunted hatred of tyranny, were 'mere sound and fury signifying nothing'.

Is not this attitude symbolic of the attitude of the Church for hundreds of years? Ever counselling humility, but sitting in the seats of the mighty; ever patching up the diseased and broken wrecks of an unjust social system, but blessing the system which made the wrecks and spread the disease; ever running divine discontent and pity into the ground as the lightning rod runs and dissipates lightning, instead of gathering it and directing it for social righteousness as the electric battery generates and directs electricity for social use. [12]

Connolly had also enumerated all the occasions when the

Catholic Church had consistently supported British 'tyranny' in Ireland, from the twelfth century down to the twentieth century. And now when it was Irishman against Irishman in a bitter economic struggle, the Church was supporting the tyranny of Irish capitalism. But Connolly's arguments apparently had no effect upon the hierarchy. In their Lenten Pastorals of 1912 the Irish Bishops continued to ignore the inferno of the slums and issued stern warnings about the dangers of Socialism: 'The evil is spreading; every year is adding new recruits to this professedly anti-Christian body; the false flag of "a heaven here below" is being waved before our Irish people by the paid agents of Socialism.' [13]

A month after the Pastorals appeared, when Larkin announced that he would go to Sligo to recruit new members for the recently formed union branch in that city, the Bishop of Elphin, Dr John Clancy, wrote a letter denouncing Larkin which was to be read at all Masses in the Roman Catholic churches of Sligo. Larkin appeared in the city on Sunday as scheduled, and after hearing himself denounced at Mass, he made the following remarks at his union meeting:

After having some breakfast I went, as I always do, to pay my respects to my Creator. I knelt down, and after some time I heard a very respected rev. clergyman read out a letter from an eminent ecclesiastic of the Catholic Church condemning James Larkin who had come down to raise the red flag of bloody revolution in Sligo. (A Voice—'We don't care about him.') Well, you must care about him. I do, and I respect him in all matters connected with the spiritual domain of the Catholic Church, as I call it. I am bound to respect him, and all those who are under him, but when he travels into the domain of politics, of historical fact or economic thought, he can go his road and I can go mine (Cheers). [14]

The Dublin strike was touched off in 1913 when William Martin Murphy, one of Ireland's leading capitalists, President of the Dublin Chamber of Commerce and spokesman for the Federated Employers of Dublin, who owned the public street-car system (the Dublin United Tram Company), two city newspapers, hotels, railroads, steamships, arbitrarily dismissed and locked out some 200 workers who had refused to sign a pledge against Larkin's union. The Press and the clergy, who had been attacking Larkin and labour all along, now increased their efforts in a campaign of editorials, sermons, and speeches, and were determined to break the strike and Larkin. One of the more out-spoken priests, Father Condon, o.s.a., delivered a series of public speeches in which he upheld the employers because 'the right of ownership' was one of the teachings of the Church, and Larkin replied:

May I point out to you, sir, that you forgot to explain that you were also speaking as a shareholder in a commercial undertaking, which is effected by the present deplorable dispute which you correctly describe as an economic war . . . What of the seventy-odd priests who are shareholders in the Dublin United Tram Company and who are responsible along with that other pillar of the Church, William 'Murder' Murphy, for horrible bloodshed and tragedy of death?[15]

Father Condon and his fellow priests had based their opposition to Larkin on religious principles, but this 'conflict of interests'— they had invested their church funds in the Tram Company, which was involved in the strike—was not calculated to strengthen their stand. Larkin also asked Father Condon why he was protesting against the strike but had remained silent about the appalling situation in the Dublin slums; and he cited a number of instances of the working and living conditions in the city, many of which were recorded in the government Housing inquiry report the following year.

After the strike had been in progress for several months Larkin and Connolly had another of many clashes with the Church. The situation had become desperate for the families of the estimated 15,000 men out on strike—the total amount of people involved numbering some 100,000, or one-third of the population—and the union had set up a plan to send some of the children, who were literally starving, to the homes of workers in England until the dispute was settled. This brought an immediate response from Archbishop Walsh who condemned the plan in a letter which appeared in all the Dublin newspapers. He appealed directly to the Catholic mothers of the city:

Have they abandoned their faith? Surely not. Well, if they have not they should need no words of mine to remind them of the plain duty of every Catholic mother in such a case. I can only put it to them, that they can no longer be held worthy of the name of Catholic mothers if they so far forget that duty as to send away their children to be cared for in a strange land without security of any kind that those to whom the poor children are to be handed over are Catholics, or, indeed, are persons of any faith at all. (16)

Besides the danger to faith and morals, the Archbishop was apparently concerned about the food and comfort the children would receive in English homes, for a week later he remarked 'that taking the children away would only make them discontented with the homes to which they returned—those who did return.' (17) Perhaps the best answer to this attitude was given by the Irish poet A E (George Russell) when, in addressing a rally in support of the Dublin strike in the Albert Hall, London, he remarked:

Ah! but I forgot; there has sprung up a third party, who are super-human beings, they have so little concern for the body at all that they assert it is better for children to be starved than to be moved from the Christian atmosphere of the Dublin slums. Dublin is the most Christian city in these islands. Its tottering tenements are holy. The spiritual atmosphere which pervades them is ample compensation for the diseases which are there and the food which is not there. If any poor parents think otherwise, and would send their children for a little from that earthly paradise, they will find the docks and railway stations barred by these super-human beings and by the police, and they are pitched headlong out of the station, set upon and beaten, and their children snatched from them. A Dublin labourer has no rights in his own children. You see if these children were even for a little out of the slums they would get discontented with their poor homes, so a very holy man has said. Once getting full meals they might be so inconsiderate as to ask for them all their lives. (18)

The plan for the children was destined to fail. Large priest-led crowds demonstrated and picketed at the railway stations and the docks, and the children were not allowed to leave the city. Arnold Wright, who saw the whole episode as a victory of Catholicism over Socialism, gave the following description of one of the scenes that took place at the North Wall quay:

A large number of priests were conspicuous in the throng and took an active part in directing what was in reality a picketing of ships. Cabs which drove up were detained until the excited Catholics had made sure that they contained no juveniles of the class marked out for deportation. In one instance a family party, including children, were detained until one of the attendant priests had assured the crowd that they had nothing to do with the Larkinites' scheme, when they were permitted to resume their journey. Eventually, after the last boat had cast off from the wharf and there was no further possibility of deporting children that night, the great crowd, now numbering many thousands, formed in processional order and marched along the quays bareheaded, singing 'Faith of our Fathers', 'Hail, glorious St. Patrick', and other sacred melodies. Thus they proceeded until they reached College Green, where a halt was called and the assembled multitude were addressed by Father Farrell, of Donnybrook, a priest who had taken a conspicuous part in the evening's operations. 'Remember', he said, 'that this great demonstration was unorganized and unprepared. It shows the love you have for the Catholic children of this city. It is a magnificent protest against the proselytizing of our children in the Socialistic homes of England.' The crowd cheered these sentiments with enthusiasm, and then dispersed to their homes with cries of 'Away with the Socialists', and 'Down with Larkin'. By general consent it was one of the most remarkable and significant uprisings of Catholics that Dublin had witnessed for many a long day. [19]

Connolly spoke for the defeated Larkinites when he fired this parting shot at Father Farrell: 'One scoundrel in clerical garb is said to have stated on Wednesday that the children were being "brought to England by trickery, fraud and corruption for proselytizing purposes". Nothing more venomous and unfounded was ever spewed out of a lying mouth in Ireland since the *seoinin* clergy at the bidding of an English politician hounded Parnell to his grave.' [20]

At this time Connolly and Larkin were not alone in their insistence that Irish clericalism not Catholicism—the Churchmen not the Church—was incompatible with Socialism. The liberal Catholic writer, W. P. Ryan, who had a number of clashes with the clergy, had much to say on the subject. Before he came to Dublin in 1907, he had edited a weekly newspaper in the Boyne Valley called the *Irish Peasant*, but after a year of publication the paper was suppressed by Cardinal Logue because, as Ryan put it in *The Labour Revolt and Larkinism* (1913), 'laics and clerics had discussed in its columns sundry questions of burning Irish interest, including the popular control of education and the respective positions and rights of the laity and the clergy in the community'.[21] Not discouraged by the suppression of this paper, Ryan went to Dublin and began another one which for four years remained an open forum for provocative issues, in spite of the fact that it was denounced as 'Satanic' by some of the clergy. Ryan's account is worth noting:

Going to Dublin, I was enabled to launch a similar organ, known in the later stages as the *Irish Nation*, and there for four years—1907–1910 —with little financial but plenty of literary resources, we fought our battle for freedom of thought and expression, some of the younger Catholic clergy assisting us earnestly, while the overt and covert opposition of the higher and conservative ecclesiastics was unceasing and unrestrained. 'A paper whose aims are "Satanic"', was part of the published description of the *Irish Nation* by a Connacht D.D., a bishop's right-hand man, while I personally loomed fearsomely in his eyes as 'A Julian and a Judas rolled into one'. So far as faith and creed were concerned, the paper stood in the main for mystical Christianity, whose essence is kindred to that of all the great religions, and for the practical application of essential Christianity in everyday life—this was denounced as Socialism. We also insisted that Churchmen were not the Church, and that ecclesiastical politics was not religion. This appeared to be the really 'Satanic' side of the publication.[22]

Since Ryan had also had many opportunities to witness the appalling conditions under which the lower classes of Dublin lived, he was solidly behind the attempts of Larkin and Connolly to erase the slums through 'the practical application of essential Christianity in everyday life'. Like them, he believed that such action was as Catholic as it was Socialistic. A year before the strike, in his book *The Pope's Green Island* (1912), Ryan pointed out that there were a number of powerful groups in the country, besides the Church, which were opposed to Larkin and Connolly: 'In the ranks of labour itself some bold and able types have arisen, notably in Dublin and Belfast. Whether they preach Socialism, co-operation, or trade unionism, they keep their eyes as

a rule on Irish conditions and characteristics. They make headway
with their own class and meet varied opposition or misunderstanding amongst sundry clergymen, farmers, manufacturers,
publicans, slum-owners, food adulterators, those who want no
change, and those who say that nothing particular can be done
pending the establishment of a national legislative authority.'[23]
Then he went on to analyze some of the inconsistencies and ironies
of the clerical attitude:

The clerical opposition is mainly to anything that seems to savour of
Socialism, though some have the singular notion, as their utterances
show, that a 'poor' class is a direct creation or design of Providence,
and to them a social state without poverty, and a measure of abject
poverty, is unthinkable. Much of what they ascribe in a cloudy way
to Sin and Devil springs from palpably anti-social, selfish, and materialistic factors. The social criticism and reconstructive theories they
have heard of late years have staggered them. . . . Bad as are great
stretches of Dublin slumdom and its borderlands, the said priests do
surprisingly little in the way of social work, though Franciscans carry
on a well-meaning temperance crusade. There are many Dublins—
Irish, non-Irish, and some that are almost non-human. I hope
there is no place else in Ireland where numbers of children are so
utterly miserable and neglected, so crying a disgrace to Church and
State. . . .
    Some younger priests see the irony and humiliation of the position, the
unchristian spectacle of Catholic ecclesiastics as impassioned defenders
of worldly property, honouring the rich or well-to-do in this world and
bidding the poor be content with the prospect of heaven in the next;
forgetting or ignoring the great fact that the Catholic ideal is collectivist,
not individualistic as the term is usually understood. . . . It is often
difficult for the young clergy to help the work forward, and dangerous
to be suspected of socialistic leanings. So sometimes in the dioceses
under old-fashioned or autocratic bishops, they look on helplessly and
pensively, feeling lonely amid the waste of life, and painfully conscious
of the fact that official Irish Catholicism is socially ineffective or a
compromise. . . . Still the crucial questions for Catholicism in Ireland
remain unanswered—Can its official theology be liberalized and
spiritualized? Can it be applied as the Catholic Bishop of Ross asked
some years ago, more practically to everyday life? At present it is far
too little either a gospel or a philosophy. So it does not enlighten and

inspire souls, or check anti-social sins and evils, as it might were it
truly evangelical, liberal, and vital. [24]

These, then, were some of the major conflicts which characterized O'Casey's Dublin, conflicts between labour and capital,
socialism and clericalism—and they all left their mark on him. By
the time of the 1913 strike he had lived through one of the most
chaotic periods in modern Irish history, and he had been exposed
to the penetrating criticisms of men like Larkin, Connolly, and
Ryan, all of whose speeches and writings he knew. It is significant
that his first writing to appear in print, an article called 'Sound the
Loud Trumpet', [25] was published in Ryan's *The Peasant and Irish
Ireland*; and he also wrote a number of articles for the *Irish Worker*,
the union paper edited by Larkin.

In the early days of the strike he was a familiar but not important
figure at Liberty Hall, where he did odd jobs around the office,
worked in the soup-kitchen, helped dispense strike benefits, and
wrote for the union paper. However, he soon had the opportunity
of working directly with Larkin. Countless instances of police
brutality in breaking up street meetings and demonstrations had
prompted the union to act in its own defence, and it formed the
Irish Citizen Army, a band of soldier-workers whose purpose it
was to protect the strikers and the people of the city from the
baton-swinging police. O'Casey was appointed Secretary of the
Citizen Army, and in that official capacity he served under Larkin.
Years later he was to look back at those days and picture Larkin as
the new Chief whom God in His infinite compassion had sent to
the troubled Irish people to replace the martyred Parnell—Jim
Larkin, 'Prometheus Hibernica'. [26]

But long before Larkin had fired his hopes for a new Dublin,
O'Casey had found two other heroes who were to have a vital influence on his life. As a boy he had discovered the new world of
drama in the plays of Shakespeare and Dion Boucicault.

2. THE FORMATIVE YEARS

Johnny Casey was ten years old when he discovered the drama
and almost had the chance to act the role of Henry VI and be murdered by Gloucester. His older brother Archie was active in ama-
teur theatricals, and little Johnny trailed after his brother spouting

the magnificent and mysterious words of Shakespeare. When Archie and one of his friends, Tommy Talton, organized some performances, the eager Johnny was taken on to play supporting parts. Little Johnny's début on the stage was scheduled to take place at a charity concert where a minstrel show and scenes from plays were to round out the entertainment. Talton was to do some speeches from one of Dion Boucicault's popular melodramas, *The Shaughraun*, while Archie and Johnny had prepared the prison-murder scene from Shakespeare's *Henry VI*, Part III, between Gloucester and Henry. By repeating his lines aloud after his brother, the ten-year-old Johnny, who was not yet able to read because of his weak eyes, learned the part of the ill-fated King. When the show was suddenly cancelled, however, on the night of the performance, after Johnny had stalked majestically through the house all day practising his part in a homemade regal costume, the heart-broken 'King' immediately flew into one of his characteristic 'tanthrums'. And so his own family had the honour of viewing his first unrehearsed performance as a frustrated monarch.

The two brothers continued to act out scenes together, and several years later when they helped organize the Townsend Dramatic Group, Johnny finally made his début as Henry VI. But it was when he was fifteen that he unexpectedly was given an opportunity to act in the old Mechanics Theatre in Abbey Street. This was the same theatre which, nine years later in 1904, was to be taken over by Yeats and, with the adjoining city morgue, rebuilt as the Abbey Theatre. It happened that a minor company of actors had been playing melodramas at the Mechanics Theatre, and when one of the players suddenly became sick a distress call went out for a last-minute replacement. Tommy Talton was in the play—it was Boucicault's *Shaughraun*, scenes from which Talton and the Casey brothers had often performed together—and he called Johnny in to take over the role of Father Dolan, the patriotic priest who protects a Fenian rebel. He played that part on the stage where twenty-eight years later his own first play was to be performed by the Abbey actors.

Shakespeare and Boucicault were most popular with the young Townsend players and their north Dublin audiences. Archie and Johnny Casey gave the Brutus and Antony funeral orations, and the Brutus–Cassius quarrel scene from *Julius Caesar*; and they played scenes from Boucicault's *The Octoroon* and the inevitable

Shaughraun. Dion Boucicault may have been a second-rate dramatist, but he was a first-rate man of the theatre. A prolific and successful playwright–producer–actor in America, England, and Ireland for fifty years—from 1841 when he scored his first comedy hit with *London Assurance* until his death in 1890—he knew how to hold and delight popular audiences with his bag of theatrical tricks and extravaganzas. He wrote or rewrote over 150 plays, most of them adaptations and free translations, cleverly borrowing and reshaping plots and characters from novels and plays, and his greatest successes were his 'Irish' plays—*The Colleen Bawn, The Shaughraun,* and *Arrah-Na-Pogue.*

But the young O'Casey only knew the works of Shakespeare and Boucicault from the lines he had picked up and memorized as an actor. By the time he was fourteen, however, he had begun an ambitious programme of self-education in order to learn to read and write. His father, a well-read man known in the neighbourhood as 'the scholar', had left behind a number of books, and Johnny, with the aid of some old primers and a dictionary, plus some coaching from his older sister Isabella, learned to read all the books, magazines, and newspapers in the house. But it was slow and painstaking labour, for he had to bend over his reading with his nose practically touching the page in order to make out the words with his weak watery eyes. He also got his first job in the stockroom of a hardware firm when he was fourteen, and this gave him spare pennies with which to buy used books. Gradually he built up a library of favourite works—Shakespeare, Dickens, Scott, Balzac, Ruskin, Byron, Shelley, Keats, Goldsmith, Sheridan, and many more. Once when he lacked the money for a copy of Milton's works which he desperately wanted, he summoned up enough courage and speed of foot to steal it from a bookstall.

He had to fight for everything he wanted, and he had also learned early in life to fight against the things he didn't want—deprivation and injustice. He quit his job in the hardware firm in protest against the long hours of dirty work for a low salary. He was fired from another back-breaking job in a stationery firm because he refused to remove his cap while collecting his meagre pay, although he had made up his mind in advance to go out with a bang. Even in those early years he was never one to remain long or suffer in silence where he felt he was being unjustly abused or exploited. And he seldom suffered fools willingly. He became disillusioned with acting and left the Townsend players because the petty jealousies and vanities of the actors too often led to quarrels over parts and performances.

Meanwhile, his mother saw to it that he attended church regularly and kept up with his religious training by reading the Bible and the Prayer Book. He was fascinated by the biblical rhetoric and legends, and he often memorized favourite passages. At the age of seventeen he made his confirmation in the Church of Ireland, and for several years thereafter he took an active part in religious functions at St. Barnabas Church, singing in the choir and teaching Sunday school. But in his early twenties he had begun to centre his interests on literature and art, and he gradually drifted away from the Church. However, he continued to maintain his close friendship with the wise and kindly Rector of St. Barnabas, the Reverend Edward Martin Griffin, who had become for him a second father.

During those early years of his life, from 1900 to 1910, O'Casey revealed that he had unusually versatile talents. He was known in his neighbourhood as one who had 'the touch' for anything that he took up, and it is likely that he might have become a scholar, musician, actor, or painter. He learned the difficult Irish language and spoke, read, and wrote it fluently, and later taught it; he learned to play the Celtic bagpipes and was a founder-member and secretary of the now famed St. Lawrence O'Toole Pipers Band; he wrote satiric songs which he sang at the weekly *ceili* at the St. Lawrence O'Toole Club, was an expert mime and comedian and acted in plays at the club; he took up painting and drew city scenes and character sketches of his friends, although his poor eyesight forced him to abandon the paintbrush for pen and ink.

At the same time that O'Casey was learning the Gaelic language and beginning to identify himself with 'Irish' Ireland, the turn of the century had already witnessed a renaissance of Irish culture. After the defeat and death of Parnell and Home Rule in 1891, Irishmen, generally disillusioned with politics and parliamentary procedures, moved in new directions. But it was mainly middle and upper class or intellectual Dublin which had become the revitalized centre of the awakened National culture—a resurgent interest and productive activity in Celtic history, mythology, poetry, drama, agrarianism, linguistics, and art, under the leadership of people like Standish O'Grady, Douglas Hyde, Arthur

Griffith, A E, Sir Horace Plunkett, Maud Gonne, W. B. Yeats, Lady Gregory, and Edward Martyn. Naturally, a self-educated common labourer like O'Casey lived in a world apart from these people who gathered and planned their work in élite circles, for instance, the famous Arts Club on the south side of the city in fashionable Fitzwilliam Square. He joined the Gaelic League and taught the language in the evenings at one of the League schools in the slums, but this was the only extent to which he was a part of the great Gaelic Revival. This movement had given Yeats the impetus to create the Irish Literary Theatre which in 1904 came to be known as the Abbey Theatre, but at this time O'Casey was still twenty years away from his first association with it. His roots were in the working class and his path was essentially that of labour —Larkin's path.

But even the path of labour soon proved to be a thorny one for O'Casey. In November 1913, a month after the organization of the Irish Citizen Army, a rival group formed the nationalistic Irish Volunteers, and in the months that followed there was deep hostility between the two groups. The Volunteers were a patriotic, middle-class organization, in no way connected with labour and the fight for improved working and living conditions; in fact, they were if anything anti-labour and even had among their members some of the very employers who had locked out the workers and tried to destroy the union during the strike. Furthermore, the Volunteers were rapidly expanding by drawing many of their recruits from the ranks of the Citizen Army.

Finally, in 1914, O'Casey, as Secretary of the Citizen Army, decided to challenge the infiltration tactics of the Volunteers, and he launched one of his characteristic fights. He brought the issue to a crisis when at a meeting of the officers he challenged the right of the Countess Markiewicz to serve as an official and member of the Citizen Army, since she was at the same time one of the leaders of the rival Volunteers. Although the Countess, an Irish woman who had married a Polish nobleman, had genuinely if somewhat romantically dedicated herself to the cause of Irish political freedom, O'Casey insisted that she was in a contradictory position which could only confuse and undermine the already diminishing ranks of the Citizen Army. But a one-vote majority of the officers supported the Countess, and when they went further and demanded that the imprudent O'Casey should apologize to her, he stubbornly refused to compromise the principle involved or bend his knee, and he promptly resigned from the Citizen Army. Larkin, although he was not particularly sympathetic to the Countess and certainly had no love for the Volunteers, nevertheless urged O'Casey to reconsider his decision, but to no avail. It was unusual for Larkin to act the role of peace-maker on this occasion, for the intransigent O'Casey had acted in a manner that was as typical of Larkin's usual behaviour as it was of his own.

This was not the first nor the last time O'Casey was to alienate himself from his countrymen over a principle. Several years earlier he had lost faith in the leaders, not the cause, of the Gaelic League, and the Irish Republican Brotherhood, of which he had also been a member, and he had left both organizations in disgust. There were too many professional patriots in these organizations to suit him, too many of the types who had, for example, led the attacks against Synge's allegedly 'immoral' and 'anti-Irish' *Playboy of the Western World* in 1907; too many cautious men who had remained silent and apparently satisfied in 1909 while the Irish bishops defeated and ruined Dr. Michael O'Hickey.

The 'martyred' O'Hickey was another of O'Casey's heroes at this time, a man who had been defeated because he had put principles before prudence. When the National University was established in 1909, a movement was started to make the Irish language an essential part of the curriculum. It was an issue of deep concern to many of the liberal clergy as well as the laity. Dr O'Hickey, D.D., Professor of Irish at Maynooth College, a Catholic seminary, became one of the leading figures in the movement, and he published a pamphlet called *An Irish University, or else—*, in which he made out a strong case for the Irish language as an integral part of Irish culture and education. Whereupon the Standing Committee of the Irish Bishops, which had all along been unsympathetic to the language revival movement, issued a statement ordering all priests to remain silent on the University question, and suppressed Dr O'Hickey. The bishops conceded that the controversy was a 'fair argument', but they were apparently determined to prevent the clergy from defending a national secular movement which the Church looked upon with suspicion. W. P. Ryan's *Irish Nation*, one of the few papers that was courageous enough to question the wisdom and the authority of the bishops, immediately entered the fight with an outspoken editorial:

Bishops, like ordinary mortals, ought to say what they mean and mean what they say. We regret to discover that in the University business certain Irish prelates are doing neither. The Standing Committee declared last week that the question of compulsory Irish in the University is a matter for fair argument. But members of the Standing Committee are 'muzzling' the priests who are friendly to the national demand. The French judge in Mr Dooley's satire first pronounced sentence on Dreyfus and then called the witnesses. Irish bishops ask for fair discussion, and straightway order the priests to be silent! . . . The priests who count are really on the side of the people this time, and certain of the bishops do not want them to show it. Poor Ireland! . . . The people must be firm and continue battling with all their might. If Ireland is to be really free and sane and natural, she must make up her mind resolutely that while rendering all due respect to bishops in their own sacred sphere, she absolutely refuses to accept their dictation in national and social matters. . . . (27)

Meanwhile Dr O'Hickey, who refused to be 'muzzled' on what he insisted was a national not a theological question, decided to act on his own in spite of the bishops' ban. Defiantly and no doubt imprudently, he published another pamphlet called *The Irish Bishops and An Irish University*, in which he directly attacked his superiors for using their considerable power for political purposes. What happened was that the bishops had not only silenced the clergy but frightened off many of the Gaelic Leaguers, who were cautious about pressing an issue that displeased the bishops. This second pamphlet put the case in the strongest possible terms, and a characteristic passage such as the following one was probably what Cardinal Logue had in mind when he later protested that Dr O'Hickey had used 'language unbecoming a gentleman and a priest':

In Ireland historical causes have given the bishops more political power, more influence in civil and social affairs, than their Episcopal brethren possess in any part of Catholic Christendom. In view of their recent pronouncement, it has become necessary to ask seriously, though regretfully, whether it is well that they should continue to wield such exceptional adventitious power; whether they have in point of fact shown themselves fit to wield that power for the true and abiding interest of the nation. (28)

The bishops considered the publication of such views an instance of flagrant insubordination, and with the backing of Cardinal Logue they prevailed upon the Trustees of Maynooth to get rid of Dr O'Hickey. He was summarily dismissed without a hearing, on the charge that he had violated the College Statutes. When it turned out that the Statutes in question were vague and had in fact expired years before the dismissal, Dr O'Hickey demanded a full hearing on his case, but he was turned down. At that point, in the summer of 1909, the *Irish Nation* started an O'Hickey Testimonial Fund, and for a year the paper continued to receive contributions (one came in from Sean O'Cathasaigh) and keep the O'Hickey case alive with editorials and articles. Then, on the advice of his friend and colleague, Dr Walter McDonald, D.D., Professor of Theology at Maynooth, Dr O'Hickey decided to appeal his case to the Vatican, and he went to Rome in 1910.

During the very month that he left Ireland, in June 1910, an important announcement was made by the Senate of the National University—it had voted to make the Irish language an essential part of the curriculum. The battle had been won, but Dr O'Hickey was its chief casualty. He was to spend the next six years of his life in Rome, frustrated by the red-tape of ecclesiastical law; and his case was doomed to fail since the Irish bishops, and Cardinal Logue himself, sent repeated warnings to the Vatican that support of the O'Hickey appeal would undermine the position of the clergy in Ireland. Finally defeated after a six-year ordeal, Dr O'Hickey returned to Ireland in the summer of 1916, and in November he died suddenly, a broken and forgotten man.

It was to be expected that his friend Dr MacDonald, who suffered a somewhat similar fate, should also have become one of O'Casey's 'martyred' heroes. At one point in his career, in 1913, Dr McDonald had been sharply reprimanded by a bishop for publicly criticizing some past Church policies in a book review he had written for a Dublin newspaper. When he tried to defend himself by stating it would be wrong to hide or falsify the facts of history, the reply came back: 'Why, then, urged the Bishop, did you not publish your criticism in a book, which would not be read by the common people, Catholic and Protestant?'[29] In reflecting on that incident he wrote: 'It was imprudent, I admit—in the sense of being calculated to get me into a scrape; but my whole life has been an act of faith in such imprudences—a protest against the

selfish prudence that will make no sacrifice for the right.'[30] This
was precisely the attitude which motivated men like Larkin,
O'Hickey, and O'Casey.

Dr McDonald did however take that bishop's advice about expressing his views on theological questions in books; but over a
ten-year period six of his works were suppressed by the Church—
'delated to the Index and condemned'. It was not until the posthumous publication in 1925 of his autobiography, *Reminiscences of
a Maynooth Professor*—he died in 1920—that the full details of his
tragic story came to light. For forty years, from 1880 to 1920, he
had been Professor of Theology at Maynooth, and during all that
time he had dedicated himself to a fight against what he called the
predominant Toryism of Irish Catholicism:

To many, if not most, of those who are acquainted with the almost
unremitting conflict that has been waged since the Union between
Irish Nationalists and the English Tory Party, it may appear strange
to hear one like me say that he was brought up in the Tory tradition.
What I mean is, that, in spite of our opposition to official Toryism,
Irish Catholics have been more Tory than the Tories—in some important respects. There is not, as far as I know—and there has not been
since the Union—a Tory leader in England who would not advocate
the principle of rebellion, given, of course, sufficient cause and a
reasonable chance of success. As against this, so conservative have we
been in Ireland, at least in our theological schools, that we have denounced as immoral in every possible case rebellion against authority,
once properly constituted.[31]

He had many 'revolutionary' ideas for liberalizing Church
policies, and when one considers some representative examples of
the issues that disturbed him it becomes apparent why six of his
books were suppressed. He was continually wrestling with the conflicts that arose between scientific truth and rigid discipline, and he
questioned the infallibility of the Church; he was sympathetic to
Socialism and the labour movement, and he attacked the clerical
attitude toward Jim Larkin; he objected to the puritanical strictures of the clergy on matters like dancing and sex generally; he
wanted sweeping reforms in the teaching methods at Catholic
schools and felt that priests should not have absolute control over
education; he believed that Church funds were too often raised for

the building of church spires and too seldom for the building of libraries. In fact, on the whole matter of Church finances he held views which could only have infuriated his superiors. Here, for example, are his frank comments on clerical behaviour and book-keeping:

I do not know whether, if the Irish people knew exactly what it costs them to support their clergy, they would or would not curtail supplies; but I am sure they are willing to make not merely a decent but a generous provision—for clergymen, who, after all, can do little service unless they show in their lives, their homes, and their surroundings, something of the poverty and the sacrifice of Christ. Well-fed, well-groomed, and well-appointed priests are of little use in a contest with the world, the flesh, and the devil; nor is it enough to give up marriage and family life, if we are addicted to the pleasures of the table and fond of show. I verily believe that the Roman palaces, of Popes and Cardinals, have cost the Church something infinitely more precious than money; and while the Catholic world, as I am sure, is quite prepared to supply the Pope with what he needs for Church purposes, the history of the Papacy justifies the faithful in being on guard against maladministration in the Roman Curia. The very best way to induce the laity to give what is wanted for the central government of the Church is to publish a budget, like other governments; and let the taxpayers—for such, in effect, they are—see what is needed, how much is received, and how it is spent. At present, it is to be feared, the burthen falls very unevenly on different parts of the Church. [32]

Professing such radical views, Dr McDonald was foredoomed to a life of frustration and silence. He was forever getting into 'imprudent scrapes' with his superiors, as a result of which he was often reprimanded and his views suppressed. As he explained in his autobiography, which he finished in the last year of his life when he knew he was dying of an incurable disease, he had always lived in the fear that he might lose his position, or, what was worse, his faith. 'It was only by God's great mercy,' he wrote, 'I did not altogether renounce the faith: as I fear I should have done ultimately had I not satisfied myself of the truth—or the tenability—of more liberal principles than those in which I was brought up.' [33] Stephen Gwynn in his *Saints and Scholars* made the following comment on this tragic and courageous remark:

'I satisfy myself.' The phrase has a Protestant ring, though coming from a Maynooth professor. That in itself would not have troubled Dr McDonald. He praised the Presbyterians for their refusal to admit to any degree of State control in ecclesiastical appointments; he pointed to the action of all Protestant Churches in publishing open accounts of all their funds as worthy and even necessary to be imitated by his own Church; he advocated the right of local committees to be associated with the clergy in the management of schools—another Protestant-sounding theory. All these were matters on which he could speak freely, though to speak in this sense was to oppose the hierarchy and to block all chances of preferment. But he wanted no preferment—neither one of the bishoprics to which his juniors on the staff of Maynooth passed on, nor the Presidency or Vice-Presidency. He wanted liberty to discuss and defend the modifications of traditional belief which he thought necessary in the cause of truth. He did not get it. He was defeated.[34]

'I satisfy myself.' The phrase has an O'Casey ring. He had read Dr McDonald's posthumous autobiography in 1925, and by the following year, when he left Ireland in self-exile, he had un-doubtedly identified himself with the man who had spent his life fighting for liberty and truth—with three brave and imprudent Irishmen: Larkin, O'Hickey, and McDonald.

3. THE FORMATIVE WRITING

In 1918 O'Casey had his first works published, aside from some earlier articles in labour journals. Fergus O'Connor, a small Dublin publisher of greeting cards, song books, and Republican and Labour literature, brought out a booklet of some of the songs O'Casey had written to amuse his friends in the St Lawrence O'Toole Club, titled: *Songs of the Wren:* Humorous and Senti-mental, by Sean O'Cathasaigh (Author of 'The Grand Oul 'Dame Britannia').[35]. It must have been fairly successful, for before the year was out two new editions of *More Songs of the Wren* appeared, fourteen songs in all. They were in the tradition of the popular street ballad, set to traditional airs, some romantic songs with such titles as, 'As I Wait in the Boreen for Maggie', 'The Bonnie Bunch of Roses, O!', and 'The Girl from the County Kildare'; but mostly they were spirited burlesques of the British with titles like, 'The Demi-Semi Home Rule Bill', 'If the Germans Came to Ireland in the Morning', and 'The Divil's Recruitin' Campaign'. The unsuccessful attempt by the British late in World War One to recruit Irishmen is the occasion of this last song, and it is an interesting example of O'Casey's earliest writing of lively satire.

THE DIVIL'S RECRUITIN' CAMPAIGN

(Air: 'Sargeant Willy Baily')

I suppose you've often heard, now, of the place that lies below—
  Too all tooral, ooral, ooral ooo!
A public meeting there was held not very long ago,
  Too all tooral, ooral, ooral ooo!
'Twas the Divil that presided, and soon it was decided
That the only way to see the matter through,
An' to keep the British Nation at its present elevation,
Was to hasten on Conscription, tooral ooo!

Ses the Divil, ' Things in Ireland, now, they will not do at all'
An' he spoke in tones of thunder, tooral ooo!
All the men that's left in Ireland, now, will have to hear the call
To get out and to get under, tooral ooo!
Ses his secretary, 'Look, sir, Home Rule's on the Statue Book, sir?
And we've only just another thing to do:
The Duke of Connaught swear in as the great High King of Eireann,
And we'll get recruits in thousands, tooral ooo!'

Ses the Divil, ' In our Empire things have reached a pretty pass,
  Tooral, ooral, ooral, ooral ooo!
With their air raids, submarines an' all their latest poison gas,
  Tooral, ooral, ooral, ooral ooo!
But I wouldn't still be carin' if it wasn't now for Erin,
And the doings of the silly Sinn Fein crew?
I'm beginnin' to feel queer, oh! with this cursed De Valera—
  Tooral, ooral, ooral, ooral ooo!

An' the Divil sent his agents out to gather in recruits,
  Tooral, ooral, ooral, ooral ooo!
To preserve the Saints in England an' destroy the German brutes,
  Tooral, ooral, ooral, ooral ooo!

You'll get a welcome hearty from the gallant Irish Party—
Tell them to spread an' preach what isn't true—
'Twas written by St. Kevin that no Gael could enter Heaven
Unless he dyed the green, red, white and blue.

After years an' years an' years of work his agents all came back,
            Tooral, ooral, ooral, ooral ooo!
They carried an old man just nicely tied up in a sack,
            Tooral, ooral, ooral, ooral ooo!
We could only just get one sir, to put the khaki on, sir—
Tho' we search'd an' search'd the country through an' through?
He'll join the British Awmy, but the doctors say he's bawmy—
            Tooral, ooral, ooral, ooral ooo!

He had a soft tenor voice and was fond of singing these songs at informal occasions and for his friends. One friend with whom he shared a tenement room in Mountjoy Square after his mother died, a Gaelic-speaking Aran Islander named Micheal O Maolain [Michael Mullen], once commented: 'His soft sweet voice would remind you of the song of the robin; low like it—not too long-drawn-out. But the little red-breasted bird had a sweetness of his own, and so it was with Sean O'Casey.'[36]

During 1918 Fergus O'Connor also published O'Casey's first book, a short dramatic narrative of the last days of Thomas Ashe, one of the martyrs of the aftermath of the Easter Rising. A slender paper-back book of fifteen pages, it appeared first as *The Story of Thomas Ashe* by Sean O'Cathasaigh, and in a slightly expanded second edition it was called *The Sacrifice of Thomas Ashe*. Ashe, a member of the Citizen Army and one of O'Casey's friends, was imprisoned in August 1917 during a round-up of suspected insurgents. In protest he went on a hunger-strike, was subjected to force-feeding and torture, as a result of which he died in September 1917. Although O'Casey had by this time alienated himself from the organizations that took part in the Rising, he was nevertheless committed to the cause of Irish liberation, and he indicated in this book that he was better able to fight with his pen than with a gun. And he fought on his own principles, stressing the fact that Ashe was a fallen hero of Irish labour and liberty as well as Irish nationalism. He tells the tragic story in a powerful and sometimes crude prose style that is charged with revolutionary rhetoric. Here is a typical example of the early O'Casey indignation which reveals that he must have had an intimate knowledge of the political writings of Milton and Shelley.

Oppression of the Bloody Hands, you cannot put a rope around the neck of an idea; you cannot put an idea up against a barrack-square wall and riddle it with bullets; you cannot confine it in the strongest prison that all your slaves could ever build.

Thomas Ashe's body, today, is covered with Irish mould, but his principles are surging into a stronger life within the minds of the Irish Proletariat, the Irish Scholar, and the Irish Worker. Death has won a poor victory! Labour has lost a champion; Irish-Ireland has lost a son; Militant Ireland has lost a soldier; but all have gained a mighty and enduring inspiration. Ashe died that Human Liberty might be vindicated and that Ireland might live. [37]

Shortly after the book on Ashe appeared, the Irish publishing firm of Maunsel contracted O'Casey to write a short history of the Citizen Army. His second book, the seventy-two-page *Story of the Irish Citizen Army*, by P. O'Cathasaigh [the 'P' was a misprint], published in 1919, was a first-hand account of the organization and activities of the Citizen Army during the 1913–14 strike and lock-out, and also covered the events leading up to and including the 1916 Rising. Jim Larkin and the Irish Labour movement dominate the first two-thirds of the book, and James Connolly, who assumed leadership of the resistance after Larkin went to America in the autumn of 1914 to raise union funds, becomes the central figure in the last part. While O'Casey recognized Connolly's ability and courage, and paid tribute to his heroic sacrifice of his life in the Rising, he felt that Connolly had gradually shifted his loyalties from the Citizen Army to the Irish Volunteers—from labour to nationalism. Perhaps this was an inevitable path for Connolly, for with Larkin away and labour losing ground, the Volunteers had become the most powerful force by 1916. But still O'Casey's loyalties belonged to labour's Plough and the Stars, the flag with the seven stars of the symbolic heavenly Plough on a background of bright St Patrick's blue, which was the Citizen Army banner, not the orange, green and white Tri-Colour of the nationalists.

He felt that the future of Ireland depended upon the ultimate unification of both groups. Labour was fundamentally democratic but not 'Irish' enough and had not sufficiently captured the popular imagination; the nationalists were fanatically 'Irish' and lacked working-class sympathies and sound democratic principles.

It is from these elements that Labour must build the future state; democratizing the national movement and Irishing itself. Labour will probably have to fight Sinn Fein—indeed the challenge seems to have been thrown down already—but the Labour leaders must become wiser and more broadminded than they at present seem to be; they must remove the beam from their own eye that they may clearly see to remove the mote from the eye of Sinn Fein, and then they will find in that organization elements that will readily yield to its penetrating forces; then the leaders of Labour in Ireland will be able to glean grapes from a tree that hitherto brought forth only wild grapes, because Labour, through the Citizen Army, has broken down the first trenches of national prejudice, and has left a deep impression on the bloody seal of Irish Republicanism. [38]

This book indirectly suggests that the War of Irish Independence, which is usually put down as the period from the 1916 Rising to the 1922 Free State 'Settlement', might more accurately be said to cover the decade beginning in 1913 with the General Strike and labour's formation of the Citizen Army, the initial organized body of protest and armed resistance. The labouring masses of Dublin under the leadership of Jim Larkin had struck the first blow, although they did not at that time foresee the chain-reaction of events which was to explode in 1916. Nevertheless, revolutionary labour had shown the way to revolutionary nationalism. But once the Nationalists took the lead, Labour was gradually squeezed out. Labour had no voice in the cease-fire and uneasy settlement of 1923, and to this day it has remained without significant power in modern Irish life and government.

Again in this second book O'Casey had written a fervent historical narrative, sometimes over-written but always alive with the emotional impact of the times. He still indulged in rhetorical excesses, as for example in his fondness for the pathetic fallacy and colour-catalogues: 'The disappearing Artist Sun had boldly brushed the skies with bold hues of orange and crimson, and delicate shades of yellow and green, bordered with dusky shadows of darkening blue. . . .' [39] However, he consistently revealed his ability to present the story through the characters and dramatic episodes that he knew so well. This sensitivity for the dramatic situation is evident in the following description of Jim Larkin preparing to address a mass meeting in front of the union headquarters at Liberty Hall.

Suddenly the window is raised, and the tense, anxious feelings of the men crowded together burst out into an enthusiastic and full-throated cheer that shatters the surrounding air, and sends up into the skies a screaming flock of gulls that had been peacefully drifting along the sombre surface of the River Liffey. Louder still swells the resonant shout as Jim Larkin appears at the window, with an animated flush of human pride on his strong and rugged face, as he brushes back from his broad forehead the waving tufts of dark hair that are here and there silvered by the mellowing influence of Time and the inexorable force of issuing energy from the human structure. Again the cheers ring out, and Larkin quietly waits till the effort to demonstrate their confidence and affection will give place to the lustful desire to hear what he has to say to them, while hidden under the heavy shadows of the towering Custom House a darker column of massive constables instinctively finger their belts, and silently caress the ever-ready club that swings jauntily over each man's broad, expansive hip. (40)

There is only a spark of the dramatist-to-be in these early writings—humorous songs and historical stories—yet the fire of O'Casey's genius which was soon to burn brightly had its source in these early expressions of his laughter and passion.

He received fifteen pounds for *The Story of the Citizen Army*, a tremendous sum for him at the time and the first money of any consequence he had earned from his writing. There was to be no celebrating, however, for his ailing mother died late in 1918, shortly after he had finished the book. Susan Casey was in her eighties when she died. It was surprising that she had survived so long, for she had literally worn herself out struggling for so many years against disease and poverty. Her death was a severe blow to her favourite son. He owed his life and what remained of his poor eyesight to her tireless energy and gentle heart. From her he had received his spiritual as well as physical strength and his deep compassion—qualities which combined with and tempered the stubborn pride and fierce courage he had inherited from his father.

After his mother died O'Casey cut adrift from his older brother Michael, a boisterous heavy-drinking man. His sister Isabella and his brother Tom were dead, and his other surviving brother Archie had married and emigrated to England. Alone now as he approached his fortieth year, he was fully determined to achieve the new goal he had set for himself—to write a play that would be performed at the famed Abbey Theatre. It was to take four years and four manuscripts before he reached this goal and launched his career as a dramatist.

He had written a play called *The Frost in the Flower*, a devastating satire on some of the leading members of the St. Lawrence O'Toole Club; and when the club's dramatic group understandably refused to perform it, he boldly sent it on to the Abbey. Since he had no money for paper and ink, he had to improvise. Several of his friends who worked in offices made off with batches of oddsized sheets of paper and a box of indelible lead pencils; and by boiling the purple lead in water he concocted a pot of home-made ink. Yeats and Lady Gregory must have been surprised when they received the crude and makeshift manuscript by an unknown author. It was rejected but came back with a terse comment: 'Not far from being a good play.' (41) With this slender encouragement, O'Casey went on to write another play, *The Harvest Festival*, which dealt with a series of conflicts between some labourers and the Church. Again the play was rejected, but this time he received a letter from Lennox Robinson, with some comments by Lady Gregory praising several scenes and particularly the characterization of a clergyman. This spurred him on to write a third play, *The Crimson and the Tri-Colour*, which was about the struggles of some labourers during the Rising. Now the rejection was accompanied by Lady Gregory's detailed critique of all the characters, most of which she liked. She had told him: 'I believe there is something in you and your strong point is characterization.' (42) She actually wanted to produce this play, with its imperfections of plot and structure, but Yeats, who held out against it, told her: 'Casey was bad in writing about the vices of the rich which he knows nothing about, but he thoroughly understands the vices of the poor.' (43)

The Abbey directors realized that in spite of the crude construction—and the added problem of trying to decipher the crabbed handwriting in poor ink on uneven sheets of paper—these plays by an unknown common labourer revealed the signs of a potential playwright. Lady Gregory was most enthusiastic and ready to help O'Casey, and Yeats joined her in urging him to concentrate on the slum-peasants that he knew so well. It was not only the advice of the directors, however, but what he had learned directly from the trial-and-error writing of these three rejected scripts which now brought the resolute O'Casey, at the age of forty-three, to the threshold of his initial success. Just as he had confidently taught himself to read literature as a boy, he was now teaching himself how to write it, without any special training in the drama.

Meanwhile, in March 1922 he had what might be called his first work of fiction published in *Poblacht Na h-Eireann* [The Republic of Ireland], a weekly Republican paper edited by Erskine Childers, who was soon to become one of the seventy-seven Die-Hard Republican leaders to be executed by the Irish Free State Government. O'Casey's allegorical tale of some 1250 words titled, 'The Seamless Coat of Kathleen', a Parable of the Ard-Fheis [*ard-esh*, the meeting of the leaders], was a satire on the many vested interests now fighting for control of the new Free State government. He mocked the various attempts to weave a new Republican coat for the unfortunate Kathleen Ni Houlihan. He later used the same theme for his comic fantasy, the one-act *Kathleen Listens In* (1923), which he wrote after *The Shadow of a Gunman*; but it received a cool reception at the Abbey, for the audience was largely composed of the partisans of all the political groups he had unmercifully parodied. In June 1922 another work of fiction appeared in a magazine called *The Gael*. This was a two-part short story of about 3,000 words called 'The Corncrake', which he had written as a free translation of a farcical Gaelic folk tale. It is an amusing story about some practical jokers who make fools of two 'arguefying' old codgers, a pair of bull-necked clowns who are roughly-sketched portraits of the kind of comic characters he was to create in his plays.

In 1923 he sent his fourth play to the Abbey and it was immediately accepted without a revision in the text. Only the title was changed from *On the Run* to *The Shadow of a Gunman*. At last he was on his way. He had knocked on the door until it opened, and now he would see some of his own pictures in the hallway. Yeats and particularly Lady Gregory had no doubt helped him open the

door with their encouragement and advice; there were some melodramatic scenes and low comedy characters that might have been
inspired by Boucicault; his fondness for Shakespeare and the Bible
probably had an indirect influence on his exuberant use of language. Yet there was an original vitality and invention in this play
that was uniquely his own, especially evident in his striking
counter-balance of the comic and tragic genres. And the broad
laughter served to humanize the sharp edge of his indignation. He
wrote then, as he went on to write in his succeeding works, like
one who had just discovered the power and poetry of the English
language and could never cease to wonder at the miracle of words.
He had created his own rich and dramatic idiom out of the common language he had heard spoken in the slums of Dublin, just as
Synge before him had used the speech rhythms and idioms of the
Aran Islanders and Wicklow peasants in his plays. Synge, however,
had approached the problem of creating an indigenous language
for the drama as a trained and sophisticated writer, not as a primitive like O'Casey who was himself a part of the world he created.
And O'Casey was following Synge instinctively, not consciously,
for while he knew of the works of his fellow countryman at this
time, he had not yet read or seen any of Synge's plays.

No, not Synge, fine as he is. It was only after the production of *The
Gunman* and *Juno* that I saw a Synge play. I never had the money to
spare to go to the Abbey. I went twice before I wrote plays—once
paying for myself in the shilling place; and once thro' the kindness of a
friend to see Shaw's *Androcles and the Lion.* I'd never seen a Shaw
play before; but I'd read his *John Bull's Other Island,* issued in a six-
penny paper-covered edition. Strindberg, yes; and the Elizabethans,
including Shakespeare; and Dion Boucicault, who wrote *Colleen Bawn,*
and *Arra na Pogue,* etc., and many others whose plays were a penny
each; and some fine ones among them; and Ibsen faintly. But I've let all
the older literature of England into my soul, and these, too, though not
dramatists, influenced me a great deal; but life always, and most forcibly
of all. [44]

If the newly discovered dramatist had any hopes of giving up his
job as a labourer and living on his earnings as a writer, they
vanished when he received his share of the receipts from *The
Shadow of a Gunman.* Most Abbey productions ran for at least a

week, but with an unknown playwright the directors decided to give the play a three-day trial run during the last week of the season. The final night was a complete sell-out and the 'House Full' sign was hung out—the first time this had happened in the history of the Abbey. The play grossed over ninety pounds, yet O'Casey's reward came to only four pounds! He had to wait a year to make his 'fortune' when his next play, *Juno and the Paycock*, drew such large crowds that it had to be extended for a second week, the first time in Abbey history that a play had run longer than a week. Furthermore, for the first time in the twenty-year history of the Abbey there were long queues outside the theatre and many people had to be turned away. Yeats thought it was a very fine play, though he remarked to Lady Gregory that it reminded him of Tolstoy, of all writers! After one of the performances an exuberant Lady Gregory stated: 'This is one of the evenings at the Abbey that makes me glad to have been born.'[45] And Lennox Robinson some years later said what everyone at that time knew; 'Those two early great plays of O'Casey, *The Shadow of a Gunman* and *Juno and the Paycock*, saved the Theatre from bankruptcy'[46]; and, one might add, artistic as well as financial bankruptcy.

O'Casey himself was none too solvent at this time, for he was still working as a labourer during the run of the play, mixing cement on a road repair job. When the two-week run ended, however, and he received the grand sum of twenty-five pounds, he decided to give up his job and hazard the chance of trying to live by his pen alone. At the age of forty-four he finally considered himself a professional writer, and thereafter he was to make his precarious living solely from his writing.

4. APOTHEOSIS AND EXILE

O'Casey did not achieve what Yeats called his 'apotheosis' until two years later. In the meantime he had written two one-act plays that were performed at the Abbey, *Kathleen Listens In* (1923) and *Nannie's Night Out* (1924), the first a comic fantasy, the second a broad farce, neither of which he has seen fit to include among his published works. Then in 1926 came the play that rocked Ireland, *The Plough and the Stars*, a genuine Irish theatrical triumph, greeted with shouts of blasphemy and obscenity, flying objects and fists, and finally the arrival of the police in the Abbey Theatre.

Controversies and riots over plays were by no means new to Dublin, nor were they to be a new experience for O'Casey in the years ahead. In 1899 Yeats's *The Countess Cathleen* had been condemned as dangerously heretical by Cardinal Logue who, somehow better qualified to pass judgement on the play for not having read it, insisted that no Irish woman, Countess or colleen, could ever sell her soul to the Devil, even to save Ireland. In 1907 irate audiences at the Abbey had interrupted performances of Synge's *Playboy of the Western World* with outraged booing and shouting at the mere mention of an Irish girl's undergarment, a 'shift', and at what they considered to be a slanderous insult to the Irish peasantry.

Now it was O'Casey's turn to offend the Irish chauvinists. He had already offended them with his satiric and anti-idealistic portraits of the Dublin slum-dwellers and would-be patriots in *The Gunman*, although they had apparently not realized it. To the puritans and sentimental patriots, Ireland was still the beautiful Queen that James Mangan, the nineteenth-century romantic poet, had glorified in his popular poem, 'Kathaleen Ny-Houlahan':

> *Think her not a ghastly hag, too hideous to be seen?*
> *Call her not unseemly names, our matchless Kathaleen?*
> *Young she is, and fair she is, and would be crowned a queen.*

But the earthy Seumas Shields in *The Gunman* had not hesitated to describe her in unseemly and unqueenly terms:

An' you daren't open your mouth, for Kathleen ni Houlihan is very different now to the woman who used to play the harp an' sing 'Weep on, weep on, your hour is past', for she's a ragin' divil now, an' if you only look crooked at her you're sure of a punch in th' eye.

Even *Juno* was received with some grumbling in Dublin, but it was after the successful two-week run, when the Abbey players put the play on at Cork, that there were signs of the trouble to come. The manager of the Cork theatre had refused to allow the play to be performed except in a badly bowdlerized version, with all references to religion eliminated and all references to sex cleaned up. Even the beautiful and poignant prayer spoken by Mrs. Tancred and Juno Boyle, one of the most important speeches in the play, was cut out; and to avoid the undesirable fact that an

Irish girl had been seduced, albeit by an Englishman, some dialogue was added to indicate that Bentham had married Mary Boyle before he deserted her.

If provincial Cork had been shocked by O'Casey's profanation of those two sanctified aspects of Irish life—religion and sex— provincial Dublin was soon to be outraged to the point of violence. [47] For in *The Plough and the Stars* he turned to the trinity of Irish taboos—religion, sex, and patriotism—and exposed them all on the Abbey stage. Now there were riots in the theatre again, as if to confirm O'Casey's genius. In this play about the 1916 Rising, he had dared to defend the victims, the women and children in the bullet-riddled tenements, rather than the 'heroes' of the rebellion; he had dared to bring the 'sacred' Republican flag into a Pub; and he had dared to portray an 'Irish' girl as a prostitute. He had the audacity to show the audience the real Ireland which they refused to recognize, and if Kathleen ni Houlihan now looked more like a 'ragin' divil' than a 'queen', the responsibility for this unflattering portrait lay not in the dramatist but in the grim and turbulent reality of contemporary life which mocked the sentimental ideals. Peter Kavanagh in his book *The Story of the Abbey Theatre* has accurately identified the 'sentimental nationalists' who regularly assailed the Abbey. And they were not limited to Ireland, for they were part of 'the world-wide army of philistines fighting its never-ending battle with the artist. . . . They resemble most closely those who today take part in the St Patrick's Day parades in American cities—who imagine Ireland to be as green and level as a lawn, where the girls go around with eyes cast down, green garlands in their hair, and Rosaries at their girdles, while the men, armed only with shillelaghs, beat heavily armed battalions of British soldiers'. [48]

Now the tin-horn patriots had the Abbey in an uproar again. The opening-night audience on Monday was on the whole enthusiastic, but if the dissenters had been stunned by the initial impact of the play, they were quick to spread the word and organize their rowdy demonstrations on the next three nights. On Tuesday and Wednesday the play was repeatedly interrupted by shouting and jeering, but on Thursday night the real trouble broke loose. There were minor incidents from the start, but by the second act the rioters were drowning out the actors with the increasing uproar of shouting, booing, whistle-blowing, and singing. The actors were forced to carry on in dumb-show and hardly a word of dialogue was heard throughout the second act. Then early in the third act the play was completely stopped. Curses, vegetables, shoes, and chairs were hurled at the stage, stench bombs were set off throughout the theatre, and at one point a group of men and women leaped on the stage and started a fight with some of the actors. Barry Fitzgerald, who was playing the role of Fluther Good, knocked one of the men back into the orchestra pit with a good 'flutherian' uppercut to the chin. The curtain was lowered, the police were summoned to restore order, and the dignified and disdainful Yeats, then a Senator as well as Director of the Abbey, strode majestically out on the stage to defend the artist and chastise the mob, just as he had done during *The Playboy* riots. It is doubtful whether many people in the theatre heard his fine speech above the uproar; however, the next day all the newspapers printed, with some variations, what he had said:

You have disgraced yourselves again. Is this to be an ever-recurring celebration of the arrival of Irish genius? Synge first and then O'Casey. The news of the happenings of the past few minutes will go from country to country. Dublin has once more rocked the cradle of genius. From such a scene in this theatre went forth the fame of Synge. Equally the fame of O'Casey is born here tonight. This is his apotheosis. [49]

But if this was O'Casey's 'apotheosis', it also marked the beginning of his complete alienation from Ireland. The 'Day of the Rabblement' had finally dawned for him, and he was soon to follow Joyce into self-exile.

For the first time in his life, Sean felt a surge of hatred for Kathleen ni Houlihan sweeping over him. He saw now that the one who had the walk of a queen could be a bitch at times. She galled the hearts of her children who dared to be above the ordinary, and she often slew her best ones. She had hounded Parnell to death; she had yelled and torn at Yeats, at Synge, and now she was doing the same to him. What an old snarly gob she could be at times; an ignorant one too. [50]

It wasn't only the Dublin mob, however, that had objected to *The Plough*. Although many of the newspaper reviewers had praised the play, there were notable exceptions among the Dublin nationalists, intellectuals, and literati. Mrs. Hanna Sheehy-Skeffington, widow of one of the 1916 martyrs, who had led one group of rioters in the theatre, roundly condemned the play in a patriotic letter to the Press, and challenged O'Casey to a debate on the whole issue.[51] Joseph Holloway, the architect who designed the Abbey, a friend of Yeats and a loyal patron of the theatre, agreed with the people who called the play 'Dirt for dirt's sake'.[52] Andrew E. Malone, dean of the Dublin critics, who had previously praised *Juno*, now called *The Plough* a cheap music-hall concoction.[53] The novelist Liam O'Flaherty attacked Yeats as well as O'Casey—Yeats for having 'pompously' insulted the Dublin audience in his speech, O'Casey for having written a 'bad play' which undermined the Irish national character. The poet F. R. Higgins belittled the play as a mere catalogue of 'Handy-Andy burlesque incidents', and charged that O'Casey 'entirely lacks the sincerity of an artist'. O'Casey had his defenders, too; particularly in editorials and letters in the *Irish Times* and AE's *Irish Statesman*, but the controversy ran on for weeks and a steady stream of abusive letters flooded the press. In a front-page article the *Evening Herald* accused O'Casey of slander,[54] and in a long editorial the *Catholic Bulletin* condemned Yeats and the Abbey as an Anglo-Irish conspiracy and O'Casey's play as 'Sewage School' drama.

Besides these bitter attacks, there were other alienating forces at work. O'Casey had often felt that as a writer and as a man there was no place for him in the Abbey literary circles. He remained a strange and angry man from the Dublin tenements—in the phrase of a hostile critic, 'the guttersnipe from the slums', a title that he readily accepted and wore proudly. Lady Gregory, his only genuine and trusted friend among the Abbey hierarchy, accepted him warmly and graciously, but Yeats always remained politely aristocratic in his relationships with the proletarian O'Casey. There was, however, no intentional malice in Yeats's aloof manner, for he more or less behaved the same toward everyone. In the speech he had made in O'Casey's behalf from the stage of the Abbey, he had, as Peter Kavanagh pointed out, defended an artistic principle more than a specific individual. He had enjoyed this new opportunity to excoriate the Dublin philistines, for he had his own vision of an exclusive poetic theatre in which there would be no place for a large

popular audience. Yeats and O'Casey had the highest respect for
each other as artists, but they lived in totally different worlds
which separated them as men. Yeats did not have writers like
O'Casey in mind when in his late poem, 'Under Ben Bulben', he
urged his creative country men to return to Ireland's aristocratic
traditions and themes:

> *Irish poets, learn your trade,*
> *Sing whatever is well made,*
> *Scorn the sort now growing up*
> *All out of shape from toe to top,*
> *Their unremembering hearts and heads*
> *Base-born products of base beds.*
> *Sing the peasantry, and then*
> *Hard-riding country gentlemen,*
> *The holiness of monks, and after*
> *Porter-drinkers' randy laughter?*
> *Sing the lords and ladies gay*
> *That were beaten into the clay*
> *Through seven heroic centuries?*
> *Cast your mind on other days*
> *That we in coming days may be*
> *Still the indomitable Irishry.* (55)

O'Casey represented a new kind of 'indomitable Irishry'—the
'base-born' yet heroic people of the Dublin tenements. O'Casey
was a proud plebeian, Yeats a proud patrician. Their opposite
social, economic, and educational backgrounds, their contrasting
experiences, habits, and temperaments, the different kinds of plays
they wrote, even the manner in which they dressed, reflected the
gulf between them. Yeats always attended the theatre in the company of the social élite and was regally attired in formal evening
clothes, while O'Casey, almost as if in reply to the patrician poet
and the social élite, invariably appeared in his democratic cap,
which he seldom removed, and his familiar turtle-neck sweater, a
plebeian uniform that he proudly continued to wear through the
years.

Nor was all peaceful behind the scenes at the Abbey. Although
Yeats and Lady Gregory had warmly accepted *The Plough*, two
members of the Abbey board of directors vehemently objected to
the play. O'Casey's language was too strong and even 'indecent';

a word like 'bitch' could not be allowed on an Irish stage; one
of the love scenes was much too passionate; the appearance
of an Irish girl as a prostitute was shockingly impossible; and
the song at the end of the second act was simply obscene and
had to go. In fact, it was all 'beyond the beyonds' and the
actors themselves would refuse to appear in such a play, warned
George O'Brien, one of the dissenting directors. He was almost
right.

During the rehearsals O'Casey once threatened to withdraw his
play when some of the actors decided to change or omit what they
felt were objectionable lines. One of the leading Abbey actresses,
who was cast as Mrs Gogan, after consulting with her priest, insisted that as a Catholic she could not say the line, 'Ne'er a one o'
Jennie Gogan's kids was born outside of th' bordhers of the Ten
Commandments'. She finally gave up the role and played a walk-
on part instead; but in later revivals of the play, when it became
one of the outstanding works of the Abbey repertory, she had no
objections to playing the part without benefit of clerical advice,
and she played it extremely well for she was a fine actress. Other
actors tried to tone down their lines or exchange their parts for less
controversial ones, and Ria Mooney, who was cast as Rosie Redmond, was warned by her friends to quit before she ruined her
career. Even that superb actor F. J. McCormick, who played the
part of Jack Clitheroe, objected to the impropriety of some of his
lines—he refused, for example, to say the word 'snotty'—and in
the heated days of argument following the riots he publicly announced that the actors should not be associated with the objectionable parts of the play.

All these difficulties were but part of the growing antagonism
which surrounded O'Casey and gradually estranged him from the
city and the people he loved. He became an alienated rebel in a
country whose whole history had been marked by rebellion and
betrayal, back-biting and sneering. He knew now what Joyce meant
in his 'Gas from a Burner', that bitter broadside in which he had
written:

> This lovely land that always sent
> Her writers and artists to banishment
> And in a spirit of Irish fun
> Betrayed her own leaders, one by one.

'Twas Irish humour, wet and dry
Flung quicklime into Parnell's eye . . .
O Ireland my first and only love
Where Christ and Caesar are hand and glove! (56)

Thus, he was also being impelled toward banishment by religious and political forces—the alliance of Christ and Caesar. His recent discovery of the McDonald tragedy, and its parallel to the O'Hickey tragedy, convinced him that the powers which had 'flung quicklime into Parnell's eye' were still in the saddle; and in the political saddle was the new Irish Government which rode along in unison with the authoritarian clergy. He felt that these combined forces had created the atmosphere and the attitudes which inspired the pietistic and patriotic fanatics to attack his play. This Ireland was not the workers' republic for which Larkin and Connolly had fought.

Many years later, in examining that period of O'Casey's estrangement, the writer Sean O'Faolain made some trenchant observations which suggest that O'Casey had interpreted the temper of the time correctly. O'Faolain began with a comparison of two Abbey riots: 'The type of people who had, long ago, protested against Synge's *Playboy* had no political power. The people who objected to O'Casey had political power.' He went on to speak about the religious nature of that power: 'Moreover, in those "old days" the Catholic Church had had only a limited amount of political power because the government had been an alien and non-Catholic government, and the foreign Gallio, like all pro-consuls, had kept the ring with the tolerance of total indifference. Now the Church could wield almost unlimited power because the native government was composed of men who respected, loved, and feared it.'(57) He then turned to the political nature of that power:

Sean O'Casey's plays are thus an exactly true statement of the Irish Revolution whose flag should be, not the tricolour, but the plough and the stars of the labouring classes. We must, finally, understand that the class that thus came to power and influence was not a labouring class; the more able among them changed their nature by changing their place in life—they graduated rapidly into *petit bourgeois*, middle-men, importers, small manufacturers, thus forming a new middle class to fill the vacuum formed by the departure or depression of the alien middle class. These men, naturally, had had very little education and could have only a slight interest in the intellectuals' fight for liberty of expression. They were ordinary, decent, kindly, self-seeking men who had no intention of jeopardizing their mushroom-prosperity by gratuitous displays of moral courage. In any case, since they were rising to sudden wealth behind protective tariff-walls they had a vested interest in nationalism and even in isolationism. The upshot of it was a holy alliance between the Church, the new businessmen, and the politicians, all three nationalist-isolationist for, respectively, moral reasons, commercial reasons, and politico-patriotic reasons. The intellectuals became a depressed group. Possibly they were also infected by the atmosphere around them. When patriotism starts to cash in it is enough to sicken anyone.

O'Casey had been sickened by the spectacle. By the spring of 1926, at the height of his turbulent success, he was anxious to escape before he became infected by the atmosphere. He wanted to leave Ireland in order to be a free Irishman, free to live and write on his own terms.

In late March, six weeks after the *Plough* riots, the news came from England that *Juno* had won him the Hawthornden Prize, an award for the best work of the previous year by a new writer. He was invited to London to receive the award, which carried with it a cheque for a hundred pounds, the most money he had seen in his life. After several exciting weeks in London, where he became friendly with men like Bernard Shaw and Augustus John, he went back to Dublin for his meagre belongings, mostly books, and by mid-April he was back in England to stay, living in a flat in London and working on a new play, *The Silver Tassie*, which he had promised to send back to Yeats and Lady Gregory. He had left Dublin, not the Abbey Theatre, although it soon turned out that the Abbey had left him when it decided to reject his new play.

He had to be free, but he had not left Dublin in order to forget it. The city and its people were to remain the centre of his life and work even in his exile. Only a man who loved his country so deeply could have hated so fiercely the conditions under which his countrymen lived. His life and his work represented a rebellion against human suffering, and exile was the heart-breaking price he had to pay for that rebellion.

According to ancient legend, Zeus employed Prometheus to

make men out of mud and water, but out of his great compassion for suffering mankind the rebellious titan stole fire from heaven and gave it to them, for which he was exiled and chained to a rock. The exiled O'Casey understood better than anyone the anger and the compassion of Prometheus, for he had created the fire of his plays from similar motives.

CHAPTER II

The Tragi-Comic Muse

> That way of Trage-Comedy was the common mistake
> of that age [Shakespeare's], and is indeed become so
> agreeable to the English taste, that tho' the severer
> Critiques among us cannot bear it, yet the generality
> of our audiences seem to be better pleas'd with it than
> an exact Tragedy. *The Merry Wives of Windsor*, *The
> Comedy of Errors*, and *The Taming of the Shrew*, are all
> pure Comedy; the rest, however they are call'd, have
> something of both kinds.
>
> Nicholas Rowe (1709)[58]

> The art of the Elizabethans is an impure art.
> T. S. Eliot (1924)[59]

1. PURE AND IMPURE DRAMA

THE ART of O'Casey is an impure art. It is a drama which is neither 'exact Tragedy' nor 'pure Comedy', and yet it is a diverse drama which boldly combines these two genres in a reconciliation of opposing forms. It is a drama in which scenes of low comedy may precede or follow, or even merge with, scenes of deep tragedy. It is a drama in which the ordinary rituals of life are presented through an extraordinary rhetorical language. It is a drama in which realistic themes are reinforced with non-realistic modes such as farce, melodrama, satire, and song. It is diverting and disturbing drama that is usually more pleasing to popular audiences than to severe critics. It is an impure drama which is inspired by the bastard muse of tragi-comedy.

Tragi-comedy may not be a problem to the playwrights who undisturbedly write it or their audiences who unashamedly enjoy it, but it has consistently remained a puzzle to critics and scholars

47

of the drama. And it has understandably been most disconcerting
to those partisans of 'pure' drama who with their aesthetic theories
or their neo-Aristotelian fondness for the rules of the game protest
that there are no fixed rules of conventions for a hybrid drama that
is neither a tragedy nor a comedy yet is *both*. It is well known that
the so-called crudities and impurities of Shakespeare's plays provoked the displeasure of the eighteenth-century critics, and while
many of those neoclassical strictures have been answered, perhaps
most notably by Dr Johnson, the case for pure drama has not remained without its champions and distinguished practitioners in
our own time. Two of the major poets and most influential literary
figures of the twentieth century, W. B. Yeats and T. S. Eliot, have
eloquently argued their theories of pure drama and have written
significant verse plays in support of their views. The plays of
Shakespeare are for Eliot 'an impure art', and for Yeats they are
impure because they are tragi-comic. In his essay, 'The Tragic
Theatre', Yeats explained it as follows:

In the writers of tragi-comedy (and Shakespeare is always a writer of
tragi-comedy) there is indeed character, but we notice that it is in
moments of comedy that the character is defined, in Hamlet's gaiety
let us say; while amid the great moments, when Timon orders his tomb,
when Hamlet cries to Horatio 'absent thee from felicity awhile', when
Anthony names 'Of many thousand kisses the poor last', all is lyricism,
unmixed passion, 'the integrity of fire'. Nor does character ever attain
to complete definition in these lamps ready for the taper, no matter how
circumstantial and gradual the opening of events, as it does in Falstaff
who has no passionate purpose to fulfil. . . . [60]

   For Yeats, then, the pure or 'unmixed' lyric passion of tragedy
is corrupted by the comic element with its intrusion of what he
calls 'the daily mood' of realistic character; thus, in a tragi-
comedy the tragedy is lost among 'our common moments' when
the comedy 'sings, laughs, chatters or looks its busy thoughts'. It
was with these guiding principles that Yeats wrote his Noh-in-
spired 'Plays for Dancers', stylized verse plays in which the impure elements of character and comedy were suppressed in favour
of the pure elements of lyricism and passion.
   While Eliot does not practise Yeats's aesthetic theories in his
own verse plays, he nevertheless shares many of Yeats's views in

his own theorizing on the drama. Eliot not only objects to Shakespeare's tendency to mix comedy with tragedy, but also objects to what he calls the general Elizabethan habit of carelessly mixing realistic or common experiences with non-realistic or symbolic conventions. He certainly moves in the direction of 'pure' Yeatsian drama when he writes in his essay, 'Four Elizabethan Dramatists':

... the Elizabethans committed faults and muddled their conventions. In their plays there are faults of inconsistency, faults of incoherency, faults of taste, there are nearly everywhere faults of carelessness. But their greatest weakness is the same weakness as that of modern drama, it is the lack of a convention. . . .
  The difference between a great dancer and a merely competent dancer is in the vital flame, that impersonal, and, if you like, inhuman force which transpires between each of the great dancer's movements. So it would be in a strict form of drama; but in realistic drama, which is drama striving steadily to escape the conditions of art, the human being intrudes.[61]

Eliot grants that the unfortunate human intrusion is necessary in the 'realistic' plays of Shakespeare and the moderns, but he goes on to make his case for a 'strict form of drama' which would be non-realistic and impersonal, or, if one likes, inhuman, and therefore not likely to escape Eliot's pure conditions of art. Doubtless Yeats with his 'integrity of fire' would have appreciated Eliot's rather Yeatsian dancer-image and the 'impersonal flame'. When Yeats rejected *The Silver Tassie* he scolded O'Casey for not using dramatic action as 'a fire which burns up everything but itself' in a process by which man and history are reduced to 'wallpaper in front of which the characters must pose and speak'.[62] What price pure flame! Perhaps it is not surprising that Eliot should have found what he called 'the perfect and ideal drama' in the sacred ritual of the Mass, and that Yeats should have found it in the ancient ritual of the Japanese Noh. Apparently they both envisioned the ultimate drama as an other-worldly art. Now the drama originally had its roots in religious ritual, but once it became secularized and flourished it was seldom a strict or pure form. Even in Greek drama there are extremely few works that adhere to the Aristotelian pattern, which is actually a descriptive analysis not a definitive theory. Sophocles' *Oedipus Rex* is an isolated example not a universal model of a unique one-act play; for no formalized theory, pure Aristotle or pure fire, has yet been established which can, or for that matter should, satisfactorily embrace the dissimilar works of Aeschylus, Sophocles and Euripides, let alone the Elizabethans and the moderns.

There is yet another sense in which the drama is an impure art. Unlike all other forms of literature, the drama is a collaborative medium, for it is dependent upon many contributions besides the text itself. It must be interpreted by directors and actors; it must be produced with sets, lighting, costumes, music, and the services of many skilled technicians; and it must finally be performed before a public audience in a theatre. Many writers have avoided the drama because of this collaborative and public 'intrusion'. Once André Gide was disturbed by one of Jacques Copeau's lectures on 'pure' drama at the Vieux-Colombier and he made a particularly significant comment on it in his *Journal*:

[Copeau] was struggling against the epoch, as any good artist must do. But dramatic art has this frightful disadvantage, that it must appeal to the public, count with and on the public. This is indeed what made me turn away from it, more and more convinced that truth is not on the side of the greatest number. Copeau, though claiming not to, was working for a select few. He wanted to lead to perfection, to style, to purity, an essentially impure art that gets along without all that. [63]

The drama is not like a lyric poem and should not be treated as if it were a sonnet or a sonata. Yeats was actually more dramatic in his lyric poetry than he was in his lyric plays. His concept of dramatic purity had inspired him to create an absolutely refined and formalized anti-drama—plays which Louis MacNeice has described as 'undramatic charades'[64]—plays in which, according to Ronald Peacock, Yeats 'refines away the material world in too many directions at once'. Eliot, on the other hand, has been more successful as a dramatist because, unlike Yeats, he does not always practise in his plays the purity he preaches in his essays. One can in fact make out a good case for most of Eliot's plays as impure drama, for instance the tragi-comic *Cocktail Party*, modelled as it was upon that striking example of impure Greek drama, Euripides' tragi-comic *Alcestis*. And S. L. Bethell has shrewdly pointed out another fortunate contradiction in the Eliot canon; '*Murder in the*

Cathedral, with its complex demands upon the audience, is the nearest approach to serious art in the popular tradition. Mr Eliot has significantly written in praise of the old music-hall, and in this play he exploits music-hall devices in the service of the highest dramatic aims. If this be inconsistent with his judgement upon the Elizabethans, it is a blessed inconsistency.'[65] It is evident, then, that Eliot talks about but does not write 'a strict form of drama'— one could add the early *Sweeney Agonistes* and the late *Confidential Clerk* to *Murder in the Cathedral* and *The Cocktail Party*—all impure plays in which he mixes music-hall devices and melodrama with poetic conventions, character and comedy with passion and poetry. It should also be remembered that Eliot once wrote: 'You cannot define Drama and Melodrama so that they shall be reciprocally exclusive; great drama has something melodramatic in it, and the best melodrama partakes of the greatness of drama.'[66] In *Poetry and Drama*, he continues to be blessedly inconsistent in coming round to the view that the modern verse dramatist must accept the *human intrusion*. He is now convinced that the dramatist who writes his plays in verse must not lose 'that contact with the ordinary everyday world with which the drama must come to terms'.[67]

Since they are seldom over-burdened with formal theories, the writers of tragi-comedy are probably not aware that there could be a conflict between art and everyday life. Art and life are not the same thing; art is a selective ordering of experience while life is commonly a series of disordered experiences. But art is not an escape from life; if it is an escape at all it is an escape *into* life. All aspects of life are fair game for the artist, and the writer of tragi-comedy above all does not hesitate to combine the sublime with the absurd, the heroic with the hilarious, the poetic with the profane—and there can be little doubt that in the process he achieves something akin to Coleridge's 'balance or reconciliation of opposite or discordant qualities'. Playwrights like Shakespeare, Chekhov, Shaw, Synge, O'Casey, Pirandello, Giraudoux, Anouilh, Sartre, Wilder, Beckett, and Ionesco have freely used 'music-hall devices in the service of the highest dramatic aims'. All of these playwrights, and many others in our time, write what is essentially impure drama. One might even say that the bastard genre of tragi-comedy has been one of the dominant forms of twentieth-century drama,[68] as illustrated by such diverse works as Chekhov's *Uncle Vanya* and *The Cherry Orchard*; Shaw's *Saint Joan* and *Heartbreak House*; Synge's *The Well of the Saints* and *The Playboy of the Western World*; O'Casey's *Juno and the Paycock* and *The Plough and the Stars*: Pirandello's *Six Characters in Search of an Author* and *Henry IV*; Sartre's *The Flies* and *No Exit*; Beckett's *Waiting for Godot* and *End Game*. A similar claim and a parallel list might be made for the modern novel as tragi-comedy, with Joyce's *Ulysses* as the archetypal work.

In another dominant type of modern drama (and this also applies to the modern novel) which is commonly described as naturalism, the writer confines himself to such a scrupulous recording of everyday life that he ultimately arrives at the opposite pole from aesthetic purity—the drama of sociological purity. The aim of this drama is 'scientific truth', as it was pronounced by Emile Zola who wrote the credo of naturalism in 1873 in his famous Preface to *Thérèse Raquin*, [69] a dramatization of one of his novels. Zola had rightly rebelled against the artificial nineteenth century melodrama of 'armour, secret doors, poisoned cups and the rest', but in his vigorous reaction against this clap-trap he borrowed Taine's social empiricism and practically reduced the art of the drama to a 'scientific' study of hereditary and environmental evidence. Fortunately, however, not all those dramatists who are neatly 'classified' as naturalists in the anthologies and histories of drama strive for or achieve the naturalistic purity that Zola demanded. In fact, Zola himself rises above the limitations of Zolaism in most of his works. And Ibsen made it a special point of protest to disaffiliate himself from Ibsenism when he wrote *The Wild Duck*. Even to this day, however, Ibsen is so often heralded and/or damned as a naturalist of social protest that one might think he never wrote plays before or after *The Doll's House* and *An Enemy of the People*, when indeed the poetic works of his early phase— *Brand* and *Peer Gynt*—and the symbolic works of his major phase—*Hedda Gabler, Rosmersholm, The Master Builder, John Gabriel Borkmann*, and *Little Eyolf*—all outsoar the confines of naturalism. Ibsen may have had too little humour and too classical a spirit to allow himself the levities and felicities of tragi-comedy, but it must be said of him that he used the highest moral values in the service of the highest dramatic aims.

Of course the writer of tragi-comedy is also concerned with the highest moral values, but because he cannot be solemn about what he feels too deeply, he must move obliquely round his subject and test the inconsistencies of a tragi-comic vision. His compassion is concealed in this irony. Dramatists like Chekhov and O'Casey—who are invariably and inaccurately 'classified' as naturalists in the anthologies and histories of drama—possess the tragi-comic sense of life, for it is only by laughing with and through their characters that they are able to cope with the overwhelming burden of reality. For them life is at the same time too brutal and too beautiful to be treated with undisguised agony or idealism. For them the double mask of tragi-comedy reveals the polarity of the human condition. Long ago Plato must have understood this polarity for at the conclusion of *The Symposium*, after a night of wild drinking and philosophic debate, his still clear-headed Socrates is explaining to the tragedian Agathon and the comedian Aristophanes, just before they fall into a drunken sleep, that there is a common ground for tragedy and comedy, 'that a skilful tragic writer is capable of being also a comic writer'.[70]

But Plato does not actually tell us that this writer may combine his tragic and comic skills in the same play. Dr Johnson does, however, for in defending Shakespeare from 'the censure which he has incurred by mixing comick and tragick scenes',[71] he states with his characteristic wisdom that the artist can always appeal from the arbitrary rules of criticism to the higher court of nature. It is in the nature of life itself, Dr Johnson tells us, that the tragi-comic writer finds his vision of a 'mingled drama':

Shakespeare's plays are not in the rigorous and critical sense either tragedies or comedies, but compositions of a distinct kind; exhibiting the real state of sublunary nature, which partakes of good and evil, joy and sorrow, mingled with endless variety of proportion and innumerable modes of combination; and expressing the course of the world, in which the loss of one is the gain of another; in which, at the same time, the reveller is hasting to his wine, and the mourner burying his friend; in which the malignity of one is sometimes defeated by the frolick of another; and many mischiefs and many benefits are done and hindered without design. . . .

That this is a practice contrary to the rules of criticism will be readily allowed; but there is always an appeal open from criticism to nature. The end of writing is to instruct; the end of poetry is to instruct by pleasing. That the mingled drama may convey all the instruction of tragedy or comedy cannot be denied. . . . [72]

It is difficult to find a better justification of tragi-comedy. It is just as difficult to find a pat definition of it. Perhaps it is inadvisable to try to define it, to establish a set of rules for a bastard genre the very existence of which is contrary to the so-called existing rules of drama. One feels about defining tragi-comedy the way Sissy Jupe felt, in Dickens's *Hard Times*, when that Gradgrind of 'facts and calculations' demanded that she define a horse. Sissy was intimidated into silence, for it is not easy to define the familiar. And like Sissy, who *knows* what a horse is from having been near horses all her life, one *knows* what tragi-comedy is from having seen and read it all one's life. A definition parallel to Bitzer's 'Quadruped. Gramnivorous. Forty teeth, namely twenty-four grinders . . .' etc. will not do. Nor will it do to distil and divide equal parts of Aristotelian tragedy and Bergsonian comedy. Eric Bentley, one of the most enlightened of the modern critics of the drama, has pointed out the danger of pontifical theorizing:

Tragedy is a topic that lures the critic into talking beautiful nonsense. On this subject even more than on others he tends to generalize from a favourite example or merely to play high-minded cadenzas. The trouble always is that tragedy has been a different thing for every major practitioner. And if anything is more elusive than a correct description of the tragic it is a correct description of the comic. [73]

And having established this caution, Bentley avoids high-sounding definitions and wisely concerns himself with an intelligent examination of specific plays. He finally concludes:

Detailed study of particular works naturally calls attention from generic to individual qualities, which is pleasant since the good things in art are essentially individual. Very well then. In the teeth of logicians and lexicographers one is content to read comedies without knowing exactly what comedy is. [74]

Very well then. One may similarly be content to read tragi-comedies without knowing exactly what tragi-comedy is. With this refreshing if precarious assumption as a starting point, it may be possible to go on to make some discoveries about the nature of tragi-comedy in the particular works of O'Casey. The reader who would know definitively what the artist knows intuitively must be prepared for surprises and mysteries. There are no predictable laws of measurement in literature. Every work of art is a kind of a mutation; even when one enjoys it and examines it the mystery is never fully fathomed. In replying to a young man who had written to him about the 'meaning' of *The Playboy of the Western World*, Synge commented: 'With a great deal of what you say I am most heartily in agreement—as where you say that I wrote the *Playboy* directly, as a piece of life, without thinking, or caring to think, whether it was a comedy, tragedy, or extravaganza, or whether it would be held to have, or not to have a purpose—also where you speak very accurately and rightly about Shakespeare's "mirror".'[75] And once when O'Casey was confronted by an elaborate analysis of one of his plays he modestly remarked that he was a dramatist not a theorist and must have built better than he knew. Perhaps most successful dramatists build better than they know. For the theoretical dramatist, however, a little pure theory could be a dangerous thing and he might end up knowing better than he builds.

2. A REVOLUTION IN THE THEATRE

'I believe that the theatre has reached a point at which a revolution in principles should take place.'[76] T. S. Eliot wrote these words in 1924, the same year that O'Casey wrote *Juno and the Paycock* and was already in the midst of creating his own unique revolution in the theatre. Of course, O'Casey's revolution was not quite what Eliot had in mind. Eliot's revolution was to be launched against prosaic realism in order to return to the pure principles and conventions of verse drama. But O'Casey's revolution— which was similarly a reaction against prosaic realism, a point that is too often overlooked—also turned out to be a return to an old but impure theatrical principle: make 'em laugh and make 'em weep. He also made 'em think deeply and he made 'em feel passionately. If there was a tone of indictment in these early plays, it was an organic part of the entertainment. And he probably picked up this 'principle' of robust entertainment from his experience of the tumultuous life of the Dublin slums and from his reading of

those two master showmen of the theatre, Shakespeare and
Boucicault. Once after he had seen a special performance of one of
Yeat's poetic Noh plays for dancers, O'Casey felt that something
vital was missing from that static form of drama, for it reminded
him of an artificial flower. He believed that: 'A play poetical to be
worthy of the theatre must be able to withstand the terror of Ta Ra
Ra Boom Dee Ay, as a blue sky, or an apple tree in bloom, withstand any ugliness around or beneath them.'[77] There is plenty of
good old 'Ta Ra Ra Boom Dee Ay' in the plays of Shakespeare,
Boucicault, and O'Casey.

In getting at the problem of what makes good drama, then,
O'Casey went back to fundamental ingredients. For him the drama
had to tell an exciting story about people whose conflicts were
colourful as well as meaningful; it had to amuse as well as amaze
an audience confronted by the mundane and profound crises of
their fellow men; it had to exploit all the elements of theatrical fun
and excitement, with low comedy that could be wildly hilarious as
well as pointedly satiric, and with melodrama that could be used to
turn the screw of tragic tension; it had to present a striking image
of man in broad dimensions of character and language which while
drawn from life were sufficiently larger than life-size to reveal an
imaginative projection of reality. Finally, O'Casey added his per-
vasive attitude toward this spectacle, his unique tone of voice, his
tragi-comic point of view. He chose to penetrate the dilemma of
suffering mankind with the compassionate shock of rich laughter.
Twenty years before O'Casey wrote his plays, his fellow countryman Synge had begun this revolution in the theatre with his wild
tragi-comedies. And Synge had also chosen the basic ingredients
of low comedy and melodrama to project his near-tragic vision of
life.

Perhaps it is fortunate that O'Casey developed his fondness for
low comedy and melodrama early in life before he had a chance to
discover that some scholars often frowned upon them as cheap and
absurd theatrical tricks. Melodrama is certainly compounded of
theatrical tricks which are calculated to shock and excite an
audience, but this is not undesirable in the theatre and it did not
prevent the Greek and Elizabethan dramatists, for example, from
exploiting these tricks in their plays. And it is doubtful whether
the blood-and-thunder devices of melodrama—those flamboyant
signs of impurity in the drama—-cheapened their works. One could

make a long and notable list of the absurdly melodramatic plots of Sophoclean and Shakespearean plays. As Eric Bentley points out in his fine essay on 'The Psychology of Farce' [78] it is misleading as well as foolish of the highbrow scholars to discredit farce and melodrama, for these techniques have consistently remained 'central to literature and drama'. Art is a reflection of life, but it is an artificial configuration which exaggerates and distorts reality in order that the complexities and mysteries of life can be observed more sharply and with greater significance. Art cannot be restricted to the so-called natural scheme of things. 'If art imitates life,' Bentley says, 'it should be added that while naturalistic art imitates the surface, "melodramatic" art imitates what is beneath the surface. It is a matter, then, of finding external representation —symbol—for what cannot be photographed or described.' While this view should not be applied indiscriminately to all melodrama, it is certainly pertinent to the O'Casey plays, for with their melodramatic actions and low-comedy antics they are infinitely more than a surface photograph of the Dublin slums. It is the trenchant life beneath the surface of poverty and patriotism that interests him, and it is in this endeavour that he enlists the mock-heroic devices of satiric comedy and the sensational devices of melodrama.

The validity of melodrama, or for that matter all artifice in literature and in the theatre, depends upon the function it serves. It has the initial and surely legitimate function of galvanizing the conflict and tension—it creates a heightened atmosphere by raising fears and building suspense—and this whirl of excitement can serve as a prelude to deeper issues below the surface which ultimately emerge from the conflict. In fact, it is possible that man's deepest emotions can best be revealed when he succumbs to the outrageous temptations of melodramatic excess. Oedipus rashly kills his father and marries his mother, yet it is through these absurdly melodramatic horrors that he is forced to make his tragic discoveries about himself and the nature of man and fate. Lear foolishly banishes the good Cordelia and trusts the evil Goneril and Regan, yet it is through these absurdly melodramatic errors that he is driven to discover his tragic reason in madness. There are countless examples of this sort, in novels as well as plays, in which melodramatic action serves a non-melodramatic purpose. But there are also many works in which the melodrama is merely an end in itself or merely furthers some trite end, particularly those sentimental plays and novels of the last half of the nineteenth century which led to the original discrediting of melodrama. In these Victorian thrillers virtue automatically triumphed over vice no matter how staggering the odds—in fact, the greater the odds the better—for in Oscar Wilde's clever jest at the expense of the prim Miss Prism, 'The good ended happily and the bad unhappily. That is what Fiction means'.

One popular practitioner of this sort of theatrical fiction throughout the last half of the nineteenth century was Dion Boucicault. Yet master of melodrama that he was, the boisterous Boucicault would certainly have offended poor Miss Prism for he was also a master of low comedy and Irish blarney. He was at heart a rowdy and exuberant clown, and although he never deviated from the Victorian formula of vice punished and virtue rewarded, he filled the theatre with as much laughter as sentimentality and was most successful in his rollicking 'Oirish' comedies. The Stage Irishman who for centuries had been passed off as the brash buffoon of English literature—and Anglo-Irish literature—became in Boucicault's plays the clever and mischievous rogue-hero. Boucicault also created his quota of stock Celtic caricatures, but he was at his best with the comic vagabond—the *shaughraun* or wanderer—who shrewdly and bravely righted all wrongs and was master of the revels. So popular was this merry court-jester turned comic-hero that Boucicault had to satisfy his audiences by constantly recreating him as Myles na Coppaleen in *The Colleen Bawn* (1859), Sean the Post in *Arrah-Na-Pogue* (1864), and Conn the Shaughraun in *The Shaughraun* (1874)—all ripe acting parts which Boucicault wrote for himself and played with a charming brogue which Bernard Shaw claimed was not to be excelled for its musical sound and irresistible insinuation or 'sloothering'. This beguiling rogue-hero was not Boucicault's original creation—he borrowed the general format from the comic novels of William Carleton and Charles Lever, Irishmen who in turn had gaelicized it from Le Sage's picaresque Gil Blas—but with his mercurial genius for comic invention and showmanship he usually surpassed his sources in theatrical if not literary qualities. In Boucicault this hero emerged as a Celtic composite of Robin Hood, Monte Cristo, and Robin Goodfellow. And since the music-hall spectacle was his main concept of theatrical entertainment, no Boucicault play was complete without its music and song, the lilting ballads by the dozen he set to traditional airs, and the big 'sensation' scenes he produced with spectacular staging techniques—Myles na Coppaleen diving from a rock in a cave down into a simulated lake of blue gauze to rescue the drowning Colleen Bawn; Sean the Post cheating the British gallows in order to be with his darling Arrah na Pogue by escaping from a mobile prison tower which sinks to indicate he is climbing its ivy walls; and finally Conn the Shaughraun, the nonpareil, out-leaping and out-laughing them all— Conn 'the soul of every fair, the life of every funeral, the first fiddle at all weddings and patterns'.

Although he was an inspired and ingenious showman, Boucicault was no Barnum for he always gave his audiences exactly what he advertized and what they seemed to want—a melodramatic circus guaranteed to produce thrills and laughs aplenty. Understandably his hurly-burly action was all on the surface since it was clearly intended to be merry Celtic moonshine. Unlike a Dickens or an O'Casey, he had neither the ability nor the desire to plumb the depths of the melodrama. But in those days before the films, before the wide-screen cinema, he worked wonders on the stage and seldom failed to give his audiences a rousing good time, that vital ingredient of sheer theatrical fun which some high-principled aesthetes of the drama tend to overlook. Tragi-comic playwrights like Synge and O'Casey had more penetrating aims and greater genius than Boucicault—though one should not belittle his achievement as is so often the case—yet they shared his fondness for low comedy and melodrama and usually wrote their plays as if they were convinced that the circus and the music-hall are indigenous to the drama. In the most general sense, Synge and O'Casey used Boucicault the way Chaucer and Shakespeare used Boccaccio, as a bountiful source of comic material which they remoulded to their own purposes. But specifically, in this remoulding process Synge and O'Casey exploited and transformed the Boucicaultian drama by colouring it with an ironic point of view; they wrung the sentimental suds out of his soap-operas and dipped them in a briny solution of satire; they retained the Stage Irishman but laughed at as well as with him while they exploited his romantic roguery.

On one of those rare occasions when Synge wrote criticism, he turned out a short note on Boucicault and Irish drama for the English magazine *The Academy and Literature*. He had gone to a performance of *The Shaughraun* at the old Queen's Theatre in Dublin in 1904, and he was so impressed by what he saw that he drew some important comparisons between Boucicault's methods and those of the Irish National Theatre Society (which during that same year moved into its new Abbey Theatre). Here is the complete note:

Some recent performances of *The Shaughraun* at the Queen's Theatre in Dublin have enabled local playgoers to make an interesting comparison between the methods of the early Irish melodrama and those of the Irish National Theatre Society. It is unfortunate for Dion Boucicault's fame that the absurdity of his plots and pathos has gradually driven people of taste away from his plays, so that at the present time few are perhaps aware what good acting comedy some of his work contains. The characters of Conn the Shaughraun and in a lesser degree those of Mrs Kelly and Moya as they were played the other day by members of Mr Kennedy Miller's company, had a breadth of naive humour that is now rare on the stage. Mr James O'Brien especially, in the part of Conn, put a genial richness into his voice that it would be useless to expect from the less guttural vocal capacity of French or English comedians, and in listening to him one felt how much the modern stage has lost in substituting impersonal wit for personal humour. It is fortunate for the Irish National Theatre Society that it has preserved—in plays like *The Pot of Broth*—a great deal of what was best in the traditional comedy of the Irish stage, and still has contrived by its care and taste to put an end to the reaction against the careless Irish humour of which everyone has had too much. The effects of this reaction, it should be added, are still perceptible in Dublin, and the Irish National Theatre Society is sometimes accused of degrading Ireland's vision of herself by throwing a shadow of the typical Stage Irishman upon her mirror.[79]

Synge had good cause to be sensitive about accusations that the Irish National Theatre Society had degraded Ireland's vision of herself, for in the previous year, 1903, Yeats's National Theatre Company had performed Synge's first play, *In the Shadow of the Glen*, in Molesworth Hall before a hostile audience. The play was greeted with hissing, and a trio of ardent nationalists, Maud Gonne, Marie Quinn, and Dudley Digges (three actors who in 1902 had played leading roles in the first performance of that parable of national idealism, Yeats's *Cathleen Ni Houlihan*), had stalked out of the hall 'in protest against what they regarded as a decadent intrusion where the inspiration of idealism rather than the downpull of realism was needed'.[80] All the Dublin newspapers had been similarly outraged by the play. The *Irish Independent* considered the plot of Synge's tragi-comedy, in which a young Irish wife leaves her crabbed old husband—who feigns death in a mock-wake—to run off with a poetic young Tramp, as 'nothing more nor less than a farcical libel on the character of the average decently reared Irish peasant woman'.[81] Arthur Griffith, founder of Sinn Fein and later President of the Irish Free State Government, wrote a sharp attack on Yeats and Synge in his nationalist weekly, *The United Irishman*,[82] which signalled the official outbreak of hostility between the nationalists and the Abbey. It was a warning of what was to come when the hyper-sensitive nationalists rioted against Synge's *Playboy* four years later and O'Casey's *Plough* twenty-three years later. The mock-dead-man incident goes back to an ancient folk tale, which Synge heard from an old *shananchie* (a storyteller) on the Aran Islands, and Boucicault had used it in *The Shaughraun* when Conn is stretched out as a mock-corpse only to sit up merrily in his shroud at the climactic moment. And the painfully comic situation of the young woman unhappily married to a decrepit husband has too many parallels in Irish peasant life as well as folk literature to be considered libellous. But at the turn of the century zealous Irishmen were so serious about their national character they were in no mood to laugh at their own image in the dramatist's satiric mirror. Although the Irish dramatic movement began as a part of the National movement, it produced in its two greatest dramatists, Synge and O'Casey, men who consistently viewed the national character with irony instead of idealism.

Thus it is no surprise that what Synge saw in Boucicault turned out to be vital to the new drama at the expense of the new nationalism. Rowdy farce and broad satire were not calculated to exalt the national ideals. Comic rogues however brave they might be were too full of mischief and irresponsibility to inspire people bent on turning their thoughts to the noble deeds of ancient Celtic heroes. But Synge saw above all Boucicault's 'careless Irish humour' and 'good acting comedy', that type of music-hall comedy which had its roots in the 'personal humour' of irreverent low comedy, as

distinct from the 'impersonal wit' of drawing-room comedy of
manners which characterized the continental theatre and which
Anglo-Irishmen like Oscar Wilde wrote for the English theatre.
Synge had correctly pointed out the direction that the new Irish
drama should and did follow. The nationalists, however, were not
at all concerned with methods of drama. Irish idealism was their
criterion for all of life and literature. To the rabid nationalist, to
a proud patriot like Maud Gonne who tended to see herself as an
Irish Joan of Arc, any Irishman on a stage who was the object or
even the instrument of low comedy could only be a Stage Irishman, which was tantamount to treason. This attitude in large
measure explains the riots in the Abbey Theatre against Synge
and O'Casey who had chosen occasions when Irish nationalism
was most sensitive and pompous and therefore most vulnerable to
write their anti-heroic plays. The Stage Irishman was their target
not their weapon, and they used Boucicaultian comedy as an
ironic method of exposing an inflated idealism. Writing twenty
years later than Synge when the follies of nationalism had increased
twenty-fold, O'Casey found larger and more numerous targets,
one of the most tempting of which was the braggart-patriot or
'Irish' Irishman of the twentieth century who had become as
mirth-provoking a straight-man as his *alter ego* the beguiling nineteenth century Stage Irishman.

As for Synge's reference to Yeats's *Pot of Broth*, that play was
undoubtedly a modest attempt to preserve the 'careless Irish
humour' but it was also a Boucicaultian farce, without irony.
Based on an old folk tale and written with considerable help from
Lady Gregory, the play is entirely uncharacteristic of the plays
Yeats had envisioned for the Abbey Theatre and the plays he later
wrote. The hero of this one-act burlesque, a roguish ballad-singing
Tramp who cods a peasant couple out of a chicken dinner, is a
close cousin to Myles na Coppaleen and Conn the Shaughraun—
and if one adds the ironic point of view, a poor relation of Synge's
Tramps and Tinkers and O'Casey's Captain Boyles and Joxer
Dalys. But Yeats, who had originally conceived of a theatre that
would produce plays which were 'remote, spiritual, and ideal',
soon gave up trying to write peasant farces, just as he gave up
writing nationalistic plays like *Cathleen Ni Houlihan*.

It was Lady Gregory who first carried on the tradition of 'careless Irish humour' in the Abbey, although her irony when present

was extremely gentle, in those delightful one-act plays which have become classics in the Abbey Theatre repertory, such farce-comedies as *Spreading the News*, *Hyacinth Halvey*, *The Rising of the Moon* and *Workhouse Ward*. And it is significant to note that even Lady Gregory with her mild comedies early ran afoul of rampant Irish idealism when the Fay brothers refused to perform *The Rising of the Moon* and one of her first plays, *Twenty-Five*. The idyllic view of Ireland as a paradise of saintly peasants was apparently a form of myopia which afflicted actors as well as zealous nationalists. In 1903 Yeats had enlisted Willie and Frank Fay, who had a Dublin dramatic group of their own, in organizing the Irish National Theatre Society. The Fays were outstanding actors and acting coaches, and they undertook the important task of training the new acting company, but their knowledge of the drama might be judged by their reaction to *Twenty-Five*, a lively little farce somewhat similar to *The Pot of Broth*, which incidentally the Fays also disapproved of. Here is the letter Frank Fay wrote to Yeats:

In my brother's opinion 'Twenty-Five' would not suit us. He thinks the dialogue is excellent, but does not think an Irish peasant, however hard up, would play a stranger for his money like old Michael does, and, even assuming the possibility of that, my brother thinks the card-playing scene too long. Again, he does not approve of card-playing as a means of getting money, and he thinks the play in the country districts might incite to emigration, on account of the glowing terms in which American life is spoken of. I may say that I myself quite agree with this verdict.[83]

Is it any wonder that Synge and O'Casey met with such antagonism if artists like the Fays did not 'approve' of Irish peasants who played cards for money or might be tempted to emigrate from their forsaken bogs to America, both of which pursuits the crafty Irish peasants had uninhibitedly been following for the past hundred years? Those who remained 'decent' usually lacked the money not the desire to gamble or emigrate. The Fays eventually consented to produce *Twenty-Five*, an unimportant work, but they had greater cause for alarm when they were confronted by the plays of Synge. Yeats and Lady Gregory had some reservations, too, about Synge's use of 'oaths' and 'strong' language, particularly in *The Playboy of the Western World*, but they did not hesitate to produce the play and they defended Synge courageously when the riots broke out. When Willie Fay and his brother Frank first read the script of *The Playboy* they were deeply upset, not only by the strong language but by the lack of 'decency' in the characters. The Fays were friends of Synge's, and no doubt they were only trying to help him when they urged him to make changes in the play. As Willie Fay tells it:

Frank and I begged him [Synge] to make Pegeen a decent likable country girl, which she might easily have been without injury to the play, and to take out the torture scene in the last act where the peasants burn Christy with the lit turf. It was no use referring him to all the approved rules of the theatrical game—that, for example, while a note of comedy was admirable for heightening tragedy, the converse was not true. [84]

Fortunately Synge was a man who put his integrity as an artist before the pleading of his actor friends. Had he listened to Willie Fay and made Pegeen 'a decent likable country girl', he would have destroyed one of his finest characters and hopelessly bowdlerized his play; and had he made his plays conform to what Willie called 'all the approved rules of the theatrical game', they would in all probability have been forgotten long ago.

Synge had a much harder time with the hyper-sensitive Irish than O'Casey. Except for *Riders to the Sea*, his one-act tragedy which was well received, all his plays met with varying degrees of stony silence or violent abuse in Dublin. *In the Shadow of the Glen* was hissed and denounced: *The Well of the Saints* was equally denounced, played to empty houses and lost sixty pounds; *The Playboy of the Western World* provoked the famous riots in the theatre; and *The Tinker's Wedding* was thought to be so pagan and blasphemous that it has to this day never been produced by the Abbey. His last play, the beautifully tragic *Deirdre of the Sorrows*, was left incomplete when he died of Hodgkin's disease at the age of thirty-eight in 1909, and it received a mixed reception when it was performed before small houses in the following year. Yeats wrote a moving tribute to Synge in the chapter of his *Dramatis Personae* called 'The Death of Synge', in which he also chastised the people who hounded Synge throughout his brief career and continued to heap scorn on him when he was in his grave. Peter Kavanagh in his *Story of the Abbey Theatre* has explained the typical reaction of Irishmen toward Synge in the following manner:

Now, Synge was the most hated of all the Abbey dramatists. Lady Gregory and Yeats were disliked by the more sentimental nationalists, mainly because they were regarded as pro-British. But Synge was detested by nationalists of every shade and degree of political thought. To them, he was a Paris bohemian who went to the west of Ireland to write slanderous plays about the peasants. His first play, *In the Shadow of the Glen,* described an unhappily married couple. There are no loveless marriages in Ireland, the nationalists cried. Such a thing cannot happen in Ireland; it is something Synge saw in Paris, and now he is imputing it to the Irish Catholic peasants. And *The Well of the Saints* was hardly less obnoxious.

Synge was naturally annoyed, and he told Willie Fay one night, 'Very well, then; the next play I write I will make sure it will annoy them.' This was *The Playboy of the Western World.*[85]

Thus Synge, like O'Casey after him, had succeeded in 'annoying' the Catholics as well the nationalists, the two most sensitive and influential moulders of public opinion and behaviour in Ireland, although they did not become all-powerful until after the settlement of 1923. George Moore has described how he went to see *The Well of the Saints* and sat in the empty stalls with barely twenty people, one of whom was the playwright and devout Catholic Edward Martyn who was deeply annoyed by what he called Synge's anti-Catholicism: 'All this sneering at Catholic practices is utterly distasteful to me,' protested Martyn. 'I can hear the whining voice of the proselytizer through it all.'[86] Not a very accurate or fair judgement of Synge or his play, but unfortunately it was too often the prevailing view, in spite of the fact that Synge was, unlike O'Casey or even Yeats, that rarest type of Irishman, a man entirely without political or religious bias. He had what Yeats called 'a complete absorption in his own   :am'—his art.[87]

It was in the development of his art that Synge began the revolution in the theatre which was later carried on by O'Casey. It was of course Yeats and Lady Gregory who established and guided the Abbey Theatre, but it was Synge and O'Casey who shaped it to their own genius, and it is their plays which represent the highest achievements of the Irish Dramatic Renaissance.

3. THE ANTI-HEROIC VISION

An anti-heroic vision of life provides the unity of theme and the diversity of character and action in O'Casey's first four plays, *The Shadow of a Gunman* (1923), *Juno and the Paycock* (1925), *The Plough and the Stars*, (1926), and *The Silver Tassie* (1928). This latter work, which was rejected by the Abbey Theatre, will presently be examined in the broader context of experimental techniques and the Yeats–O'Casey controversy, for here we must centre our attention upon the first three plays which are similar in technique as well as theme and may be said to form a tragi-comic trilogy.

These first three plays are initially linked by the fact that they are all pacifist plays in which the main characters are not the National heroes actually engaged in the fighting but the noncombatants in a city under military siege, a tragic experience which has by mid-twentieth century become terrifyingly familiar to too many people in all parts of the world. O'Casey's 'open city' is Dublin during the Irish War of Independence; the setting of *The Gunman* is 1920 during the guerrilla warfare between the insurgent Irish Republican Army and the British forces, mainly the ruthless Auxiliary troops known by their uniforms as the Black and Tans; the setting of *Juno* is 1922 during the Civil War between the Irishmen who supported the Free State Settlement and the diehard Irish Republicans who rejected partition; the setting of *The Plough* is 1916 during the Easter Rising against the British. The action in each succeeding play is built around an ever-expanding radius of involvement. In the first play the conflict arises when a poet and a pedlar inadvertently become involved in the war; in the second play a whole family is caught in the cross-fire of the battle; and in the third play all the people in the tenements are trapped by the war that now covers the whole city which is in flames at the end of the play.

In all these plays the theme revolves around a series of illusions of heroism which point to the basic conflict. Donal Davoren in *The Gunman* thinks he is a lofty poet, his neighbours think he is a brave 'gunman' on the run'. But he is actually a 'shadow' of a poet, a 'shadow' of a gunman—a shadow-man who doesn't know who he is. All the tenement-dwellers in the play suffer from a variety of dreams and deceptions which serve as contrasts to

Davoren's self-deception and self-discovery. When his neighbours mistake him for an I.R.A. gunman he foolishly encourages the deception and vainly enjoys it, especially when he is with the impressionable Minnie Powell—'the Helen of Troy come to live in a tenement'—who has fallen in love with the romantic image of the poet-gunman she thinks he is. But Davoren isn't much of a poet either, for most of the time he sighs like a 'stricken deer' trying to flee from the stupid 'herd', trying to isolate himself from his neighbours and the war in order to write his sentimental verses in a watered-down imitation of Shelley. Throughout the play he indulges his mock-heroic fancies as masquerading gunman and romancing poet, with the result that his vanity and detachment defeat him and lead to the tragic death of Minnie Powell.

Davoren tries to see himself as a dreamy poet who 'lives on the mountain-top'. O'Casey had borrowed Davoren's romantic idealism from Louis Dubedat's creed in Shaw's *The Doctor's Dilemma*: the belief in 'the might of design, the mystery of colour, and the belief in the redemption of all things by beauty everlasting'. Davoren repeats these words when he tries to escape to his mountain-top, but the world in which he lives will not allow him to assume the romantic attitudes of the grandiloquent and dying Dubedat. It is only the shock of Minnie Powell's death that makes Davoren see himself and his world with terrifying clarity.

It is his droll pedlar friend Seumas Shields who really understands the chaotic world in which they are trapped. Seumas understands that poetic and patriotic poses will not help, even though he is in his own way just as ineffectual as Davoren, for he is a lazy, blustering, amiable coward who resorts to the efficacy of prayer or the comfort of his bed when trouble comes. Yet he understands and is the ironic Chorus character in the guise of a bumbling clown, a wise-fool who sees the truth. He has better reasons than Davoren for not becoming involved in the war since he was once active in the Irish Republican movement but left it when the fanatical nationalism and the terror of indiscriminate bloodshed began to destroy the people it was supposed to save. Seumas makes this point in an episode which thematically links the plays of the trilogy.

SEUMAS. I wish to God it was all over. The country is gone mad.
Instead of counting their beads now they're countin' bullets; their

Hail Marys and paternosters are burstin' bombs—burstin' bombs, an' the rattle of machine-guns; petrol is their holy water; their Mass is a burnin' buildin'; their De Profundis is 'The Soldier's Song', an' their creed is, 'I believe in the gun almighty, maker of heaven an' earth'—an' it's all for 'the glory o' God an' the honour o' Ireland'.

DAVOREN. I remember the time when you yourself believed in nothing but the gun.

SEUMAS. Ay, when there wasn't a gun in the country; I've a different opinion now when there's nothin' but guns in the country—an' you daren't open your mouth, for Kathleen ni Houlihan is very different now to the woman who used to play the harp an' sing 'Weep on, weep on, your hour is past', for she's a ragin' divil now, an' if you only look crooked at her you're sure of a punch in th' eye. But this is the way I look at it—I look at it this way: You're not goin'—you're not goin' to beat the British Empire—the British Empire, by shootin' an occasional Tommy at the corner of an occasional street. Besides, when the Tommies have the wind up—when the Tommies have the wind up they let bang at everything they see—they don't give a God's curse who they plug.

DAVOREN. Maybe they ought to get down off the lorry and run to the Records Office to find out a man's pedigree before they plug him.

SEUMAS. It's the civilians who suffer; when there's an ambush they don't know where to run. Shot in the back to save the British Empire, an' shot in the breast to save the soul of Ireland. I'm a Nationalist meself, right enough—a Nationalist right enough, but all the same— I'm a Nationalist right enough; I believe in the freedom of Ireland, an' that England has no right to be here, but I draw the line when I hear the gunmen blowin' about dyin' for the people, when it's the people that are dyin' for the gunmen! With all due respect to the gunmen, I don't want them to die for me.

For Seumas as for the women in *Juno* and *The Plough*, for Juno Boyle and Nora Clitheroe, life is more sacred than patriotic slogans; human realities are more meaningful than fanatical abstractions, particularly when in the name of the national honour the revolution devours its own children. When Juno's son Johnny, who had his hip crippled in the Easter Rising and lost an arm fighting with the I.R.A. in the Civil War, boasts about the sacred 'principles' and insists he would sacrifice himself again for Ireland, she promptly offers her opinion about such heroics.

JOHNNY. I'd do it agen, ma, I'd do it agen; for a principle's a principle.
MRS BOYLE. Ah, you lost your best principle, me boy, when you lost your arm; them's the only sort o' principles that's any good to a workin' man.

Juno sees life in terms of the essential human situation—bread on the table and love in the heart; these are the only realities that have any meaning for her and she fights for them without any heroics. And when she loses her son, when Johnny is finally shot, she follows Mrs Tancred and keens the heart-breaking lament of the universal mother for a dead son.

MRS BOYLE. . . . Maybe I didn't feel sorry enough for Mrs Tancred when her poor son was found as Johnny's been found now—because he was a Die-hard! Ah, why didn't I remember that then he wasn't a Diehard or a Stater, but only a poor dead son! It's well I remember all that she said—an' it's my turn to say it now: What was the pain I suffered, Johnny, bringin' you into the world to carry you to your cradle, to the pains I'll suffer carryin' you out o' the world to bring you to your grave! Mother o' God, Mother o' God, have pity on us all! Blessed Virgin, where were you when me darlin' son was riddled with bullets, when me darlin' son was riddled with bullets? Sacred Heart o' Jesus, take away our hearts o' stone, and give us hearts o' flesh! Take away this murdherin' hate, an' give us Thine own eternal love!

But the men go on sacrificing themselves for principles and the 'murdherin' hate' continues. In the second act of *The Plough*, Commandant Jack Clitheroe and two of his comrades, after listening to the speeches about 'the sanctity of bloodshed . . . and the exhilaration of war', drink a toast to Ireland before they go out to battle. The stage directions indicate that 'they speak rapidly, as if unaware of the meaning of what they say. They have been mesmerized by the fervency of the speeches'.

CLITHEROE. You have a mother, Langon.
LIEUT. LANGON. Ireland is greater than a mother.
CAPT. BRENNAN. You have a wife, Clitheroe.
CLITHEROE. Ireland is greater than a wife.

But the mothers and wives of Ireland think otherwise, and in the third act when the pregnant Nora Clitheroe returns from a desperate search for her husband, she replies for all Irish women, for women of all countries who lose their men in wars.

NORA. I could find him nowhere, Mrs Gogan. None of them would tell me where he was. They told me I shamed my husband an' th' women of Ireland be carryin' on as I was—— They said th' women must learn to be brave an' cease to be cowardly—— Me who risked more for love than they would risk for hate—— My Jack will be killed, my Jack will be killed! He is to be butchered as a sacrifice to th' dead! . . . An' there's no woman gives a son or a husband to be killed—if they say it, they're lyin', lyin', against God, Nature, an' against themselves! . . . I cursed them—cursed the rebel ruffians an' Volunteers that had dhragged me ravin' mad into th' sthreets to seek me husband! . . . An' he stands wherever he is because he's brave? No, but because he's a coward, a coward, a coward! . . . I tell you they're afraid to say they're afraid—— Oh, I saw it, I saw it, Mrs Gogan—— At th' barricades in North King Street I saw fear glowin' in all their eyes—— An' in th' middle o' th' sthreet was somethin' huddled up in a horrible tangled heap—— His face was jammed again th' stones, an' his arm was twisted round his back—— An' I saw they were afraid to look at it—— An' some o' them laughed at me, but th' laugh was a frightened one—— An' some o' them shouted at me, but th' shout had in it th' shiver o' fear—— I tell you they were afraid, afraid, afraid!

Juno and Nora are against war not Ireland. As wives and mothers they realize there can be no victory in war for them if they lose their men and homes. They repudiate war and the illusion that the soldiers alone are the chief sufferers, the illusion that the soldiers die bravely and beautifully for their country, the illusion that the women willingly send their men out to die. For centuries romantic Irishmen had nurtured these illusions by celebrating in poems and stories the glorious deeds of rebel patriots who kissed their beloved colleens farewell and went off to sacrifice themselves for a greater love, Kathleen ni Houlihan. But now O'Casey was mocking all these illusions by looking at the brutality of war through the realistic eyes of working-class Irishwomen instead of through the haze of sentimental patriotism.

This is O'Casey's underlying theme; and yet his anti-heroic vision of life encompasses infinitely more than an argument against war and the illusions of Irishmen. Because he is sceptical about rampant heroism, he is at heart more concerned about the individual nature of his people than the causes they are heroic about. He creates a unique and diversified world, a human comedy, as well as an incisive theme. Once he establishes his controlling theme he moves freely and even discursively around it, playing tragi-comic variations on it, developing it broadly through an ensemble of characters rather than closely through a few central characters. The structural pattern of his plays is loose not tight, contrapuntal not dialectical.

O'Casey's world is chaotic and tragic but his vision of it is ironically comic. It is in this war-torn world of horrors and potential tragedy that he finds the rowdy humour which paradoxically satirizes and sustains his earthy characters: they are the victims of their follies yet they revel in their voluble absurdities. And it is clear that O'Casey himself enjoys his people no less for their follies, as he intends his audiences to enjoy them. There is a sharp tone of outrage in his Daumier-like portraits of life in the slums of a beleaguered city, and this tone becomes even stronger in his later plays, but he was not dramatizing case histories. His plays do not follow the documentary principles of Naturalism—of Hauptmann's *Weavers* or Galsworthy's *Strife*. Low comedy is not one of the handmaidens of Naturalism. Even when he is in a serious mood O'Casey is likely to be satiric not solemn, poignant not pathetic. And when the tragic events or consequences of war and poverty become most crucial he will open up the action and counterbalance the incipient tragedy with a music-hall turn or a randy ballad or a mock-battle. While everyone awaits a terrifying raid by the Black and Tans in *The Gunman* the well-oiled Dolphie Grigson parades into the house spouting songs and biblical rhetoric in drunken bravado. Just when Mrs Tancred is on her way to bury her ambushed son in *Juno* the Boyles have launched their wild drinking and singing party. While the streets ring with patriotic speeches about heroic bloodshed in *The Plough* the women of the tenements have a free-for-all fight about respectability in a Pub.

This pattern of ironic counterpoint is maintained as a tragi-comic rhythm throughout the plays. For each tragic character there are comic foils who constantly bring the action round from the tragic to the comic mood; for Davoren there is Seumas Shields, for Juno there is the 'Paycock', for Nora there is Bessie Burgess. Actually, Bessie and Nora exchange roles in the last act of the *Plough* when the mad Nora is reduced to ironic babbling and the previously sardonic Bessie achieves tragic dignity. For all the mock-heroic clowns in the plays there is a retinue of boisterous drunkards, liars, cowards, braggarts, parasites, hypocrites, viragos, and snobs; in *The Gunman* there is Tommy Owens, Mr and Mrs Grigson, Mr Mulligan, Mrs Henderson, Mr Gallogher; in *Juno* there is Joxer Daly, Masie Madigan, Needle Nugent; in *The Plough* there is Fluther Good, Peter Flynn, the Covey, Mrs Gogan, Rosie Redmond. In a turbulent world crowded with these broadly comic and satiric characters it is not surprising to find that the comic spirit often dominates the action. But O'Casey would have it so precisely because the humour in his plays reveals a native vigour and shrewdness in his characters which ironically becomes a means of survival in a shattered world. It is this attitude which keeps his plays from becoming melancholy or pessimistic. His humour saves him and his characters from despair. In the midst of anti-heroic laughter there can be no total catastrophe. Where there is suffering and death no happy endings are possible, but where there is also laughter life goes on.

War and poverty create the terrible conditions that force O'Casey's people to reveal their resourcefulness in wild scenes of tragi-comic irony in which the grotesque laughter seems to mock at death. For instance, the third act of *The Plough* is set among the crumbling tenements during the week of the Easter Rising; now the speeches about 'the glory of bloodshed' in the previous act have been transformed into a terrible reality. The streets are a battlefield and the sickening whine of bullets fills the air. The British gunboat *Helga* has begun to shell the city. The hysterical Nora Clitheroe collapses after her unsuccessful attempt to find her husband at the barricades. The shrivelled little Mollser, unable to get proper food or medical care, is dying of tuberculosis. Lieutenant Langon is carried in dying of a stomach wound. And in the midst of this chaos O'Casey presents the looting of the shops by the ragged and hungry slum-dwellers who scramble amid bursting bombs and bullets to grab the only trophies that have any meaning for them—food and clothing. These people have been deprived of the bare necessities for so long that those who are not shot stagger away from the shops overburdened with luxuries and strange assortments of ridiculous items. Rushing in with a new hat, a box of biscuits, and three umbrellas, Bessie Burgess sets the tone of humour amid horror with her breathless announcement:

They're breakin' into th' shops, they're breakin' into th' shops! Smashing windows, battherin' in th' doors, an' whippin' away everything! An' th' Volunteers is firin' on them. I seen two men an' a lassie pushin' a piano down th' sthreet, an' th' sweat rollin' off them thryin' to get it up on th' pavement; an' an oul' wan that must ha' been seventy lookin' as if she'd dhrop every minute with th' dint o' heart beatin', thryin' to pull a big double bed out of a broken shop-window! I was goin' to wait till I dhressed meself from th' skin out.

With this call to action the Covey soon reels in carrying a huge sack of flour and a ham, and Fluther, as might have been expected, comes in roaring drunk after having launched a raid on a Pub. Bessie is about to go out for another haul with a neighbour's pram when she is intercepted by the eager Mrs Gogan, and the two women rage at each other in a mock-battle over which of them has the proper right to use the pram for looting. Their intentions with the pram are equally set on plunder, yet both women assume an indignant legal attitude, characterized by Mrs Gogan's sense of outrage: 'Moreover, somethin's tellin' me that th' hurry of inthrest you're takin' in it now is a sudden ambition to use th' pram for a purpose that a loyal woman of law an' order would stagger away from.'

The comic absurdity of this fight between two viragos over the jurisdiction of the pram, like the similar brawl in the Pub in the previous act, when contrasted with the fighting at the barricades, irreverently mocks the 'holiness' of the war. The heroes at the barricades are deflated by this profane farce in which the pram and the looting take precedence over patriotism, and thus the anti-heroes of the tenements become heroes by comic proxy.

But before long these anti-heroes begin to earn their ironic heroism. The two women finally go off together with the pram, and as the intensity of the war increases a significant change occurs among these people. Although they all continue to quarrel and 'twart' each other with reckless delight, they also begin to

unite against what they gradually recognize as their common
enemy—the war. Fluther, before he gets drunk, risks his life to
find Nora and bring her back safely from the fighting area. The
sharp-tongued but compassionate Bessie Burgess—who grows
larger in stature as the play progresses and might finally be said to
earn the role of main hero, as the Juno of this play—silently gives
the suffering Mollser a bowl of milk, helps the prostrate Nora,
whom she has so bitterly abused, into the house, and then risks
her life in the machine-gunned streets trying to get a doctor for
Mollser, the daughter of her favourite sparring-partner, Mrs
Gogan. And in the last act, when Mollser has died and the dis-
consolate Nora has lost her baby prematurely, all the people in the
house take refuge in Bessie's attic flat. It is Fluther again who
dodges the bullets to make arrangements for the burial of the two
children, and it is Bessie who nurses the deranged Nora through
three sleepless days and nights, only to be shot trying to protect
Nora. Finally it is Ginnie Gogan who carries on and takes Nora
down to Mollser's empty bed.

In this manner the women who are the main victims of the war
rise to become the main heroes. This pattern is repeated in all the
plays as some of the women die for their neighbours and others
live to rebuild a new life out of the ruins. Minnie Powell dies trying to save Donal Davoren, and Bessie Burgess dies trying to save
Nora Clitheroe; Juno Boyle and Ginnie Gogan endure everything.
This is the only kind of untainted heroism that O'Casey recognizes. These women are his Ireland. They are not the patriotic
Ireland that made an exhilarating epiphany of the ritual of bloodshed. They are not the romantic Ireland that idealized Kathleen
ni Houlihan of the beautiful green fields and the harp. They are
not the sweet blushing colleens whose fabled existence is exalted
in the guise of the Stage Irishwoman. They are the Ireland of
tenacious mothers and wives, the women of the tenements—
earthy, shrewd, laughing, suffering, brawling, independent women.
O'Casey found them in the Dublin slums, but they have their
counterparts in Synge's peasant women, like Pegeen Mike in *The
Playboy of the Western World* and Mary Byrne in *The Tinker's
Wedding*; in Joyce's Molly Bloom; in Yeats's Crazy Jane; in the
eighteenth-century Brian Merriman's peasant girl of 'The Midnight Court'.

Juno Boyle has the name of a classical heroine, and she has many of the qualities of that Roman goddess, but O'Casey uses the allusion in such a way as to give her the heroic stature of her namesake and the earthy reality of a Dublin housewife of the tenements. When Bentham hears her name he is reminded of the 'ancient gods and heroes', however, the Captain explains how she got her name: 'You see, Juno was born an' christened in June; I met her in June; we were married in June, an' Johnny was born in June, so wan day I says to her, "You should ha' been called Juno', an' the name stuck to her ever since".' Furthermore, O'Casey was aware of the fact that the classical Juno was always associated with peacocks, the patron birds who are often near her or draw her chariot, but he used this aspect of the legend in a completely ironic way by giving his Juno a peacock of a husband who takes his name from the common association of strutting vanity. Thus, the 'Paycock' becomes Juno's parasite not her protector.

The women in O'Casey's plays are realists from necessity, the men are dreamers by default. The men are frustrated and gulled by dreams which they are unable and unwilling to convert into realities. And as if in mock-defence of those dreams they revel in their romanticizing and bragging and drinking. In *John Bull's Other Island* Shaw may have gone to the root of the Irishman's curse when he made Larry Doyle pour out his embittered confession:

Oh, the dreaming! dreaming! the torturing, heart-scalding, never satisfying dreaming, dreaming, dreaming, dreaming! No debauchery that ever coarsened and brutalized an Englishman can take the worth and usefulness out of him like that dreaming. An Irishman's imagination never lets him alone, never convinces him, never satisfies him; but it makes him that he cant face reality nor deal with it nor handle it nor conquer it; he can only sneer at them that do, and be 'agreeable to strangers', like a good-for-nothing woman on the streets. It's all dreaming, all imagination. He cant be religious. The inspired Churchman that teaches him the sanctity of life and the importance of conduct is sent away empty; while the poor village priest that gives him a miracle or a sentimental story of a saint, has cathedrals built for him out of the pennies of the poor. He cant be intelligently political; he dreams of what the Shan Van Vocht said in ninetyeight. If you want to interest him in Ireland you've got to call the unfortunate island Kathleen ni Houlihan and pretend she's a little old woman. It saves thinking. It saves working.

It saves everything except imagination, imagination, imagination; and imagination's such a torture that you cant bear it without whisky. [88]

O'Casey's Irishmen suffer from the symptoms of this outcry, and as a result there is an undercurrent of tragedy in the plays. But most of O'Casey's Irishmen possess the grotesque symptoms without Larry Doyle's awareness of them, and as a result there is also an abundance of comedy in the plays. Herein lies one of the many differences between tragedy and comedy: the tragic figure becomes truly tragic when he is able to see his own image; the comic figure becomes absurdly comic when he is unable, or pretends to be unable, to see his own image. When the women in O'Casey's plays finally see themselves and their world clearly they become tragic figures, like Juno Boyle and Bessie Burgess. Of the men, only Davoren as the self-confessed 'poltroon' makes Larry Doyle's discovery, at the very end of the *Gunman* after he has fully indulged his aery dreams, but he is the only non-comic character in the play.

There is, however, one unique figure who dominates all three plays, the mock-heroic character who proudly wears his motley and is satisfied to see as much of himself and the world as he expediently chooses to see. This character is first formulated in Seumas Shields in the *Gunman*, and he is fully developed in Captain Jack Boyle in *Juno* and Fluther Good in the *Plough*— those two falstaffian rogues who epitomize the triumphant anti-hero.

Captain Jack Boyle may lack the girth of Captain Jack Falstaff, but he has the same flamboyant humour and glorious mendacity, the ingenious sense of self-indulgence and self-preservation. Both men are bragging scoundrels whose disrespect for the truth stems not only from an instinctive love of licence but from an empirical conviction that a virtuous life invariably leads to dullness and an heroic life often leads to death. Falstaff can point to a corpse on the battlefield and say, 'there's honour for you', or counterfeit death because 'The better part of valour is discretion, in the which better part I have saved my life'. Boyle, living like Falstaff in a time of Civil War when men's lives are valued cheaply, sets too high a price on his own sweet skin to care about honour or become involved in the fighting. And he has his counterfeit game for saving himself from the deadly virtues of work: he automatically develops a powerful pain in his legs at the mere mention of a job. When Jerry Devine goes looking for him in all the Pubs with news of a job, his discretionary wrath erupts and protects him: 'Is a man not to be allowed to leave his house for a minute without havin' a pack o' spies, pimps an' informers cantherin' at his heels? . . . I don't want the motions of me body to be watched the way an asthronomer ud watch a star. If you're folleyin' Mary aself, you've no pereeogative to be folleyin' me.' (*Suddenly catching his thigh.*) 'U-ugh, I'm afther gettin' a terrible twinge in me right leg!' Furthermore, Boyle has what he considers a good reason to regard a man like Devine with suspicion: 'I never heard him usin' a curse word; I don't believe he was ever dhrunk in his life— sure he's not like a Christian at all!'

Captain Boyle's account of his adventures on the sea has that comic touch of fantastic imagination which characterized Captain Falstaff's version of his exploits on Gadshill. Juno Boyle knows her husband for the 'struttin' paycock' that he is, and she pointedly explains his seafaring record; 'Everybody callin' you "Captain", an' you only wanst on the wather, in an oul' collier from here to Liverpool, when anybody, to listen or look at you, ud take you for a second Christo For Columbus!' But this fact does not prevent the 'Captain' from telling his 'buttie' Joxer what it was like to be an adventurous sailor on the high seas.

BOYLE. Them was days, Joxer, them was days. Nothin' was too hot or too heavy for me then. Sailin' from the Gulf o' Mexico to the Antanartic Ocean. I seen things, I seen things, Joxer, that no mortal man should speak about that knows his Catechism. Often, an' often, when I was fixed to the wheel with a marlin-spike, an' the wins blowin' fierce an' the waves lashin' an' lashin', till you'd think every minute was goin' to be your last, an' it blowed, an' blowed—blew is the right word, Joxer, but blowed is what the sailors use——

JOXER. Aw, it's a darlin' word, a daarlin' word.

BOYLE. An' as it blowed an' blowed, I often looked up at the sky an' assed meself the question—what is the stars, what is the stars?

JOXER. Ah, that's the question, that's the question—what is the stars?

A clever parasite full of comic platitudes, the ingratiating Joxer is a perfect foil for the braggart Captain; he spaniels at the Captain's heels most of the time, but he too sees as much of himself and the world as it is profitable for him to see. Joxer is capable of reversing the game and fooling the Captain when he has something to gain. Together they insulate themselves from the world of terrible realities by living in an illusory world of fantasies and drunken bravado. O'Casey satirizes them unsparingly for the shiftless rascals that they are, yet because he also sees the amusement of a universal frailty in them—they are fools not knaves—he is able to laugh with as well as at their hilarious mischief. And audiences laugh with as well as at them because they too recognize the common frailties of man in the Boyles and Joxers of this world—Boyle the universal braggart-warrior, Joxer the universal parasite-slave, both of them derived from the well-known clowns of Roman and Elizabethan comedy. It is also possible that many men are more than amused by the 'paycock's' game and secretly envy the Captain and his 'buttie' their merry pranks. The average man who realizes he cannot cope with his besetting problems on an heroic scale may well have an unconscious desire to get rid of his problems entirely by emulating the Captain in his irresponsible and therefore irresistible dreaming and singing and drinking. A frustrated non-hero might if he dared forsake his responsible suffering and seek the uninhibited pleasures of a clowning anti-hero; however, he probably settles for the vicarious pleasure of sitting in a theatre and watching a Captain Boyle thumb his red nose at responsibility. Much is made of the frustrated clown who yearns to play Hamlet, but the average man is more likely a frustrated Hamlet who if he had the strength of his weakness would cheerfully assume the role of an uninhibited Falstaff or Boyle.

The women in O'Casey's plays may be uninhibited creatures, too, but they always remain close to the realities of life and when there is a call for responsible action they put aside self-gratification and act. Even Juno has her fling. When the Boyles have their wild party Juno joins the celebration on borrowed money and time, and after the mourning Mrs Tancred interrupts them, Juno temporarily agrees with the Captain and remarks that maybe Mrs Tancred deserved to lose her Die-hard son. But when her own son is killed, when her daughter is seduced, Juno assumes her burdens; she repeats Mrs Tancred's prayer and rejects the Captain. When her daughter cries out against a God who would allow such tragic things to happen, Juno replies: 'These things have nothin' to do with the Will o' God. Ah, what can God do agen the stipidity o' men!' And she abandons the Captain. When Prince Hal becomes King he assumes the burdens of state and rejects the dissolute Falstaff.

> *I know thee not, old man : fall to thy prayers :*
> *How ill white hairs become a fool and jester!*
> *I have long dream'd of such a king of man,*
> *So surfeit-swell'd, so old, and so profane.*
> *But being awak'd, I do despise my dream.*

In a somewhat similar manner, Juno, being awake, forsakes all dreams and rejects her foolish jester of a husband. Her elegaic prayer brings her to a condition of tragic awareness.

Yet O'Casey does not end the play with Juno. Maintaining the anti-heroic theme and contrapuntal rhythm of the whole work, he concludes on a tragi-comic note by contrasting Juno's heroic condition with the Captain's mock-heroic condition. For it is his play as well as Juno's; together they represent the tragi-comic cycle of O'Casey's world; together they reveal the ironic cross-purposes of life. As Juno and Mary leave to start a new life, the Captain and Joxer stagger drunkenly into the barren room, roaring patriotic slogans as they collapse in a state of semi-coherent bravado. It is a final scene of horrible humour. The Captain remains the 'struttin' paycock' in his glorious deterioration; even in his drunken raving he remains a magnificently grotesque anti-hero. Juno must reject him, yet we can forgive him, for he maintains his falstaffian spirit to the end.

Fluther Good is also drawn in the falstaffian mould, but he is sufficiently different from Captain Boyle to emerge with the stamp of his own individuality. He too is a roistering fellow, a drinking and bragging clown, but he is more impetuous than the Captain, more aggressive and daring, in his guarded way. He is more of a blustering gamecock than a 'struttin' paycock'. He has more stomach for a fight then the wily Captain, though his fighting is discreetly confined to rhetorical invective. He has no trouble annihilating little Peter Flynn—that ridiculous 'patriot' clad in the full-dress uniform of a National benevolent association—when 'oul' Pether' brags about never having missed a pilgrimage to Bodenstown to the shrine of Wolfe Tone. But he has to 'sing on the high notes' of his ignorance when he gets into a shouting contest with the clever Covey [a 'covey' is Dublin slang for a 'smart aleck'] who dumbfounds Fluther with materialistic catechisms from his vade-mecum, Jenersky's *Thesis on the Origin, Development and Consolidation of the Evolutionary Idea of the Proletariat*, a tome which understandably fills the Covey with a proletarian fervour that makes him impervious to the protests of Fluther, patriots, and prostitutes.

And yet the windy Fluther is capable of courageous deeds where women are concerned, for he is a knight-errant of the tenements—he rescues pregnant women in distress and defends the honour of insulted prostitutes. All the women had a good word for Fluther. Mrs Gogan praises him for risking his life to arrange the decent burial of poor Mollser: 'An' you'll find, that Mollser, in th' happy place she's gone to, won't forget to whisper, now an' again, th' name o' Fluther.' When he gallantly protects Rosie Redmond and her venerable profession from the 'twarting' Covey, she describes him as a man 'that's well flavoured in th' knowledge of th' world he's livin' in'. Perhaps Nora Clitheroe, who is constantly in his debt, pays him the highest compliment when she calls him 'a whole man'.

Taken in his 'wholeness', Fluther the 'well-flavoured' man is a magnificent mixture of contradictions. He has the heart of a Don Quixote but the hide of a Sancho Panza. Among the ladies he is a protector and a peace-maker, but with the men he is full of himself and his inimitable flutherian wrath, or full of Irish whiskey. His roar is worse than his bite; he starts more arguments than he can settle; he rages and boasts, lies and threatens when he is cornered; he swears abstinence then drowns himself in drink when the shops are looted, crying 'Up the Rebels' and 'th' whole city can topple home to hell' in the same drunken breath; he can defend a prostitute's good name, and then go off to spend the night with her—'well-flavoured' man that he is, Fluther knows that there are times when Dulcinea must give way to Doll Tearsheet.

As a man of many frailties and fine parts, as a prince of buffoonery as well as errantry, Fluther the Good is the mock-hero of the play. In a terrible time of war, he is too shrewd to be a patriot, too wise to be an idealist; yet in his comic anti-heroism he plays the fool for man's sake. In his vitality and humour there is a hope that man may endure.

4. THE CONTROL OF HIS CRAFT

In examining O'Casey's gradual development and control of his craft—his dramatic technique and artistic intention—it will first be helpful to consider what some of his critics thought he was doing or should have been doing, and then see what he actually achieved. He can be a careless writer and there are flaws as well as virtues in his craftsmanship, but that there are some misconceptions about both can be observed in the following testimony by two critics of the drama, Andrew E. Malone and Joseph W. Krutch, who saw his plays when they were first performed in Ireland and America; and two scholars of the drama, Raymond Williams and Ronald Peacock, who have more recently commented on the plays in their studies of dramatic literature.

When O'Casey's plays were first produced at the Abbey Theatre they were performed as tragi-comedies, in the judgement of Andrew E. Malone, the drama critic of the *Dublin Magazine*. According to Mr Malone, however, this was a serious mistake, for he insisted that the plays were 'hideous tragedies' not tragi-comedies. Writing in 1925 in his regular column, 'From the Stalls', he was disturbed by the fact that 'O'Casey's meaning failed to get across the footlights'. Mr Malone had just read the first two plays, *The Gunman* and *Juno*, which had been brought out by Macmillan, and he insisted that the published texts supported the views he had formed when he had seen the first performances. He blamed the crude audiences for laughing too often and at the wrong times—for in the early days the Abbey had been supported mainly by a small coterie of intellectuals who seldom filled the theatre and presumably seldom laughed, according to Mr Malone; whereas the popular plays of O'Casey now packed the theatre with the 'less discriminating' Dubliners of the lower orders. He also accused the Abbey actors of deliberately playing for laughs and misleading the untutored audiences. Apparently the high-minded Mr Malone saw little cause for laughter in the plays:

Life is a rollicking comedy to the audiences and a hideous tragedy to the dramatist, but it is not entirely the fault of the audiences that the hideousness of Sean O'Casey's tragedies failed to affect them. As played at the Abbey Theatre it was the tragi-comedy rather than the truly

tragic aspects of his plays that were emphasized, and the superb acting
of F. J. McCormick and Barry Fitzgerald as Joxer and the Captain
veiled the tragic significance of Juno as played by Sara Allgood. The
audiences took the two typical Dublin loafers to their hearts, more
easily, perhaps, because that type had never found itself on the stage of
the Abbey Theatre before . . . Why do theatre audiences laugh at the
wrong things? Why, in fact, do they laugh in the theatre at the things
which excite their pity in daily life? Why do they laugh at Joxer and the
Captain in the theatre and treat them as a problem when they worry the
newspapers with their letters?[89]

Why do they laugh? One can only reply that there must be
something wrong with the ability of actors who play the parts of
the Captain and Joxer and cannot provoke hilarious laughter; and
there must be something wrong with the sensibility of audiences
that cannot respond with uninhibited laughter. One might as well
ask, why did audiences laugh at the mock-heroic adventures of the
miles gloriosus, the braggart warrior of Roman and Elizabethan
comedy, or why did audiences laugh at the antics of the clever
parasite-slave of Roman and Elizabethan comedy, for certainly the
Captain and Joxer trace their mirth-provoking ancestry back to
those mischievous rogues. And O'Casey's characters are no less
humourous for the fact that they are sharply satirized for indulging their follies in a world that is in 'a terrible state o' chassis'.
Audiences can laugh in the theatre at characters who might
'excite their pity in daily life' because life and art are not the
same thing; because the artist organizes the disorder of life; and
because the artist's point of view is there to guide them. Perhaps
the laughter that the O'Casey characters provoke is only embarrassing to someone who insists the plays are 'hideous tragedies'.
Four years later, in his book, *The Irish Drama* (1929), Mr Malone
decided that not only the plays of O'Casey but those of Synge, too,
and in fact 'almost every play at the [Abbey] Theatre was reduced
to the level of farce' by the actors.[90] Even the great Arthur Sinclair, he claimed, had been guilty of playing for laughs in 'serious'
plays: 'The audience could be induced to laugh uproariously at
Sinclair even in such plays as *The Shadow of the Glen* or *The Playboy of the Western World;* the greatest tragedy in the repertory of
the theatre could be made the occasion for laughter.'[91]
Even such plays as *In the Shadow of the Glen* and *The Playboy*

of the Western World? One can hardly call these two works tragedies! They may contain some dark elements, but they are too rich with scenes of broad farce and characters of grotesque satire not to be devastatingly humorous. If Mr Malone had caught the actors playing for laughs in Synge's two tragedies, *Riders to the Sea* and *Deirdre of the Sorrows*, which is most unlikely, one might understand his objection. And since Arthur Sinclair, a great comedian, played the role of Dan Burke, the boorish old peasant husband who is farcically stretched out as a mock-corpse and finally cuckolded in *In the Shadow of the Glen*, and the role of Michael James, the red-nosed publican in *The Playboy of the Western World*, it is difficult to see how he could do anything but induce uproarious laughter. Granted that even the best actors, especially in comic roles, need a firm directorial hand so that—in Hamlet's warning to the players—'your clowns speak no more than is set down for them'. But the point is that Mr Malone, one of the early historians of the Abbey Theatre and a highly respected critic, failed to recognize the comic values in the works of Synge and O'Casey. Somehow he overlooked the evidence which indicated that the Abbey repertory was not mainly composed of 'great tragedies'; that, in fact, the outstanding Abbey plays were comedies and tragi-comedies; and that it followed quite naturally that the outstanding Abbey actors should have been masters of comedy. Yeats himself, in summing up the achievements of the Abbey in his 'Letter to Lady Gregory', pointed out that the Abbey players 'at their best, were great comedians'.[92] Turning from actors to playwrights, the Irish genius for comedy has for three centuries been so formidable that a list of great 'English' comedies would be largely composed of the plays of such celebrated Irishmen as Congreve, Farquhar, Goldsmith, Sheridan, Wilde, and Shaw. And returning to the two most formidable Abbey playwrights, however one tries to deal with the ironic undercurrent of tragic themes in the plays of Synge and O'Casey, it is impossible to deny that their works are also exuberant manifestations of the comic spirit.

Another highly respected critic who recorded his reactions to the O'Casey plays when they first appeared was Joseph W. Krutch. After having seen productions of *Juno* and *The Plough* in 1927 in America, Mr Krutch, then drama critic of *The Nation*, registered a long list of complaints. Unlike Mr Malone, he did recognize and even admire the comedy in the plays, but he saw little else of merit. Mr Krutch concluded:

No one can deny that O'Casey has an extraordinary gift for racy dialogue or that he can hit off the foibles of the Irish character with malicious wit, but his plays lack form, lack movement, and in the final analysis lack any informing purpose. They bustle with characters, generally amusing enough in themselves, but the series of sketches which go to make up one of his dramas is strung upon the skimpiest thread of melodramatic action, and though each of his plays has its moments neither of the two seen here [*Juno* and *The Plough*] produces any unified or lasting effect. To this day I do not know just where the author's sympathies lie, and I defy anyone, after six months have passed, to recall the play [*The Plough*] in any form except that embodied in a jumbled memory of rather confused events. [93]

In the years since Mr Krutch wrote this review he has not modified his hard conclusions. One of his most recent comments on O'Casey appeared in his book *Modernism in Modern Drama* (1953); one never finds out whether he thinks O'Casey is not 'modern' enough, too 'modern,' or even 'modern' at all, for Mr Krutch disposes of him in several quick sentences at the end of a chapter on Synge, merely adding to his earlier charges of confusion and lack of purpose, a lack of 'hope' in the plays: 'O'Casey offers no solution; he proposes no remedy; he suggests no hope.'[94] The world and O'Casey have changed in the past half century, but not Mr Krutch.

In another book on modern drama, Raymond Williams, an English scholar of some discernment, has something to say about O'Casey's plays—but not too much, for his remarks appear in a 'Note' at the end of a chapter on Synge. Mr Williams calls his book *Drama From Ibsen to Eliot* (1952), and he devotes full chapters to Ibsen, Strindberg, Chekhov, Shaw, Synge, Pirandello, Yeats, and Eliot. For O'Casey there is the 'Note' in which Mr Williams states that the language and characters of the plays suffer from the limitations of Naturalism; and as a result the misplaced comedy in the plays breaks down into 'Naturalistic caricature . . . a particularly degenerate art'.[95] Doubtless Mr Malone would have objected to the use of the term 'degenerate', but he too saw O'Casey as a Naturalist, a 'photographic artist', whose plays are 'all "slices of life" in the strictest and most literal sense of the term'. And futhermore, like many of the Dublin literati, as well as some modern critics, Mr Malone had reservations about the music-hall elements in O'Casey's plays. He was not convinced that music-hall humour had a place in the drama. George Jean Nathan made the following comment on this sort of 'critical snobbery'.

The derogation of O'Casey by certain critics, first among them his fellow countryman and fellow-playwright, Ervine, as—in the instance of *Juno and the Paycock*—mere superb music-hall seems to me not only obvious critical snobbery, for superb music-hall remains nonetheless still superb, but equally obvious critical superficiality, inasmuch as it overlooks the play's rare comedy scenes' deep roots in dramatic character, their deep penetration into human eccentricity, and withal their beautiful, drunken dramatic literature. They are Molière full of Irish whiskey, now and again, Shaw off dietetic spinach and full of red meat. Flanagan and Allen (if such critics insist) in the classical garb of Falstaff and Dogberry. Furthermore, to derogate O'Casey as a mere hint of a poet, which these same critics do, is an even larger betrayal of critical sense. Where in the drama of living Irishmen is there greater and more genuine dramatic poetry than you will find in the mighty sweep of *The Plough and the Stars*, or in the boozy low measures of parts of *Juno*, or in the riff-raff of *Within the Gates*, in their periodic utterance, or in the speech of the workmen in *Purple Dust*, or even in passages of the otherwise largely dubious *Star Turns Red*? The answer is: nowhere. [96]

Finally, there is Ronald Peacock's important book, *The Poet in the Theatre* (1946). Although Mr Peacock writes about poetic drama, he analyses the work of five prose dramatists—Henry James, Ibsen, Shaw, Chekhov, and Synge—because he realizes that the 'poet' in the theatre does not necessarily create the poetry of the drama by writing his plays in lyric verse; but it is unfortunate that he overlooks O'Casey as a poetic dramatist. When he does mention O'Casey it is only to point out that his plays are 'symptomatic' of what is wrong with modern drama and the modern world in general; it is an ominous indictment:

. . . in the present age, which is one of social disintegration . . . the individual is overshadowed by the conflict of impersonal forces, of which he is more and more the victim and less and less even so much as the agent. Moreover, the moral judgements of the time bear upon the non-personal, the social situation; the question of the rightness or wrongness, the luck or ill-luck, of individual behaviour is disregarded and is often impossible of determination. A private crisis has little significance for a public eye dazzled by revolution and international vicissitudes. The 'tragic hero' has in consequence disappeared. The tragic plays of O'Casey are symptomatic of this situation. His characters, vivid as some of them are, are not as important as the larger political tragedy of which they are fortuitous victims. In themselves they are not in the least inevitable and unique tragic persons, like those of tradition; any set of Dublin people would do.[97]

One might challenge the notion that a human crisis can be so private that it has no public involvement, or wonder why a social situation must be non-personal; but whatever one thinks of Mr Peacock's somewhat Spenglerian view of disintegrating modern man, it is difficult to see how he could so completely have misunderstood the relationship between O'Casey's characters and the disordered world in which they live. If O'Casey says nothing else, in most of his plays, he certainly insists that his people are *more important* than 'the larger political tragedy' which threatens to destroy them. It is precisely this threat which inspires his women—Juno Boyle, Ginnie Gogan, Nora Clitheroe, Bessie Burgess—to fight for their families and friends, to fight against poverty and war; it is this threat which makes the quarrelling tenement-dwellers unite against their common enemies. Perhaps the usually perceptive Mr Peacock had some difficulty seeing this, but not the outraged patriots who rioted at the performances of *The Plough* because they saw all too clearly that O'Casey was more concerned with human beings than with national politics. But one does not have to be an outraged Irish nationalist to see that the personal tragedy is more important than the political tragedy in these plays. Yes, 'any set of Dublin people will do', any set of human beings anywhere will do—wherever or whatever they are, they are more important than the forces that threaten to destroy them.

And of course the people in O'Casey's plays are not like the 'tragic persons of tradition'. Presumably Mr Peacock is invoking the dogma of Aristotle and the drama of the Greeks and Elizabethans. But to what purpose? Would he have us believe that O'Casey tried and failed to write classical plays 'like those of tradition'? It is not likely that O'Casey either could or tried to imitate what goes under the general classification of 'traditional tragedy'; to say nothing of the fact that the genre of tragedy takes so many different forms in the 'traditional' works of Aeschylus, Sophocles, Euripides, Marlowe, Shakespeare, and Webster. O'Casey wrote in a new genre which cannot be measured in the Procrustean beds of tradition. Eric Bentley has given us a refreshing antidote to the academician's automatic invocation of the traditional muse:

Is it not the classical error of academicism to classify first-rate examples of a new genre as secondary examples of an old genre? And of all the old genres has not Shakespearean drama been the greatest hindrance to all new departure? 'It is when you are not able to write *Macbeth* that you write *Thérèse Raquin*,' said Robert Louis Stevenson. If he meant that you write a second-rate work when you are not able to write a first-rate work he is right but not very profound. If he meant that you only write a modern play when you can't write an Elizabethan play he was talking a kind of nonsense that makes one understand, and to a large extent support, Bernard Shaw's assault on Shakespeare.[98]

Mr Williams is like Mr Peacock a traditionalist, but in his strictures against O'Casey he invokes the social muse of Naturalism and then reduces all the comedy to cheap caricature. Yet O'Casey's exploitation of the comic spirit is too rich and penetrating to be reduced to caricature—Mr Williams ignores the main current of mock-heroic humour and satire in the plays, and the underlying comedy of character. And the abundance of humour and merriment can hardly be said to create the proper mood or material for the Naturalist bent on exposing social 'truths'. In fact, Mr Malone believed that comedy undermines Naturalism, and he scolded the Abbey actors for stressing the comic values in O'Casey's plays because he felt they were Naturalistic tragedies.

If Mr Malone had had his way O'Casey might have shared Chekhov's complaint. Too often Chekhov's plays have been performed as if they were Naturalistic tragedies. Even the great Stanislavsky muted the comic values in Chekhov's tragi-comic trilogy, *Uncle Vanya* (1899), *The Three Sisters* (1901) and *The Cherry Orchard* (1904), by playing more for tragic pathos than for comic irony, as if the plays had been written by Gorki instead of

Chekhov. On numerous occasions Chekhoz complained about
Stanislavsky's productions of his plays at the Moscow Art
Theatre, and he wrote to his friends: 'You tell me that people cry
at my plays. I've heard others say the same. But that was not why
I wrote them. It is Alexayev [Stanislavsky] who makes my characters into cry-babies . . . I am describing life, ordinary life, and not
blank despondency. They either make me into a cry-baby or into
a bore.' [99]

No doubt Mr Malone wanted to see more 'blank despondency'
in O'Casey's 'hideous tragedies'. But Mr Krutch complained
that there was too much despondency—no hope and no purpose,
only confusion. For him the plays were merely a series of sketches
'strung upon the skimpiest thread of melodramatic action', with
no form, no movement, no unity, and no purpose. Mr Krutch was
also confused about O'Casey's sympathies, and he defied anyone
to recall a play like *The Plough* after six months' time 'in any form
except that embodied in a jumbled memory of rather confused
events'. And a quarter of a century later he was still disturbed because he felt O'Casey offered no 'solution', proposed no 'remedy',
suggested no 'hope'. Confronted by such a melancholy indictment of those high-spirited plays, one can only wonder if the confusion did not originate with the critic instead of the artist. O'Casey
portrays a world of disorder, but he creates it within the controlled
framework of artistic order. His control is at times imperfect, it is
seldom mis-directed. It is not his intention to 'solve' the human
predicament—any more or less than a Shakespeare or a Chekhov
or an O'Neill portrays a disordered world in order to propose
remedies or solutions for it—but he does come to terms with it, he
tries to understand and evaluate it. And in that evaluation the
people in his plays represent an affirmative vision of man. He is
not pessimistic about man's fate, even amid poverty and war; but
he is no easy optimist either, and none of his characters are so
virtuous that they escape his satiric observations. Even Juno Boyle
and Bessie Burgess must earn their salvation.

The extent to which O'Casey gradually mastered the disci-
plines of dramatic form can be seen in the development of his craft
with each succeeding play. At the beginning, in *The Gunman*, he
probably had more genius than talent—a daring and original insight into the tragi-comic life of his characters, but a rather
cautious and conventional approach to the form and development

of the action. He confined his characters to a single set in a tenement room, using only two acts, both of which are constructed in
similar patterns of inter-linking episodes. In both acts Davoren
and Shields are alone at the start, and they are continually interrupted by their boisterous neighbours who gradually draw them
into the conflict. The first act ends with the death of Maguire, a
person close to Shields; the second act ends with the death of
Minnie Powell, a person close to Davoren. Davoren and Shields
are structurally as well as thematically the centre of the play; they
give the play its unity and its direction. Davoren moves in a cycle
of tragic irony, Shields moves in a cycle of comic irony. If anything
there is probably too much similarity in this recurring pattern of
action within the confines of a nineteenth century box-set; too
much unity in the sense that the repetitive pattern of both acts has
a tendency to become mechanical. There is, to be sure, a vigorous
and varied movement in the play, but it arises from the propulsive
life of the characters not the conventional arrangement of the form.
It must be remembered, however, that O'Casey had started writing entirely on his own, with no formal education and no practical
training in the drama or the theatre. Thus, he apparently had the
good sense to proceed cautiously in the handling of form, about
which he did not know too much, and to take his risks with his
characters, about whom he knew all there was to know.

But within the limitations of the conventional and repetitive
structure, he created a diversity of episodes. There are eight episodes in the first act, nine in the second act—episodes in which
eleven flamboyant characters are involved—and all these serio-
comic episodes spin the plot along, creating a mingled atmosphere
of comic and tragic moods. This double atmosphere of ironic
humour and incipient horror reveals O'Casey's controlling point of
view, his method of showing us that even in a disordered world of
poverty and war man's individual and eccentric traits cannot be
rubbed away. This tragi-comic point of view penetrates all the
material of the play and gives it its over-all unity.

Melodrama also contributes significantly to the total effect of
the play, sometimes awkwardly but on the whole successfully.
Most of the suspense and surprise generated by melodramatic
events is related to the mysterious Maguire, with his butterflies in
Knocksedan and his bag of threads and hairpins, which turns out
to be a bag of bombs. The Stop Press at the end of the first act,

suddenly announcing Maguire's death in an ambush near Knock-sedan, is a good shocker but an improbable device, for it is not likely that a newspaper could have reported the news so soon after Maguire's departure earlier in the act. The surprise bag of bombs is also a melodramatic device—however, it is a highly successful one; it is a coincidence which not only contributes to the suspense of the second act but reveals the cowardly self-deception of Davoren. O'Casey does not introduce melodrama for gratuitous thrills or happy resolutions. His bag of bombs is as effective and relevant a stage prop as Shakespeare's famous handkerchief, for in drama the moral end justifies the melodramatic means.

Furthermore, the laconic Maguire serves a vital function in the anti-heroic theme which is more important than his bag of bombs. In a world of voluble cowards, hypocrites, braggarts, and pseudo-patriots, he stands out in ironic contrast as a quiet and genuine patriot, that rare person who is a man of action and a man of few light words. Tommy Owens is a tin-horn patriot full of national-istic songs and slogans who does his fighting and bragging in the local pub; Adolphus Grigson is a patriotic Orangeman whose love of biblical rhetoric and liquor does not hide his cowardly hypocrisy; Seumas Shields is a shrewd ex-patriot turned pedlar who covers up his cowardice and laziness with a torrent of philosophical words; Donal Davoren is an ineffectual poet masquerading as a dangerous gunman. But Maguire is a real patriot, a gunman masquerading as a simple pedlar.

Finally, something must be said of the manner in which O'Casey uses Davoren as a unifying link for all the episodes. Davoren establishes the anti-heroic theme of the play, but this theme is ex-panded and vitalized by the comic characters, and in their rowdy presence, with Seumas Shields in the forefront as the wisest fool in the tenement bedlam, poor Davoren is often limited to playing the role of straight-man. He sets up the ironic humour which others exploit. Perhaps we see too much of him, since he takes part in all the action and never leaves the stage. It may be consis-tent with his brooding nature that he does nothing but try to write poems and indulge his romantic illusions; but after two acts of this one wishes he would finally bestir himself when he makes his discovery at the end of the play, beyond merely passing judge-ment upon himself and Shields.

Davoren is less animated than the other characters in the play because O'Casey, like most masters of the comic spirit, took a closer measure of and a greater delight in his eccentrics than his straight-men. His comic characters are all scene-stealers, and they dominate their world for the same reasons that the Wife of Bath, Falstaff, and the Pickwickians dominate their worlds. They are all uninhibited and eloquent individuals, free-wheeling madcaps whose comic eccentricity usually reveals a natural shrewdness in their apparent folly. There is in their egregious humour an irreverence for the ordinary conventions of life which allows them to speak with a candour that both shocks and delights the ordinary citizen. They are drawn in the broad dimensions of caricature as well as the strong lines of character, and while they possess the foibles of the ordinary citizen they are not 'real' people; they are larger than real people, better than real people. And in his next two plays O'Casey had the good judgement to make these comic eccentrics his main characters.

Thus, in *Juno* and *The Plough* there is not only an advance in O'Casey's dramatic techinque but a re-location of the main plot in the comic characters. Non-comic characters like Johnny Boyle in *Juno* and Jack Clitheroe in *The Plough*, who might have been counterparts to Davoren, are now secondary figures. In his excellent book, *Some Versions of Pastoral* (1950), William Empson discusses the prevalence of double plots in English drama, and the manner in which the main or 'serious' characters are contrasted with comic characters who on a lower level provide 'a sort of parody or parallel in low life to the serious part'.[100] This describes the situation in *The Gunman*, but O'Casey reverses the parallel in his next two plays where the main plots are given over to the comic characters and are contrasted with the under-plots or serious parts of the plays. The central focus has shifted to the eccentrics who mock the serious business of war. Furthermore, there are main characters in both plays, like Juno Boyle in *Juno* and Bessie Burgess in *The Plough*, who function on both levels, the comic and the tragic, and link the two.

In *Juno* we see the Boyle family in a fuller development of character, in sharper transitions, in a wider range of actions than was the case with the characters in *The Gunman*. O'Casey has solved the problem of the brooding Davoren, for now in the more flexible three-act structure we see all the Boyles in contrasting moods, struggling and roistering in tragi-comic conflict with each other and their friends, the Captain and Joxer leading the ironic revels while the family is in a state of moral and economic collapse. But the use of the legacy indicates that O'Casey still relied upon well-worn material for his plot and suspense. The legacy itself, however, stock device of melodrama that it is, like the bag of bombs in *The Gunman*, serves its function in the development of the tensions and the complication of the plot. It gives the Boyles a false reprieve and cause for extravagant celebration—pride soaring before a fall—and thus gives them a chance to hasten their own collapse. It is Bentham, the manipulator of the legacy and the seducer of Mary, who is the one weak link in the play. He is an artificial character, a Stage Englishman as petty villain who is unconvincing and unmotivated. And there is another sign that O'Casey was still learning his craft. In the original version of the play he had written an extra scene for the third act in which he described the actual shooting of Johnny Boyle by the I.R.A.; however, it was wisely cut out by the Abbey directors during rehearsals. The visualization of Johnny's death is not so important as its impact upon Juno, and it is enough that she hears the tragic news for at that point she has become the central figure in the play.

It is in *The Plough* that O'Casey achieves a firm control of his craft. Structurally he allows himself a more flexible use of time, place, and action—*The Gunman* covers two days in one set and two acts, *Juno* covers two months in one set and three acts, *The Plough* covers six months in four sets and four acts. The inter-action between the characters is more complex, and since we see them in a greater variety of moods and situations, the individual characters stand out in sharp relief against the tragi-comic panorama. O'Casey now reveals a resourceful command of staging techniques and makes the most of the theatrical element of spectacle, already pointing the way to the technical experiments and innovations he went on to develop in plays like *The Silver Tassie, Within the Gates, Red Roses For Me*, and *Cock-a-doodle Dandy*. The first act, like the early acts of *Juno*, establishes the norm of the tenement life. But in the second act the symbolic shadow of the Speaker with his inflamatory words blaring out of a loudspeaker hovers over the Pub in which the brawling people of the tenements ignite their own ironic riots. In the third act in front of the crumbling Georgian houses the brutal street fighting is interrupted by the tragi-comic parade of the looters. The eerie fourth act in a bare attic room is a requiem for the burning city and the dying people.

The form of *The Plough* is more expansive and varied than the conventional form of *The Gunman* because the greater scope and intention make greater demands upon the treatment of the material. And as O'Casey gained more confidence and control of his craft with each play, he dared to set himself greater aims in his next work. Each succeeding play he wrote posed different problems in dramatic technique, and his next experiment in *The Silver Tassie* was not so much a departure from his past work as a continuation of his search for new methods of handling old and new material.

CHAPTER III

The Playwright's Not For Burning

> We hope to find in Ireland ... that freedom to experiment which is not found in theatres of England, and without which no new movement in art or literature can succeed.
>
> W. B. Yeats (1898)

> The desire to experiment is like fire in the blood.
>
> Lady Gregory (1914)

I. THE EXPERIMENTAL PLAYWRIGHT

WHEN Yeats rejected *The Silver Tassie* in 1928 he administered a serious blow to the future of the Abbey Theatre as well as to the future of Sean O'Casey. The adamant position he took in his letter of rejection to O'Casey raised a series of crucial problems concerning: the aims of the Abbey Theatre, the themes that a playwright should and should not write about, the opinions that a playwright could and could not express in his work, and the nature of a playwright's experiments with new techniques. The immediate result of Yeats's decision was a blistering point-by-point reply from the outraged O'Casey, and the battle-lines were drawn; two of the leading figures of Irish theatre had clashed over their opposing theories of drama. Perhaps it would be more accurate to say that Yeats had the theories and O'Casey had a new play which did not happen to fit Yeats's current theories. But once provoked, O'Casey, in attacking Yeats's theories and defending his play, was able to muster some potent counter-theories of his own. The full significance of this clash must be seen against the background of O'Casey's development as a playwright, and Yeats's evolving theories and experiments as a playwright and as a director of the Abbey.

Just as Yeats the poet experimented with various myths and

94

techniques of verse on his lifelong journey from Innisfree to Byzantium, Yeats the playwright experimented with various myths and techniques of drama on his life-long journey from the Celtic Twilight to the Japanese Twilight. He began by writing nationalistic plays in prose and verse; he experimented with the peasant idiom in some prose plays; he wrote mythic plays in blank verse about Celtic heroes; and finally he discovered the ancient Japanese Noh tradition and wrote his highly stylized lyric plays for dancers.

From the start, his Irish Literary Theatre, which became the Abbey Theatre, had been conceived as an experimental art theatre not merely as an instrument of the Celtic Revival. He wanted a non-commercial theatre dedicated to the writing and producing of poetic plays which would be measured by their artistic success, not the caprices of popular favour or the pressures of financial success. Yeats made these terms clear in everything he wrote about the theatre, and most spectacularly in his speeches from the stage of the Abbey when he had to chastise a rioting mob. The initial direction of the theatre was set in the statement of principles that he drew up in 1898, with the help of Lady Gregory:

We propose to have performed in Dublin, in the spring of every year certain Celtic and Irish plays, which whatever their degree of excellence will be written with a high ambition, and so to build up a Celtic and Irish school of dramatic literature. We hope to find in Ireland an uncorrupted and imaginative audience trained to listen by its passion for oratory, and believe that our desire to bring upon the stage the deeper thoughts and emotions of Ireland will ensure for us a tolerant welcome, and that freedom to experiment which is not found in theatres of England, and without which no new movement in art or literature can succeed. [101]

If in their allusion to the theatres of England Yeats and Lady Gregory appeared to have overlooked J. T. Grein's Independent Theatre, an off-West End experimental art theatre which had been established in London in 1891, it was because their Irish theatre was in part a reaction against the prose realism and didacticism of Ibsen and Shaw, playwrights whose works were first performed at Grein's Independent Theatre.

In 1902 in *Samhain*, the occasional magazine of the Irish

theatre, Yeats spoke of creating 'A People's Theatre', and he proclaimed, 'Our movement is a return to the people',(102) a return to folk myths told in the rich folk idiom. But this did not mean that the new Irish theatre was to be a Popular Theatre, for it was conceived as an exclusive theatre for the right people. Yeats had made this view clear in 1899 in an essay called 'The Theatre':

We must make a theatre for ourselves and our friends; and for a few simple people who understand from sheer simplicity what we understand from scholarship and thought. We have planned the Irish Literary Theatre with this hospitable emotion, and that the right people may find out about us, we hope to act a play or two in the spring of every year; and that the right people may escape the stupefying memory of the theatre of commerce which clings even to them, our plays will be for the most part, remote, spiritual, and ideal. (103)

Yeats wrote many volumes on the theatre and many volumes of plays, but those three esoteric qualities always remained the basis of his theory of drama—'remote, spiritual, and ideal'. Celtic mythology, especially the Cuchulain legends, had already provided him with themes that were sufficiently 'remote, spiritual, and ideal', but it wasn't until he discovered the ritualistic Noh plays that he found what he believed to be the ultimate form of drama—a pure stylized form which he adapted to his own use. Now, by grafting themes from the Celtic Twilight on a form from the Japanese Twilight, he had created a new dramatic form. It was at this point, in 1916, that Yeats exulted in his discovery: 'I have invented a form of drama, distinguished, indirect, and symbolic, and having no need of mob or Press to pay its way—an aristocratic form.' (104)

It was through a translation of the Japanese Noh plays by Ernest Fenollosa and Ezra Pound that Yeats first became acquainted with this fourteenth-century Japanese genre. The plays were a ceremonial form of drama, religious rituals that were originally performed by young nobles and princes in honour of the Shinto shrines, and later taken over by an élite of specially trained actors who played them before small court audiences. Unlike the popular Kabuki plays which were the drama of the groundlings, the aristocratic Noh plays were as 'remote, spiritual, and ideal' as any art form could be. They were plays of formalized diction and symbolic gestures, with masks, dances, choruses, and music—a ritualistic folding and unfolding of the cloth to the accompaniment of primitive string and percussion instruments. It was under the influence of this stylized drama that Yeats began to write his 'Plays for Dancers', works like *At the Hawk's Well* and *The Only Jealousy of Emer*, and he described his 'new' drama in the following manner:

I hope to have attained the distance from life which can make credible strange events, elaborate words. I have written a little play that can be played in a room for so little money that forty or fifty readers of poetry can pay the price. There will be no scenery, for three musicians, whose seeming sun-burned faces will, I hope, suggest that they have wandered from village to village in some country of our dreams, can describe place and weather, and at moments action, and accompany it all by drum and gong or flute and dulcimer. Instead of the players working themselves into a violence of passion indecorous in our sitting-room, the music, the beauty of form and voice all come to a climax in pantomimic dance. [105]

Thereafter most of Yeats's experiments in the drama were to be further refinements of this ritualistic form, and he only regretted that he had not discovered it sooner: 'My blunder has been that I did not discover in my youth that my theatre must be the ancient theatre that can be made by unrolling a carpet or marking out a place with a stick, or setting a screen against a wall.' [106] Now he was free to write plays that would be like poetic séances for fifty kindred spirits in a sitting-room. Yeats had finally created his own private vision of a theatre, an aristocratic and decorous sitting-room theatre which would present crepuscular plays about 'some country of our dreams', free from the 'violence of passion', and achieving their 'climax in pantomimic dance'. It was an exclusive theatre so remote, so spiritual, so ideal, that it might best be described as a distillation of the theatre as pure poetic ritual—the theatre as anti-theatre.

It is in the light of Yeats's dedication to this new dramatic form that one finds some of the main reasons for his rejection of O'Casey's new dramatic form in *The Silver Tassie*. The nature of his own experiment apparently made it difficult for him to accept

O'Casey's experiment. For Yeats the form of the Noh play had become the ultimate form of drama, and he appeared to be offering
O'Casey an alternative: he could go on writing realistic plays
like his first three works; or, if he must experiment with new forms,
he could do so providing he wrote plays that were 'remote,
spiritual, and ideal'. But O'Casey was not content to repeat the
mixture as before, and Noh drama was not his porridge.

   In all probability Yeats had expected O'Casey to continue in his
old path, to use his past triumphs as a formula for future successes.
Certainly that would have been the safe and easy way. But the self-
schooled O'Casey had never been one to follow the safe or easy
path, in his life or his art, and in his characteristic way he had set
himself a new challenge in his new play. Perhaps he hadn't exhausted the material of the Dublin slums, but he was not the
writer to exploit his material to the point of exhaustion.

   Since his new play was a pacifist play about the First World
War, it was emotionally and thematically related to all his previous
work. His first three plays had dealt with the Irish Civil War,
from the point of view of the chief sufferers of the Dublin slums,
the women. He now turned to a larger war of even greater horrors
and more universal implications, again using the point of view of
the chief sufferers, the infantry soldiers. But while the general
theme of his new play was an extension of his past work, the
dramatic form, particularly in the symbolic second act, was a bold
experiment in the revolutionary techniques of Expressionism, the
non-realistic and surrealistic movement in modern drama which
had been developed by Strindberg and the German dramatists
early in the twentieth century.

   O'Casey was familiar with the Expressionistic plays of writers
like Strindberg, Toller, and the Strindberg-influenced O'Neill,
and in the symbolic stagecraft of these experimental dramatists he
found a method of projecting the nightmare tragedy of the battle
zone on the stage. In *The Dream Play* (1902) and *The Ghost
Sonata* (1907) Strindberg had created non-realistic characters and
scenes so that he could symbolically 'reproduce the disconnected
but apparently logical form of a dream'.[107] In *Masses and Man*
(1921) and *The Machine Wreckers* (1922) Ernst Toller had used
allegorical figures, group chanting, and surrealistic tableaux to represent the rebellion of individual man in a mechanized society.
In *The Emperor Jones* (1920) and *The Hairy Ape* (1922) Eugene

O'Neill had experimented with dream techniques in order to reveal the submerged torments of his allegorical characters.

While O'Casey used many of these techniques in *The Silver Tassie*, he did not become a doctrinaire Expressionist. He did not construct a theory of drama to explain his experiment. He had found a new form, not the ultimate form of drama, and he reshaped and modified it according to its function in his symbolic second act. Furthermore, unlike Strindberg and O'Neill who used a minimum of straight realism in their symbolic plays, O'Casey extended his experiment by mixing realistic and non-realistic techniques in his plays—a mingled form which he was to use in all his later plays, and which has subsequently been used by most modern dramatists, to mention some representative examples, Obey's *Noah* (1931), Wilder's *Our Town* (1938), Giraudoux's *Madwoman of Chaillot* (1945), Williams's *The Glass Menagerie* (1944), Miller's *Death of a Salesman* (1949).

2. A WORLD ON WALLPAPER

In the spring of 1928 O'Casey sent his new manuscript to the Abbey, confident that he had written a universal anti-war play in an experimental technique which opened new possibilities for the drama. But when Yeats and the Abbey said no, particularly in the terms of Yeats's letter of rejection, he was bewildered and enraged. He felt that the Abbey was not only rejecting his play but denying him the artist's right and need to experiment. This must have been especially ironic to O'Casey since it appeared that Yeats was reserving for himself the freedom to experiment as he pleased. Even Lady Gregory had experimented with her Folk History plays, Wonder Plays, and translations of Molière into Kiltartan dialect, the idiom of the Galway peasants. It was when she departed from her popular one-act farces to try her hand at new forms that Lady Gregory had remarked, 'The desire to experiment is like fire in the blood'.[108]

O'Casey now had plenty of fire in his blood, not only for his experimental play but for a vindication of it. Actually he had no quarrel with Lady Gregory who, although she had her doubts about his play, was still his most helpful and loyal friend at the Abbey. It was Lady Gregory who had sent him all the correspondence containing the Abbey directors' views of the play. Lady

Gregory and Lennox Robinson had been impressed by the symbolic second act, and Robinson had recognized O'Casey's need to experiment when he wrote to Lady Gregory: 'I'm glad he's groping towards a new manner . . . he couldn't go on writing slum plays forever and ever'.[109] Robinson, however, had one important reservation about O'Casey's new manner upon which he based his rejection: 'I don't think the mixture of the two manners—the realism of the first act and the unrealism of the second—succeeds, the characters who were Dublin slum in the beginning of the play end by being of nowhere.' Another director, Walter Starkie a Professor of Italian and Spanish literature at Trinity College, who was abroad when the decision on the play was reached, came home too late to insist that, even though the play had flaws, it should have been accepted. 'He is groping after a new drama outside the conventional stage,' Starkie said; 'at any moment he may make a great discovery.'[110]

It was Yeats's rather academic argument and condescending manner that really rankled O'Casey, and he quickly dispatched his blazing point by point counter-argument. Yeats had let it be known indirectly, through Lady Gregory, that O'Casey could make a public announcement that he himself had decided to withdraw his play for revision, thus being spared the embarrassment of an outright rejection. But this inept gesture of appeasement only added fuel to the fire. 'There is going to be no damned secrecy with me surrounding the Abbey's rejection of the play,'[111] O'Casey wrote to Robinson. 'Does he [Yeats] think that I would practise in my life the prevarication and wretchedness that I laugh at in my plays?' If Yeats had expected O'Casey to follow such an ignominious course, and with proper humility rewrite the play to please him, he had sadly misjudged the man as well as his play. O'Casey always believed with Blake that 'The tygers of wrath are wiser than the horses of instruction'.

Thus, still bristling in the knowledge that Yeats's decision was unalterable, and seeking some possible redress of his grievances, O'Casey decided to let the world know all the 'facts' of the rejection and judge who was right. In a daring if undiplomatic move, he sent Yeats's letter and the letters of the other Abbey directors, without their permission, to the London *Observer* and the *Irish Statesman*, together with his own roaring reply. Yeats and his associates were indignant. O'Casey felt that he was now a vindicated if rejected playwright. All the London and Dublin newspapers and magazines cheerfully reprinted the Yeats–O'Casey duel as a headline feature, and the battle was on. The heart of the argument, as stated in the letters, might be examined in the form of a dialogue on the nature of the dramatist's craft:

YEATS. Your play was sent to me at Rapallo by some mistake of the Theatre's. It arrived just after I had left, and was returned from there to Dublin. I found it when I myself reached Dublin four days ago. Enclosed with it were the opinions of my fellow-directors, but those opinions I shall not read until I have finished this letter; the letter, however, will not be posted unless their opinion concurs with mine. I had looked forward with great hope and excitement to reading your play, and not merely because of my admiration for your work, for I bore in mind that the Abbey owed its recent prosperity to you. If you had not brought us your plays just at that moment I doubt if it would now exist.

O'CASEY. There seems to me to be no reason to comment upon whether you read my play in Rapallo or Dublin, or whether you read my play before or after reading your fellow-directors' opinions, or whether the Abbey owed or did not owe its prosperity to me—these things do not matter, and so we'll hang them up on the stars.

YEATS. I am sad and discouraged; you have no subject. You were interested in the Irish Civil War, and at every moment of those plays wrote out of your own amusement with life or your sense of its tragedy; you were excited, and we all caught your excitement; you were exasperated almost beyond endurance by what you had seen or heard, as a man is by what happens under his window, and you moved us as Swift moved his contemporaries. But you are not interested in the Great War.

O'CASEY. Now how do you know I am not interested in the Great War? Perhaps because I never mentioned it to you. Your statement is to me an impudently ignorant one to make, for it happens that I was and am passionately and intensely interested in the Great War. Throughout its duration I have felt and talked of nothing else; brooded, wondered, and was amazed. In Dublin I talked of the Great War with friends that came to see me, and with friends when I went to see them. I talked of the Great War and of its terrible consequences with Lady Gregory when I stayed at Coole. I have talked of the Great

War with Doctor Pilger, now the cancer expert in Dublin, who served as surgeon at the front. Only a week before I got your letter I talked of the Great War to a surgeon here. And yet you say I am not interested in the Great War. And now will you tell me the name and give me the age and send me the address of the human being who, having eyes to see, ears to hear and hands to handle, was not interested in the Great War?

YEATS. You never stood on its battlefields or walked its hospitals, and so write out of your opinions.

O'CASEY. Do you really mean that no one should or could write about or speak about a war because one has not stood on the battlefield? Were you really serious when you dictated that—really serious, now? Was Shakespeare at Actium or Philippi? Was G. B. Shaw in the boats with the French, or in the forts with the British when St Joan and Dunois made the attack that relieved Orleans? And someone, I think wrote a poem about Tir na nOg who never took a header into the Land of Youth.

YEATS. You illustrate those opinions by a series of almost unrelated scenes as you might in a leading article.

O'CASEY. I don't know very much about leading articles, though I may possibly have read them when I had the mind of a kid, so I don't quite get your meaning here.

YEATS. There is no dominating character, no dominating action, neither psychological unity nor unity of action, and your great power of the past has been the creation of some unique character who dominated all about him and was himself a main impulse in some action that filled the play from beginning to end.

O'CASEY. Now, is a dominating character more important than a play, or is a play more important than a dominating character? . . . I remember talking to Lady Gregory about 'The Plough and the Stars' before it was produced, and I remember her saying that 'The Plough' mightn't be so popular as 'Juno', because there wasn't in the play a character so dominating and all-pervading as Juno, yet 'The Plough' is a better work than 'Juno'.

YEATS. The mere greatness of the World War has thwarted you; it has refused to become mere background, and obtrudes itself upon the stage as so much deadwood that will not burn with the dramatic fire. Dramatic action is a fire that must burn up everything but itself; there should be no room in a play for anything that does not belong to it; the whole history of the world must be reduced to wallpaper in front of which the characters must pose and speak. Among the things that the dramatic action must burn up are the author's opinions; while he is writing he has no business to know anything that is not a portion of that action.

O'CASEY. Your statement[s] about '. . . psychological unity and unity of action . . . Dramatic action is a fire that must burn up everything but itself . . . the history of the world must be reduced to wallpaper in front of which the characters must pose and speak . . . while an author is writing he has no business to know anything that isn't a part of the action . . .' are, to me, glib, glib ghosts. It seems to me they have been made, and will continue to be spoken for ever and ever by professors in schools for the culture and propagation of the drama. (I was nearly saying the Gospel.) I have held these infants in my arms a thousand times and they are all the same—fat, life-less, wrinkled things that give one a pain in his belly looking at them.

YEATS. Do you suppose for one moment that Shakespeare educated Hamlet and King Lear by telling them what he thought and believed? As I see it, Hamlet and Lear educated Shakespeare, and I have no doubt that in the process of that education he found out that he was an altogether different man to what he thought himself, and had altogether different beliefs. A dramatist can help his characters to educate him by thinking and studying everything that gives them the language they are groping for through his hands and eyes, but the control must be theirs, and that is why the ancient philosophers thought a poet or dramatist Daimon-possessed.

O'CASEY. Whether Hamlet and Lear educated Shakespeare, or Shake-speare educated Hamlet and Lear, I don't know the hell, and I don't think you know either . . . And was there ever a play, worthy of the name play, that did not contain one or two or three opinions of the author that wrote it? And the Abbey Theatre has produced plays that were packed skin-full with the author's opinions—the plays of Shaw, for instance.

YEATS. I see nothing for it but a new theme, something you have found and no newspaper writer has ever found. What business have we with anything but the unique?

O'CASEY. And so when I have created the very, very thing you are looking for—something unique—you shout out: 'take, oh, take this wine away, and, for God's sake, bring me a pot of small beer' . . . I have pondered in my heart your expression that 'the history of the world must be reduced to wallpaper', and I find in it only the pretentious bigness of a pretentious phrase. I thank you out of mere politeness, but I must refuse even to try to do it. That is exactly, in my opinion (there goes a cursed opinion again), what most of the Abbey dramatists are trying to do—building up, building up little worlds of wallpaper, and hiding striding life behind it all . . . It is all very well and very easy to say that 'the dramatic action must burn up the author's opinions'. The best way, and the only way, to do that is to burn up the author himself. [112]

As far as O'Casey was concerned, the playwright was not for burning. Nor were his 'opinions'. It is difficult to understand why O'Casey's 'opinions' on the subject of war and human suffering had suddenly disturbed Yeats, since this new play, except for the experimental techniques, did not contain radically different 'opinions' from those in O'Casey's three previous anti-war plays which Yeats had accepted and praised as the work of a genius. In order to be consistent, Yeats should have rejected the first three plays also, for the war in Ireland is not reduced to 'mere background' in those works and they defy his 'wallpaper world' theory of drama as clearly as does *The Silver Tassie*. By invoking his new concept of drama, in which the characters had to pose and speak against an abstract, non-historical background, Yeats would have had to reject a number of his own plays, not only the nationalistic *Countess Cathleen* and *Cathleen Ni Houlihan*, but his translation of Sophocles' *King Oedipus*, which he published in 1928, the same year he said no to O'Casey. To put it bluntly, he would have had to reject practically all the major works of drama, beginning with the Greeks and Elizabethans, for there are extremely few plays in which the worldly conflicts of history are not central to the action— certainly more than a mere background of wallpaper. The handful of non-heretical plays that could escape his Index Aestheticum would be his own Noh plays for dancers, probably the baleful mysteries of Maeterlinck, and no doubt Villiers de l'Isle Adam's gallic pastiche, *Axel*, a favourite play of Yeats's younger days when he was fond of quoting Axel's line: 'As for living, our servants will do that for us.' [113]

A year after he had rejected *The Silver Tassie*, Yeats wrote in his manuscript-book that he did not believe that literature should be written on a theme that deals with the history of the times and

'bulks largely in the news'. It was just after the London production of *The Silver Tassie* in 1929, and Yeats was still trying to
justify his stand against the play:

We were biased, we are biased by the Irish Salamis. The war as Casey
has conceived it is an equivalent for those primary qualities brought
down by Berkeley's secret society, it stands outside the characters, it is
not part of their expression, it is that very attempt denounced by
Mallarmé to build as if with brick and mortar with the pages of a book.
The English critics feel differently. To them a theme that 'bulks largely
in the news' gives dignity to human nature, even raises it to international importance. We on the other hand are certain that nothing can
give dignity to human nature but the character and energy of its expression. We do not even ask that it shall have dignity so long as it can burn
away all that is not itself. [114]

Yeats was still calling for purification by fire. But he was also
admitting a double bias. First his Irish bias allowed him to accept
the Irish Salamis—the Irish Civil War—but made him reject a
World War in which Ireland had not participated. As for his
aesthetic bias, it may have been valid for Mallarmé and the French
Symbolist poets, and for Yeats the poet, but it is a bias that is more
appropriate to lyric poetry than drama. The Symbolist poets had a
profound influence upon modern poetry, but they knew little
about the drama and did not concern themselves with the craft of
playwriting. Yeats could claim, therefore, that a lyric poem would
arise like the phoenix from the purifying fire of the aesthetic process, but a drama needs the vital 'brick and mortar' of human
history, whether it 'bulks largely in the news' or deals with war or
any other contemporary theme. The drama is probably the most
social of all art forms, in its public presentation before an audience
and in its treatment of worldly themes; it deals with man in relation to society as well as to himself.

To a certain extent, then, the issue narrows to Yeats's personal
bias against the use of war, especially a non-Irish war, as a theme
for poetry or drama. When he edited *The Oxford Book of Modern
Verse* in 1936 he arbitrarily omitted Wilfred Owen and other
World War poets. He explained his distaste for war poetry in his
Introduction in the following manner: 'If war is necessary, or
necessary in our time and place, it is best to forget its suffering as

we do the discomfort of fever, remembering our comfort at midnight when our temperature fell, or as we forget the worst moments of more painful disease.'[115] 'Tis a consummation devoutly to be wished, but the tragic disease of war is not so easily forgotten. Nor can one make it disappear by thinking of the comforts of peace, by editing it out of books, or by rejecting plays that deal with it.

Another type of escapist attitude toward the Great War was prevalent when O'Casey wrote his play. Many people who could not find comfort in forgetting the carnage or rejecting it from their thoughts, found solace in looking back on it with an attitude of nostalgiac patriotism. For instance, one of the biggest hits in the West End in 1928 was R. C. Sherriff's *Journey's End*, a sentimental tribute to the British soldiers who presumably fought the war like gentlemen cricketers and quoted *Alice in Wonderland* before they died beautifully and bravely for the greater glory of England. O'Casey called *Journey's End* 'a play of false effrontery'[116] because it presented the war as 'a pleasant thing to see and feel'; this may be a hard judgement, but it must be remembered that O'Casey had already written three anti-heroic plays in which he had exposed the excesses of Irish patriotism, and he was in no mood to look favourably upon its British equivalent. The fact that British chauvinism was more charming then Irish chauvinism did not make O'Casey any happier about it. Although *The Silver Tassie* was written several months before Sheriff's play, it was a timely reply to those people who sentimentalized the tragedy of the war and took a cavalier attitude toward human suffering.

On the matter of an author's 'opinions' in a work of art, Yeats raised a number of problems. First of all, he simply did not believe that a writer should have any 'opinions' about such a distressing subject as war. Experiment or no experiment, he invoked his arbitrary objection when he told O'Casey: 'I see nothing for it but a new theme, something you have found and no newspaper writer has ever found.' If some people must write about war, Yeats seemed to be saying, let newspaper men do it in leading articles—it is a subject for journalists not artists.

Then Yeats went on to use the term 'opinions' in another sense which did not help his argument. He made a specious distinction between a writer's first-hand contact with an event and his second-hand knowledge of it, the former being a valid experience, the latter only an 'opinion'. It is strange to see Yeats, of all writers, trying to defend the cult of literal experience. 'You never stood on its battlefields or walked its hospitals, and so write out of your opinions.' O'Casey's reply is devastating, punctuated by his ironic reference to a verse play Yeats wrote about that unvisited country of Irishmen's dreams, *The Land of Heart's Desire*. And there are countless writers beside Shakespeare and Shaw who wrote about wars without having stood on the battlefields—one thinks immediately of Stephen Crane who wrote a graphic novel about the American Civil War which was fought before he was born.

To be sure, O'Casey had strong 'opinions' about war, whether the Irish Civil War or the World War, but he used them as an organic part of his theme. His characters are naturally influenced by their experiences in the war, which is the centre of the dramatic action. He had written a play not a tract. His 'opinions' were not superimposed or merely stated in leading-article fashion; nor were they debated in point-blank range of the subject in the dialectical manner of a Shaw. But even if O'Casey had followed Shaw and written what has come to be called a 'drama of ideas'— too often a pejorative and misleading term—one might still question this final aspect of Yeats's stand against an author's ideas or 'opinions' in a play, or any type of literature.

Unfortunately too many literary battles have been fought over the respective merits of aesthetics and ideas—form and content— in a work of art, as though these qualities represented a dualism rather than the mutually dependent parts of an organic whole. *What* a writer says should not be separated from *how* he says it. Ideas or 'opinions' are not necessarily limited to abstract concepts or leading articles, and they are not in themselves alien to literature; on the contrary, they can usually be found in the best literature of all ages. Lionel Trilling has analysed this relationship between aesthetics and ideas with extraordinary wisdom in his essay 'The Meaning of a Literary Idea', in *The Liberal Imagination* (1950):

The most elementary thing to observe is that literature is of its nature involved with ideas because it deals with man in society, which is to say that it deals with formulations, valuations, and decisions, some of them implicit, others explicit . . . what drama does not consist of the opposition of formulable ideas, what drama, indeed, is not likely to break out into the explicit exposition and debate of these ideas? . . . The form

of the drama *is* its idea, and its idea *is* its form . . . Intellectual power
and emotional power go together. (117)

In the light of this 'elementary' synthesis of form and content,
it may be accurate to say that Yeats's theory of drama was singu-
larly applicable to his own verse plays for dancers. His theory had
little relevance to the plays of O'Casey. In its own right and for its
own purposes it may envision a valid form of ceremonial drama;
but it is based upon an eastern tradition and is a genre apart from
the mainstream of western drama.

Certainly Yeats's theory was consistent with the attitudes—one
is tempted to say 'opinions'—which can be found in all his work,
especially his poems. For example, he has recorded his unhappy
relationship with the politically active and 'opinionated' Maud
Gonne in several poems, particularly in 'A Prayer for My
Daughter', where he indicates what can happen to a beautiful
woman who has strong opinions, and he warns his daughter that
'opinions are accursed':

> *An intellectual hatred is the worst,*
> *So let her think opinions are accursed.*
> *Have I not seen the loveliest woman born*
> *Out of the mouth of Plenty's horn,*
> *Because of her opinionated mind*
> *Barter that horn and every good*
> *By quiet natures understood*
> *For an old bellows full of angry wind;* (118)

Yeats wrote this poem in 1919 at the time of and in relation to
Maud Gonne's activities in the Irish Civil War, the very period
about which O'Casey had written his first three plays, which
Yeats had praised so highly. It would seem, then, that he first put
the curse of 'opinions' on women, but by 1928 he applied this
prejudice to everyone, particularly playwrights.

And yet, with all his prejudices and his intricate system of
theories and ideas, Yeats himself probably had more personal
'opinions' than any modern writer of his stature. The poet and the
dramatist, Yeats had told O'Casey, must be Daimon-possessed.
But perhaps different mediums require different Daimons. Yeats's
Daimon gave him a mythic vision and inspired him to write some
of the outstanding poetry of modern times. He did bring a con-

temporary as well as a mythic sense of history to many of his best poems, particularly his later work, but in his plays he was too faithful to his otherworldly theories and confined himself to the distant country of noble dreams. The Daimon of lyric poetry limited his power as a playwright, for Yeats was so possessed with the purifying fire of dramatic action that he burned away the material life and active presence of his characters, leaving them in their abstract purity to pose and speak as mystical figures in a remote world on symbolic wallpaper.

O'Casey's Daimon of the drama gave him a vision of modern history and inspired him to write some of the outstanding plays of our time on some of the major crises of modern man.

3. A WORLD AT WAR

Harry Heegan, the symbolic hero of *The Silver Tassie*, is a herculean young athlete and infantry soldier who dominates and provokes the action of the play, even when he is not on the stage. Before he makes his victorious appearance from the football field late in the first act, the other characters, particularly Harry's father Sylvester and his old 'buttie' Simon, exalt the legend of Harry's impulsive courage and strength. Like two comic chorus-characters the old codgers offer a vivid catalogue of Harry's fabulous deeds as champion runner, strong-man, fighter, and football hero. And from the moment Harry bursts on the stage, surrounded by his admirers and carrying 'the silver tassie', the trophy which he has almost single-handedly helped the Avondales.win, he *is* the play.

In the first act Harry's tumultuous spirit shines through the mundane world like the image of a legendary hero. He is an open-hearted primitive, an instinctive hero who glories in the joy of his uninhibited emotions and the vigour of his powerful limbs. Like Synge's Christy Mahon, he is a conquering 'playboy of the western world', victor in all games, races, and fights, and the darling hero of all the girls. O'Casey, however, introduced his tragic hero at the point where Synge's comic hero departed. Christy had discovered his primitive powers at the conclusion of *The Playboy of the Western World*. At the beginning of *The Silver Tassie* Harry has already gone 'romancing through a romping lifetime', and he is in the full flush of a new victory when we first see him. Harry is on the heights from which he will soon fall when he is wounded in the war and abandoned by his friends and the girl he loves. Christy, however, is only able to become the real 'playboy' when he is abandoned by his friends and the girl he loves. The comic movement of Christy's life goes from impotence to liberation and triumph; the tragic movement of Harry's life goes from liberation and triumph to impotence.

Symbolically Harry is the universal soldier destroyed in a world war, but he is also a particular Irishman; except for the second act, which takes place in the war zone in France, the other three acts are set in Dublin. Thus, although the play is in a sense a morality play—a conflict between the good life that Harry represents and the evil of war—O'Casey avoids the allegorical abstractions of the old morality plays by allowing his universal theme to develop out of individualized characters in a particular time and place. With this particularized locale he is also able to reveal in the last half of the play how the people who stay at home are spiritually wounded by the war.

As in his previous works, O'Casey begins this play on a broad comic note, but with an undercurrent of tragic implications that will presently emerge and darken the mood of the last three acts. The first act is a comic-ironic prologue that builds up to the moment of Harry's triumphant arrival. Much of the satiric humour grows out of a running quarrel between the two old men and Susie Monican. Sylvester and Simon are continually defending the natural joy and exuberance that Harry represents against what Sylvester calls Susie's 'persecutin' tambourine theology'. Susie is a fire-and-brimstone religious fanatic with a thou-shalt-not fear of life, largely a result of her frustrated love for Harry, and the more she hurls her hysterical warnings at Sylvester and Simon— 'I can hear some persons fallin' with a splash of sparks into the lake of everlastin' fire'—the greater their excitement flares over Harry's heroic deeds. And later Susie's fanaticism will be contrasted with the genuine religious feeling of the soldiers.

As rambunctious clowns Sylvester and Simon have the hilariously vulnerable traits of the roguish Captain Boyle and Joxer, and they are not immune from O'Casey's satire, for he laughs at as well as with them. They appear to be shrewd enough to cope with Susie's attempts to 'claw' them into the kingdom of heaven, but their own attitude toward religion is a kind of genial hypocrisy characteristically illustrated in the following scene:

SIMON. In a church, somehow or other, it seems natural enough, and even in the street it's alright, for one thing is as good as another in the wide-open ear of the air, but in the delicate quietness of your own home it, it——

SYLVESTER. Jars on you!

SIMON. Exactly!

SYLVESTER. If she'd only confine her glory-to-God business to the festivals, Christmas, now, or even Easter, Simon, it would be recommendable; for a few days before Christmas, like the quiet raisin' of a curtain, an' a few days after, like the gentle lowerin' of one, there's nothing more—more——

SIMON. Appropriate——

SYLVESTER. Exhilaratin' than the singin' of the Adestay Fidellis.

Harry and his neighbour Teddy Foran are home from the trenches on furlough, and while Harry is out on the football field, Teddy has a brawl with his wife who seems too glad to see him go back to the war. In an uproarious scene, after he has smashed all the dishes in the upstairs Foran flat, Teddy chases his wife into the Heegan rooms where the bold Sylvester protects her by hiding under the bed with her. And Simon, still excited about the way Harry stretched out a Bobby with a right to the jaw, had gone upstairs to take care of the raging Teddy—'Phuh, I'll keep him off with the left and hook him with the right'—but after a discreet reconsideration of the odds he disappeared.

All these preludes to Harry's entrance serve to create the vivid background of his life, and they are also ironic pointers of what lies ahead of him. Teddy Foran's relationship with his wife is a foreshadowing of what will later happen to Harry and his girl Jessie Taite. The religious theme will reappear in a more serious vein throughout the play as the dazed soldiers struggle to find comfort and understanding. And Sylvester and Simon by exalting Harry's natural powers establish a norm with which we can contrast the tragic consequences of the war when he comes back wounded.

When it is almost time for the troopship to take the men back to France, Harry's teammates carry him and his girl Jessie on their shoulders through the streets and the chant of the crowd is heard outside—'Up Harry Heegan and the Avondales!' Harry comes in explaining excitedly how he kicked the winning goal, and he and Jessie celebrate by kissing and drinking wine from the tassie, which Harry calls the 'sign of youth, sign of strength, sign of victory'. Before they march off, Harry and Barney, another of his soldier friends, sing the Scottish ballad by Robert Burns, 'The Silver Tassie'—'the song that the little Jock used to sing . . . the little Jock we left shrivellin' on the wire after the last push':

> *Gae bring to me a pint of wine,*
> *And fill it in a silver tassie;*
> *That I may drink before I go,*
> *A service to my bonnie lassie.*

> *The boat rocks at the pier o' Leith,*
> *Full loud the wind blows from the ferry;*
> *The ship rides at the Berwick Law,*
> *An' I must leave my bonnie Mary.*

> *The trumpets sound, the banners fly,*
> *The glittering spears are ranked ready;*
> *The shouts of war are heard afar,*
> *The battle closes thick and bloody.*

> *It's not the roar of the sea or shore,*
> *That makes me longer wish to tarry,*
> *Nor shouts of war that's heard afar—*
> *It's leaving thee, my bonnie lassie.*

The first stanza is from an old folk ballad and Burns added the remaining stanzas. There is a legend that Burns composed the song after seeing a young soldier part from his sweetheart on the pier of Leith; and while O'Casey introduces the song in a generally similar situation at the end of the first act, he associates the tassie itself with Harry in a special way, as the cup of victory as well as love. And in the rest of the play the tassie is used as a symbol of Harry's lost love and forgotten triumphs.

Ironically, there is no protesting or keening as the men leave for the trenches. The lassies in the play seem to be glad that their men are going back to the war. Harry is too intoxicated by his victory in the game and the wine he has drunk to see through Jessie, who merely regards him as a prize catch and hates his mother for preventing her from marrying him to get his allowance cheques. Susie and Mrs Heegan are fiercely jealous of Jessie, and Mrs Heegan's greatest concern is that her son should not miss the boat, in which case she might miss his allowance cheques. When the justifiably outraged Teddy Foran turns on his flighty wife and smashes the dishes, it is Mrs Heegan who remarks: 'You'd imagine, now, the trenches would have given him some idea of the sacredness of life.' But none of the women in the play seem to understand 'the sacredness of life' or the tragedy of war. O'Casey here departs from his earlier sympathetic treatment of women because he is writing about an aspect of war which is not directly their tragedy, the holocaust of the battle-front. Also, the insensitivity of the women increases the tragic isolation of the soldiers, for it is their tragedy, their play.

We feel the full impact of this tragic isolation in the second act when we are suddenly brought into the no-man's land of the war zone. There is a violent change of technique to parallel the violent change of mood—from comic reality to tragic surreality. Here O'Casey creates the shock of the war in a horrible transfiguration scene. In the second act of *The Plough* he had been confronted with a somewhat similar problem but he solved it by using off-stage devices, a huge shadowy figure and a loudspeaker voice to blare out exhortations of bloodshed; and later in that play he had a number of characters rush in from the barricades to describe the gory street fighting. But these methods were now too limited for his new play. Instead of *telling* the audience through exposition that war is hell, he had found in the techniques of Expressionism a way of *showing* them a symbolic nightmare of that hell—a new method of developing the tortured figure that the once herculean Harry has become in the last two acts. There are many variations in the Expressionistic methods of Strindberg, Toller, Kaiser, and O'Neill, and they have been very accurately summarized by Allardyce Nicoll in the following statement:

Short scenes took the place of longer acts; dialogue was made abrupt and given a staccato effect; symbolic (almost morality-type) forms were substituted for 'real' characters; realistic scenery was abandoned, and in its place the use of light was freely substituted; frequently choral, or mass, effects were preferred to the employment of single figures, or else single figures were elevated into positions where they became representative of forces larger than themselves.[119]

With some modifications O'Casey incorporated most of these elements in his second act. He used one long act with a fixed set instead of a series of short tableaux. The symbolic soldiers are very close to morality types. Several figures stand out above the choral mass of soldiers and lead the antiphonal chanting of songs and staccato phrases, especially the Croucher who is on a ramp above the other men. Predominantly red lighting and the black barrel of a huge howitzer gun create the representational battlefield just behind the front lines beside the ruins of a monastery which now serves as a Red Cross Station. When the enemy breaks through at the end of the act the firing of the gun and the general barrage of shells is simulated by wild flashes of light, without sound effects. In one of the jagged monastery walls there still remains a single unbroken stained-glass window of the Virgin, and, just above it, a life-size Crucifix, one arm of which has been loosened by a shell and now leans outstretched toward the Virgin. The symbols of the Virgin and the Gun stand out as opposing forces. While an organ is heard from behind the ruined monastery wall, where a celebration of the Mass is in progress, the Croucher, a half-crazed soldier, dreamily intones his litany as the act begins. The Notes explain that 'The Croucher's make-up should come as close as possible to a death's head, a skull; and his hands should show like those of a skeleton's. He should sit somewhere *above* the group of soldiers'. Here is the opening scene:

CROUCHER. And the hand of the Lord was upon me, and carried me out in the spirit of the Lord, and set me down in the midst of a valley.

And I looked and saw a great multitude that stood upon their feet, an exceeding great army.

And he said unto me, Son of man, can this exceeding great army become a valley of dry bones?

(*The music ceases, and a voice, in the part of the monastery left standing, intones*) · Kyr ... ie ... e ... eleison. Kyr ... ie ... e ... eleison (*followed by the answer*) : Christe ... eleison.

CROUCHER (*resuming*). And I answered, O Lord God, thou knowest. And he said, prophesy and say unto the wind, come from the four winds a breath and breathe upon these living that they may die.

(*As he pauses the voice in the monastery is heard again*) : Gloria in excelsis Deo et in terra pax hominibus bonae voluntatis.

CROUCHER (*resuming*). And I prophesied, and the breath came out of them, and the sinews came away from them, and behold a shaking and their bones fell asunder, bone from his bone, and they died, and the exceeding great army became a valley of dry bones.

(*The voice from the monastery is heard, clearly for the first half of the sentence, then dying away toward the end*) : Accendat in nobis Dominus ignem sui amoris, et flammam aeternae caritatis.

(*A group of soldiers come in from fatigue, bunched together as if for comfort and warmth. They are wet and cold, and they are sullen-faced. They form a circle around the brazier and stretch their hands toward the blaze.*)

1ST SOLDIER. Cold and wet and tir'd.

2ND SOLDIER. Wet and tir'd and cold.

3RD SOLDIER. Tir'd and cold and wet.

4TH SOLDIER (*very like Teddy*). Twelve blasted hours of ammunition transport fatigue!

1ST SOLDIER. Twelve weary hours.

2ND SOLDIER. And wasting hours.

3RD SOLDIER. And hot and heavy hours.

1ST SOLDIER. Toiling and thinking to build the wall of force that blocks the way from here to home.

2ND SOLDIER. Lifting shells.

3RD SOLDIER. Carrying shells.

4TH SOLDIER. Piling shells.

1ST SOLDIER. In the falling, pissing rine and whistling wind.

2ND SOLDIER. The whistling wind and falling, drenching rain.

3RD SOLDIER. The God-dam rain and blasted whistling wind.

1ST SOLDIER. And the shirkers sife at home coil'd up at ease.

2ND SOLDIER. Shells for us and pianos for them.

3RD SOLDIER. Fur coats for them and winding-sheets for us.

4TH SOLDIER. Warm.

2ND SOLDIER. And dry.

1ST SOLDIER. An' 'appy. (*A slight pause.*)

BARNEY. An' they call it re-cu-per-at-ing!

1ST SOLDIER (*reclining near the fire*). Gawd, I'm sleepy.

2ND SOLDIER (*reclining*). Tir'd and lousy.

3RD SOLDIER (*reclining*). Damp and shaking.

4TH SOLDIER (*murmuringly, the rest joining him*). Tir'd and lousy, an' wet an' sleepy, but mother call me early in the morning.

1ST SOLDIER (*dreamily*). Wen I thinks of 'ome, I thinks of a field of dysies.

THE REST (*dreamily*). Wen 'e thinks of 'ome, 'e thinks of a field of dysies.

1ST SOLDIER (*chanting dreamily*).

> I sees the missus paryding along Walham Green,
> Through the jewels an' silks on the costers' carts,
> Emmie a-pulling her skirt an' muttering,
> 'A balloon, a balloon, I wants a balloon',
> The missus a-tugging 'er on, an' sying,
> 'A balloon, for shime, an' your father fighting:
> You'll wait till 'e's 'ome, an' the bands a-plying!'
>   (*He pauses.*)

(*Suddenly*). But wy'r we 'ere, wy'r we 'ere—that's wot we wants to know!

2ND SOLDIER. God only knows—or else, perhaps, a red-cap.

In the Croucher's prophetic speeches O'Casey has ironically paraphrased but reversed the meaning of the biblical passages from the Book of Ezekiel. In Chapter 37 of that Book, the Lord offers the wandering Israelites a prophecy of hope and renewal; their dried bones shall be revived and they shall arise a 'great army'. Ezekiel 39:9 actually reads: '. . . come from the four winds, O breath, and breathe upon these slain that they may live'. And Ezekiel 37:10 reads: '. . . and a breath came into them and they lived, and stood up upon their feet, an exceeding great army'. But the Croucher, intoning through his death-mask, sees only a wasted battlefield of dried bones.

For a contrasting treatment of the same biblical allusions—in this case an orthodox view—one can turn to T. S. Eliot's 'Ash Wednesday'. In this poem of renewed faith Eliot uses these same phrases from Chapter 37 of Ezekiel, but of course he does not reverse the meaning. He wrote this poem in 1930 (two years after O'Casey's play), after his conversion, when he no longer saw the modern world as a sterile valley of dead bones. However, in 'The Waste Land' (1922) where he had also used an allusion from Ezekiel—this time in a context of despair—there is a closer parallel to what O'Casey does in the above scene. Perhaps the second act of The Silver Tassie might be called an 'objective correlative' for O'Casey's 'waste land'. Eliot's line' I will show you fear in a handful of dust' might have been spoken by the Croucher.

At the same time that the Croucher intones his fateful dithy-rambs, the incantation of the Kyrie is heard—the plea to God for mercy. But the only response is the bitter chant of the exhausted soldiers, an ironic antistrophe. In their chanted cockney diction, here and throughout the act, O'Casey creates a special mock-lingo which fixes the mood of the action at a strident non-realistic pitch and reinforces the grotesque anonymity of the soldiers. And yet there are some deeply poignant links with the outside world of reality, as for example in the 1st Soldier's dream of his missus and his little girl Emmie wanting a balloon. The Soldiers try to reject the hopeless prophecy of the mad Croucher, the death's head figure; they try to pray, they try desperately to convince them-selves that they can escape from this valley of death. The 1st Soldier insists, 'There's a Gawd knocking abaht somewhere.' But though they have not been able to find Him on the battlefield, they go on believing in Him, and in the weapons of war that might save them. Just before the enemy break-through at the end of the act the Soldiers sing their songs to God and the Gun—'We be-lieve in God and we believe in thee.' And it is the Wounded on the Stretchers, the mutilated and dying, who remind us that 'the image God hath made' and the war is destroying, is the image of 'power and joy' which Harry Heegan symbolized in the first act:

> The power, the joy, the pull of life,
> The laugh, the blow, and the dear kiss,
> The pride and hope, the gain and loss,
> Have been temper'd down to this, this, this.

There are four songs and five extended chants in the act. In the Notes, O'Casey explains that all the chanted passages are to be in-toned antiphonally in the simple Plain Song of Gregorian chant, with the traditional three-part division, the Intonation, the Meditation, and the Ending. Thus, by following the responsive pattern of the Mass at the beginning, and the recurring intonation of Gregorian chant throughout the act, O'Casey sets the tradi-tional rituals of the church against the terrible rituals of the war in a dissonant struggle between the forces of good and evil. In this manner he was able to develop his anti-war theme as an organic part of his symbolic form.

In the second act, the dehumanizing forces of war win the tragic struggle, and in the last two acts we see the realistic consequences of the war as the wounded soldiers also lose the struggle on the home front. Absolute war corrupts absolutely—those who ignored it at home as well as those who were crippled by it in the trenches.

The third act takes place in a hospital ward back in Dublin with all the individualized characters of the first act now in a new situation. Harry was wounded in the spine and is confined to a wheelchair, paralysed from the waist down. Teddy was blinded. Susie Monican has become a nurse, but her patients are little more than bed-numbers to her and she releases her repressions in love games with the young doctor. The fickle Jessie Taite has abandoned the invalid Harry for the healthy Barney, who has now won Harry's girl as well as the Victoria Cross for carrying him out of the line of fire. Harry's mother now finds great comfort in the knowledge that she will get the maximum disability allowance.

Sylvester and Simon are also patients in the hospital, and their imaginary pains and fears represent a series of comic contrasts to the tragic condition of Harry and Teddy. The two old clowns are given many opportunities to create an atmosphere of sheer theatrical fun with their capers. Their bath episode in the third act and telephone episode in the fourth act are excellent examples of the *tour de force* comedy that is such a characteristic part of every O'Casey play. Once he sets the direction of his main plot, he often steers a circuitous course of action with his comic sub-plots. It is his way of maintaining contact with the hurly-burly traffic of life, and what he called the 'Ta Ra Ra Boom Dee Ay' element of the drama.

Gradually, however, the tragic implications of the main plot dominate the action as the abandoned and bitter Harry tries to fight back. When the operation he is to undergo in the third act proves a failure, he turns up at the Avondales' War Victory Dance in the final act, his once powerful body now impotent in a wheelchair. The unfaithful Jessie deserts him for Barney, and Harry calls for red wine, remembering the wine of victory he had earlier drunk when he was the hero of the Avondales. Now he drinks an ironic toast:

To the dancing, for the day cometh when no man can play. And legs were made to dance, to run, to jump, to carry you from one place to another; but mine can neither walk, nor run, nor jump, nor feel the merry motion of a dance. But stretch me on the floor fair on my belly, and I will turn over on my back, then wriggle back again on to my belly; and that's more than a dead, dead man can do!

The red wine of life has lost its meaning for the crippled Harry, and he speaks for all the sad-mad soldiers wounded in body and spirit by the war. Later he drinks wine from the symbolic tassie and cries out to everyone, to the world:

Red wine, red like the faint remembrance of the fires in France; red wine like the poppies that spill their petals on the breasts of the dead men. No, white wine, white like the stillness of the millions that have removed their clamours from the crowd of life. No, red wine; red like the blood that was shed for you and for many for the commission of sin. (*He drinks the wine.*) Steady, Harry, and lift up thine eyes unto the hills.

Implicit in the second act, the martyred soldiers are now directly associated with Christ in the blood-and-wine ritual 'for the commission of sin'. All the symbolic rituals in the play are eventually exposed to tragic irony—the ritual of the triumphant hero, the ritual of the Mass, the ritual of the war, the ritual of red wine drunk from the tassie. And at significant points in the semi-realistic last two acts there are ironic echoes of the symbolic chanting in the second act. For example, the older people try to calm Harry by asking him to play his ukulele and sing a Negro spiritual, and the scene is presented with antiphonal voices:

SYLVESTER. An' give him breath to sing his song an' play the ukelele.
MRS HEGAN. Just as he used to do.
SYLVESTER. Behind the trenches.
SIMON. In the Rest Camps.
MRS FORAN. Out in France.
HARRY. I can see, but I cannot dance.
TEDDY. I can dance, but I cannot see.
HARRY. Would that I had the strength to do the things I see.
TEDDY. Would that I could see the things I've strength to do.

HARRY. The Lord hath given and the Lord hath taken away.
TEDDY. Blessed be the name of the Lord.
MRS FORAN. I love the ukelele, especially when it goes tinkle, tinkle, tinkle in the night-time.

Softly Harry sings his Negro spiritual—it is 'Swing Low, Sweet Chariot' in the text, although there is a suggestion in the notes that 'Keep Me From Sinkin' Down' might be more suitable to Harry's present frame of mind—and the song is a preparation for Harry's stoical exit. He has one more burst of rage in a fight with Barney, and then he goes off with the blind Teddy. The two of them are finally prepared to conquer their self-pity as they leave:

HARRY. What's in front we'll face like men! The Lord hath given and man hath taken away.
TEDDY. Blessed be the name of the Lord!

Harry changes one significant word, and it is *man* and man-made war that have destroyed what God created. God is the guardian, but man is the measure. This conclusion reminds one of Juno Boyle's reply to her daughter: 'Ah, what can God do agen the stipidity o' men.'
While Juno is the universal mother and Harry is the universal soldier, she is above all a realistic character who finally becomes symbolic in the most general sense, he is above all a symbolic character who is at all times both realistic and representational. Juno speaks for all mothers in war-time, Harry speaks for all soldiers; but O'Casey felt he had to use different forms and techniques in telling their analogous yet different stories. O'Casey realized that the dramatist cannot limit himself to a single approach; he must suit the theme and character to the form, and the particular emphasis and technique depend upon the total intention. In *Juno and the Paycock* the character defines the theme; in *The Silver Tassie* the theme defines the character. The methods and forms are different, and the result is that in the one play he created a noble woman, in the other a noble theme.
Among the important discoveries O'Casey made in his new experiment, he found that it was not only possible but necessary to combine realistic and non-realistic techniques, as he had already combined comic and tragic material in his previous work. He

found that he could set a large theme in a framework of reality and at the same time develop it allegorically through the methods of Expressionism. He found that he could bring a sharper tone of moral passion to his theme by projecting it through the symbolic second act, as well as through Harry Heegan in the other three acts, thus making his play an ethical as well as an emotional spectacle, giving it moral as well as imaginative power. As a result *The Silver Tassie* is one of the most original and powerful anti-war plays ever written—a passionate morality play for modern man.

Since O'Casey had now set his aims so high it was to be expected that there would be some flaws and partial failures in a work of such magnitude. Yeats had complained that the war does not become 'mere background', which is precisely what O'Casey did not want it to become; however, a valid objection could be raised about the fact that some of the characters serve as 'mere background'. Harry is a dynamic and sharply drawn character as well as a symbol, and some of the people around him have their own individuality apart from their relationship to him—the fanatical and frustrated Susie, the raw-boned Teddy, his sloppy and garrulous wife, the two irascible jesters Sylvester and Simon. But Mrs Heegan, Jessie, Barney, and Dr Maxwell are little more than flat characters painted black, like minor vices in opposition to Harry; they merely serve as negative symbols. Perhaps of this group at least Mrs Heegan should have undergone some development and change in the last two acts.

Then, one wonders if it was necessary to eliminate Harry from the second act. O'Casey stresses the fact that the war has robbed the soldiers of their identity, yet he names the relatively minor Barney outright and indicates that the 4th Soldier is 'very like Teddy'. Surely Harry is too important to be dropped completely. Perhaps there could have been a soldier 'very like Harry', or possibly Harry, with his ukulele, could have been represented in distortion by a figure somewhat like the Croucher.

Another aspect of the experiment involves the handling of the language. In the first act and the last two acts where O'Casey uses the Dublin idiom he is in control, although there are a few awkward moments when he seems to be toying with a 'literary' diction, as when the earthy Sylvester speaks of 'the frost beads on the branches glistening like toss'd down diamonds from the breasts of the stars '. In the second act O'Casey is particularly successful with the chanted passages when he uses biblical rhetoric or the cockney idiom, yet there are several instances where he is hard pressed to sustain the staccato incantations and he falls into a laboured, semi-literary diction. This straining for effect is evident, for example, toward the end of the act when the soldiers say they are

> Crouching to scrape a toy-deep shelter,
> Quick-tim'd by hell's fast, frenzied drumfire.

or when they begin their Song to the Gun,

> Hail cool-hardened tower of steel emboss'd
> With the fever'd, figment thoughts of man.

Fortunately there are not many stilted passages like these, and actually O'Casey made some changes in the final version of the play. [120] After the London production in 1929, he cut out twenty of the chanted lines at the end of the second act, eliminating a number of strained passages and quickening the action just before the enemy break-through. O'Casey was not aware of these flaws until he saw the play performed.

It is with respect to this need for a theatre as a workshop that Yeats's rejection did O'Casey the greatest disservice: by denying him the use of the Abbey for his new play and thus preventing him from seeing the play through the important stages from rehearsal to production when modifications are often made; by discouraging him from writing his future plays for the theatre that he had rescued from artistic and financial ruin. It meant that one of the Abbey's greatest playwrights would never again write a play for that theatre, even though he went on to write eight more plays. It meant that he would have to write most of his remaining plays for a publisher instead of a theatre.

4. POPULAR AND VULGAR DEVILS

Although he certainly did not plan it that way, Yeats's decision also had a damaging influence upon the future of the Abbey Theatre. Through the years since the rejection of *The Silver Tassie*, O'Casey moved with a changing world and went on to exciting if not always successful experiments with each new play, but the Abbey marked time as a conservative national theatre, disinclined to experiment with new techniques of writing and staging and acting, content to go on producing mediocre plays in the worn-out mould of kitchen-comedy realism. Today in Dublin the Abbey kitchen clichés are among the chief targets of abuse by the literary scholars and wits, and the chief targets of parody by the music-hall comedians. The Abbey Theatre has been reploughing the same furrow of quaint realism for so long that it would now have great difficulty trying to work in some of the new fields of modern drama.

It is ironic that Yeats himself had apparently foreseen this trend a decade before the *Tassie* incident. In 1919 in his 'Letter to Lady Gregory' he commented sadly on the growing popularity of the Abbey as a theatre of commonplace realism: 'Yet we did not set out to create this sort of theatre, and its success has been to me a discouragement and a defeat.' [121] This was a time when Yeats was fully absorbed with his verse plays for dancers, but perhaps he also had reason to remember the prophetic comment Joyce had made two years after the Irish Literary Theatre had been organized.

At that time, in 1901, Joyce was a nineteen-year-old Dublin University student, and he had written an essay called 'The Day of the Rabblement', which he published privately with a friend as a twopenny pamphlet. In the essay the brash and unknown young Joyce, who was an enthusiastic disciple of Ibsen and continental drama, warned the established and Celtic-minded Yeats that he was too fine a poet to compromise his artistic integrity for a nationalistic movement led by a 'rabblement' of Irish chauvinists. Joyce believed that the Irish Literary Theatre, by refusing to perform European masterpieces and confining itself to the kind of plays that would further the national movement, 'by its surrender to the trolls, has cut itself adrift from the line of advancement'. [122] And Joyce identified the 'trolls' or 'devils' in the following manner:

The Irish Literary Theatre gave out that it was the champion of progress, and proclaimed war against commercialism and vulgarity. It had partly made good its word and was expelling the old devil, when after the first encounter it surrendered to the popular will. Now, your popular devil is more dangerous than your vulgar devil. Bulk and lungs count for something, and he can gild his speech artly. He has prevailed once more, and the Irish Literary Theatre must now be considered the property of the rabblement of the most belated race in Europe. [123]

Here was Joyce, like a Celtic Dr Stockmann, warning Yeats against the tyranny of a rising nationalist majority. Joyce felt that insidious as the 'vulgar devil' of commercialism was to the artist, it was not so dangerous as the 'popular devil' of nationalism.

Actually, Yeats did not need to be reminded of this danger. Although he had written several nationalistic plays in that early period, he never succumbed to the 'popular devil', and indeed through all his years as an active director of the Abbey he made it his special task to fight against the constant antagonism and intimidation of the nationalistic rabblement. Yeats had encouraged and defended the two greatest Abbey dramatists, Synge and O'Casey, whose plays had satirized the national illusions. As early as 1903 when Arthur Griffith assailed Synge's first play, *In the Shadow of the Glen*, as a libellous attack on the national character, Yeats had replied by giving his own version of the 'popular devils' in the hope that their identification might make them more vulnerable to defeat. 'It will save some misunderstanding in the future,' he began with what proved to be unfounded optimism, 'If I analyse this obscurantism.' [124] Yeats then identified 'three sorts of ignorance' that were a threat to his theatre:

1st. There is the hatred of ideas of the more ignorant sort of Gaelic propagandist, who would have nothing said or thought that is not in country Gaelic. One knows him without trouble. He writes the worst English, and would have us give up Plato and all the sages for a grammar. 2nd. There is the obscurantism of the more ignorant sort of priest, who, forgetful of the great traditions of his Church, would deny all ideas that might perplex a parish of farmers or artisans or half-educated shopkeepers. 3rd. There is the obscurantism of the politician and not always of the more ignorant sort, who would reject every idea which is not of immediate service to his cause. [125]

It was not long before Yeats realized that misunderstandings between the Abbey and these burgeoning obscurantists were inevitable. He did not need to be reminded that even the shy and detached Synge had been provoked to write a mock-revenge broadside called 'The Curse', [126] as a reply to one of the obscurantists or 'popular devils'. Synge addressed his sardonic verses 'To a sister of an enemy of the author's who disapproved of "The Playboy"':

> Lord, confound this surly sister,
> Blight her brow with blotch and blister,
> Cramp her larynx, lung, and liver,
> In her guts a galling give her.

> Let her live to earn her dinners
> In Mountjoy with seedy sinners:
> Lord, this judgement quickly bring,
> And I'm your servant, J. M. Synge.

And when the 'popular devil' lowered its horns at performances of *The Playboy* and *The Plough*, Yeats stood his ground magnificently. However, his famous excoriation of the rabblement from the stage of the Abbey in 1926—'You have disgraced yourselves again'—was to be one of his last public battles.

By 1928 Yeats was a tired and sick man of sixty-three, and he was no longer able or willing to sacrifice his health or his own work for the arduous job of managing the Abbey. Joseph Hone says of this period in his life: 'The days when Yeats had been largely employed in managing the Abbey Theatre, and writing for it, were long over. But he still read, or had read to him, every new play before its production, he attended all the Board meetings, and exercised, when he wished to do so, the decisive influence upon policy.'[127] It was in October of 1927 that Yeats had his breakdown, the first serious illness since his childhood. A bad cold had developed into a high fever and recurring lung haemorrhages, and he also suffered from general exhaustion. His doctors told him that he must withdraw from public life and avoid all mental strain—he was at the time a member of the Irish Senate as well as an active poet and semi-active director of the Abbey. And so he left Ireland late in 1927 to spend a quiet winter of recuperation in Spain, the French Riviera, and Rapallo. He was to spend every winter in the mild Mediterranean climate. It was when he returned from Rapallo in the spring of 1928 that he read O'Casey's new play. A year later he wrote to a friend that he would welcome 'the happiness of finding idleness a duty—no more opinions, no more politics, no more practical tasks'.[128]

At this time Lady Gregory was an aged woman of seventy-six and although she was still as active at the Abbey as a woman of her years could be, the practical tasks of running the theatre were largely in the hands of Lennox Robinson. It was a year after the rejection of *The Tassie*, after Lady Gregory had seen the London production of the play in 1929, that she wrote to Yeats telling him they should have accepted the play: 'I believe we should have taken it—we could not have done the chanted scene so well, it was very moving, but we could have done the other acts better.'[129] And she continued to brood about it in her *Journal*: 'But my mind goes back to *The Tassie*—we ought not to have rejected it. We should have held out against Lennox Robinson that last evening the order to return it was given.'[130]

Bernard Shaw wrote a letter to Lady Gregory in 1928 attacking Yeats for his stand against the play, and he also wrote a similar letter to O'Casey, offering his moral support and a shrewd comment on Yeats:

My dear Sean, what a hell of a play! I wonder how it will hit the public. Of course the Abbey should have produced it, as Starkie rightly says —whether it liked it or not. But the people who knew your uncle when you were a child (so to speak) always want to correct your exercises; and this was what disabled the usually competent Yeats and Lady Gregory. Still it is surprising they fired so very wide, considering their marksmanship . . .

If Yeats had said 'It's too savage; I can't stand it', he would have been in order. . . . Yeats himself, with all his extraordinary cleverness and subtlety, which comes out when you give him up as a hopeless fool, and (in this case) deserts him when you expect him to be equal to the occasion, is not a man of this world; and when you hurl an enormous chunk of it at him, he dodges it, small blame to him. However, we can talk over it when we meet. Cheerio, Titan—G.B.S.[131]

If, as Shaw says, Yeats was 'not a man of this world', after 1928 he drifted even farther away from public and practical tasks, particularly as they affected the affairs of the Abbey. He continued to disassociate himself from the 'rabblement' in his poems and plays, but it was now a private not a public matter.

Shortly after *The Tassie* was rejected, the Abbey also rejected a new play about Robert Emmet written in the Expressionistic technique by Denis Johnston, then an unknown young playwright. Whereupon Johnston retitled it *The Old Lady Says 'No'* and had it accepted in 1929 by the newly formed Dublin Gate Theatre. Under the leadership of the extraordinarily talented and daring Hilton Edwards and Michael MacLiammoir, the Gate went on to become a dynamic and famous theatre, producing experimental plays and continental classics while the parochial Abbey went on serving up the old realistic mixture as before. In fact, after 1928 when the Gate Theatre was formed the Abbey was safer than ever in its nationalistic conservatism because it could claim that experimental plays or 'foreign' classics were the province of the Gate Theatre. Certainly the Abbey's rejection of the O'Casey and Johnston plays must have made it clear to any playwrights with new ideas that they would find no welcome at the Abbey.

There was one other crucial factor with respect to the Abbey's nationalistic conservatism which Yeats and Lady Gregory had under-estimated. While they were busy fighting the 'rabblement' in the theatre itself, they had allowed the legal representative of the 'popular devil' to move into the front office. Back in the early 1920's when the Abbey was in financial trouble, Yeats was prepared to give up the theatre, but Lady Gregory had appealed to the newly formed Free State Government for a subsidy, just before the success of the O'Casey plays ironically made it unnecessary. In 1925 the Abbey received its first government grant, plus a government-appointed director to look after the national interests, for the Abbey was thereafter to be the Irish National Theatre. Significantly, it was that first government-appointed director, Dr George O'Brien, a Professor of Economics, who had strongly objected to *The Plough and the Stars* in 1926. On the first occasion when the interests of the Abbey and the interests of the government seemed to be in conflict, Lady Gregory spoke for Yeats and herself when she said: 'Our position is clear. If we must choose between the subsidy and our freedom, it is our freedom we choose.' [132] But in a letter to Yeats, Dr O'Brien had drawn up a long list of his objections to *The Plough*, and he had concluded with the subtle hint that he was only trying 'to prevent the outbreak of a movement of hostility that would make it difficult or impossible for the Government to continue or to increase its subsidy'. [133]

If Yeats and Lady Gregory had reacted to that intimidation and its future implications as they should have, by actually choosing their freedom and promptly handing Dr O'Brien and the subsidy back to the government, the recent history of the Abbey might have been a brighter picture. Instead they chose the temporary expedient of out-voting Dr O'Brien at the directors' meeting.

Yeats and Lady Gregory had won a minor skirmish, they had not settled the fundamental conflict, for as long as the government remained in the theatre it was destined to have its way in the end. It was inevitable that the government position would grow stronger through the years, when Yeats was gradually losing his health and his interest in the affairs of the theatre, when Lady Gregory died in 1932, and when Yeats himself died in 1939. Thereafter it was safe to assume that the Abbey Theatre would become a national monument of decency and respectability, a National Theatre which would not produce plays that embarrassed the government or criticized the national ideals. Peter Kavanagh points out that this edifying spectacle was already taking shape as early as 1928 when the recuperating Yeats was casting his mind on other things:

The government subsidy was having a subtle effect on Abbey Theatre policy. It was turning into an institution as conservative as the National Gallery or the National Museum. The Abbey was now secure against failure and was gradually becoming conscious of its national importance in a bourgeois sense. It was tending to interest itself in how it looked to the world. The seeds of decline were already sown, and Yeats was too interested in other things to have the energy to uproot those seeds. [134]

Upon several occasions the Abbey directors tried to uproot those seeds of decline and assert their independence, as when they had a change of heart about O'Casey and in the face of bitter opposition from the 'popular devil' finally produced *The Silver Tassie* in 1935. In 1934 O'Casey had gone back to Dublin for a brief visit, and to his surprise he received a gracious letter from Yeats inviting him to spend a day with the poet. To show that he had forgiven and forgotten old wounds, Yeats had made the opening gesture of friendship, and O'Casey accepted it. The two reconciled warriors now found that they had many 'opinions' in common, particularly when they talked about 'how tiresome the customary Abbey play was becoming; how the Theatre needed new life through a newer type of play'. [135] It was in this mood that Yeats now asked for one of O'Casey's newer plays, and it was decided that the Abbey would produce *The Silver Tassie*.

The play ran for only one week, and it touched off a typical Dublin controversy, with the main attack against O'Casey, Yeats, and the Abbey led by the Catholic and nationalistic 'rabblement'. Many Catholic organizations denounced O'Casey's 'blasphemous' play. For instance, the Catholic Young Men's Society of Galway passed the following resolution: 'That we condemn vehemently the dramatic work of the Abbey Theatre in so far as it infringes the canons of Christian reverence or human decency and so far as it infringes the nation's prestige at home and abroad.' [136] The newspapers were flooded with angry editorials and letters. The *Irish Catholic* wanted to pass a law against O'Casey: 'Those who relish the rank sort of fare that Mr O'Casey provides ought to be denied by law the opportunity of indulging their debased tastes.' [137] And that newspaper found some consolation in the 'fire' of abuse to which O'Casey's play had been exposed: 'If *The Silver Tassie* withstands the test of fire to which it has been subjected within the last ten days, then, though it would not thereby be proved genuine silver, the base metal of which it is composed is at least equivalent to asbestos.' [138] O'Casey and his play had been scorched but not destroyed, for they were not for witch burning.

The Standard went on from its attack upon the 'revolting' and 'immoral' play to demand that the Abbey must get rid of Yeats: '*The Silver Tassie* has given us a golden opportunity of improving our stage, and of reconsidering the value of our literary heroes who have been set up for our admiration. Mr W. B. Yeats is no literary leader for a Catholic country.' [139] The President of the Gaelic League, P. T. McGinley [*Cu Uladh*, the Hound of Ulster], one of the chief spokesmen of the national movement, issued a public statement condemning the play, which he had not seen, and demanding that the Abbey be abolished: 'The Abbey Theatre at its best was never an exponent of Irish national ideals. At its worst, it is intolerable, and must be swept aside. I have never seen its latest horror; but I remember some years ago going to see *The Plough and the Stars*, and having to leave before the second act from a fit of nausea. As to the Abbey itself, I am inclined to echo the prayer that I once heard an embittered old farmer utter on hearing of the death of his landlord: "A speedy race down with him." ' [140]

A surprise attack also came from within the Abbey itself, for one of the newly appointed directors, novelist and playwright Brinsley Macnamara, wrote a long letter to the *Irish Independent* denouncing his fellow-directors as well as the play. When the decision to produce the play was made over his protest, Macnamara insisted that all 'objectionable' scenes should be cut out of the performances, but he was out-voted; and when the controversy broke he explained in his I-told-you-so letter that he had been vindicated in his fight for 'Catholic cleanliness and wholesome entertainment in a theatre which our Catholic Government is subsidising'. (141)

What a far cry from the principles upon which Yeats had established the Abbey were all these pietistic demands for a wholesome National Catholic theatre. The time was ripe for a mighty defence of those principles, but Yeats was now a tired old man and he did not step forward to proclaim the freedom of the artist and the independence of his theatre. Even in his aging isolation, however, Yeats had lost none of his poetic powers, and in November of 1935, three months after the *Tassie* controversy, he wrote a poem called 'Parnell's Funeral' in which, remembering the fall of 'the uncrowned King', he lamented the betrayal of Ireland's heroes and ideals, first by 'strangers', the English, but later and more tragically by the 'popular rage' of the Irish themselves.

> *An age is the reversal of an age:*
> *When strangers murdered Emmet, Fitzgerald, Tone,*
> *We lived like men that watch a painted stage.*
> *What matter for the scene, the scene once gone:*
> *It had not touched our lives. But popular rage,*
> Hysterica passio *dragged this quarry down.*
> *None shared our guilt; nor did we play a part*
> *Upon a painted stage when we devoured his heart.*
> *Come, fix upon me that accusing eye.*
> *I thirst for accusation. All that was sung,*
> *All that was said in Ireland is a lie*
> *Bred out of the contagion of the throng.* (142)

And now the throng that had devoured Parnell's heart was turning its *hysterica passio* on the Abbey Theatre, on O'Casey and Yeats. The 'popular devil' was raging for blood again, and Yeats had further reasons to feel the tragic guilt of his countrymen. And Joyce's prophetic 'day of the rabblement' had arrived again.

> *O Ireland my first and only love*
> *Where Christ and Caesar are hand and glove!*

CHAPTER IV

The Playwright as Prophet

Rouze up, O Young Men of the New Age! set your foreheads against the ignorant Hirelings! For we have Hirelings in the Camp, the Court & the University, who would, if they could, for ever depress Mental & prolong Corporeal War.

William Blake (1804)

The experience of mankind on earth is always changing as man develops and has to deal with new combinations of elements; and the writer who would be anything more than an echo of his predecessors must always find expression for something which has never yet been expressed, must master a new set of phenomena which has never yet been mastered. With each such victory of the human intellect, whether in history, in philosophy or in poetry, we experience a deep satisfaction: we have been cured of some ache of disorder, relieved of some oppressive burden of uncomprehended events. [143]

Edmund Wilson (1940)

I. 'THE ACHE OF DISORDER'

SHORTLY after *The Silver Tassie* opened in London during the second week of October 1929, an economic disaster occurred in America which set off a chain reaction of universal disorder: the Wall Street stock market crashed in the last week of October 1929. Only ten years after the end of the First World War, this new disaster led to the tragedy of a World Depression in the 1930's and sowed the seeds of yet another World War. The suffering and confusion of the depression years provided the background of

O'Casey's next play, *Within the Gates*, which he wrote in 1933. Thus, he was still intent upon using the major events of his time as the material for his plays. His preoccupation with the crises of modern history was his moral commitment to the fate of modern man in a world of disorder. It was therefore understandable that after writing a play about the Great War he should have turned to the Great Depression.

During the worst time of the depression decade, in 1932, some twenty-five million people in America and Europe were unemployed—over twelve million in America, over six million in Germany, nearly three million in Great Britain, and about four million in the other European nations. After the First World War the economy of Europe had been largely built up by American capital, and the collapse of the American economy had far-reaching effects. It was the worst economic disaster that the capitalist world had experienced. Great masses of idle and hungry people were on public relief, barely surviving on doles and bread-lines. There were violent demonstrations of protest and mass hunger-marches in all countries. In London, for example, in March 1932, a parade of National Hunger Marchers from all over Britain converged on the city and was welcomed in Hyde Park by 100,000 people.

It was a time of political as well as economic upheaval, and in Germany the economic collapse prepared the way for Hitler's Fascist putsch. Inevitably the tragic events of this period prepared the way for yet another and more terrible World War in 1939. Imperialist and Fascist nations launched open acts of aggression and the ineffectual League of Nations disintegrated. Japan invaded Manchuria, Italy invaded Abyssinia, and Germany prepared to over-run central Europe. The scourge of Fascism was spreading everywhere. In some of the democratic countries it emerged as a threat if not a decisive force; Sir Oswald Mosley's Black Shirts were openly active as the British Union of Fascists, and even in little Ireland there was a brief threat from General Eoin O'Duffy's Blue Shirts in the mid-1930's. In 1936 the Spanish Civil War broke out and eventually led to the victory of General Franco's Fascists. Everywhere men were being enslaved and destroyed by economic and political forces, by brutal acts of oppression and aggression leading up to another Great War.

Ten years before these events, writing about the universal

disorder of the twentieth century in the early 1920's, Yeats in his prophetic poem 'The Second Coming' had described the under-lying spiritual crisis which loosed the material chaos:

> *Things fall apart ; the centre cannot hold ;*
> *Mere anarchy is loosed upon the world,*
> *The blood-dimmed tide is loosed, and everywhere*
> *The ceremony of innocence is drowned ;*
> *The best lack all conviction, while the worst*
> *Are full of passionate intensity.* [144]

Yeats had sounded a general truth in his bleak conclusion about the 'best' and the 'worst' men; however, there were still those exceptional men like O'Casey, Malraux, Picasso, and Casals, who as the 'best' retained their convictions with passionate in-tensity. Many of the 'best' artists in the period leading up to and during the Second World War acted upon the urgency of John Donne's great sermon: they knew the bell was tolling for everyone and they used their creative work or moral suasion as weapons.

A close analogue for O'Casey's passionate reaction to 'the ache of disorder' during these years can be found in Blake's Preface to his poem 'Milton'. Blake begins with a prose exhortation—'Rouze up, O Young Men of the New Age!'—and then he girds himself for the battle against 'the dark Satanic mills':[145]

> *Bring me my Bow of burning gold :*
> *Bring me my Arrows of desire :*
> *Bring me my Spear : O clouds unfold !*
> *Bring me my chariot of fire !*
> *I will not cease from Mental Fight,*
> *Nor shall my Sword sleep in my hand*
> *Till we have built Jerusalem*
> *In England's green & pleasant Land.*

Would to God that all the Lord's people were Prophets. Numbers XI. Ch. 29: v.

And so O'Casey was now ready to assume the role of a visionary poet and chastising prophet in the struggle for the new Jerusalem of the world. It was a role which Blake and Shelley and Byron had assumed for the Men of England and the Isles of Greece; and later the Mental Fight for freedom had been carried on by prophets like Carlyle and Ruskin, Dickens and Morris, Shaw and the Fabians. O'Casey had read and admired all these writers, and it was in part from them and from his early background in Dublin that he inherited his prophetic moral passion. Before he had heard of Marx, he had developed the socialist conscience from his experiences in the inferno of the Dublin slums, from his work in the Dublin labour movement and his contact with empirical Socialists like Larkin and Connolly, and from those prophetic English writers of the nineteenth century. The following remarks by Shaw might be used as an illustration of what O'Casey found in these prophets and how he was now to follow them:

If you read Sociology, not for information but for entertainment (small blame to you!), you will find that the nineteenth-century poets and prophets who denounced the wickedness of our Capitalism exactly as the Hebrew prophets denounced the Capitalism of their time, are much more exciting to read than the economists and writers on political science who worked out the economic theory and political requirements of Socialism. Carlyle's Past and Present and Shooting Niagara, Ruskin's Ethics of the Dust and Fors Clavigera, William Morris's News from Nowhere (the best of all the Utopias), Dickens's Hard Times and Little Dorrit, are notable examples: Ruskin in particular leaving all the professed Socialists, even Karl Marx, miles behind in force of invective. Lenin's criticisms of modern society seem like the platitudes of a rural dean in comparison. [146]

In his younger days O'Casey had read writers like Ruskin and Dickens, and Shaw himself, for entertainment; but since they had fired his indignation as well as his imagination, they had also given him information about the 'wickedness of Capitalism' which was still pertinent to the times. The problem for O'Casey now was, how to use this information and invective as entertainment in the drama. Shaw had done it with his devilish wit and dialectical satire. In his earlier plays O'Casey had done it with the mock-heroic satire of tragi-comedy. But now, in a world of increasing tensions and disorders he sought to master 'new combinations of elements'; he retained his satiric vision of life but he sought to use the revolutionary ideas of Socialism and techniques of Expressionism in a new way and with a new prophetic vision of the good life. He set out to use his art as a celebration of life.

As a result he wrote a group of four prophetic plays beginning with the Great Depression and ending with the second Great War: *Within the Gates* (1933), *The Star Turns Red* (1940), *Red Roses For Me* (1942), *Oak Leaves and Lavender* (1946). They are all in a general sense modern morality plays, for, following in the direction of *The Silver Tassie*, they are plays about symbolic characters who like Harry Heegan represent and project a large theme. And it is in all four plays a theme which has its origin in the primitive and exultant joy of Harry Heegan: it is the joyous dance of life, the liberation of mind and body, the joyous *élan vital* which O'Casey celebrates in opposition to the anarchic and negative forces of modern life. This dance of life was also to become the theme of his last four plays, the comic fantasies, and it is most spectacularly symbolized in the fantastic figure of the joyous Cock in *Cock-a-doodle Dandy*.

Thus, while his prophetic plays deal with what can generally be called the 'sociology' of the times—the relationship between man and society—he locates 'the ache of disorder' in man's spirit as well as his body. He turns his invective against economic slavery and those who condone it with their pious hypocrisy, as he has always done, but above all he condemns the mean and narrow view of life as a vale of tears. He offers instead his joyous dance of life as a prophetic and poetic vision. Before she dies, the young whore Jannice in *Within the Gates* leaves her mark upon the microcosmic world of Hyde Park with a frenzied dance to life. In *Red Roses For Me*, Ayamonn and the poor people of Dublin break into a spontaneous ballet on the banks of the river Liffey when for a moment the city is mystically transformed in an epiphany of joy.

When in such instances O'Casey uses his 'Bow of burning gold' to create a poetic image of the new Jerusalem, he is in control of his prophetic and dramatic vision. However, when he swings his 'Sword' angrily in the 'Mental Fight' against the allegorical dragons of Capitalism and Fascism, his drama suffers from heavy-handed didacticism. He cannot play Shaw's game of devil's advocate and his attempt at dialectical combat is not as entertaining as Shaw's. This is evident in *The Star Turns Red* and *Oak Leaves and Lavender*, his two most didactic and weakest plays. In his truculent didacticism he sets up an over-simplified conflict between the whiteness of Communism and the blackness of Fascism, and as a result the dramatic values in these two plays suffer from an excess of sentimental morality. There is too much good and too much evil, too much sound and too much fury. When the prophet snarls, the dramatist nods—and so does the prophet.

Yeats's earlier warning to O'Casey that the playwright should not impose his 'opinions' upon a play has a certain relevance to these two works, not because, as Yeats assumed, 'opinions' did not belong in the drama, but because O'Casey had been so carried away by his bitter invective that he over-stated his 'opinions' in terms that were too transparent and sentimental. In these two plays he used Swift's revulsion and anger without Swift's subtlety and irony. Considering the intensity of O'Casey's feelings toward Fascism at the time, his extreme partisanship may be commendable, but it did not aid the dramatic craftsmanship of the plays. It is one of the paradoxes of the creative process that the artist must feel 'the ache of disorder' intensely and yet achieve a sufficient detachment from it so that he can bring a pattern of order to it—what Coleridge called 'a more than usual state of emotion, with more than usual order'. But in most of his plays O'Casey was able to do this.

During that first decade of his exile in England his personal life was beset with an unusual amount of disorders and anxieties. He was an ingrained Irishman cut adrift from his native land. He was an established playwright without a theatre, an Irish playwright cut off from the Abbey Theatre. He had a wife and children to support on an uncertain income which was more dependent upon the sporadic sales of his published plays than productions of them. Shortly after he arrived in London in 1927 he had met a young Irish actress named Eileen Reynolds Carey, who was playing the role of Nora Clitheroe in the London production of *The Plough*, and they were married later that same year. He was forty-seven years old and his bride was in her early twenties. He was a 'lapsed' Protestant but she was then a practising Catholic, and they were married in a Catholic church. Their three children were baptized Catholics, although they were apparently not raised as Catholics— Breon born in 1928, Niall in 1936 [147], and Shivaun in 1939.

Throughout those uneasy years when he was hard-pressed in raising and trying to support his family, he wrote only one full-length play, *Within the Gates*, but he also wrote three books:

Windfalls (1934), a collection of early poems, four short stories, and two one-act plays; *The Flying Wasp* (1937), a collection of essays on the London theatre; and *I Knock at the Door* (1939), the first volume of his six-volume autobiography. The poems in *Windfalls* are some of his early exercises in naïve romanticism, none of them particularly distinguished, and they indicate that O'Casey, like Synge, could be more genuinely poetic in prose than in verse. The best things in the book are the two lively one-act farces, 'The End of the Beginning' and 'A Pound on Demand', and one of the short stories, 'The Star-Jazzer', a powerful tale of frustration in Dublin which has the lyric and tragic qualities of Joyce's stories in *Dubliners*. The autobiography will be examined in a later chapter; *The Flying Wasp* offers a spirited illustration of O'Casey's views on the drama in the 1930's, particularly his attack on the entrenched realism of the London theatre and his defence of his own attempts to move in a new direction.

It was almost a repeat performance of his fight with Yeats and the Abbey directors over *The Silver Tassie*, only this time the occasion of the battle was *Within the Gates* and his adversaries were the London critics led by James Agate. Actually, the seeds of the controversy were sown in 1931 when James Agate, the drama reviewer of the *Sunday Times* and probably the most influential critic in London, came out with high praise for Noel Coward's *Cavalcade*, a maudlin pageant of British chauvinism. Mr Agate unashamedly called it a 'first-class' play, and he may well have been inspired by the sentiments of Noel Coward's curtain speech, which Mr Agate felt summed up the 'meaning' of the play: 'I hope that this play has made us feel that despite our national troubles it is still a pretty exciting thing to be English.'[148] Mr Agate in his review hoped that the play would run for hundreds of nights and that he would be able to see it again and again. It had a long run of 405 performances, no doubt aided by the Agate imprimatur. At a time when the economy of the country was collapsing and rapidly growing worse, when it was not very exciting to be English for the millions of destitute and unemployed, the theatre-going people of England apparently preferred to escape with Messrs Coward and Agate into a glow of nostalgia over the glories of the British Empire.

But aside from the impoverished masses who could not afford this type of luxury, there was a minority of Englishmen who did not approve of it—the artists and intellectuals of Chelsea and Bloomsbury, as Mr Agate identified them, and they irritated him. After enduring two years of this irritation from the 'highbrows' who wanted more than 'Noelisms' and patriotism in the theatre, Mr Agate slapped back at them in an article called 'Swat that Wasp!' in which he again defended *Cavalcade* and the state of the London theatre: "There is a nest of wasps,' he wrote, 'which must be smoked out because it is doing the theatre infinite harm . . . I refer to a small coterie of highbrows which makes a point of running down everything that does not happen to live at the top of their particular street. Waspishness set in with "Cavalcade", which it declared to be bad art grating on everything that one would most want to forget.'(149) Little did Mr Agate realize that he was poking a nest from which a lowbrow Irish wasp would presently emerge with a devastating sting.

Nine months after he swatted that nest of wasps, Mr Agate took a wild swat at *Within the Gates*. When *Juno* and *The Plough* were produced in London he had praised them without reservations, but now he objected to the fact that O'Casey's new play was not just like those earlier works. He opened his review with a long paragraph on Sainte-Beuve (he regularly delighted in making allusions to the French and quoting in French), and then announced that the O'Casey play was 'pretentious rubbish', a phrase which he went on to clarify in the following manner: 'But first we must do a little ground-clearing and explain that "pretentious rubbish" is not nearly so offensive as it sounds. Grandeur of form may well go with vacuity of content, and it is the latter which makes the thing rubbish and the combination of the two which makes that rubbish pretentious.'(150) If Mr Agate had been more consistent and less excitingly English, he might more accurately have applied this standard of judgement to a play like *Cavalcade* and discovered that it was a pretentious play of patriotic rubbish. But the urbane critic was in no mood to consider seriously a play like O'Casey's which attacked the basic premises of the collapsing British society—that was 'vacuity of content' to him. On the matter of 'grandeur of form', Mr Agate was constitutionally unsympathetic to all forms of modern art which were not 'rational' to him and realistically recognizable. Thus he went on to take his stand against modern painting, music, and drama:

Within the Gates is obviously a work of art, just as some pictures are works of art in which everything judged by any but artistic rule is manifestly cock-eyed. Now carry this a step farther. We know to our amazement that pictures which make no appeal to the eye may still be works of art, and we have learned to our chagrin that musical compositions which make no appeal to the ear are to be placed in the same category. Is it similarly laid down that a play which runs counter to the mind in its rational functioning may still be a work of art in virtue of its appeal to eye and ear? [151]

Since O'Casey's play was a calculated assault upon the so-called 'rationally functioning' British mind, Mr Agate probably had cause to feel amazed and chagrined, although his general reaction to the development of modern art and his curious remarks on 'artistic rule' and 'cock-eyed' art are perhaps something less than rational. As for drama, he had a habit of classifying symbolic or non-realistic plays as 'pretentious' art, and among the plays he dismissed in this fashion were Pirandello's *Henry IV*, which he called 'pretentious nonsense', O'Neill's *Strange Interlude*, which he called 'pretentious and wearisome'. As 'pretentious rubbish', *Within the Gates* obviously belonged in this 'cock-eyed' category.

Although a minority of the London critics was favourably impressed by *Within the Gates*, the majority seemed to agree with Mr Agate, and so did the theatre-goers. The play closed after twenty-eight performances. There was one particularly notable review in *The Times* which indicated that some people did understand what O'Casey was trying to do, and it is worth quoting in part:

> Mr O'Casey's fierce play is that very rare thing—a modern morality play that is not a pamphlet, but a work of art. In substance it is a violent attack on the whole fabric of civilization, which Mr O'Casey represents as a tottering edifice with its foundation of hypocrisy, false compromise, and fear . . . A little writer, impelled to this theme, would have fallen inevitably into shrill and bitter screaming, and there are moments when Mr O'Casey himself weakens; but except on those rare occasions his art purges the dross from his controversy. [152]

But O'Casey was preparing to take up his own defence in *The Flying Wasp*, a title inspired by Mr Agate's alarum over the 'nest of wasps'. The book has a unique and expansive sub-title which describes O'Casey's mood and subject: 'A laughing look-over of what has been said about the things of the theatre by the English dramatic critics, with many merry and amusing comments thereon, with some shrewd remarks by the author on the wise, delicious, and dignified tendencies in the theatre of today.'[153] Although O'Casey had primarily set out to sting Mr Agate into an awareness of his own pretentiousness, he buzzed merrily over the whole field of the London theatre in the mid 1930's, pricking the English public for ignoring Shakespeare and over-stuffing themselves with the bittersweet blancmangery of Noel Coward and Frederick Lonsdale, swatting the conservative critics for their insistence upon just-like-life realism and their belief in the inviolability of the box-set and the proscenium arch. The pugnacious O'Casey was in another brawl and he was enjoying every minute of it. Here are some representative examples of the flying wasp's sting.

On seeing Mr Agate hoist with some of his own canards:

Pictures that are not 'manifestly cock-eyed' can, I suppose, be discerned as works of art without the conjuring up of any artistic rule, but, Mr Agate, do tell us what is the artistic rule by which we can tell that a dramatic criticism is a work of art, though manifestly cock-eyed.[154]

Mr Agate fails to see propaganda lepping about all round us. Most literature is livened with propaganda. Shakespeare has it. *The Trojan Women* is propaganda. So are the Bible and the Koran, the rule-book of Y.M.C.A., the philosophy of Spinoza and Schopenhauer, and the hymn-books of the Salvation Army. Mr Agate's articles are propaganda, and this article is propaganda against the propaganda of Mr Agate.[155]

I do not know what Mr. Agate's opinions are, politically, socially, or theologically. He has never expressed them, as far as I know; but even if I did know them I could give no assurance that any opinions I may express or hint at in future work will readily copulate with his.[156]

On those critics who insisted that 'the theatre is a place for plain statement' and those who wanted 'real plays about real people':

We do not want merely an excerpt from reality; it is the imaginative transformation of reality, as it is seen through the eyes of the poet, that we desire. The great art of the theatre is to suggest, not to tell openly; to dilate the mind by symbols, not by actual things; to express in Lear a world's sorrow, and in Hamlet the grief of humanity . . . This rage for real, real life on the stage has taken all the life out of the drama. If everything on the stage is to be a fake exact imitation (for fake realism it can only be), where is the chance for the original and imaginative artist? Less chance for him than there was for Jonah in the whale's belly. The beauty, fire, and poetry of drama have perished in the storm of fake realism. (157)

On the Public Death of Shakespeare in the London theatre:

Nietzsche has said that God is dead, and were he living today, he would add to the name of God the name of Shakespeare, for Shakespeare, as far as the writing of drama, the speaking of drama, the acting of drama, the production of drama, are concerned, is as dead as Queen Anne. He is gone and almost forgotten, and with dead Shakespeare, English drama lies dead too. All the sirens, hooters, buzzers, and recording clocks of the theatre will immediately cry out that this is nonsense. Let us see who have been the highlights and the limelights and the leading lights of the English Theatre during the past ten years or so. Here they are, standing to attention with their chests out: Coward, Lonsdale, Phill-potts, Sherriff, with Beverley Nichols peeping round the corner. And their plays: *Bitter-Sweet* and *Cavalcade*; *Maid of the Mountains* and *Spring Cleaning*; *The Farmer's Wife* and *Yellow Sands*; *Evensong*. Here we have the highest mountain peak and the deepest sea of modern English drama. (158)

On those critics who limited their reviews to impressionistic rhapsodies about 'good theatre' and 'good acting', meanwhile forgetting that drama is also a form of literature:

A good acting play that is not also good enough to be enjoyed in the study is not worth a dying tinker's damn. (159)

On putting the clock ahead instead of back, in reply to a critic who wrote: 'The Reinhardt gang has never realized that to venture one inch beyond the proscenium arch destroys the whole illusion so laboriously created. This is the age of the picture stage, and even if you are twelve German producers rolled into one, you cannot put the clock back':

The truth seems to be, nay, madam, it is, that the critics are still in the picture-frame age; they have lived all their lives there, and they want to die on the old doorstep. But they mustn't object if we refuse to lie down and die with them. Perhaps some kindly manager will in some theatre electrify the proscenium border so that any actor that steps over it will be immediately electrocuted. . . .

Sculpture, architecture, literature, poetry, and the domestic arts are effectively walking about in new ways, and drama isn't going to stay quietly in her picture-frame gazing coyly out at changing life around her, like a languid invalid woman looking pensively out of a window in the fourth wall. (160)

On Noel Coward's *Design for Living*, which Mr Agate and his colleagues held up as a model of exciting drama and praised for 'the original and profound philosophy underlying Mr Coward's great wit'; and which O'Casey summed up as an inane charade of musical beds, or a 'Design For Dying':

The principal persons in the play, whose 'lives are diametrically opposed to ordinary social conventions', barge at each other in the most conventional way possible, without one curious twist or word or turn of phrase . . . and passing through a period of four years, all the arguments, all the explaining away of the sun and moon and life and death have been the screaming of Otto because Gilda went to bed with Leo, and the screaming of Leo because Gilda went to bed with Otto, and the screaming of Ernest because Gilda decides to leave him, and return to her orbital movements from Leo to Otto and from Otto to Leo till the final curtain puts a veil over these poor wincing worms in a winecup. (161)

Perhaps Noel Coward did not entirely earn the swatting he received through three chapters of *The Flying Wasp*, but it should be remembered that O'Casey was using the 'Coward Codology' (162) to attack the concept of featherweight drama prevalent in London at the time. Just as he had fought the Abbey directors, he was once again defending the dramatist's need to explore new forms and provocative themes. He was blasting Mr Agate and his critical colleagues for applauding the innocuous works of Coward, Lonsdale, Phillpotts, and Nichols, while damning the important works of Strindberg, Pirandello, O'Neill, Toller, and O'Casey. He was demanding that the drama should have some relevance to life in a changing and chaotic world. He was pointing out the direction that the drama should take at a time when the universal 'ache of disorder' was impelling most of the significant dramatists and leading figures in the allied arts to turn away from safe subjects and stock realism.

A glance at the bold and original development of modern drama outside England during the past generation will reveal the prophetic nature of O'Casey's views in the mid 1930's. In comparison with modern French and American drama, for example, modern English drama has largely remained a tepid and trivial art. Where are the English playwrights to compare with Obey, Giraudoux, Anouilh, Sartre, Camus—O'Neill, Odets, Wilder, Williams, Miller? The field of drama in England has practically been abandoned to a handful of daring poets, to the brief efforts of Auden and Isherwood, the major efforts of T. S. Eliot, and the minor efforts of Christopher Fry. The 'angry' plays of John Osborne arrived about thirty years too late.

During those years the English tradition of acting produced some outstanding performers of Shakespeare and Restoration comedy. But there has been no significant English tradition of modern drama, and there have been no outstanding playwrights, save perhaps T. S. Eliot. And the Irish Wasp stopped stinging long enough to offer his highest praise for an isolated play like *Murder in the Cathedral*. But the rest was 'codology'.

Perhaps O'Casey was in a position to be a prophetic critic because he was practising what he preached in a prophetic play like *Within the Gates*—prophetic in technique and theme.

2. A PARABLE IN HYDE PARK

Like the old morality plays, *Within the Gates* is about the struggle of opposing forces for the body and soul of a symbolic character— here it is young Jannice, the everywoman of O'Casey's parable in Hyde Park. The Park is a microcosm of the chaotic world of the early 1930's, and the symbolic characters in it suffer from spiritual as well as economic depression. For O'Casey believes, with Shaw, that the failure of Capitalism is in large measure the failure of Christianity. This belief is fundamental to the theme of the play, for in a secular and even heretical sense, it is a deeply religious play. It is a play about O'Casey's humanistic vision of salvation.

During the five years since he wrote his last play, the primitive and joyous life-force which Harry Heegan symbolized seemed to have grown stronger in his mind. But he realized now that this life-force could be destroyed short of a war, that it had to be defended daily in the market-place. And so, maintaining this aspect of his earlier theme, he shifted the setting of his new play from the military battleground to the battleground of everyday life.

In *The Tassie* he had experimented only partially with the symbolic methods of Expressionism, but now he constructed his whole play as a non-realistic configuration of the real world as he saw it in a transmuted vision. The four stylized scenes or tableaux are set in a park which resembles London's famous Hyde Park, and they represent a cyclical pattern of life—a Spring Morning, a Summer Noon, an Autumn Evening, a Winter Night. All the people in the park are representational characters—the Young Whore Jannice, the Dreamer, the Atheist, the Bishop, the Bishop's Sister, the Gardener, the Chair Attendants, the Nursemaids, the Guardsman, the Evangelists, the Salvation Army Officer, the Old Woman, the Policewoman, the Man with the Stick, the Man in the Bowler Hat, the Man in the Trilby Hat, the Man in the Straw Hat, the Down-and-Outs, the Chorus of Young Man and Maidens. O'Casey has stated that he visualized these people as symbolic but living characters, going about their individual ways in the stylized world of the park as they might in a semi-realistic film. He conceived of 'the film as geometrical and emotional, the emotion of the living characters to be shown against their own patterns and the patterns of the Park'.(163) It suggests the technique of a Chaplin film like *Modern Times*, in which the emotional patterns of the characters are seen against the geometrical patterns of the Machine World. It was O'Casey's intention, therefore, to construct a symbolic design of modern life in the park, life that is representational and yet linked to reality.

The play begins with the symbolic rebirth of nature and ends with the symbolic death of Jannice. The main action centres around Jannice's attempts to save herself from sin and death, to identify herself with the spirit of life. When the Park Gates open on the first scene it is a bright Spring Morning and the formalized flowers and trees are in blossom, reflecting the fertility of nature and life. A Chorus of Young Boys and Girls, 'representing trees and flowers', enters singing one of the Dreamer's songs, 'Our Mother the Earth is a maiden again'. This pastoral ballad is sung to the tune of 'Haste to the Wedding', and for most of the songs in the play O'Casey uses the music of folk ballads with his own lyrics. 'Jannice' is sung to an old Irish folk tune, 'Sing and Dance' is sung to the air of 'Little Brown Jug', 'The Song of the Down-and-Out' is set to 'The Foggy Dew', the 'Gardener's Song' to 'Moll Roone'. With several of the men Jannice sings 'London Bridge is Falling Down', and the Salvation Army group sings the hymn 'There were Ninety and Nine'. All these songs contribute to the theme and spirit of the play, for the world of the park that O'Casey envisions and exalts is a singing world, and he reinforces this view by using the tradition of folk balladry, the songs of the people. As the writer of many of the songs, the poetic Dreamer is the champion of music and dancing, youth and beauty, love and joy. Jannice is the main character in the play, but the Dreamer is O'Casey's chorus-character who represents the good life and tries to win her over to his side.

This decision, however, is a difficult one for the tormented Jannice who is confronted by a succession of would-be saviours before she makes her final choice. She is the Bishop's illegitimate daughter, but hypocrisy and cowardice made him cover up this indiscretion of his student days. Now, when he comes to the park 'to get close to the common people', he discovers who she is and tries to save her and his conscience by bringing her back to the church. He had left her as a child in a convent, but the Atheist, her step-father, explains why he took her away from the church: 'When a few years old, the kid was shoved into a church institootion, where the nuns, being what she was—a child of sin—paid her special attention; an' the terrors an' dangers of hell became the child's chief enjoyment.' When she grew up she was still haunted by the terrors of hellfire and damnation. Restless and driven by fear, she left the Atheist, then tried for a while to live with her alcoholic mother, the Old Woman, and finally drifted into prostitution, her present occupation. In the first scene she is desperate and close to hysteria, suffering from a sense of guilt and a weak heart, a condition which seems to be related psychosomatically to her halluci-

nations of hell. She paints the horrors in her mind when she appeals
to the Atheist for help:

YOUNG WOMAN. I can't live alone any longer, Dad. When I lie down
in bed and stretch out in search of sleep, the darkness reddens into
a glow from the fire that can never be quenched.
ATHEIST. Oh, the old, false, foolish fear again!
YOUNG WOMAN. Green-eyed, barrel-bellied men glare and grin at
me; huge-headed, yellow-eyed women beckon to me out of the glow
from the fire that can never be quenched. Black-feathered owls, with
eyes like great white moons, peck at me as they fly through the glow
from the fire that can never be quenched. Save me, Dad, oh, save
me!

But the Atheist is unable to save her, for like so many of the
others in the park-world he can only offer her a mechanical
'system' which overlooks the basic needs of the human heart. He
knows what is wrong with the unchristian Christians, he scorns
their hypocrisy and bigotry, but he does not have enough to offer
in place of what he would wipe out. It is the Dreamer, the touchstone of the play, who tells us what is lacking in the Atheist's way
of salvation:

ATHEIST. . . . I did my best for 'er, takin' awye a supernatural 'eaven
from over 'er 'ead, an' an unnatural 'ell from under 'er feet; but she
never quite escaped. D'ye know, one time, the lass near knew the
whole of Pine's *Age of Reason* off by 'eart!
DREAMER. And did you bring her into touch with song?
ATHEIST. Song? Oh, I had no time for song.
DREAMER. You led her from one darkness into another, man. Will
none of you ever guess that man can study man, or worship God, in
dance and song and story!

For the Dreamer, the search for faith and freedom is not to be
found in the institutionalized dogma of the Church or the materialistic dogma of the Anti-Church. With Blake he believes that 'Art
is the Tree of Life. Christianity is Art'.[164] The two hapless Chair
Attendants, like cockney Joxers, are the Bishop's questionable and
comic allies. They are mis-shapen products of his creed, but they
often indicate how they have absorbed his doctrines. They can see

no joy in life, and the older one, 'Erbert, in an argument with the Dreamer tries to put man in his proper place: 'Wot's you or me in the general scheme of things, eh? Speck o' dust, blide o' grass, a nought, a nothing.' But the Dreamer's humanistic 'heresy' lies precisely in his rejection of this view of man as an insignificant speck of dust.

Still, the view that man is 'a nothing' seems to prevail in the park. When the young Guardsman and the Nursemaid try to embrace, they are assailed by the Evangelists and the Policewoman.

1ST EVANGELIST. Remember, brother and sister, it's a terrible thing when it comes.

GUARDSMAN. Wot is? When wot comes?

1ST EVANGELIST. Death, brother, Death!

2ND EVANGELIST. An' after death The Judgement!

1ST EVANGELIST. Oh, be converted before it is too late.

2ND EVANGELIST. Before it is too, too late, too late.

1ST EVANGELIST. It may be upon you today, in an hour, in a moment.

GUARDSMAN. Wot mye?

1ST EVANGELIST. Death, brother, death!

NURSEMAID (*indignantly*). We want to be left alone. We've important business to talk about an' do, so push off, please.

1ST EVANGELIST. Left alone! Devil's desire that, sister. You won't be left alone in hell.

GUARDSMAN (*rising angrily and pushing them away*). Here, git! We wants privacy, so git!

NURSEMAID (*rising from the bench as he is about to sit down again, having got rid of the Evangelists*). Let's sit dahn on th' grass, 'Arry— it's more comfortable.

GUARDSMAN. So it is.

(*They recline on the slope. He puts his arms round her, kisses her, and is about to kiss her again, when the Policewoman appears opposite, and stares reprovingly at them. She goes over to them.*)

POLICEWOMAN. You can't do the likes of that 'ere. Control yourselves. It doesn't allow such conduct in a public place.

GUARDSMAN (*embarrassed, but trying to be defiant*). Wot dorsent?

POLICEWOMAN (*sharply*). Th' lawr, young man, the lawr!

Although nature is in full bloom on this bright Spring morning and seems to be encouraging everyone to embrace joyously, love is

forbidden in the park-world, by church and state. And of course
young Jannice has difficulty trying to sell it. She is not strong
enough to follow the Dreamer, and too frightened of 'the fire that
can never be quenched' to follow the Bishop. She has hopes that
the Gardener will save her by marrying her, but he is not interested in permanent relationships. When the Gardener rejects
her to go back to his job of setting up a Maypole for a celebration
of Spring, the Man with the Stick, who is a bit of a sly covey,
'twarts' him about the symbol of the Maypole: 'It represents life,
new life about to be born; fertility; th' urge wot was in the young
lass you hunted away.' But now at the end of the scene the Maypole stands as an ironic symbol in the park, for 'new life' has not
had much of a chance to thrive on this Spring morning. To complete the irony, as the Gates close the Policewoman arrests Jannice
for having tempted the Gardener into sin; this one time she had
actually proposed marriage.

The repression of life, in contrast with the Dreamer's celebration of life, establishes the conflict of the play, a conflict which
Jannice must resolve. In the second and third scenes she alter-
nately tests the paths of salvation offered to her by the Bishop and
the Dreamer, and in the final scene just before her death she makes
a choice which is an attempt to come to terms with the forces that
both men represent—God and Joy.

The Bishop is a sorely tempted man, and although his official
position has led him to assume a pompous and artificial manner,
he really wants to get close to the common people, he is capable of
deep compassion, he is genuine about his remorse, and he reveals
the deeper side of his nature before the play ends. But he must
work out his own fate as painfully as Jannice works out hers, and
he is understandably slow to change. When she confronts him with
her plea for help in the second scene, he can only offer her pious
platitudes. When she demands more than this from 'a priest of the
most high God', he is embarrassed and threatens to call the police,
but she stuns him with a bitter accusation: 'When you go to where
your God is throned, tell the gaping saints you never soiled a hand
in Jesu's service. Tell them a pretty little lass, well on her way to
hell, once tempted you to help her; but you saved yourself by the
calm and cunning of a holy mind, an' went out into the sun to pick
the yellow primroses, leaving her, sin-soddened, in the strain, the
stain, the horrid cries, an' the noisy laugh of life.'

She understands why the Dreamer is against the Church, but she is not ready to accept what he offers her. He dedicates a song to her and offers it to her with his love; however, she only flirts with him, and at the end of the scene she goes off with the Salvation Army Officer who offers her 'peace everlasting'. The need for 'peace' has become an obsession and she continually repeats the word, asking where she can find it, peace without fear.

It isn't long before she realizes that the Salvation Army's 'peace' is no better than the Bishop's. The God-fearers turn out to be life-fearers. So in the third scene she finally goes over to the Dreamer and they spend a week of joy and love together. But it is now an Autumn Evening, and although she seems to be happy Jannice is close to death. Her heart has grown weaker, she is pale and suffers from fainting spells. Her discovery of the Dreamer's way of life has come too late, and there is a hysterical fear in her voice as she sings and dances wildly through the park. 'Death has touched me', she says after a dizzy spell, 'and is telling me to be ready.' She insists she will die dancing, but in her 'readiness' for death she moves inevitably toward a reconciliation with God.

While this main theme of Jannice's salvation unfolds, O'Casey also develops a series of comic sub-plots, low-level parodies of the relationship between man and God. Whenever the Dreamer and the Bishop go off after one of their struggles for the soul of Jannice, the crowd of multifarious people who wander through the park moves in to argue and make speeches about the fate of man, the soul, God, the universe, and relativity. They assail each other with a comic barrage of half and quarter truths, and they speak in the distorted cockney lingo, which underscores the parody. For example, one of these sustained episodes occurs in the final scene. Earlier, the Man in the Trilby Hat had explained the mystery of the universe with the statement that 'Gord myde . . . all the wunnerful things we see 'en 'ears arahnd us—on the earth 'en above us in the sky'. But now the Man with the Umbrella tries to account for the mystery with his unique version of the theory of relativity. The language here may be different from the Dublin idiom, but it is not too difficult to imagine Captain Boyle and Joxer Daly, or Fluther Good and the Covey, going at each other in an episode like this.

MAN WITH UMBRELLA. . . . Spice-time gives a noo meanin' to th' universe. Spice is relative to time, en' time is relative to spice—there's nothin' easier to understand.

MAN WEARING TRILBY (*dubiously*). Yes, quite; I gets thet, but——

MAN WITH UMBRELLA (*interrupting impatiently*). Wyte, 'old on a second. Don't question me yet. Listen carefully; let your mind foller wot I sye, en' you'll get th' idear.

GUARDSMAN. Listen cautiously to wot th' gentleman's asyein—'e knows wot 'e's torking abaht.

NURSEMAID (*tugging at the Guardsman's sleeve*). Aw, c'm on, Harry; you knows I 'as to be back by ten. (*The Guardsman takes no notice.*)

MAN WITH UMBRELLA (*pompously*). Now try to remember that all th' old idears of the cosmos—Greek for all things th' 'uman mind knows of—are buried with Copernicus, Kepler, Newton, en' all that crew.

GUARDSMAN (*emphatically*). 'Course they is, en' deep too.

MAN WITH UMBRELLA. Now we all know that the clock created time, en' the measuring-rod created spice, so that there is really neither spice nor time; but there is such a thing as spice-time. See? Get that?

MAN WEARING TRILBY (*with confidence*). Quite; that much is perfectly clear.

MAN WITH UMBRELLA. Right. Now suppose that one night, when we all slept, th' universe we knows sank down to the size of a football, an' all the clocks began to move a thousand times quicker—no, slower—it wouldn't make the slightest difference to us, for we wouldn't realize that any difference 'ad tyken plice, though each of us would live a thousand times longer, en' man couldn't be seen, even under a microscope.

GUARDSMAN (*jocularly*). Could a woman be seen under a microscope?

MAN WEARING CAP (*to Guardsman*). Levity's outa plice, friend, when men are trying to think out th' truth of things.

GUARDSMAN. But 'ow could th' world sink dahn to th' size of a football? Doesn't seem a sife thing to me.

MAN WITH UMBRELLA (*with cold dignity*). I said *if* it did, friend.

GUARDSMAN (*trying to find a way out*). Yes; but if a man couldn't be seen under a microscope, wot abaht 'is kids?

MAN WITH UMBRELLA. I simply styted a hypothenuse, friend.

MAN WEARING CAP (*to Guardsman*). It's only en hypothenuse, you understand? (*To Man with Umbrella.*) But it's en impossible one, I think. D'ye mean that under your hypothenuse, en hour of the clock would stretch aht into ten years of time?

MAN WITH UMBRELLA. Exactly that in spice-time; en 'undred years if you like.

MAN WEARING CAP. Wot? Then in your spice-time, a man doin' eight hours would be workin' for eight 'undred years!

GUARDSMAN (*to Man with Umbrella*). You're barmy, man! Wot abaht the bloke doin' penal servitude fer life? When is 'e agoin' to get aht? You're barmy, man!

NURSEMAID (*to Guardsman—chucking his arm*). Are you comin', Harry? If you don't 'urry, I'll 'ave to go, en' you'll 'ave to go withaht even a firewell squeeze.

MAN WITH UMBRELLA (*annoyed—to Guardsman*). Look, friend, if I was you, I'd go with the girl; for it's pline your mind 'asn't been educyted yet to grasp the complicyted functions of wot we know as spice-time problems.

GUARDSMAN (*with heat*). 'Oo 'asn't a mind? 'Oo're you to sye I 'asn't a mind? I 'asn't a mind as would warnt to tern th' world into a foot-ball. It's a punch on the jawr you warnts for thinkin' people warnts the world to be a football. Wye's there different thoughts in every mind, en' different rules in every country? Becorse people like you 'as th' world turned upside dahn! Wot do I mean when I syes th' world is upside dahn? Why, I means th' whole world is upside dahn, en' ennyone as 'as a mind'll unnerstend me!

The flustered Guardsman speaks better than he knows about the park-world. His phrase, 'th' whole world is upside dahn', echoes Captain Boyle's equally prophetic statement uttered in the heat of unknowing folly: 'th' whole worl's in a terrible state o' chasis'. The whole world within the gates is 'upside dahn'. O'Casey often exploits the irony which brings wisdom from the lips of fools. Later the tipsy Old Woman mockingly tells the Bishop: 'Truth is bent in two, and hope is broken. O Jesus! Is there no wisdom to be found anywhere!'

It is a Winter Night now in the upside-down park-world, particularly for Jannice. For now that the Dreamer has shown her a way to live, she is dying; and she must find a way to die.

YOUNG WOMAN (*tremulously*). I'm bad, Dreamer; please go and find the Bishop for me . . . Things are twisting before my eyes. (*Frightened.*) Get the Bishop, go for the Bishop.

DREAMER. Aren't you safer in the arms of the Dreamer than you are at the Bishop's feet?

YOUNG WOMAN (*tonelessly*). While I had life—yes; but I feel close to death now, and I have a lot to answer for, Dreamer.

But when the Bishop comes to her he refuses to bless her, he urges her to seek penance by joining the Down-and-Outs, the mortifying poor who appear with their ominous drum-beat and their chanted 'misereres'.

BISHOP (*to Young Woman—slow, but with decision*). You must go where they go, and their sighing shall be your song!

DOWN-AND-OUTS (*chanting*):
> She must be merry no more; she must walk in the midst of the mournful;
> Who've but a sigh for a song, and a deep sigh for a drum-beat!

(*The Young Woman has stiffened with resentment as she has listened, and now stands facing the Dreamer, looking at him for encouragement.*)

DREAMER (*to Young Woman*). Turn your back swift on the poor, purple-button'd dead-man, whose name is absent from the book of life. Offer not as incense to God the dust of your sighing, but dance to His glory, and come before His presence with a song!

YOUNG WOMAN (*with reckless defiance*). I'll go the last few steps of the way rejoicing; I'll go, go game, and I'll die dancing!

DREAMER (*exultantly*). Sing them silent, dance them still, and laugh them into an open shame!

Jannice and the Dreamer dance together to a mysterious tune of flutes and strings—it is a tragic epiphany of joy. When she collapses the Bishop goes to her and, at her dying request, guides her hand in making the sign of the cross so that, as she says in her last words, 'I may whisper my trust in the golden mercy of God.' In her death she has resolved the conflicting faiths of the Dreamer and the Bishop, she has gone to God with a dance and a prayer. The Dreamer and the Bishop may worship God in different ways, but Jannice has earned the grace of both their creeds, which for her have become manifestations of the one God.

At the end of the play the Bishop is a changed man, for Jannice's tragic death has brought him round to a more compassionate view of life. Like Jannice he has gone through a spiritual crisis, and while kneeling before her body he sends his sister away with an anguished cry: 'Go home, go home, for Christ's sake, woman, and ask God's mercy on us all!' He speaks now with a universal sense of guilt, and he appeals for the salvation of everyone in the park-world.

If, then, O'Casey has written a morality play that is a criticism of religion, it is a criticism of what he believes to be unchristian Christianity. He believes with Shaw that Christianity would be an excellent way of life if Christians would practise it. If, through the Dreamer, O'Casey places most of his emphasis upon man in this world, it is because he believes that institutional religion tends to ignore social and economic realities and places too much emphasis upon the soul in the next world—particularly as it urges the poor and unemployed to accept their depression with meekness and mortification, like the Down-and-Outs. He refused to reduce the spectacle of life to a transitory journey of fear on the way to heaven. His Dreamer-Poet presents his alternative: 'Offer not as incense to God the dust of your sighing, but dance to His glory, and come before His presence with a song!'

With its devastating criticism of religion and life, this play was not likely to appeal to the urbane critics and complacent audiences of London. O'Casey had set out to shock them all, and if he hadn't succeeded he could only take sad comfort from the knowledge that prophetic writers always run the risk of being scorned. In his criticism of the hypocritical foundations of modern society he was taking his place among the Socratic gadflies, and Irish wasps, who felt it was their moral duty to sting the slumbering horse of the State into an awareness of its failures. The fact that the Athenians gave Socrates a cup of hemlock for his pains, or that Englishmen had consistently ignored the warnings of prophetic gad-flies like Swift, Carlyle, Ruskin, Shaw, and were now prepared to ignore the latest Irish nuisance, only magnifies the tragic failure of men to live by the faith they profess.

The play was also a criticism of the type of polite drawing-room and bedroom drama which titivated West End audiences. O'Casey had broken the conventions of box-set realism by expanding the physical and visual dimensions of the theatrical illusion. Instead of reproducing a photograph of life on a picture-frame stage, he had created a symbolic design of life on a cycloramic stage. By using the architecture of the stage poetically instead of literally, he had conceived his symbolic park in a series of cyclical images, stylized and transfigured, of a potentially beautiful yet stricken world. This revolutionary form was an organic part of his revolutionary theme. It did not mean, however, that he had written an *avant-garde* drama for an aesthetic or revolutionary élite. The form and theme were departures from the theatrical conventions of the time, but O'Casey had aimed at a popular audience, even though as it turned out he had apparently written an unpopular play for the popular theatre.

Yet for all its fierce integrity and imaginative power, the play has its flaws, some of which can probably be attributed to the handicap under which it was written. O'Casey no longer had direct contact with a theatre that he knew intimately, and he had been forced to write the play for a publisher. And since it was not produced until a year after Macmillan published it, he had to make extensive changes for the 'Stage Version'—as he called the amended text—eliminating superfluous characters and enlarging others, rearranging episodes and rewriting speeches. For example, in the original version he had allowed himself to indulge in some gratuitous word play, but upon reconsideration he eliminated a park Foreman who had at one point rattled on aimlessly about 'dandy women, randy women, candy women, ready women, heady women, steady women, beddy women, weddy women, splendid women, mended women, ended women, boyish women, toyish women, coyish women'. (165) He struck out this sort of gush. He re-wrote some of the Dreamer's dialogue, and cut out such lines as the following in which the sound of the words had dominated the sense: 'These quiet, Christian maenads bind the hands to blast the minds with yearning.' (166) Even in the changed version, however, O'Casey could not avoid a melodramatic overstatement of the allegorical conflict, which is often the case in a morality play. This type of genre demands clear-cut issues on the matter of damnation versus salvation, and here O'Casey was handicapped by the sentimental theme of the redemption of a fallen woman.

While they are intended to be symbolic figures not 'real' people, the noble prostitute and the idealistic poet cannot entirely escape the well-worn sentiments that cling to such types. O'Casey was aware of this danger for he tried to bring a spirit of vigour and toughness to the characterization of Jannice and the Dreamer in a partially successful attempt to save them from sentimentality. The use of a Bishop with an illegitimate daughter, though it is intended to be symbolic of hypocrisy in high places, rather tips the scale against the 'enemy'. It may strain credibility, but still the Bishop is far from a stock villain and his suffering is on a level with Jannice's spiritual crisis. The least satisfactory character in the play is the Old Woman, Jannice's mother. Through the first three scenes she is an unsympathetic slattern who beats and abuses Jannice, yet she is treated sympathetically in the last scene, particularly when she puts the Bishop in his place. Then, she interrupts the action of the play at an inopportune moment to place a wreath on a war memorial and utters a long and irrelevant speech on the forgotten war dead. The episode seems out of place and she seems out of character.

There is no such faltering, however, in the satiric episodes of the play, for O'Casey's genius for creating a variety of comic characters and farcical situations seldom deserts him. With rich invention he uses his minor characters to develop satiric variations on his main theme of salvation—characters like the groaning Chair Attendants, the chattering Nursemaids, the blustering Guardsman, the crafty Man with the Stick (who is also the Man with the Umbrella), and those belligerent orators, the Men in Bowler, Trilby, and Straw Hats.

It is undoubtedly true that O'Casey's dramatic genius flourished more readily in the realm of satiric comedy than moral prophecy. Nevertheless, he accepted the challenge of working in a new genre, with new techniques, because he had not been able to separate his responsibility to society from his responsibility to his art. He believed that he not only could but had to do both, amuse and judge his fellow men, at a time when the tragic disorders of society demanded this double commitment from the artist. And a play like *Within the Gates* seems to have justified his belief, even though the powerful morality is sometimes handled crudely in comparison with the controlled treatment of the comedy. A writer who, like O'Casey, was prompted to mix satiric amusement and moral judgement in his work was Dickens, and a novel like *Hard Times* is in this respect similar to *Within the Gates*. In that devastatingly critical and comic novel, incidentally not one of his more popular works, Dickens had both amused and passed judgement on mid-Victorian England. Ruskin once commented on these aspects of the novel in a manner that may shed some light on

O'Casey's play. Strong moralist that he was, Ruskin wanted less satiric amusement and more severe judgement; he did not believe that amusement and morality should be mingled in a 'serious' work of art; but even with this bias his views are worth noting:

I wish that he [Dickens] could think it right to limit his brilliant exaggeration to works written only for public amusement; and when he takes up a subject of high national importance, such as that which he handles in 'Hard Times', that he would use severer and more accurate analysis. The usefulness of that work (to my mind, in several respects the greatest he has wiitten) is with many persons seriously diminished because Mr Bounderby is a dramatic monster, instead of a characteristic example of a worldly master; and Stephen Blackpool a dramatic perfection, instead of a characteristic example of an honest workman. But let us not lose the use of Dickens's wit and insight, because he chooses to speak in a circle of stage fire. He is entirely right in his main drift and purpose in every book he has written; and all of them, but especially 'Hard Times', should be studied with close and earnest care by persons interested in social questions. They will find much that is partial, and, because partial, apparently unjust; but if they examine all the evidence on the other side, which Dickens seems to overlook, it will appear, after all their trouble, that his view was the finally right one, grossly and sharply told. [167]

Like Dickens, then, O'Casey had given a partial account of the disorder of English life which even in its partiality was a just view; he had exaggerated his theme by setting up a conflict between a Bishop who is not quite a 'dramatic monster' and a Dreamer who is close to a 'dramatic perfection', but he was 'right in his main drift and purpose'; he had been severely critical and yet highly amusing on a 'subject of high national importance', for he had chosen to speak his truth through the techniques of artistic exaggeration, 'in a circle of stage fire'. Perhaps neither Dickens nor O'Casey had reached his highest artistic achievement in these works; both men had on other occasions written works of greater objectivity and greater amusement. Perhaps in daring to depart from their accustomed paths in order to write impassioned if imperfect works they had brought their art into the arena of social controversy; but they had acted out of concern for their fellow men rather than for their reputations. Art should be more than a tract; it should also be more than a retreat. Art is not so sacred that it cannot serve the cause of human freedom, particularly when the urgency of the times compels the artist to take a stand in the market-place. A novel or a play created under such conditions may or may not represent the highest achievement of art, but it can represent the deepest conviction of man.

Nevertheless, it should also be clear that for the artist this conviction, this passionate intensity alone is not enough.

3. MORALITY AS ENTERTAINMENT

In his two least satisfactory plays, *The Star Turns Red* and *Oak Leaves and Lavender*, O'Casey unintentionally went on to prove that passionate intensity alone is not enough. These plays were unquestionably inspired by a deep sense of conviction, but they remain angry tracts for the times, full of smoky rage which never quite breaks into a 'circle of stage fire'. Or, to continue the fire image and give Yeats his belated due, in these two didactic plays the fire of dramatic action fails to burn through O'Casey's 'opinions' on Fascism and Communism. A comparison of these two failures with a largely successful play like *Red Roses For Me*, a work of lyrical power which completes this group of prophetic plays, will lead to some useful observations on the nature of morality as entertainment in the drama.

It is fairly obvious that *The Star Turns Red* was written as a piece of straight anti-Fascist propaganda. Although the play is about a strike that closely resembles the 1913 Dublin strike, the conflict is not so much one between capital and labour as between Fascism and Communism. The storm-troopers of the Saffron Shirts combine with the Catholic priests of the Christian Front to represent the evils of Fascism, and the striking workers under the leadership of 'Comrade Chief' Red Jim represent the virtues of Communism. The allegorical action takes place on Christmas Eve in a city very like Dublin, 'Tomorrow, or the next day'. All the material of the play—sets, props, and people—is presented through the 'symbolic' references and slogans of the two opposing camps. The dominant colours in the room of the opening scene are literally black and white; on one wall is a sketch of a Bishop, on another is a sketch of Lenin; outside the window a church tower can be seen, but beside it in the sky shines a large silver star that will turn red when the workers strike; one of the sons of the Old Man and Woman, Kian, is a die-hard Fascist with a Hitlerian moustache and a goose-step walk, and dressed in the uniform and insignia of the Saffron Shirts, the Circle and the Flash, while the other son, Jack, is a die-hard Communist who wears a red star on his jacket and plays 'The Internationale' on his cornet.

Everything conforms to this mechanical opposition, and the transparent plot follows the stock pattern of proletarian literature. When the storm-troopers threaten Jack, his girl friend Julia slaps the Leader of the Shirts and she is dragged off to be horse-whipped to the satisfaction and sanction of the Purple Priest. Julia's father Michael tries to rescue her but Kian shoots him, and the dying Michael tells Jack to take care of Julia and carry on the Communist cause. Meanwhile the union officials, at the bidding of the Purple Priest, scheme to betray Red Jim and sabotage the strike. But Red Jim learns of the evil plan and denounces the traitors, whose names incidentally sound like hisses, sneers, and grunts— Sheasker, Caheer, and Eglish. The well-meaning but helpless Brown Priest, who is a friend of the workers, warns Red Jim that the Purple Priest has mobilized the Saffron Shirts and the police in a move to break the strike and enslave the workers. Consequently the Saffron Shirts raise their arms in Fascist salute and shout, 'Hail, the Circle and the Flash', and the workers reply with a Communist salute, 'the massed majesty of the Clenched Fist'. The inevitable war breaks out, and there are a number of allusions to the Spanish Civil War. During the simulated battle scenes 'Glazounov's Preamble to his "Scènes de Ballet", Op. 52 is played to represent the heat, the firing, and the stress of battle'— perhaps a refreshing change from the William Tell Overture. The stage is strewn with corpses which 'lie around with a stiffened clenched fist held high'. At the end of the play the war continues, but the symbolic Star Turns Red in the sky on Christmas morn as the workers sing 'The Internationale' and fight on.

Even if one makes allowances for the fact that rampart Fascism was at the height of its power when O'Casey wrote this play, it is difficult to accept it as either successful propaganda or drama. There are times when the play threatens to assume the epic violence of Picasso's 'Guernica', but too often O'Casey's moral outrage is spent in sentimental invective and as a result the play seldom rises above the level of a proletarian thriller. On several occasions the play does come to life, especially in the treatment of some of the minor characters. There are brief flashes of vivid dialogue when the Hunchback comes out with this speech: 'Where's his "Workers of the world, unite!" now? Hid in the dust of his mouth and lost in the still pool of his darken'd eyes.' When the Woman with the Baby says: 'The clergy are out to save any sensible man from trusting himself to the danger of walking on a country road with a sex-hilarious lassie eager to pillage him bare of all his holy hesitation.' When the old man, swaying precariously on a ladder, says: 'Well, I'm not going to let myself go cantering down through space with nothing definite but the air to stand on!' But these moments are all too rare, and they are lost in the allegorical struggle. Perhaps one of the main troubles is that there is little to choose between the ruthless fanaticism of the two slogan-shouting groups. The Communist fist is as ominous as the Fascist salute, and the snarling epithets of both sides are practically interchangeable—the Fascists call the Communists 'melting snails' and 'oozy scum', the Communists call the Fascists 'envy-stippled titivated toads' and 'slug-souled renegades'. At one point the Old Man and Woman damn both of their fanatical sons in a momentary display of wisdom:

OLD WOMAN. What about our own two boys, always at each other's throats for the sake of a slogan? What with the Saffron Shirts prodding us on one side, and the Communists pouncing at us on the other, life's lost everything but its name.

OLD MAN. Ask your Communist son, Jack, and he'll tell you that, to the workers, life is nothing but a name.

OLD WOMAN. What about your Fascist son, Kian, going about as if he was the deputy of God Almighty?

OLD MAN (shouting). I never held with either of them! I never held with either of them!

But O'Casey did not pursue this incisive attitude, nor did he anticipate that the audience might agree with the old couple. One cannot help wondering how the women of his early plays, the Juno Boyles and Nora Clitheroes, whose compassionate concern for human values made them reject the abstract slogans and 'principles' for which their men sacrificed themselves, would have reacted to all this proletarian blood and thunder about 'the massed majesty of the Clenched Fist'. And one cannot help feeling that in his use of Jim Larkin as a model for Red Jim, O'Casey had failed to recreate the volatile and great-hearted hero of the Dublin strike.

The Star Turns Red is an angry and humourless parable lacking in those characteristic qualities of ironic compassion and satiric comedy which distinguish not only the early tragi-comedies but *The Silver Tassie* and *Within the Gates*. An O'Casey play without the saving grace of laughter is a play without the O'Casey genius. The one type of literature which is admirably suited to moral protest is satire, and yet there is almost no effective satire in *The Star Turns Red*. O'Casey is a master of low comedy, but this play has nothing of the farcical ridicule which, for example, allowed Charlie Chaplin to make his protest against Fascism in a satiric film like *The Great Dictator*. O'Casey was apparently so consumed by his hatred of Fascism that he wrote a bald political tract which is too much of an unrelieved tirade to be an artistic protest.

When the play was first produced in London in 1940 at the left-wing Unity Theatre, it received high praise from a critic who was least likely to endorse it, none other than Mr James Agate! Perhaps one cannot entirely blame the once-stung Mr Agate for not taking any chances this time; he wrote a rave notice proclaiming the play 'A Masterpiece'. [168] It is an interesting commentary on the fallibility and/or discretion of critics. Needless to say, it illustrated that O'Casey had proved to be more potent as a wasp than a playwright.

In *Oak Leaves and Lavender*, writing about the Battle of Britain early in the Second World War, he avoided some but not all of the pitfalls of proletarian rage and over-simplification. In its general conception and structure the play represents yet another of O'Casey's original innovations, with its masque-like Prelude and Epilogue that link the semi-realistic plot to the realm of prophetic fantasy. The scene is Dame Hatherleigh's old Manorial House in Cornwall which serves as a headquarters for the Home Guard, air-raid wardens, Land Army girls, and is also a first-aid post and rest-camp. But the house is haunted by elegant ghosts from the past, and in the Prelude these lavender-scented spirits in silks and powdered wigs dance a sad minuet. They lament the passing of England's old glories, a Young Son of Time warns that England

is now in more serious danger, and a Young Girl weaves among
the ghosts selling lavender—the musty symbol of decay and
death throughout the play.

After these dancing spirits fade from view, the house becomes
alive with people busily preparing air-raid defences. Feelim
O'Morrigun, a sly Irishman who has come to England to serve as
Dame Hatherleigh's butler and major-domo, is more or less in
charge of all this activity. When he and his crew of eccentric
Cornish helpers are on stage, the play sparkles with comic invention and vitality. Trying to get the house in order and spouting
his stream of sense and nonsense, the garrulous Feelim seems to
combine the characteristics of an Admirable Crichton and a
Fluther Good—or one might say a combination of Charles
Laughton and Barry Fitzgerald, if that is possible. And he has
worthy competition from Mrs Watchit, the scatter-brained
housekeeper; Sillery and Dillery, the two pompous Constables;
and Michael, the Home Guard in charge of poultry. Since he was
living next to Cornwall in Devon, O'Casey had an opportunity to
catch the comic flavour of the Cornish dialect, with its mixed
pronouns and unexpected elisions. For example, when a government order is issued calling for an increase in the output of eggs,
Michael stands up for the independence of overworked hens:
'Well, us knows what us's sayin', but no-one wants t'listen t' uns.
Us'll soon 'ave Inspectors be'ind every bush watchin' hens layin'.
What's become of that 'ere Magna Charta, us asks?'

Unfortunately, these comic characters are subordinate to the
main plot which overwhelms them, and the play, with its heavy
proletarian 'message'. Although it is ostensibly about the Battle of
Britain, the play often breaks down into a verbal battle on the
virtues of Communism and the evils of Fascism. It is Feelim's son
Drishogue, an R.A.F. pilot and rabid Communist, who manipu-
lates the debate as O'Casey's mouthpiece character. He becomes
indignant when anyone suggests that he is fighting for England,
for which he insists he has no love. He tells his Cornish girl
friend: ' I'm fighting for the people. I'm fighting against the stormy
pillagers who blackened the time-old walls of Guernica, and tore
them down; who loaded their cannon in th' name of Christ to kill
the best men Spain could boast of; who stripped the olive groves
and tore up orange trees to make deep graves for men, heaping the
women on the men, and the children on the women. I was too

young then to go out armed for battle, but time has lengthened an arm long enough to pull the Heinkels and Dorniers out of the sky, and send them tumbling down to hell!' Then there is his savage brawl with Mrs Deeda Tutting.[169] She is simply identified as 'a visitor' who comes to the house for no apparent reason other than to argue with Drishogue. The fate of England is forgotten while these two hurl venomous insults at each other. The semi-Fascist Deeda calls Russia 'a chaos of incompetence, a mass of sullen terror, a swamp of ignorance' that should be wiped out; and Drishogue replies that Russia 'will slash open the snout, and tear out the guts of any power crossing her borders!' This snarling sounds as if O'Casey were trying to rewrite his worst play, *The Star Turns Red*, and at times he almost succeeded.

Feelim and the Cornish Celts bring a quality of eccentric freshness to the play, but they are too often pushed aside and the main conflict is resolved through a series of allegorical signs. When Drishogue and Dame Hatherleigh's son Edgar go out to their death in an air battle, a trumpet sounds the first line of ' Deutschland uber Alles ', and, as the stage directions indicate, 'The rush of German warplanes is heard in the rushing swing of the music of "The Ride of the Valkyries"'. But all the people, led by Feelim and Dame Hatherleigh, become more determined to carry on the fight—'The house must change; but it must not die.' In the last act the house is symbolically transformed into a factory; stylized belts and lathes and drop-hammers and cranes replace the oak beams and furniture as the scent of lavender foreshadows the death of the decaying past and the birth of a new way of life lies ahead. The half-whimsical, half-chimerical Dame Hatherleigh believes that 'British Israel' will resurrect the Ark of the Covenant, win the war and fulfill the destiny of the Ten Lost Tribes. As the house is transformed, she wanders among the dancing ghosts in the fantastic Epilogue, thinking about her dead son but finding comfort in the belief that the best of England's past will merge with the victorious future.

In an allusion to Yeat's objection to *The Silver Tassie*, O'Casey gave *Oak Leaves and Lavender* the sub-title: 'A Warld on Wallpaper'. He may have won the argument with his earlier play, but he clearly lost it with this one, for he had allowed his political 'opinions' to dominate his artistic judgement. There was undoubtedly the making of a fine satiric play in the theme of a 'lavender world' presented as a 'wallpaper world'—see how well he brought it off in *Purple Dust*—but the idea was weakened here by the inartistic intrusion of a proletarian 'message'. Furthermore, the trouble with Drishogue is that he can sometimes be a bore as well as an intrusion. And so the prophetic 'moral' of the play fails to grip or entertain an audience.

Nevertheless, O'Casey had already indicated that he could write plays like *The Silver Tassie* and *Within the Gates* which were dramatic entertainments as well as moral indictments, and he did it again when he wrote *Red Roses For Me*. In this play, which was written two years after *The Star Turns Red*, he again used the background of the 1913 Dublin strike. But now he discarded abstract political slogans and cardboard characters, creating instead a valid world of credible people who are capable of achieving symbolic stature because they live unmanipulated lives of their own. *Red Roses For Me* is his most autobiographical play, for he draws much of his material from his own experiences and people he knew. His hero Ayamonn Breydon is a freely drawn self-portrait; Mrs Breydon is a woman very much like his mother; the Protestant Rector, the Reverend E. Clinton of St Burnupus Church is modelled after the man who had been the foster-father and spiritual guide of his youth, the Reverend E. M. Griffin of St Barnabus Church.

One of the most striking characters in the play, however, is old Brennan o' the Moor, a new type of character in the O'Casey canon. He takes his name from the legendary hero of a popular Irish ballad, 'Brennan on the Moor', a song about a colourful Robin Hood type of highwayman—'He robbed the rich, he helped the poor, like Turpin and Black Bess.' O'Casey's Brennan is like the ballad hero in spirit, but he is a man of uniquely original parts. He had great compassion for the poor of Dublin's dirty highways, but he is also a crafty man with a shilling; he has saved the money he earned as a house-painter and now owns 'a few oul' houses', but he secretly offers gifts to the needy and gives the children toys for Christmas; he is an argumentative Ulsterman and at times reveals his gruff Protestant prejudices, but he does not hesitate to help his needy Catholic neighbours. He is a bald-headed old man of seventy-six, a scheming and singing codger with a long white beard who looks and acts like a bowler-hatted Father Christmas turned wandering minstrel. Seldom without his melodeon, always ready with a song, he arranges the air of the title song of the play which Ayamonn has written.

In the ordeals and hopes of Ayamonn, a young labourer with poetic aspirations, O'Casey has crystallized his vision of the good life, already introduced in *The Silver Tassie* and *Within the Gates*. Now this vision is dramatized on the banks of the Liffey, through Ayamonn who is an articulate Harry Heegan, a practical Dreamer. And like Johnny Casside—in the Autobiography—Ayamonn is active in the labour movement and spends his spare time 'sketchin', readin', makin' songs, an' learnin' Shakespeare'. Ayamonn's song, 'Red Roses For me', serves a function similar to *The Silver Tassie* in the earlier work—it foreshadows the symbolic action of the play:

> *A sober black shawl hides her body entirely,*
> *Touch'd by th' sun and th' salt spray of the sea;*
> *But down in th' darkness a slim hand, so lovely,*
> *Carries a rich bunch of red roses for me.*

> *Her petticoat's simple, her feet are but bare,*
> *An' all that she has is but neat an' scantie;*
> *But stars in th' deeps of her eyes are exclaiming*
> *I carry a rich bunch of red roses for thee!*

> *No arrogant gem sits enthron'd on her forehead,*
> *Or swings from a white ear for all men to see;*
> *But jewel'd desire in a bosom, most pearly,*
> *Carries a rich bunch of red roses for me!*

The black-shawled woman of this ballad is Ireland, a Kathleen ni Houlihan of the Dublin slums offering her red roses as the token of a new life for her people. Ayamonn creates this vision of her in his song as in a dream; and the action of the play grows out of his struggle to merge the real and the ideal Kathleen. There are two 'miraculous' events in the play which suggest that some kind of transformation may be possible; one is secretly arranged by Brennan when he repaints the statue of the Virgin, the other is mysteriously invoked by Ayamonn as the sun sets over the banks of the Liffey.

Ayamonn works in the railroad yards and is one of the leaders in the union's attempt to seek a shilling increase in wages. At the start of the play the workers fear their demand will be rejected and they are preparing to raise money for a strike fund with a minstrel show and scenes from Shakespeare's *Henry VI*. Ayamonn's mother is helping him rehearse the part of Gloucester (it is the scene that Johnny Casside and his brother Archie once played). But he is soon interrupted by friends and neighbours who have their own notions about the way to achieve the dream of a new Ireland. He is a Protestant but his sweetheart Sheila is a Catholic and the daughter of a policeman. She loves Ayamonn but is against the plans for a strike. And she tells him how often her parents warn her about being in love with a Protestant; her mother 'chatters red-lined warnings and black-bordered appeals into my ears night and day, and when they dwindle for lack of breath, my father shakes them out of their drowsiness and sends them dancing round more lively still, dressed richly up in deadly black and gleaming scarlet'. Ayamonn's mother has similarly warned him about seeing the Catholic Sheila, but he replies to both women, to everyone, that faith and love must be joined in 'a song all men can sing'.

The argument is extended when some of Ayamonn's friends arrive with their plans for saving Ireland. The Catholic Roory O'Balacaun is a fiery Nationalist, a 'zealous Irish Irelander' who believes that only militant Fenianism and the Gaelic 'Sword of Light' can rescue the Irish people. The cynical Mullcanny, a freethinker who is against political and religious solutions, claims that only scientific materialism can lead the way to salvation. Brennan interrupts the arguments when he arrives with the news that he has finished the air for the new song Ayamonn has written for the ministrel show. He has brought along the shy young singer Sammy—he's 'extravagant in shyness' but 'a second Count Mc-Cormack in the makin''—and he sings the title song. But only Ayamonn and Brennan are able to envision the Kathleen of the Red Roses. Roory stands by his Fenian literature, Mullcanny waves his copy of Haeckel's *Riddle of the Universe* (it is his 'Jenersky'). Ayamonn tries to convert Roory to the working man's side by reading a passage from Ruskin's *Crown of Wild Olive*, but Roory is suspicious of Ruskin—'Curious name; not Irish is it?' Meanwhile poor Sheila has left in despair; Ayamonn's sharp-tongued friends have bewildered her more than he has. And finally Ayamonn's three Catholic neighbours, Eeada, Dympna, and Finnoola, rush in lamenting that someone has stolen their statue of the Virgin, the Queen of Eblana's Poor. By the end of the first act all visions of salvation have been rudely shaken.

Early in the second act Brennan confesses he had taken the statue. It had become soiled and faded with the grime of the tenements, and when the women were unable to restore its beauty by washing it, Brennan decided to take it home and repaint it. Now he has secretly brought it back, and when the women find it, its colours radiantly restored, they call it a miracle. 'Many have lived to see a strange thing this favoured night', Eeada says, 'an' blessin' will flow from it to all tempered into a lively belief.' Ayamonn, however, is having a difficult time trying to bring off his 'miracle' of Kathleen of the Red Roses.

Roory and Brennan have a comic battle about whether St Patrick was a Catholic or a Protestant. Mullcanny taunts everyone with his glib lectures on evolution—for which he is later beaten up by a mob of irate believers—and when he gives his copy of Haeckel to Ayamonn, the incensed Roory condemns the book and Mullcanny. In reply Ayamonn makes a strong statement which defines the theme of the play:

Roory, Roory, is that th' sort o' freedom you'd bring to Ireland with a crowd of green branches an' th' joy of shouting? If we give no room to men of our time to question many things, all things, ay, life itself, then freedom's but a paper flower, a star of tinsel, a dead lass with gay ribbons at her breast an' a gold comb in her hair. Let us bring freedom here, not with sounding brass an' tinkling cymbal, but with silver trumpets blowing, with a song all men can sing, with a palm branch in our hand, rather than a whip at our belt, and a headsman's axe on our shoulders.

But Ayamonn has no sooner finished with Roory when Sheila returns, pleading with him to give up his foolish songs and dreams, and particularly to give up the plan for a strike. She brings information that he can get a foreman's job if he leaves the union. Again Ayamonn is forced to take a stand:

D'ye know what you're asking me to do, woman? To be a blackleg; to blast with th' black frost of desertion the gay hopes of my comrades. Whatever you may think them to be, they are my comrades. Whatever you may say or do, they remain my brothers and sisters. Go to hell, girl,

I have a soul to save as well as you. (*With a catch in his voice.*) Oh, Sheila, you shouldn't have asked me to do this thing!

While Ayamonn is trying to save his love and his soul, the Rector enters. He is Ayamonn's most faithful friend, and he brings news that the police intend to use force to break up the strike scheduled for the next day. Sheila pleads with the Rector to forbid Ayamonn to take part in the strike, to warn him that 'God's against it'. But he replies: 'Who am I to say that God's against it? You are too young by a thousand years to know the mind of God. If they be his brothers, he does well among them.' As the Rector leaves at the end of the act, Ayamonn is ready to fight for his dream, Sheila is weeping, and a group of people from the tenement are singing softly before the statue of the Virgin.

> *Oh, Queen of Eblana's poor children,*
> *Bear swiftly our woes away,*
> *An' give us a chance to live lightly*
> *An hour of our life's dark day.*

This prayer is answered in the symbolic third act when Dublin's poor children, as in a dream-vision, are given a prophetic glimpse of the life that might be theirs. The scene is the banks of the Liffey, where a bridge spans the river and rises in the background to meet the towers of the city—the Dome of the Four Courts, Nelson's Pillar, a church spire, and the gaunt frames of dark tenements. Pedlars, beggars, and homeless people are huddled together in various groups along the river bank. In the shadows sit the three black-shawled women, Eeada, Dympna, and Finnoola, selling their violets, apples, and cakes. They are the Kathleen of the Sorrows.

EEADA (*drowsily*). This spongy leaden sky's Dublin; those tomby houses is Dublin too—Dublin's scurvy body; an' we're Dublin's silver soul. (*She spits vigorously into the street.*) An' that's what Eeada thinks of th' city's soul an body!

DYMPNA. You're more than right, Eeada, but I wouldn't be too harsh. (*Calling out in a sing-song way.*) Violets, here, on'y tuppence a bunch; tuppence a bunch, th' fresh violets.

EEADA (*calling out in a sing-song voice*). Apples an' cakes, on'y tuppence a head here for th' cakes; ripe apples a penny apiece!

DYMPNA. Th' sun is always at a distance, an' th' chill grey is always here.

FINNOOLA. Half-mournin' skies for ever over us, frownin' out any chance of merriment that came staggerin' to us for a little support.

EEADA. That's Dublin, Finnoola, an' th' sky over it. Sorrow's a slush under our feet, up to our ankles, an' th' deep drip of it constant overhead.

DYMPNA. A graveyard where th' dead are all above th' ground.

EEADA. Without a blessed blink of rest to give them hope. An' she cockin' herself up that she stands among other cities as a queen o' counsel, laden with knowledge, afire with th' song of great men, enough to overawe all livin' beyond th' salty sea, undher another sun be day, an' undher a different moon by night.

The women lapse into drowsiness but they are half-awakened when some of the homeless men drop the word 'prophet' in an argument about horses—'Copper Goose'll leave him standin', if I'm e'er a thrue prophet.' The women drift in a reverie of Ireland's past and present heroes, and Dympna says: 'Th' prophets we once had are well hidden behind God be now, an' no wondher, for we put small pass on them, an' God in His generous anger's showin' us what it is to be saddled with Johnnies-come-marchin'-home, all song an' shirt an' no surity.'

There is an initial sign of a change in this somber mood when Brennan enters with his melodeon and sings a gay pastoral ballad about two young lovers. But the weary people mock the 'pagan' song, and so does Roory, who has wandered in with Ayamonn. Roory believes in the 'marching' prophets, and he calls for 'Gun peal and slogan cry'. Only Ayamonn defends Brennan's song. When Roory leaves in disgust, Ayamonn turns to the drowsing people and beckons them to awake.

AYAMONN. Rouse yourselves; we hold a city in our hands!

EEADA (*in a very low, but bitter voice*). It's a bitther city.

DYMPNA (*murmuring the same way*). It's a black an' bitther city.

FINNOOLA (*speaking the same way*). It's a bleak, black, an' bitther city.

IST MAN. Like a batthered, tatthered whore, bullied by too long a life.

2ND MAN. An' her three gates are castles of poverty, penance, an' pain.

AYAMONN. She's what our hands have made her. We pray too much and work too little. Meanness, spite, and common pattherns are

woven thick through all her glory; but her glory's there for open eyes
to see.

Presently the sceptical people begin to open their eyes, for something strange and mystifying has begun to happen as the sun sets
over the Liffey. The sky, which has been growing darker all along,
suddenly brightens as Ayamonn speaks. A ray of sunlight breaks
through the gloom and shines on his head, which looks strangely
like a mythic visage out of the Celtic past. The inspired Ayamonn
calls to the three women:

Friend, we would that you should live a greater life; we will that all
of us shall live a greater life. Our sthrike is yours. A step ahead for us
today; another one for you tomorrow. We who have known, and know,
the emptiness of life shall know its fullness. All men and women quick
with life are fain to venture forward. (*To Eeada.*) The apple grows for
you to eat. (*To Dympna.*) The violet grows for you to wear. (*To Finnoola.*) Young maiden, another world is in your womb.

As the strange 'miracle' continues the whole city becomes
transformed with bright colours and the towers in the background
glisten brilliantly in the sunset. The people's faces shine and their
black clothing changes to vivid green. Everyone gathers round
Ayamonn as he proclaims the prophetic vision in an epiphany of
joy.

AYAMONN. There's th' great dome o' th' Four Courts lookin' like a
    golden rose in a great bronze bowl! An' th' river flowin' below it, a
    purple flood, marbled with ripples o' scarlet; watch th' seagulls
    glidin' over it—like restless white pearls astir on a royal breast. Our
    city's in the grip o' God!
1ST MAN (*emotionally*). Oh, hell, it's grand!
EEADA. Blessed be our city for ever an' ever.
AYAMONN (*lifting his right hand high*). Home of th' Ostmen, of th'
    Norman, an' th' Gael, we greet you! Greet you as you catch a passing
    hour of loveliness, an' hold it tightly to your panting breast! (*He
    sings.*)
            Fair city, I tell thee that children's white laughter,
            An' all the red joy of grave youth goin' gay,

Shall make of thy streets a wild harp ever sounding,
Touch'd by th' swift fingers of young ones at play!
THE REST (*singing*).
We swear to release thee from hunger an' hardship,
'From things that are ugly an' common an' mean;
Thy people together shall build a brave city,
Th' fairest an' finest that ever was seen! [171]

As the song ends all the people join in a spontaneous ballet of joy. Ayamonn and Finnoola, who has been transformed into a beautiful young woman in a bright green dress, lead the dance on the bridge and along the river banks in a pool of golden light. It is a moment of visionary glory, not unlike that ecstatic moment in Beethoven's Ninth Symphony when the choral voices finally burst into song—'Freude!'—with the stirring words of Schiller's 'Ode to Joy'. It is O'Casey's Ode to Joy in honour of the people of Dublin, his first and only love.

Then suddenly the people are brought back to the real Dublin as the sky darkens again and the sound of marching feet is heard in the distance. It is the police who are getting ready to break up the strike in the morning. It is also a warning for Ayamonn who must now get ready to fight for his ideal vision in the real world. He kisses Finnoola and leaves her with these words: 'You're lovely stayin' still, an' brimmin' over with a wilder beauty when you're dancin'; but I must go. May you marry well, an' rear up children fair as Emer was, an' fine as Oscar's son; an' may they be young when Spanish ale foams high on every hand, an' wine from th' royal Pope's a common dhrink! Good-bye.' The promise of Spanish ale and Papal wine for everyone adds an extra significance to these allusions from Mangan's 'Dark Rosaleen'. Throughout this scene, from the time the women think they hear the prophets of ancient Ireland, to the moment when Ayamonn appears to them like a figure out of the mythic past, the vision is reinforced with memories of the Celtic heroes—Finn MacCool, Goll MacMorna, Caoilte, Milesius, Emer, Oscar, and Osheen. When Ayamonn leaves, the three women drift back into the shadows, but they continue to brood about their strange 'dream' and the spirit of Osheen:

EEADA (*murmuringly*). Penny each, th' ripe apples. Who was it that spoke that time? Jasus! I musta been dhreamin'.

DYMPNA (*in a bewildered voice*). So must I, th' way I thought I was lost in a storm of joy, an' many colours, with gay clothes adornin' me.

FINNOOLA (*puzzled and dreamy*). Dhreamin' I musta been when I heard strange words in a city nearly smothered be stars, with God guidin' us along th' banks of a purple river, all of us clad in fresh garments, fit to make Osheen mad to sing a song of the revelry dancin' in an' out of God's own vision.

EEADA (*murmuringly, but a little peevishly*). For God's sake give over dwellin' on oul' songs sung by Osheen, th' way you'd be kindlin' a fire o' glory round some poor bog-warbler chantin' hoarse ditties in a sheltered corner of a windy street. (*Very sleepily.*) Th' dewy violets, here, on'y tuppence a bunch—Jasus, apples I mean.

(*Now the tramp-tramp of marching men is heard more plainly.*)

In the last act we are back in the Dublin of black-shawled women and marching men. Armed with rifles and batons, the mounted police charge the strikers, and in the riot Ayamonn is killed. Many innocent bystanders are wounded, and the injured Finnoola staggers to the church, where the last act takes place, to tell the Rector Ayamonn's dying words: 'He said this day's but a day's work done, an' it'll be begun again tomorrow. You're to keep an eye on th' oul' woman. He wants to lie in the church tonight.'

The bigoted Protestant vestrymen, Dowzard and Foster, the two 'scabs' who had gone to work in the railroad yard in spite of the strike which they call a 'Popish' plot, try to prevent the people from bringing Ayamonn's body into the church. But the Rector ignores them and prepares for the service, chanting softly:

> When Charon rows him nigh to shore,
> To see a land ne'er seen before,
> Him to rest eternal steer.
> Jesu, Son of Mary, hear!

Perhaps Ayamonn had already caught a glimpse of that 'land ne'er seen before' in his vision of truth on the banks of the Liffey. This seems to be the belief of the crowd of people watching as his bier is carried into the church: one man whispers: 'He died for us.' When another adds that 'It was a noble an' a mighty death', the Inspector, who ordered the police to charge, remarks: 'It wasn't a very noble thing to die for a single shilling.' The final judgement, however, is left to Sheila. She expresses the point of the play when she replies: 'Maybe he saw the shilling in th' shape of a new world.'

Sheila has painfully come to a realization of the things for which Ayamonn lived and died. At last she understands his vision of 'a new world'. She carries a bunch of red roses which she places on his body. At the end of the play Brennan appears with his melodeon and softly sings a chorus of 'Red Roses For Me' at the open door of the darkened church as a last farewell to his dead friend. Ayamonn died that his vision might live on in the hearts of these people. It is a melodramatic ending, but it is right for the moral judgement of the play. He dies that the people of Dublin might carry on his fight to make the dream a reality. The play is a prophetic allegory for modern man as well as for Dublin. It is O'Casey's most lyrical and affirmative work.

In this play he completes the visionary theme he had introduced in *The Silver Tassie* and *Within the Gates*. His first three tragicomedies were chiefly concerned with the world as it is; these three morality plays are chiefly concerned with the world as it might be. And *Red Roses For Me* is finally an attempt to come to terms with both the real and ideal worlds. In this play O'Casey borrowed and reshaped techniques and attitudes from his earlier plays. Structurally, the third act follows the fantastic technique of the second act in *The Tassie*, although of course the point of the spectacle is reversed; and the other three acts are organized very much in the manner of the loosely linked tragi-comic episodes in the first three plays. Thematically, Ayamonn's situation is somewhat like Davoren's in *The Gunman*; however, when Ayamonn's poetic aspirations are threatened by the chaotic world around him he becomes the man Davoren might have been because he is able to relate his aspirations to that world. It should be pointed out, however, that Ayamonn, in some of his romantic reflections, occasionally sounds like Davoren. O'Casey can be careless with his language. He sometimes strains for alliterative effects, or he gives Ayamonn several speeches that have the quality of 'literary' jargon. 'Time's a perjured jade,' Ayamonn says at one point, 'an' ever he moans a man must die.' It is a stale expression. But when Ayamonn is aroused and fixes his mind upon the vision of a new life, when he summons up the images of the Celtic heroes and awakens the Dubliners, his mood and his language become sharp and vivid.

Ayamonn's celebration of the joy of life is clearly an extension of the aspirations of Harry Heegan and the Dreamer; but now this romantic theme culminates in a great epiphany which merges it with the golden age of Celtic myth. Ayamonn has fired the imagination of the people with the power and the glory of the legendary Celtic heroes, and in the process he himself becomes a modern mythic hero. And he wins over women like Finnoola and Sheila, not with arguments about principles but through his visionary act of faith.

O'Casey succeeds for the same reason—because his play is an act of faith not any angry argument; because he presents his moral judgement through the incantation and mystery of dramatic revelation. This is what he had failed to do in a prophetic play like *The Star Turns Red*, where he had allowed dialectical fury to over-rule the dramatic vision and diminish the entertainment. But in *Red Roses For Me* he had appealed to the higher court of visionary truth.

A play may be more than an entertainment, but it should not be less than an entertainment. A playwright may introduce symbolic ideas or 'opinions' in his work, but he should allow them to develop out of the life of each character. And when a symbolic character like Ayamonn Breydon can assume his own identity and evoke his visionary idea of the good life in an epiphany of joy, the dramatist can successfully combine moral judgement and imagin-ative entertainment.

CHAPTER V

The Comedies: A Catharsis and a Carnival

> Well, I will scourge those apes,
> And to these courteous eyes oppose a mirror,
> As large as is the stage whereon we act;
> Where they shall see the time's deformity
> Anatomised in every nerve, and sinew,
> With constant courage, and contempt of fear.
> Ben Jonson in *Every Man Out of His Humour*

> We couldn't live without comedy. Let us pray: Oh,
> Lord, give us a sense of humour with courage to
> manifest it forth, so that we may laugh to shame the
> pomps, the vanities, the sense of self-importance of the
> Big Fellows that the world sometimes sends among
> us, and who try to take our peace away. Amen.
> Sean O'Casey in *The Green Crow*

I. SCOURGING THE APES

IF IN his prophetic plays O'Casey set himself the task of writing moralities that were also entertainments, he reversed the process in his comedies and wrote entertainments that were also moralities. For comedy, particularly the type of satiric fun and fantasy he now wrote, is a celebration and a criticism of life—a romp and a riposte. His celebration of sheer fun and joy releases a cornucopia of comic experiences; his criticism of folly and knavery reveals an incisive moral judgement which points to an ideal way of life. And this visionary way of life is invariably invoked with a fanfare of supernatural agencies and an uninhibited Ta Ra Ra Boom Dee Ay. In these four comedies, *Purple Dust* (1940), *Cock-a-doodle Dandy* (1949), *The Bishop's Bonfire* (1955), *The Drums of Father Ned* (1958), O'Casey again set out in a new direction. In his early tragi-comedies he had used a form of anti-heroic irony to mock the

175

national excesses and yet affirm his faith in the Irish people. In his prophetic plays he had used varying forms of anti-realistic symbolism to present a moral protest against spiritual and social disorder, and a vision of Ireland and the world as they might be. Now in his late comedies he used a form of satirical and fantastical entertainment to continue his protest and his vision in a mood of ripening humour. In all these groups of plays he had moved on to cope with new problems in stagecraft and dramatic technique. His general themes in all these plays are inter-related—they begin with the world as it is and finally point to the way it might be— but the methods of presentation always indicate a fresh departure, a boldness and originality of conception.

Now he had set out to unify a variety of comic experiences— comedy of humours and errors, comedy of satire and the music hall, comedy of fantasy and the circus. These diverse elements of the comic spirit are brilliantly united in *Purple Dust* and *Cock-a-doodle Dandy*, and they are handled with varying degrees of success in the other two plays. All the plays take place in 'imaginary' Irish villages, but, to paraphrase Marianne Moore, they are imaginary villages with real toads in them. The plays are specifically concerned with Irish and English follies; yet they can be said to deal with the universal vanity of human wishes, the universal quest for freedom and happiness.

O'Casey ridicules 'the time's deformity', he 'anatomises' the vanities and villainies of the Big Fellows, and the Little Fellows, 'who try to take our peace away'. These plays, then, are intended to restore our peace through fun and satire, through merry and malicious laughter. And in that restoration of peace we may gain a temporary victory over deformity and disorder. Thus, O'Casey's comedy is a form of courage; for to laugh to is conquer fear, just as to be laughed at is to be defeated.

The scourge and defeat of the ridiculous apes is one of O'Casey's aims, and in this respect he follows Jonson who saw comedy as a catharsis:

> *O, I would know 'em ; for in such assemblies*
> *They are more infectious than the pestilence :*
> *And therefore I would give them pills to purge,*
> *And make them fit for fair societies.* [172]

O'Casey did not write 'pure' Jonsonian comedies of humours,

but there is a strong element of this Jonsonian 'purge' in his plays. Baudelaire and Bergson have also lent some weight to this concept of satiric comedy as a catharsis, although they were concerned with laughter, a result of comedy rather than comedy itself. Baudelaire believed that 'Laughter is satanic: it is thus profoundly human',[173] and proclaims man's superiority over the apes. Bergson believed that laughter is a social 'corrective' by which 'society avenges itself for the liberties taken with it'.[174] According to these views, comedy is subversive in a constructive sense, it is an avenging force, for it wages satanic laughter against knaves and fools who must be purged of their folly before they can be accepted as 'fit for fair societies'. An unscourged Volpone, Malvolio (even the 'gentle' Shakespeare could on occasion use satire as a purge), Tartuffe, Shanaar (the old crawthumper in the *Cock*), or any of the general species of Yahoos, might be a menace to society.

This view of comedy as a corrective may leave out some aspects of the comic spirit, and it may not account for all aspects of comedy in O'Casey's plays. But it can serve—in Kenneth Burke's phrase— as 'a way in' to the plays; and once we find our way in we will discover that satire can up-end fools and chastise knaves without always aiming to correct them; that farce can provoke laughter that is gratuitous as well as pointed fun. We will also discover those comic characters whose shrewd folly is a protection against the stupid knavery of others—those sly Irish peasants who have their Dublin counterparts in a Captain Boyle or a Joxer Daly. It is the characters who might be called comic 'villains'—Stoke and Poges in *Purple Dust*, Shanaar and Father Domineer in the *Cock*—that are closest to the 'humorously' obsessed types of Jonsonian comedy.

The first of the comedies, *Purple Dust*, was published in November 1940, just nine months after *The Star Turns Red*, and it reveals O'Casey in a more genial and robust mood than he had been in when he wrote the earlier play. Now he put aside his savage anger and called upon the comic spirit for his inspiration. *Purple Dust* is a satire of pastoral affectations, but it also ranges merrily over a variety of human frailties. The plot develops out of the addle-brained attempt of two 'English' Englishmen, Bails Stoke and Cyril Poges, to resurrect a crumbling old Tudor mansion in the little Irish village of Clune na Gerra. Wealthy financiers from

London on a misguided lark in Ireland, they have illusions about the glories of the Elizabethan age and plan to live as dashing country squires amid the amiable Irish peasants. It is no surprise that they prove to be less than dashing and the peasants prove to be more than amiable. They are such monumental fools that their rustic masquerade would have collapsed soon enough if they had been left on their own, but the crafty Irish peasants are eager to mock their ridiculous affectations and hasten their downfall.

In the two ring-leaders of the peasants, Jack O'Killigain and Philib O'Dempsey, O'Casey creates a pair of shrewd Celtic foils for the English buffoons. O'Killigain and O'Dempsey are primitive playboys, high-spirited rustics who provide a norm of genuine pastoral life. Stoke and Poges are so hopelessly carried away by their absurd obsession for old relics and old customs, neither of which they even vaguely understand, that their pastoral utopia never becomes more than a heap of 'purple dust'. In contrast, O'Killigain and O'Dempsey have a wise and mystical understanding of the traditions and values of the old Celtic heroes; and when they ride off into the hills with the girls in the fantastic conclusion, they go to seek a pastoral utopia which offers a new vision of an old way of life.

At the start of the play, while the Irish workmen are trying to patch and paint the ruined mansion, Stoke and Poges enter with their entourage of mistresses and servants, all singing and dancing to celebrate the new venture. It is a burlesque scene that establishes the tone of the play. Each of them wears a white smock on which appears a stylized picture of a pig, a hen, a cow, a duck, a sheep, and a cock. Stoke, wearing plus-fours under his smock, carries a little rake; Poges, wearing morning clothes under his smock, carries a little spade; Avril, Stoke's mistress, carries a dainty shepherd's crook; Souhaun, Poges' mistress, carries a little hoe decorated with ribbons; Cloyne, the maidservant, carries a little hayfork; Barney, the butler, carries a little reaping-hook. City folk disguised as rustics, they dance in 'what they think to be a country style', and sing a parody of a pastoral ditty:

POGES (*singing*). Rural scenes are now our joy:
  Farmer's boy,
  Milkmaid coy,
  Each like a newly-painted toy,

ALL. In the bosky countrie!

AVRIL (*singing*). By poor little man the town was made,
   To degrade
   Man and maid;
   God's green thought in a little green shade
   Made the bosky countrie!

ALL (*chorus*). Hey, hey, the country's here,
   The country's there,
   It's everywhere!
   We'll have it, now, last thing at night,
   And the very first thing in the morning!

BASIL (*singing*). Our music, now, is the cow's sweet moo,
   The pigeon's coo,
   The lark's song too,
   And the cock's shrill cock-a-doodle-doo,

ALL. In the bosky countrie!

                    (*Chorus.*)

O'Casey here alludes to Marvell's 'Thoughts in a Garden', in which the poet retreats from the turmoil of the city to the idyllic peace of nature—'Annihilating all that's made/To a green thought in a green shade.' And of course he named the two Englishmen after the churchyard of Gray's 'Elegy'—Stoke Poges. These references to genuine pastoral experiences, in contrast to the above burlesque of pastoral affectations, reinforce the comic failure of this band of masquerading city folk to understand 'the bosky countrie'. The disenchantment of these pseudo-rustic apes is satirized throughout the play as they are confronted by real cows and cocks and defeated by genuine rustics. The Irish peasants, when they are not mocking the antics of Stoke and Poges, perform their own songs and dances, folk ballads and Irish reels. O'Killigain sings and flirts with Avril in an attempt to woo her away from Stoke, and O'Dempsey eventually wins Souhaun away from Poges.

Philib O'Dempsey is a proud and dreamy-eyed Irishman, a man of the soil and something of a natural scholar 'who knows everything worth knowing about Ireland past and present'. His friend O'Killigain appropriately calls him 'a wandherin' king holdin' th' ages be th' hand'. With his rich store of knowledge he easily makes a shambles of the pseudo-learning of the Englishmen, who think that Brobdingnag was a Celtic god—'the fellow that ate the nine nuts—or was it seven?—plucked from the tree hanging over the well near the world's end '. And the Irish workmen make sport of their ignorance, humouring them and assailing them by turns. When Poges tries to put through a call to London on a phone that hasn't been connected, the 1st Workman explains that the connection depends upon 'how long it'll take to get the sthrame o' sound from here flowin' safely to whatever other end there may be fixed for it to be heard in'. The exasperated Poges shouts 'fool' at the 2nd Workman, who is O'Dempsey, and Philib replies as if he were a Celtic king annihilating an upstart Anglo-Saxon:

2ND WORKMAN. Comin' over here, thinkin' that all the glory an' grandeur of the world, an' all the might of man, was stuffed into a bulgin' purse, an' stickin' their tongue out at a race that's oldher than themselves by a little like a thousand years, greater in their beginnin' than they are in their prime; with us speakin' with ayse the mighty language o' the world when they could barely gurgle a few sounds, sayin' the rest in the movement of their fingers.

POGES (*shouting in rage*). Go to the devil, man, and learn manners!

2ND WORKMAN (*going on vehemently, but moving slowly to one of the entrances*). Hammerin' out handsome golden ornaments for flowin' cloak an' tidy tunic we were, while you were busy gatherin' dhried grass, an' dyin' it blue, to hide the consternation of your middle parts; decoratin' eminent books with glowin' colour an' audacious beauty were we, as O'Killigain himself will tell you, when you were still a hundhred score o' years away from even hearin' of the alphabet. (*Beside the entrance.*) Fool? It's yourself's the fool, I'm sayin', settlin' down in a place that's only fit for the housin' o' dead men! Settlin' here, are you? Wait till God sends the heavy rain, and the floods come!

There is a Shavian ring in this lampoon of the English, but there is also a strange air of mystery in Philib, and his prophetic remark about the floods prepares the final resolution of the play. The Englishmen, however, are too harassed to pay any attention to his warning. The word has gone around the village that they intend to set up a farm and they are besieged by bargain offers of fowl and live-stock. The 1st Workman, for example, has some 'entherprisin' hins' for Poges: 'Listen, here, sir: if it's genuine poultry you

want, that lay with pride an' animation, an' not poor, insignificant
fowls that set about th' business o' laying like a member o' Doyle
Eireann makin' his maiden speech, I have a sthrain o' pullets
that'll give you eggs as if you were gettin' them be steam!' And
when Poges brushes him aside with the remark that he will get his
poultry from the Department of Agriculture, all the Workmen are
horrified:

1ST WORKMAN. Oh, listen to that, now! Didja hear that, ma'am? The
    Department of Agriculture, is it? Wisha, God help your innocence,
    sir. Sure, it's only a tiny time ago that the same Department sent
    down a special sthrong covey o' cocks to improve the sthrain, an'
    only afther a short probation, didn't they give the hins hysterics?
POGES. Hysterics? Good God!
3RD WORKMAN. Ah, an' hadn't the frightened farmers to bring guns
    to bear on the cocks when they found their hins scatthered over hill
    an' dale, lyin' on their backs with their legs in the air, givin' their last
    gasp, an' glad to get outa the world they knew so well! The few mighty
    ones who survived were that stunned that there wasn't an egg in th'
    place for years!

These jesting Irishmen carry on in the mischievous spirit of
Conn the Shaughraun, and indeed this and the following scenes
have the distinct flavour of what Synge called Boucicault's 'careless Irish humour'. While Poges tries to cope with the disconnected
phone and the 'enterprisin' hins', Stoke orders some horses and
goes off for a ride with Avril. However, since Irish horses are as un-
predictable as the Irish people, it is not surprising that Stoke is
soon carried back into the house bruised and covered with mud
after being tossed by his horse. And as if this were not enough
trouble, Cornelius, the Yellow-bearded Man, suddenly breaks a
hole in the ceiling and pokes his hairy head down into the room
to ask: 'Hay, hay there; is this where yous want the light to go?'
Of course he has broken through the wrong end of the ceiling, but
he calmly assures the desperate Poges that it was only a slight mis-
calculation and that he will 'hit th' right spot one o' these days'.
    This bedlam of comic errors builds up to a riotous first-act cur-
tain. When Stoke has sufficiently recovered from his shock, he
announces sadly that Avril has cantered away with O'Killigain.
The workmen overhear him say, 'Naked and unashamed the vixen

went away with O'Killigain'; and although Stoke means this figuratively, they misunderstand and assume she has gone off on a Godiva-like ride about the countryside. Alternating between mock-indignation and delight, some of them protest that they actually saw her canter off stark naked. But it is the incredulous Cornelius, still breaking holes in the ceiling and heartbroken when he learns he has missed the great event, who steals the scene.

1ST WORKMAN (*excitedly*). Did yous hear that, eh? Did yous hear what he just let dhrop? That the lassie o' th' house went off with O'Killigain riding naked through the locality!

2ND WORKMAN. Stark naked she was, too. Didn't I know well be th' cut of her jib that she was a hop, step, an' lep of a lassie! An' right well she looked too!

1ST WORKMAN. Th' sight near left me eyes when I seen her go prancin' out without so much as a garther on her to keep her modesty from catchin' cold.

3RD WORKMAN. This'll denude the disthrict of all its self-denyin' decency.

1ST WORKMAN (*excitedly jumping upon a seat to get nearer to the hole in the ceiling*). Cornelius, eh, there, Cornelius!

(*The yellow-bearded head is thrust through the hole again.*)

YELLOW-BEARDED MAN. What's up?

1ST WORKMAN. Didja hear th' terrible thing that's afther happenin'?

YELLOW-BEARDED MAN. No; what terrible thing?

1ST WORKMAN. The lassie o' th' house's gone careerin' all over th' counthry on horseback with only her skin as a coverin'!

YELLOW-BEARDED MAN (*horrified*). G'way!

3RD WORKMAN (*up to him*). An' th' poor men workin' in th' fields had to flee to th' ditches to save th' sight of their eyes from th' shock o' seein' her!

YELLOW-BEARDED MAN (*with aggravated anguish in his voice*). Oh, isn't it like me to be up here outa sight o' th' world, an' great things happenin'!

CURTAIN

Cornelius may have one of the shortest roles in the play, but it is a brilliant piece of comic invention. Each time he pokes his yellow-bearded head through the ceiling, great things happen—the world rocks with laughter.

Although it is clear to everyone else that Stoke and Poges are not long for this wild Irish world, they stubbornly refuse to give up their heap of purple dust. However, they are beginning to crack, small wonder. When we see them at the start of the second act, the realities and inconveniences of the rustic life, thanks to the obliging workmen, are catching up with them. They are shivering in their tomb-like mansion without heat, lights, plumbing, or telephone. And they haven't been able to sleep because of what they call the 'deafening jungle noises' made by owls, cuckoos, cocks, cows, swine, and sheep. Stoke is still suffering from his encounter with the horse and the humiliation of Avril's canter with O'Killigain. But since he has settled five hundred pounds a year on her for life, he can no longer control her; and Poges is in the same predicament with Souhaun. The girls are Irish, but they were 'corrupted' in London, and now O'Killigain and O'Dempsey are rehabilitating them in the old Irish ways.

Each time the frustrated Englishman try to make light of their troubles, new ones appear. When Cornelius's cow, which he has brought along to sell to them, happens to wander into the house, Stoke, armed with a gun, and Poges, screaming for help, prepare for a battle to the death with a 'wild bull'. In the midst of the confusion, some rats frighten Avril and Souhaun into breaking some of Poges' antique treasures. Full of grief and determined to do something constructive, Poges sets out to level the lawn with a huge roller and ends up by crashing a tremendous hole in a wall of the house. This crash prompts the workmen to shout up the latest great happening to Cornelius, who is still banging away at the ceiling trying to find the right spot for the light. But Cornelius thrusts his shaggy head through the hole and growls angrily: 'Didn't I think it was an earthquake! An' don't be tellin' me these things while I'm up here. Can't you wait till I'm down in th' world o' men, and can enjoy these things happenin'!' Poor Cornelius is missing most of the fun; but he is creating a fair share of it himself.

Meanwhile, Stoke is out hunting the 'wild bull'—he has already had one unhappy encounter with an Irish horse and he seems determined to settle the score at the expense of an Irish cow—and Poges, seeking relief from the calamitous happenings in the world of men, has been encouraging Philib O'Dempsey to tell him about the great happenings in Ireland's heroic past. This gives Philib an opportunity to develop the counter-theme of the play: the supernatural link between the past and the present, the mysterious hint that men like O'Dempsey and O'Killigain might ride off into the hills to live the pastoral life in the heroic style of the mighty Finn MacCoole; Dagda the Good, Chief of the Dana; Lugh, father of Cuchulain and wielder of the Invincible Sword.

2ND WORKMAN.... That was in the days o' Finn MacCoole, before his hair was scarred with a hint o' grey; the mighty Finn, I'm sayin', who stood as still as a stone in th' heart of a hill to hear the cry of a curlew over th' cliffs o' Erris, the song of the blackbird, the cry o' the hounds hotfoot afther a boundin' deer, the steady wail o' the waves tumblin' in on a lonely shore; the mighty Finn who'd surrendher an emperor's pomp for a place with the bards, and the gold o' the King o' Greece for a night asleep be the sthream of Assaroe!

POGES (*solemnly*). A great man, a great man, surely; a great man gone for ever.

2ND WORKMAN (*sharply*). He's here for ever! His hallo can be heard on the hills outside; his spear can be seen with its point in the stars; but not with an eye that can see no farther than the well-fashioned edge of a golden coin.

POGES (*moving back a step—a little awed*). You see these things, do you?

2ND WORKMAN. I hear sthrange things be day, an' see sthrange things be night when I'm touched be the feel of the touch of the long-handed Lugh. When the Dagda makes a gong o' the moon, an' th' Sword o' Light shows the way to all who see it.

Philib goes on to say that he also 'sees' Wolfe Tone and Parnell out in the hills, and that there will be others soon to come who will lead the people to take their own again. But this prophetic vision means nothing to Poges, or to his friend Stoke who finally shoots Cornelius's cow at the end of the second act.

The last act brings the fulfilment of Philib's prophecy. The heavy rains have begun, the Englishmen are hanging on grimly, and the workmen are cheerfully wrecking the house. In a slapstick episode that recalls the zany antics of the Marx Brothers, the workmen ram Poges' quattrocento desk through a narrow passageway, tearing down the columns that support the passage and ruining the desk. Then, while Poges tearfully surveys the debris. Philib, who doesn't care if the desk is a 'squattrocento or nottrocento', gets that wild gleam in his eyes again and tells Poges about the things that really matter in the world: 'There is sweet music in the land, but not for th' deaf; there is wisdom too, but it is not in a desk it is, but out in th' hills, an' in the life of all things rovin' round, undher th' blue sky'.

It is not only Stoke and Poges who are unable to perceive the music and wisdom in the land; Canon Creehewel also fails to grasp the joy and freedom of Philib's vision. In fact, he is waging a puritanical campaign against the 'dangerous' spirit of gaiety in the village, and he asks the Englishmen to help him. The Canon wants to instil a proper fear of God and life in the impulsive people, and his chief aim is to get rid of 'the devilish dance halls' and O'Killigain—the 'snake in our garden'.

But O'Killigain and O'Dempsey are preparing to ride off with the women into the enchanted hills to live like the Celtic heroes of the past. There they will be safe from the Canon, the Englishmen, and the ominous floods. Philib calls to Souhaun as if he were beckoning her to *Tir na Nog*, the Land of Youth:

Come, then, an' abide with th' men o' th' wide wathers, who can go off in a tiny curragh o' thought to the New Island with th' outgoin' tide, an' come back be th' same tide sweepin' in again ... With firm-fed men an' comely, cordial women there'll be laughter round a red fire when the mists are risin', when th' roads an' fields are frosty, an' when th' nights is still.

And O'Killigain offers a similar promise to Avril of a free and joyous life:

An' you, young girl, sweet bud of an out-spreading three, graft yourself on to the living, and don't stay hidden here any longer. Come where the rain is heavy, where the frost frets, and where the sun is warm. Avril, pulse of me heart, listen to me, an' let longin' flood into your heart for the call of life. The young thorn-three withered away now, can awaken again, an' spread its fragrance around us. Spit out what's here, an' come where love is fierce an' fond an' fruitful. Come, lass, where there's things to say an' things to do an' love at the endings!

In both of these speeches O'Casey seems to be echoing the visions of Synge's poetic tramps and playboys. At first the girls are reluctant to go dashing off into the stormy night with these two inspired Celts; but they finally give in, unlike Synge's Pegeen Mike, and they ride off to 'go romancing through a romping life-time' with their playboys.

Defeated by the peasants, deserted by the girls, frightened by the rising wind and rain, Stoke and Poges are left alone in the crumbling mansion with a garrulous Postmaster to await the avalanche of water which inundates them at the close of the play. The stage darkens and a fantastic Spirit appears suddenly in a flash of lightning, a Figure that represents 'the spirit of the turbulent waters of the rising river'. The Figure announces that the Deluge has come, and only those 'who have lifted their eyes unto the hills' will be spared. And on this note of prophetic fantasy the play ends, with O'Killigain and his friends singing in the background as they head for the hills, with Stoke and Poges lamenting their fate 'as the green waters tumble into the room'.

What O'Casey has done in this comedy, then, is to scourge the ridiculous apes and liberate the worthy Celts. He has sought to resolve 'the time's deformity' in two ways: by exposing it to satirical and farcical laughter, and by offering a visionary alternative in the form of a fantasy. In creating the mood and theme of this fantasy, he used the biblical myth of a great Deluge and the pagan myths of the Celtic heroes. For the overall theme of pastoralism, he drew upon a romantic spirit akin to Synge's pantheism and paganism. O'Killigain and especially O'Dempsey have the mystical longings for nature and freedom that we find in Synge's rustics. The speeches in which O'Killigain and O'Dempsey call to the women to go away with them contain that poetic quality of nature-mysticism that characterized the Tramp's appeal to Nora Burke in *In the Shadow of the Glen* and Christy Mahon's call to Pegeen Mike in *The Playboy of the Western World*. O'Casey had earlier begun to develop something close to this theme in characters like Harry Heegan and the Dreamer, but now he reinforced this impetus by identifying it with the enchanted hills of Ireland where all the mythic and historic heroes, from Finn MacCoole to Parnell, become for him living symbols of the good life. And he developed parallel qualities in a visionary Dubliner like Ayamonn Breydon in *Red Roses For Me*.

O'Dempsey is a more rounded and more natural character than O'Killigain. It is clear that O'Dempsey is a wild-eyed, dreamy sort of a man, and O'Killigain is a high-spirited, practical man; but in several instances O'Casey seems to be using O'Killigain to express views which are not directly relevant to the action. For instance, there are some comments on O'Killigain's having fought in the Spanish Civil War, and while these references reflect the political climate of the time when the play was written, they hardly fit into the theme of the play. In these brief instances O'Casey allowed his political bias to override the dramatic situation. And it was apparently a similar motive which led him to write the speech in which O'Killigain attacks Wordsworth as a Tory renegade. This assault on Wordsworth's politics is also an inappropriate intrusion, particularly since O'Dempsey, and even O'Killigain himself, have much in common with the nature-mysticism of Wordsworth's poetry, whatever O'Casey may personally feel about Wordsworth's apostasy.

But these are minor intrusions in an exuberantly comic play which is on the whole a triumph of theatrical ingenuity. In its variety of comic invention, in its mythic and fantastic climax, the play represents a new and original development of O'Casey's stagecraft—and of modern drama. He used the stage as if it were a combination music hall and circus ring, whirling through a profusion of burlesque turns and clowning acts, and bringing the whole performance to a spectacular conclusion with a supernatural extravaganza. Finally, in shaping all this material around his pastoral theme, he had found a new way to dramatize his faith in man; in Philib O'Dempsey's wild dream of a free and joyous life in the enchanted hills he had illustrated that magical line from an Old Play which had attracted Yeats—'In dreams begins responsibility'.[175]

2. THE ENCHANTED COCK

In his seventieth year O'Casey wrote *Cock-a-doodle Dandy*, a comic-fantasy which most imaginatively and most sharply sums up his view of life. In this play he extended the mythic visions of *Purple Dust* and *Red Roses For Me*, consummating them in the apocalyptic figure of an enchanted Cock—his comic symbol of the life-force. The whole play is a fantastic extravaganza, a satiric parable which celebrates man's freedom and joy in the life-sized image of a dancing bird out of the beast-fable tradition. The Green Crow had created his *alter ego* in the form of a gorgeous Cock.

During the same year that he wrote this play, 1949, O'Casey also published the fourth volume of his autobiography, *Inishfallen Fare Thee Well*, and this could be an appropriate sub-title for the play. Both works record the reasons for his self-exile from Ireland some twenty years earlier. The theme of exile grows out of the main conflict of the play which is presented as a mock-battle between allegorical forces of good and evil. The Cock-a-doodle Dandy is a barnyard Dionysian turned loose in a joyless little Irish village where the priest-led people have been taught to fear him as an incarnation of the devil. The 'demon' Cock and his followers, mostly beautiful young women, are banished at the end of the play, but not before he scourges the puritanical apes led by Father Domineer and Shanaar and shows them up as a dangerous crew of crawthumping bigots. Ireland itself is represented as an unhappy land of thou-shalt-not's—a land of denial that 'bites away some of the soul'. And yet it is more than an 'Irish' play, for it is a comic morality with a universal theme for men of all countries. At a time when so much of modern literature has been obsessed with Original Sin, O'Casey expressed his faith in what might be called Original Joy.

In the beginning there was Joy, O'Casey seems to be saying, and he would have man rediscover it in dance and song, in love and laughter, and in the freedom of the mind as well as the heart. As the merry champion of these primordial virtues, the enchanted Cock is an inspired magician. He can make chairs and flagpoles and houses collapse; he can make whiskey bottles go dry and glow red-hot; he can imitate cuckoos and corncrakes; he can take the shape of a top-hat or a beautiful woman; he can create a powerful wind that blows off men's trousers; he can bring down thunder and lightning and cast all sorts of mischievous spells on holy objects and on the people who oppose the way of life he represents. The name of the village he bewitches is Nyadnanave, which means in Gaelic, Nest of Saints; and the name also contains the ironic pun, Nest of Knaves. The Cock is the satiric mocker of Nyadnanavery.

The three scenes of the play take place in the garden in front of Michael Marthraun's house, and at the opening curtain, before anyone appears, the Cock enters and weaves his spell over the place by dancing merrily around the garden. 'He is of a deep black plumage, fitted to his agile and slender body like a glove on a lady's hand; yellow feet and ankles, bright-green flaps like wings, and a stiff cloak falling like a tail behind him. A big crimson crest flowers over his head, and crimson flaps hang from his jaws. His face has the look of a cynical jester.' As soon as he disappears, Marthraun and his friend Sailor Mahon come in arguing about the mysterious pranks that have upset the whole neighbourhood. The appearance of two 'oul' butties' has become a trade-mark of an O'Casey play, and these characteristic old clowns are in a disagreement about the 'sinisther signs appearin' everywhere'. Mahon, an old buck who still loves his pleasures, is sceptical, but Marthraun is convinced that the three women in his house—his young wife Lorna, his daughter by a previous marriage, Loreleen, and Marion the maid—have been bewitched by an evil spirit. When Mahon insists that 'there's nothin' evil in a pretty face', Marthraun tells him about the wind that follows Loreleen through the house and turns the holy pictures with their faces to the wall. 'Oh, man,' he warns, 'your religion should tell you th' biggest fight th' holy saints ever had was with temptations from good-lookin' women.'

But Marthraun soon finds an ally when old Shanaar pokes his way into the garden. In Shanaar, O'Casey created a merciless burlesque of the religious quack. He is described as 'a very wise old crawthumper, really a dangerous old cod . . . a very, very old man, wrinkled like a walnut, bent at the shoulders, with longish white hair, and a white beard—a bit dirty—reaching to his belly'. The name Shanaar means Old Man in Gaelic (*Shan ahr*); but there is a biblical reference to Shinar, the land of confused languages where the Tower of Babel was built (Gen. 11: 2, 9), which is a particularly appropriate allusion for Shanaar's confusion of superstitious nostrums, medieval *exempla*, and bog-Latin. He is an expert on the exorcizing of evil spirits, and this early scene in which he offers his compendium of sage advice and tries to put a proper sense of fear into Sailor Mahon, with eager support from Marthraun, and some demonic disruptions by the obliging Cock, illustrates the rich satiric spirit of the play:

SHANAAR (*shoving his face closer to Mahon's*). Ah, me friend, for years an' years I've thravelled over hollow lands an hilly lands, an' I know. Big powers of evil, with their little powers, an' them with their littler ones, an' them with their littlest ones, are everywhere. You might meet a bee that wasn't a bee; a bird that wasn't a bird; or a beautiful woman who wasn't a woman at all.

MICHAEL (*excitedly*). I'm tellin' him that, I'm tellin' him that all along!

MAHON (*a little doubtfully—to Shanaar*). An' how's a poor body to know them?

SHANAAR (*looking round cautiously, then speaking in a tense whisper*). A sure sign, if only you can get an all-round glimpse of them. (*He looks round him again.*) Daemones posterior non habent—they have no behinds!

MICHAEL (*frightened a lot*). My God, what an awe-inspiring, expiring experience.

MAHON (*frightened too, but trying to appear brave*). That may be, but I wouldn't put innocent birds or bees in that category.

SHANAAR (*full of pitying scorn for ignorance*). You wouldn't! Innocent birds! Listen all: There was a cuckoo once that led a holy brother to damnation. Th' cuckoo's call enticed th' brother to a silent glade where th' poor man saw a lovely woman, near naked, bathin' her legs in a pool, an' in an instant th' holy man was taken with desire. Lost! She told him he was handsome, but he must have money, if he wanted to get her. Th' brother entered a noble's house, an' demanded a hundhred crowns for his convent; but the noble was a wise old bird, an' said he'd have to see the prior first. Thereupon, th' brother up with an axe, hidden undher his gown, an' cleft th' noble from skull to chin; robbed th' noble, dhressed himself in rare velvets, an' searched out all th' rosy rottenness of sin with th' damsel till th' money was gone. Then they caught him. Then they hanged him, an', mind you (*the three heads come closer together*), while this poor brother sobbed on the scaffold, everyone heard th' mocking laughter of a girl and th' calling of a cuckoo!

(*As Shanaar is speaking the last three things, the mocking laughter of a girl is heard, the call of a cuckoo, and a young man's sobbing, one after the other, at first, then they blend together for a few moments, and cease. Shanaar stands as stiff as his bent back will allow, and the other two rise slowly from their chairs, stiff, too, and frightened.*)

SHANAAR (*in a tense whisper*). Say nothing; take no notice. Sit down. Thry to continue as if yous hadn't heard!

MAHON (*after a pause*). Ay, a cuckoo, maybe; but that's a foreign bird; no set harbour or home. No genuine decent Irish bird would do a thing like that on a man.

MICHAEL. Looka here, Sailor Mahon, when th' powers of evil get goin', I wouldn't put anything past an ordinary hen!

SHANAAR. An' you'd be right, Mr Marthraun, though, as a rule, hens is always undher th' eye an' comprehension of a Christian. Innocent-looking things are often th' most dangerous. Looka th' lad whose mother had set her heart on him bein' a priest, an' one day, at home, he suddenly saw a corncrake flyin' into a house be an open window. Climbin' in afther it, he spied a glittherin' brooch on a table, an' couldn't resist the temptation o' thievin' it. That lad spent th' next ten years in a reformatory; his mother died of a broken heart, and his father took to dhrink.

(*During the recital of Shanaar's story, the 'crek crek, crek crek' of a corncrake is heard.*)

MICHAEL (*in a tense whisper—to Mahon*). D'ye hear that, Sailor Mahon?

SHANAAR (*warningly*). Hush! Take no vocal notice. When yous hear anything or see anything suspicious, give it no notice, unless you know how to deal with it.

MICHAEL (*solemnly*). A warnin' we'll remember. But supposin' a hen goes wrong, what are we to do?

SHANAAR (*thoughtfully*). It isn't aysey to say, an' you have to go cautious. The one thing to do, if yous have the knowledge, is to parley with th' hens in a Latin dissertation. If among th' fowl there's an illusion of a hen from Gehenna, it won't endure th' Latin. She can't face th' Latin. Th' Latin downs her. She tangles herself in a helluva disordher. She busts asundher, an' disappears in a quick column of black an' blue smoke, a thrue ear ketchin' a screech of agony from its centre!

MICHAEL (*tremendously impressed*). Looka that now. See what it is to know!

Well, Shanaar has no sooner explained his unique remedy for exorcizing evil fowl when the Cock springs into action again. A great commotion of cackling and crowing arises from the house, and Marion rushes out with the news that a strange flying thing, a wild goose or a duck or a hen, is tearing the house apart. It has kicked over the altar light and clawed the holy pictures. When they hear this, the three frightened men are ready to retreat behind the garden wall, particularly the expert on such deviltry, Shanaar.

MICHAEL (*pleadingly—to Mahon*). You've been free with whales and dolphins an' octopususas, Sailor Mahon—you run in, like a good man, an enthrone yourself on top of th' thing!

MAHON (*indignant*). Is it me? I'm not goin' to squandher meself conthrollin' live land-fowl!

MICHAEL (*to Shanaar—half-commandingly*). In case it's what we're afraid of, you pop in, Shanaar, an' liquidate whatever it is with your Latin.

SHANAAR (*backing towards the wall*). No good in the house; it's effective only in th' open air.

At first the women do not understand what the Cock is up to and they are afraid of him. It isn't until the Messenger, who works in the local post office, arrives to quiet the 'gay bird' that the women realize the Cock is their friend. While the Messenger— his name is Robin Adair and he is in love with Marion the maid— goes into the house to calm the Cock, the three old boyos head for cover. Just before he hides behind the wall, Shanaar makes a desperate attempt to liquidate the 'demon' with a burst of bog-Latin: '*Oh, rowelum randee, horrida aidus, sed spero spiro specialii spam!*' But the Cock replies by thrusting his head out of a window and letting out a triumphant cock-a-doodle-doo.

Robin Adair finally leads the pacified Cock out of the house, and he explains to Lorna: 'Looka, lovely lady, there's no danger, and there never was. He was lonely, an' was only goin' about in quest o' company. Instead of shyin' cups an' saucers at him, if only you'd given him your lily-white hand, he'd have led you through a wistful an' wondherful dance.' Now fascinated by the brightly plumed Cock, Marion steps forward bravely to admire him, and Robin says to her: 'Just a gay bird, that's all. A bit unruly at times, but conthrollable be th' right persons.' It becomes clear throughout the play that Robin Adair and the three young women are the 'right persons'; and the only other person in Nyadnanave who is capable of being saved is Sailor Mahon.

There is little hope for superstitious fools like Marthraun and Shanaar. After the Messenger goes off with the Cock and the women return to the house, the wizened old quack whispers a final warning to Marthraun about the ungodliness of women, for, as he puts it, 'th' circumnambulatory nature of a woman's form often has a detonatin' effect on a man's idle thoughts'. He also urges

Marthraun to call in a priest to have the house 'purified an' surified' of the Cock's evil influence, and as he leaves he intones a
special blessing: '*Ab tormentum sed absolvo, non revolvo, cockalorum credulum hibernica!*' To which Marthraun, deeply moved,
replies: 'You too, Shanaar oul' son, you too!'

But the sceptical Sailor Mahon isn't taken in by all this crawthumping puritanism. Like Fluther Good, the Sailor is a 'well-
flavoured man' who can appreciate the joys and beauties of life.
And he has a good deal of Fluther's angry eloquence when he tells
Marthraun what he thinks of the old quack:

MAHON (*viciously*). That Latin-lustrous oul' cod of a prayer-blower is
a positive danger goin' about th' counthry!
MICHAEL (*startled and offended*). Eh? I wouldn't go callin' him a cod,
Sailor Mahon. A little asthray in a way, now an' again, but no cod.
You should be th' last to call th' man a cod, for if it wasn't for his holy
Latin aspirations, you mightn't be here now.
MAHON (*with exasperation*). Aw, th' oul' fool, pipin' a gale into every
breeze that blows! I don't believe there was ever anything engen-
derogically evil in that cock as a cock, or denounceable either!
Lardin' a man's mind with his killakee Latin! An' looka th' way he
slights th' women. I seen him lookin' at Lorna and Marion as if they'd
horns on their heads!
MICHAEL (*doubtfully*). Maybe he's too down on th' women, though you
have to allow women is temptin'.
MAHON. They wouldn't tempt man if they didn't damn well know he
wanted to be tempted!

Whenever any of the men glare at the women as if they were evil
temptresses with horns on their heads, the mischievous Cock
obligingly sees to it that a pair of real horns suddenly appear on
their pretty heads.

Besides this main conflict over the Cock, two sub-plots are also
introduced in the first scene. The first one involves the intended
strike of turf workers who are demanding a shilling raise in wages.
Since Marthraun owns the turf bog, and Mahon owns the lorries
that transport the turf to town, both men carry on a running
argument over which of them should make up the extra shilling.
The second sub-plot is introduced at the end of the scene when
Lorna's sister Julia, who is dying of an incurable disease, is carried

into the garden on a stretcher. She is on her way to Lourdes in the hope of finding a miracle that will save her life. Father Domineer enters to lead a prayer so that 'Julia will bring us back a miracle, a glorious miracle'. The rest of the play becomes a contest between the miracles of Father Domineer and the miracles of the Cock.

In the second scene the whole village has been mobilized by Father Domineer to fight the Cock. When Marthraun and Mahon get into an argument with the Messenger, their chairs mysteriously collapse under them; and when they try to find relief from their troubles with a drink, the 'bewitched' whiskey bottle first appears to be empty and then glows red-hot in their hands. Even the Sailor thinks the joke has gone too far now: 'You'd think good whiskey would be exempt from injury even be th' lowest of th' low.' But as the Nyadnanaves intensify their campaign against the Cock, the mischievous pranks continue. A pompous Porter delivers Marthraun's new tall-hat with a bullet-hole in it; for the local police, who are spraying the countryside with rifle-shot in their hunt for the Cock, mistake the hat for the Cock. Presently a volley of shots is heard and the Police Sergeant, a bumbling Dogberry, enters with his rifle and tries to explain what happened:

SERGEANT. Three times I shot at it; three times th' bullets went right through it; and twice th' thing flew away crowing.

MICHAEL (*excitedly*). Did you get it th' third time, did you get it then?

SERGEANT. Wait till I tell yous: strange things an' unruly are happenin' in this holy land of ours this day! Will I ever forget what happened th' third time I hot it! Never, never. Isn't it a wondher an' a mercy of God that I'm left alive afther th' reverberatin' fright I got!

MICHAEL (*eagerly*). Well, what happened when you hot it then?

MAHON (*eagerly*). When you hot it for th' third time?

SERGEANT. Yous could never guess.

MICHAEL (*impatiently*). Oh, we know we'd never guess; no one can go guessin' about demonological disturbances.

MAHON. Tell us, will you, without any more of your sthructural suggestions!

SERGEANT. As sure as I'm standin' here; as sure as sure as this gun is in me left hand (*he is holding it in his right one*); as sure as we're all poor, identified sinners; when I hot him for th' third time, I seen him changin' into a——

MICHAEL and MAHON (*together*). What?

SERGEANT (*whisperingly*). What d'ye think?

MAHON (*explosively*). Oh, we're not thinkin'; we can't think; we're beyond thinkin'! We're waitin' for you to tell us!

SERGEANT. Th' soul well-nigh left me body when I seen th' unholy novelty happenin': th' thing that couldn't be, yet th' thing that was. If I never prayed before, I prayed then—for hope; for holy consideration in th' quandary; for power to be usual an' spry again when th' thing was gone.

MICHAEL. What thing, what thing, man?

MAHON (*despairingly*). Thry to tell us, Sergeant, what you said you said you seen.

SERGEANT. I'm comin' to it; since what I seen was seen by no man never before, it's not easy for a man to describe with evidential accuracy th' consequential thoughts flutterin' through me amazed mind at what was, an' couldn't be, demonstrated there, or there, or anywhere else, where mortals congregate in ones or twos or crowds astoundin'.

MICHAEL (*imploringly*). Looka, Sergeant, we're languishin' for th' information that may keep us from spendin' th' rest of our lives in constant consternation.

SERGEANT. As I was tellin' you, there was th' crimson crest of the Cock, enhancin' th' head lifted up to give a crow, an' when I riz th' gun to me shouldher, an let bang, th' whole place went dead dark; a flash of red lightning near blinded me; an' when it got light again, a second afther, there was the demonized Cock changin' himself into a silken glossified tall-hat!

As the trembling men stare at Marthraun's tall-hat, the garden is suddenly plunged into darkness; there are flashes of lightning: the hat disappears and the Cock is seen standing in its place; then the Cock gives a lusty crow and when the lights come back on the Cock and the hat have both vanished. And the men, moaning of sulphur and brimstone, are stretched out on the ground.

In this burlesque of the tall-hat O'Casey has aimed his satire at the masquerade of bourgeois Irish politicans. As the local Councillor, gombeen man, and Knight of St Columbanus, Marthraun has his formal hat ready for an audience with the President of Ireland. Himself a proud wearer of the working-man's cloth-cap, O'Casey says in *Inishfallen Fare Thee Well* that 'the terrible beauty of the tall-hat is born to Ireland'. [176] In this book he describes catholic-bourgeois-capitalists like Marthraun as the new power in the country—'the new Irish aristocracy—the devalerians'. He sees modern Ireland as a theocratic state, an alliance between the 'purple biretta' of the Roman Catholic Church and the 'tall-hat' of the De Valera politicians, and he echoes Joyce's warning that 'Christ and Caesar are hand and glove'. And his reaction to the De Valera is personal as well as political and religious: 'He couldn't see De Valera abandoning himself to sweat and laughter in the dancing of a jig, nor could he see him swanking about in a sober green kilt and gaudy saffron shawl; or slanting an approving eye on any pretty girl that passed him; or standing, elbow on counter in a Dublin Pub, about to lower a drink, with a Where it goes, lads. No, such as he would be always in a dignified posture at Dail or Council, or helping to spray prayers at a church gathering.' [177]

The Nyadnanaves, then, are 'devalerian' puritans under strict orders from their politicians and priests to beware of the joyous temptations of the 'devilarian' Cock. While the men are still recovering from the shock of the demonic tall-hat, the Bellman enters, dressed as a fireman, ringing his bell frantically, and shouting the Cock's latest 'miracle'—'Th' Cock's comin'! In the shape of a woman! Gallus, Le Coq, an' Kylelock, th' Cock's comin' in th' shape of a woman! Into your houses, shut to th' windows, bar th' doors!' Marthraun urges Mahon and the Sergeant to follow Shanaar's instructions and take no notice of 'he or she'; he then pleads with Mahon to sing one of his sea shanties to bolster their courage, and in the midst of the song about long ago 'when men were men', Loreleen appears mysteriously in a beam of golden light. Soon Lorna and Marion join her, wearing gay costumes for a fancy-dress ball, and the three women, with the help of the Cock, proceed to bewitch the men. The women take drinks of whiskey, for they are on friendly terms with the Cock and his 'lesser boyo in the bottle', and the men drink too. Robin Adair appears in the background and strikes up a tune on his accordion, and the three couples whirl about in a lively dance, during which the head-dress of the women has curved upward to simulate horns.

When the dance reaches a peak of excitement, Father Domineer enters in a rage at the unholy spectacle; a lusty cock-a-doodle-doo rings through the garden, and the priest roars at the dancers:

Stop that devil's dance! How often have yous been warned that th' avowed enemies of Christianity are on th' march everywhere! An' I find yous dancin'! How often have yous been told that pagan poison is floodin' th' world, an' that Ireland is dhrinkin' in general doses through films, plays, an' books! An' yet I come here to find yous dancin'! Dancin', an' with th' Kyle-loch, Le Coq, Gallus, th' Cock rampant in th' disthrict, destroyin' desire for prayer, desire for work, an' weakenin' th' authority of th' pastors an' masters of your souls! Th' empire of Satan's pushin' out its foundations everywhere, an' I find yous dancin', *ubique ululanti cockalorum ochne, ululo!*

With this outburst of hysterical Nyadnanavery, O'Casey's satire turns savage and the mood of the play darkens. Thematically, it is a preparation for the ominous climax of the second scene, for Father Domineer next turns on Sailor Mahon and commands him to dismiss one of his lorry drivers who, according to the priest, is 'livin' in sin with a lost an' wretched woman'. But Mahon refuses to obey the order, insisting that the man is one of his best workers. When Jack, the lorry driver, comes in at the end of the scene to report to Mahon on the strike situation, Father Domineer turns on him viciously and utters a curse that God should strike him dead. It is the priest, however, not God, who presently fulfills the curse, for he suddenly lunges at the unrepentant Jack in a burst of fury and hits him a fatal blow on the head.

The second scene closes with this brutal act of violence, and it is the turning point in the battle between the symbolic forces of good and evil; it indicates that Nyadnanavery can be ruthless as well as ridiculous. The satiric sport continues in the final scene, but the comedy is now darkened by tragic implications: the Cock will be defeated and the women banished. The puritanical vigilantes are now terrorizing the whole countryside. Father Domineer has come to rid Marthraun's house of its evil influences, and his assistant, One-eyed Larry, carries the holy equipment—bell, book, and candle. The half-blind and half-idiotic Larry is another religious crawthumper, a younger version of Shanaar. Although it is common knowledge that he lost his eye in a childhood accident, his account of how it happened is worthy of Shanaar's quackery:

It was the Demon Cock who done it to me. Only certain eyes can see him, an' I had one that could. He caught me once when I was spyin' on

him, put a claw over me left eye, askin' if I could see him then; an' on
me sayin' no, put th' claw over th' other one, an' when I said I could see
him clear now, says he, that eye sees too well, an' on that, he pushed an'
pushed till it was crushed into me head.

   One-eyed Larry and Marthraun creep behind Father Domineer
as the three of them go into the house for the exorcizing, and soon
the whole house begins to shake and rumble as the mock-battle
with 'evil spirits' rages. Flashes of lightning and drums of thunder
break from the house, followed by the screeching and cackling of
barnyard fowl. Suddenly, One-eyed Larry bolts out of the house,
battle-scarred and filled with terror: 'They're terrible powerful
spirits. Knocked the bell outa me hand, blew out th' candle, an'
tore th' book to threads! Thousands of them there are, led be the
bigger ones—Kissalass, Velvethighs, Reedabuck, Dancealong, and
Sameagain'.
   After a final flash of lightning and a burst of thunder from the
collapsing house, all is silent, then the priest and Marthraun limp
out, bruised and battered. The smoke-stained Father Domineer
announces that 'evil things have been banished from the dwel-
ling'. But the eye-blackened Marthraun remembers that the
women have some dangerous books hidden in their rooms, and so
the house is finally 'purified an' surified' when the evil books are
brought out to be destroyed—one about Voltaire and one called
'Ullisississies, or something'. This is a signal for the Cock—who
has a few more tricks left before he is driven out of the land—to
pirouette through the garden while everyone remains transfixed,
as if stuck to the ground. The garden goes dark again, there are
thunder-bolts and rifle-shots, and when the light returns Father
Domineer has been carried off by the Cock and everyone else is
stretched out.
   Now burlesque pandemonium has broken loose. Marthraun and
Mahon groan that they have been shot, and they dig cigar-shaped
bullets out of their breast-pockets. One-eyed Larry runs in,
clutching his trousers, to proclaim 'a miracle', for Father Domineer had been rescued from the Cock, carried home on the back
of a white duck. The Bellman runs in, clutching his trousers, to
warn everyone that the angry Cock has created a great wind with
his wings, because Father Domineer was saved by a speckled duck.
The Sergeant runs in, minus his trousers, to describe how the

powerful wind denuded him, and to announce that Father Domineer was saved by a barnacle goose. They get into a wild argument over what kind of a bird saved the priest, and suddenly a gale-like wind blows up and bounces them about the garden. At this point the limping and dishevelled Father Domineer returns to lead his trouser-clutching troops in a mock-assault on the wind, which now subsides with a sad wail. Nyadnanavery is victorious.

Meanwhile, young Loreleen, who has been denounced by Father Domineer as the personification of those evil spirits— 'Kissalass, Velvethighs, and Dancealong'—has been attacked by a mob of vigilantes. Sailor Mahon has tried to help her escape from the country; however, both of them were caught and beaten. Now Loreleen is dragged into the garden by the lynch-mob, her clothes torn and her face bleeding. Father Domineer condemns her to be driven out of the country—'*de cultus feminarum mulifico eradicum*'. Loreleen goes, but she tells the priest: 'When you condemn a fair face, you sneer at God's good handiwork. You are layin' your curse, sir, not upon a sin, but on a joy.' Lorna, Marion, and Robin Adair follow her into exile. When Robin tries to kiss Marion as they leave, she tells him: 'But not here, Robin Adair, oh, not here; for a whisper of love in this place bites away some of th' soul.' The Cock-a-doodle Dandy is silent now as his young allies go to seek love and freedom and joy in some other land.

At the end of the play Julia returns from Lourdes, alone and full of despair. All the Nyadnanaves who saw her off with their 'somersaultin' prayers' have forgotten her now, for they are too busy proclaiming their miraculous victory over the Cock and the women. But there was no miracle for Julia who has come back with a tale of pain from Lourdes—'the Coney Island of misery, agony, and woe'[177] as O'Casey described it in *Inishfallen Fare Thee Well*. When Marthraun, who suddenly realizes his women have left him to face a bitter and lonely life, asks the departing Robin Adair what he should do, Robin answers: 'Die.' The curtain falls as Robin goes away singing a gay love ballad.

This is not a very joyous conclusion for a play about joy because O'Casey is too uncompromising a satirist to succumb to rosy optimism. He refused to soften the point of his parable because he wanted to warn his audience that the free and joyous life cannot be won cheaply. His funniest play is also his bitterest play because he was partly in a Swiftian mood when he wrote it. In a general sense, it has the paradoxical spirit of *Gulliver's Travels*; it can delight young innocents and disturb as well as delight their elders; it contains the fantastic satire of the first three books of Swift's work, and the savage satire of Book IV. O'Casey's blistering attack on the Nyadnanaves has a parallel in Swift's fierce blast at the Yahoos; the magnificent Cock is an alternative to Nyadnanavery, as the noble Houyhnhnms are an alternative to Yahooism. Both writers are so uncompromising in their search for ideal values, so hard in their hatred of inhumanity, that they become bitter when man disappoints them. Perhaps they expect too much from all-too-fallible man. It is paradoxical that they are provoked to great hatred because they are motivated by great love, for there is a quality of compassionate heart-break in their rage for a better life.

In his well-known letter to Pope, Swift wrote: 'The chief end I purpose to myself in all my labours is to vex the world rather than to divert it.' It has been suggested that O'Casey's mood in his play was only in part Swiftian because his chief end was to vex *and* divert the world. And what a carnival of comic diversion there is in the *Cock*! It is more richly inspired than *Purple Dust* in its extravagant exploitation of farce and satire. It rings the changes on a variety of comic traditions in the drama, and strikes some new ones. The fantastic village of Nyadnanave, that Nest of Knaves and Quacks, was conceived with something of the irreverent mockery that led Aristophanes to ridicule Athenian mythology when in *The Birds* he created Nephelococcygia, that Cloud-Cuckoo Land which is literally and figuratively, for the birds. O'Casey's bedlam of hocus-pocus miracles and prat-falls follows the traditional antics of the music hall and circus theatre, the low comedy of Plautus and Shakespeare and Boucicault. Religious quacks like Shanaar and One-eyed Larry have their secular counterparts in Plautine and Jonsonian comedy. Irish buffoons like Marthraun, Mahon, the Sergeant, the Dellman, and the Porter, can be found in Boucicault, and they have their Anglo-Saxon counterparts in Shakespeare. In fact, all these traditionally comic devices and characters have been reshaped and recreated with the mark of O'Casey's originality: his theatrical instinct for uninhibited fun, his mock-heroic deflation of the pompous and the absurd.

Most original of all is the creation of that Wizard of Joy, the

Cock-a-doodle Dandy. He is drawn in the mock-epic tradition, and yet there is no creature quite like him among all the Chanticleers of the beast-fables. He has many ancestors, but he is a unique and original myth—a fabulous bird of freedom and joy. Chaucer's vainglorious Cock is the butt of the comedy, whereas O'Casey's dancing Cock has an Aesopian shrewdness and Dionysian spirit which make him the instrument of the comedy. He is a symbol and a scourge, a joyous bird and an avenging jester. And his mythic stature is enhanced by his votaries, those legendary figures out of the popular ballads, Robin Adair and maid Marion.

In contrast to the Cock, Father Domineer, as his name too clearly indicates, is too much of a straight 'villain' to be an entirely satisfactory symbol. The nonhuman Cock is credible as a mythic creature, but the inhuman priest is too obvious a sign-post to be completely convincing as a symbol or a man. It may fit the fable-genre to have the 'enemy' represented as a monster; however, O'Casey was also writing a drama. The devils in the early morality plays and the malcontents in Elizabethan drama were very funny fellows, and perhaps O'Casey could have made Father Domineer more of a comic villian. Shanaar and One-eyed Larry are excellent cases in point; they are satirized unmercifully, and they are no less dangerous for all their comic crawthumping. They are dangerous enough to help Father Domineer defeat the Cock.

After this final turn of the action, the defeat of the Cock by the Nyadnanaves, O'Casey brings us out of the comic realm of fable and back to the shock of reality. He breaks the spell of fantasy at the end in order to remind us that the Cock is after all a poetic myth, a state of mind. The revels are over and the force of the parable is now clear. The gay bird can ridicule Nyadnanavery, he can mock it with his miracles, but he cannot destroy it. He can only encourage us to go on fighting it.

And here it must be pointed out that the dangers of Nyadnanavery are not limited to Ireland. The vigilantes of fear and repression can be found everywhere in the modern world, and O'Casey stressed this universal aspect of his play when he commented on it:

The play is symbolical in more ways than one. The action manifests itself in Ireland, the mouths that speak are Irish mouths; but the spirit is to be found in action everywhere: the fight made by many to drive the joy of life from the hearts of men; the fight against this fight to vindicate the right of the joy of life to live courageously in the hearts of men. It isn't the clergy alone who boo and bluster against this joy of life in living, in dance, song, and story (many clerics, even Bishops, are fair, broad-minded, and help the arts; like the Catholic Bishop of Ferns and Leighlin, who is the worthy Patron of the Wexford Opera Festival); and who interfere in the free flow of thought from man to man . . . Political fellas, too, in the United States, in the Soviet Union, in England and, especially, in Ireland—everywhere in fact—political fellas run out and shout down any new effort made to give a more modern slant or a newer sign to any kind of artistic thought or imagination; menacing any unfamiliar thing appearing in picture, song, poem, or play. They are fools, but they are menacing fools, and should be fought anywhere they shake a fist, be they priest, peasant, prime minister or proletarian. [179]

So the enchanted Cock's dance of life is a comic ritual for all men who would be free. O'Casey's merry fantasy is a parable and an entertainment—a catharsis and a carnival.

3. BONFIRES AND DRUMS

From their reactions to O'Casey's two latest comedies, *The Bishop's Bonfire* (1955) and *The Drums of Father Ned* (1958), some Dubliners seemed intent on proving that Nyadnanavery is a force to be reckoned with in Ireland. The first play received its world première in Dublin, but the second one, though it had been accepted by the Tostal Council for the Dublin International Theatre Festival, was dropped when the Archbishop of Dublin refused to give it his blessing. Both plays provoked a storm of criticism and abuse, and O'Casey continued to be the occasion of controversy in his native country.

Even before Cyril Cusack's production of *The Bishop's Bonfire* opened at the Gaiety Theatre—there was no chance that the Abbey directors would do it, or that O'Casey would allow them to if they wished—the *Standard* launched a vigilante campaign against the playwright and his play. He was damned and his play was prejudged as dangerous. In front-page lead articles the paper printed photographed excerpts from his autobiography illustrating his 'false' and 'cynical' comments on the Roman Catholic

Church and Irish puritanism. The first article ended with a warning: 'Mr O'Casey's name is now in the public eye—his bishop's bonfire is shortly to be ignited. Is it inflammable material?'[180] At this time, two weeks before the play opened, the *Standard* itself was the most inflammable material in Dublin. A week later it became even more incendiary as it boasted: 'It is rather an understatement to write that the article on Sean O'Casey which appeared in last week's *Standard* aroused considerable interest. It goes without saying that people were shocked by the full realization of the bitter venom with which O'Casey regards the Faith and its ministers. . . . It was our intention to shock and in this we succeeded.'[181] But shock was not the paper's only aim, for it was clearly determined to prevent the production of the play if it could, or at the very least create a climate of hostility toward it. 'It is one of the contradictions of modern life,' the article concluded, 'that he should be offered a stage in the capital city of the country most steadfastly ranged against the enemies who are his friends . . . Where is the nation's self-respect?' Fortunately for the nation's self-respect, most of the other papers withheld comment until they had seen the play; but the *Standard*'s shock-treatment had had its effect on the ultra-religious and chauvinistic elements in the city.

There was an air of excitement and anxiety at the theatre on the opening night and extra forces of police were on hand to control the huge crowd, in the event there was a repetition of the famous Abbey riots. Hours before the curtain went up there were some 2,000 people jammed in South King Street and overflowing around the corner by Mercer's Hospital, but most of them were turned away since there were only 300 unbooked seats in the gallery. The London critics had come over to review the play and O'Casey's wife and daughter were present, but the seventy-five-year-old playwright remained at home in Devon, ill and unable to risk the strain of a long journey.

Except for some outbursts of booing and hissing during the performance and at the final curtain, there were no riots in the theatre. But a reviewers' riot broke out in the newspapers the following morning and during the rest of the week, for the play was unanimously attacked in the Irish press. The English critics, however, were of a different mind, as the *Irish Times* reported several days later: 'Much favourable criticism and some real enthusiasm have been evoked in the British press by Sean O'Casey's new play. . . . While the Irish reception ranged from cool to openly hostile, the strong corps of British drama critics seem to have found their journey to Dublin well worth while.'[182] This split-decision along national lines led to further skirmishes when some of the unhappy Irish critics sniped back at the English critics for enjoying the play and showing surprise at the hostile Irish reception.

No one insisted that it was a great play, but the Englishmen were able to respond to its uproarious humour and vitality, even though some of them pointed out weaknesses in the writing. Kenneth Tynan began his review in the *Sunday Observer* by chastising the Irish: 'Truly, the Irish never forgive those they have insulted. Back from long exile came Sean to Dublin, and his compatriots hissed his play at the curtain fall. At the first night of Mr O'Casey's *The Bishop's Bonfire* there were more stage Irishmen in the house than in the cast, and by the first interval venomous tongues were already lamenting the play's failure. Those who had uprooted the author now charged him with having forgotten his roots; those who had expelled him from the parish charged him with being too parochial.'[183] Mr Tynan went on to say that the play was written in a 'manic-depressive' mood: '. . . here were two plays, one ghastly, one gorgeous, in unhappy juxtaposition. The depressive (or serious) theme is youth's subservience to authority . . . What matters is the maniac half of the play. Here dealing with the wild inconsequent rustics who are redecorating Ballyoonagh for one of the bishop's impending visits, Mr O'Casey hits his full stride, as the old mocker and fantastic ironist, ever happier with tongue in cheek than with hand on heart. Broad comedy of protest was always the best Irish vein, and Mr O'Casey strikes it rich. ...'

But the Irish critics were not amused. Their reactions ranged from the report in the *Evening Press*: 'The general effect is boring . . . A sad evening in the theatre, if ever there was one!'[184] to the comment in the *Standard*: 'Cock-a-snoot anti-clericalism . . . This is not art, this is not drama. This is but crude vulgar abuse which will ring as harshly in the ears of decent Protestants as in those of conscientious Catholics.'[185] In a special dispatch to the *Christian Science Monitor*, London's Harold Hobson called it a 'clumsy play' with 'flashes' of the old O'Casey genius, but he too had something to say about the Irish reception: 'The protests of much of the audience and of influential parts of Irish opinion were not aesthetic, but political and religious. Mr O'Casey is a rebel socially and philosophically; he is essentially a Protestant in the sense that he protests; and he protests with passion, with eloquence, with perversity, and with fire. This does not go down well in Ireland, where orthodoxy is more highly regarded than it is, for example, in England or France . . . If the Irish saw their clergymen portrayed on the stage as curates are shown in English farces, I really believe they would burn the theatre down.' [186]

There were some further hissing and booing incidents during the run of the play, but there were no attempts to make a bonfire of the theatre. On the whole, the Dublin audiences were apparently not as hostile as the Dublin critics for they packed the Gaiety for five weeks, when the play had to close in the midst of a successful run to make way for the previously committed Dublin Opera Company. One night a group of dissenters jumped up in the gallery and started to protest when O'Casey's young priest advises a frustrated girl to abandon her vows of chastity; but a little old lady in the back of the gallery shouted at them—they were obviously outraged Catholics—in a clear voice that rang through the theatre: 'Get out ye bloody Protestants!' She might have been a character in the play and the audience roared with laughter.

Now for the play itself. Kenneth Tynan's 'manic-depressive' gambit is a bit too glib, yet there is some point to his suggestion that O'Casey had actually written two plays. In all his works he uses multiple plots in a loosely unified form, mingling comic and tragic themes, farcical and melodramatic incidents, and playing them against each other in ironic counterpoint. He had reconciled these discordant qualities in plays like *Juno and the Paycock* and *The Plough and the Stars* by creating characters who were capable of responding to both comic and tragic experiences. He maintained this technique with some of the characters in the later plays, with Harry Heegan, for example, in *The Silver Tassie*, but mostly, in moralities like *Within the Gates* and *Red Roses For Me*, and comedies like *Purple Dust* and *Cock-a-doodle Dandy*, he treated his characters as 'humorous' types—comic heroes and fools, satiric villains and knaves—using the catalytic agencies of symbol, myth, and fantasy to achieve a unified form. The point about *The Bishop's Bonfire*, then, is not that he used two plots, one farcical and the other melodramatic, as he had done so often in the past, but that this time he did not entirely succeed in reconciling them. Perhaps one of the difficulties is that there is no symbolic or mythic equivilent of the 'cock ex machina' in this play, even though the spirit of the Cock is often present. That spirit of joyous fun propels the main plot and gives the play its enormous vitality and humour; however, the depressing tone of the secondary plot, treated as it is as grim melodrama without the saving grace of satire, leads to the weakest part of the play, the pseudo-tragic conclusion.

Like all of the comedies, the main action of the play is built around a festive occasion. It is the eve of Bishop Bill Mullarky's visit to his native village of Ballyoonagh. Feverish preparations are being made in the home of the tall-hatted Councillor Reiligan, the richest man in town—politician, gombeen man, and pillar of the church—who has just been made a Papal Count in honour of the event. The whole house is being redecorated for the Bishop by a group of bumbling workmen who practically sabotage the affair. They drink and argue, sing and dance, and generally keep the house in a state of hilarious confusion. There is the Prodical, an intemperate Protestant who prefers brawling and drinking to work. His chief sparring-partner is Rankin, a pious Catholic who is an equally rambunctious fellow. Codger Sleehaun is an eighty-four-year-old poacher and all-round handyman who, somewhat like Brennan o' the Moor in *Red Roses For Me*, is a merry old bird full of wise advice and songs for all occasions. Daniel Clooncoohy is a nervous young workman with a quick temper that hides an inferiority complex, and Hughie Higgins is a drunken Railway Porter with a penchant for making long and not entirely coherent speeches. The Bishop himself does not appear in the play, and all these men mock his expected arrival with their house-wrecking antics. Their festival of fun effectively satirizes the official occasion, which is intended to be formal rite, touched off by a huge bonfire of 'evil' literature.

The theme of the play arises out of the conflict between these two ways of celebrating—the official celebration sponsored by the Church and State, and the unofficial celebration improvised by the village clowns. It is another variation of the theme that appears in all the later plays—repression and pietism versus freedom and joy. In the main plot these forces clash with an explosion of comic pandemonium; in the secondary plot they grind against each other with bitter attrition.

The secondary plot deals with Councillor Reiligan's two young daughters and the men they love. Both daughters are frustrated by their father's fanatical, and profitable, pietism. Keelin is forced to give up the lower-class Daniel, who himself fears he is unworthy to marry a Papal Count's daughter, when a match is arranged for her with a wealthy old farmer who happens to be the Bishop's brother. Fooraun has taken vows of perpetual chastity in spite of the fact that she loves Manus Moanroe, who abandoned his study of the priesthood because he loved her. The sympathetic young curate, Father Boheroe, tries to help both couples. O'Casey's priests are either Domineers or Boheroes, black or white types with no subtle shades of grey. And so Father Boheroe is a flat chorus-character. He often expresses the theme of the play, as, for example, when he declares that 'merriment may be a way of worship'. He warns Keelin and Daniel—and Ireland—to beware of 'the terrible beauty' when he says: 'You've escaped from the dominion of the big house with the lion and unicorn on its front; don't let yourselves sink beneath the meaner dominion of the big shop with the cross and shamrock on its gable.' He urges Fooraun to abandon her vows and marry Manus: 'When we have problems, Fooraun, ourselves are the saints to solve them.' But Bollyoonagh's version of Nyadnanavery eventually defeats them all and banishes merriment. Reiligan and the Canon are determined to purify the town for the Bishop.

Thus it can be seen that the two plots are certainly interrelated. The trouble arises, however, at the end of the play when O'Casey moves away from the main plot and decides to resolve his theme through the secondary plot in a sudden burst of melodramatic fury. The bitterly disillusioned Manus breaks into the house and steals the church funds, and when Fooraun tries to stop him he shoots her. Then, in an operatic death scene, while she moans, 'You ruffian! Oh, Manus, darling, I think I'm dying', she takes the gun, writes a suicide note absolving him, and dies. One of the London critics suggested that there is a 'Chekhovian atmosphere of humorous sadness' in the play. How that improbable ending cries out for a Chekhovian touch, with Manus shooting and missing! Or an O'Casey touch of inspired fantasy such as he used at the conclusion of *Purple Dust*. The young lovers in

Cock-a-doodle Dandy were defeated, but they went off into exile on their own terms.

It is only the comic characters in *The Bishop's Bonfire* who are able to live on their own inimitable terms. They redeem the play in spite of the unconvincing conclusion. Their humour is their method of survival, and they keep it active by consuming generous quantities of gin. O'Casey once said that laughter 'is the hilarious declaration made by man that life is worth living', [187] and the laugh-provokers in the play offer abundant proof of this. The Prodical, who is always making and breaking vows of temperance, does not need to be encouraged to break his latest vow when the Codger arrives gloriously drunk and carrying a keg of gin. When Rankin warns him of his vow, the Prodical works himself into a hilarious declaration of independence:

RANKIN. You said a short time ago that it was goin' to be never again with you.

PRODICAL (*protestingly*). I'm not to blame for you overhearin' silent things. What I murmured was sotto vossie. I'm not a factotum to me own whisperin's into me own ear.

RANKIN. It wasn't said sotto vossie. It was outspoken, an' next door to a vow.

PRODICAL (*indignantly*). It was no vow! It had no habiliments of any vow on it. It was a *sub rosa* understandin' or misunderstandin' with meself.

RANKIN (*plaintively to Prodical*). Your good angel's trying to pull you back, Prodical; but if you once get to the keg, you're cornered! It's an occasion of sin, an' may do immortal harm to your poor soul!

PRODICAL (*coming over to Rankin and thrusting his face upwards towards Rankin—indignantly*). Looka, me good angel, I won't have you hoverin' over me soul like a saygull over a fish too deep for a dive down! I'm not goin' to let foreign bodies write down messages on me soul the way a body writes down things on a Christmas card. (*Preparing to jump from the scaffold.*) Me soul's me own particular compendium. Me soul's me own spiritual property, complete an' entire, verbatim in all its concernment.

Independent clowns like the Prodical with their unique souls are not likely to be intimidated or restrained by witch-hunting politicians and priests. It is no surprise, therefore, that these rude mechanicals continually frustrate the plans of Reiligan and the Canon. They launch monumental arguments about souls and bricks, saints and soldiers, and who should pluck the plovers and the fifty ducks; they get drunk on the Codger's keg of gin and spill a bag of cement over a new carpet; they throw potted palms around the house and wreck the furniture; they carry on a mock-battle with the statue of St Tremolo, the Bishop's patron saint. The statue represents a martyred Roman Legionary, famous for the miraculous powers of his horn or *buccina*, and the men call him 'the buckineeno boyo'. The drunken Porter, who accompanies his disconnected remarks with a rocking step-dance, gives a mad account of his battle with the statue; he has the job of delivering it, and every time he touches it, it gives out strange trumpet blasts. The other men hear the blasts whenever they make 'blasphemous' comments, and when they hide a whiskey bottle under the statue.

When the Codger complains that the country is over-populated with images of saints, Reiligan's son Michael, a Lieutenant in the Irish Army, insists that they need soldiers not saints to protect themselves from the Russians. And this touches off one of the wildest scenes in the play as they all argue about the Lieutenant's fantastic jeep-plan for the defence of Ireland, elaborated with dead-pan logic.[188]. Here is O'Casey striking it rich with superb comic invention:

LIEUTENANT. You see, men, Ireland's so important, geographically, that, in a war, the Russians would need to take her over within an hour, within an hour. Does that ring a bell?

DANIEL (*convinced*). Yis; a whole peal of them. But then, wha'?

LIEUTENANT. Well, man, we'd have to get help at once.

PRODICAL. Then what about England?

LIEUTENANT. England! Why, man alive, she'd be fightin' for her life, an' couldn't let us have even a policeman from point-duty! I'm an Army Officer; I know these things.

DANIEL (*wisely—to Prodical*). You see, Prodical? He's an Army Officer —he knows. (*To Lieutenant.*) Well, then, wha', Mick?

LIEUTENANT. America's our only man, Dan, for what we need is swarms an' swarms of jeeps.

CODGER (*incredulous*). Jeeps?

LIEUTENANT. Yes, jeeps; each with a driver, a spare driver, a commander, an' a wireless operator. Every able-bodied man in Ireland in a jeep here an' a jeep there, with a sten-gun, a hammer an' pliers, head-phone, an' a jeepsie walkie-talkie—that's the one solution, Dan.

CODGER (*testily*). An' what would the ordinary cars an' pedestrians do, an' the roads buzzin' with jeeps? There wouldn't be a man, woman, child, or chicken left alive in the country!

DANIEL (*rapping the table*). Order, order, Codger; order!

LIEUTENANT (*hotly—to the Codger*). An' even if they were all done in aself, wouldn't death on our own roads be better than exportation be the Bolsheviks to an unknown destination?

CODGER. What exportation are you walkie-talkiein' about?

DANIEL. Don't talk like an eejut, Codger.

LIEUTENANT (*hotly*). Looka, a nation like Russia that did so much to her own people wouldn't cast a thought about eliminatin' a few thousand Irishmen an' Irishwomen, or wait to think twice about exportin' the rest of us.

CODGER (*fiercely*). An' where would the Bolsheviks find the ships an' trains to export four million of us? Siberia's a long way off, if you ask me!

LIEUTENANT (*to the Codger*). Looka, man, the Bolsheviks wouldn't be dreamin' of Siberia, an' the Isle of Man only a few feet away from our own green border.

DANIEL (*to Codger*). Aha, that's bet you! You see, now, Codger, don't you?

CODGER (*vehemently*). No, I don't see now! If Russia be anything like what the clergy make it out to be, any Russians flutterin' down from the Irish skies on to our emerald sod will be poor divils seekin' an asylum.

PRODICAL. An asylum? It's a lunatic asylum you must be meanin'?

CODGER (*rattily*). No, no, man; an ordinary asylum, an ordinary asylum!

PRODICAL. There's no ordinary asylum. When anyone says, We've taken a certain party to the asylum, we mean a lunatic asylum, don't we?

CODGER. Yes, yes; but——

PRODICAL. There's no but about it. An asylum's an asylum—there's no but about it.

CODGER (*raising his voice*). I'm tellin' you, there's different asylums; for instance, a deaf an' dumb asylum!

PRODICAL (*raising his voice higher than the Codger*). The paratroopers droppin' from our skies won't be deaf an' dumb, will they?

DANIEL (*louder than the other two*). Order, order—let Mick speak!

LIEUTENANT (*resignedly*). Aw, let the eejuts talk, Dan.

PRODICAL (*angrily—to the Lieutenant*). Eejut yourself! Wantin' to flood the country with jeeps! Will you tell us who's goin' to provide the hundreds of thousands of jeeps to gallopin' round, an' lay out every man-jack an' every woman-lizzie of us, dead as mackerel on the roads of Eireann, bar the boyos who have the good fortune to be sittin' in them?

CODGER (*fiercely—to Lieutenant*). An' if we put into every one of them a driver, a spare driver, a commander, and a wireless operator with his walkie-talkie, addin' all them laid out flat an' dead on the roads, will you tell us who's goin' to look after the common things that have to be done to keep the country goin'?

PRODICAL (*to Lieutenant*). Aha, you're silent now. That's bet you!

LIEUTENANT (*in a rage as he goes swift from the room, banging the door after him*). Aw, go to hell, you pair of eejuts!

CODGER. You see, he turns to abuse when he's bet. Couldn't face up to unconfutable arguments.

PRODICAL. Him an' his jeeps! Another thing—while America might be droppin' the jeeps, what's to prevent the Bolshies at the same time from droppin' their paratroops an' fillin' the jeeps as they touch down, to let them go scamperin' all over the roads?

CODGER (*emphatically*). Nothin'. An', maybe, takin' over the Turf Board, the Tourist Association, the Hospitals Sweep, the Catholics Young Men's Society, the Protestant pulpits, an' the President's residence; endin', maybe, with the plantin' of a Red Flag in the hand of Saint Patrick's Statue standin' helpless on a windy hill in the centre of the lonely Plains of Meath!

DANIEL. Don't be actin' the eejut, Codger!

CODGER (*angrily*). Who's actin' the eejut?

DANIEL (*as angrily*). You are, the way you're talkin'!

CODGER (*close up to him*). Eejut yourself!

DANIEL (*placing a hand to Codger's chest, and shoving him backwards*). Aw, go away!

CODGER (*rushing back, putting a hand to Daniel's chest, and shoving him backwards*). You go away!

DANIEL (*swiftly returning, and giving the Codger a fiercer shove backwards*). You go away!

PRODICAL (*remonstrating*). Gentlemen, easy! Can't yous see yous are turnin' your own opinions into *ipso factos*?

In the midst of such inspired buffoonery, all the preparations for the Bishop's visit are forgotten and undermined. God help the man who would try to control the blathering 'eejuts' of Bally-oonagh. When Reiligan finds them all arguing, their work abandoned and the house half destroyed, he gives an order: 'From this out, there's to be no talkin'; and if anyone does talk, everybody is to listen to nobody.' And this is precisely what happens—they all go on talking, everybody listening to nobody, and all orders and opinions are turned into *ipso factos*. O'Casey ridicules repression and pietism most successfully when he creates this mad world of merriment, a festival of glorious fools.

The Dubliners who were not amused by this merriment had a chance to strike back at O'Casey three years later when his newest play, *The Drums of Father Ned*, was scheduled to receive its world première at the Dublin International Theatre Festival. This Theatre Festival, which was part of the annual Tostal, or Spring celebration, had been inaugurated the previous year in 1957, and its director, Brendan Smith, had planned an ambitious programme for 1958. The works of three outstanding Irish writers were to be performed: O'Casey's new play; a version of Joyce's *Ulysses*, called *Bloomsday*, dramatized by an Ulster playwright, Alan McClelland; and three mime plays by Samuel Beckett, plus a reading of his radio drama, *All That Fall*. As it turned out, however, none of these plays were produced, the Theatre Festival was postponed and eventually abandoned for that year. The controversy that led to this fiasco is worth examining because it illustrates some of the very aspects of Irish life which O'Casey had been describing in his plays and autobiography.

The first sign of trouble appeared early in January 1958 when the newspapers announced the Archbishop's disapproval of the O'Casey and Joyce works. He refused to open the Tostal with the celebration of the Mass, as he had regularly done in the past, if works by these two writers were to be performed. On 10 January the *Irish Times* reported: 'For the past week, there has been some doubt whether these two plays would be part of the festival programme. Last week the Council became aware that the Most Rev Dr McQuaid, Archbishop of Dublin, did not approve of their inclusion in the programme. As a result of their inclusion, this year's Tostal will not be marked by an official opening Mass.'[189] The Archbishop had rejected the suggestion by some of the Council members that he perform a special Votive Mass, and he also withdrew the customary Low Mass. The Tostal Council took note of the Archbishop's action, but at this stage they decided to go ahead with the plays as planned. Nevertheless, strong opposition to the programme had arisen following the Archbishop's pronouncement. On 12 January the *New York Times* printed a special dispatch from Dublin, in which it was stated that 'there have been rumblings among strongly militant Catholic societies in Dublin that indicate trouble. Some of these threatened today to boycott the festival if the Tostal Council proceeded with the production of what they term "plays of doubtful morality".' And the dispatch continued: 'It was reported today that some members of the Dublin Corporation may vote against spending on street decorations for the Tostal unless the O'Casey and Joyce plays are expunged from the programme.'

During the following month it became apparent that the Tostal Council was weakening under heavy pressure and was coming round to the realization that it would be hazardous to go against the Archbishop's wishes. On 12 February the break came when the *Irish Times* reported a series of charges and counter-charges: O'Casey announced that he was withdrawing his play; the Council simultaneously announced that it was dropping the play. Although the man who was to produce the play for the Globe Theatre Company had recently come back from a visit to O'Casey in Devon, and both had been in agreement about the production, the Council now claimed that O'Casey had refused to allow 'certain structural alterations' to be made in Dublin: 'A spokesman for the Council said yesterday—"The Dublin Tostal Council, through its festival director (Mr Brendan Smith), rejected this play because it was not allowed to make structural alterations to make it suitable for the Dublin public."' There was no indication of what these alterations were—though one might venture a guess from that phrase, 'suitable for the Dublin public'—and it was not surprising that O'Casey was in no mood to let anyone rewrite his play for him so that it would be acceptable to the Dublin public, and presumably the Archbishop.

In that same issue of the *Irish Times*, in the column adjoining the report that the play had been dropped, there was another prominent news story which shed some significant light on the whole issue. The headlines read: 'Unions To Protest At Tostal Plays.

Archbishop's Letter Read to Dublin Unions.'[190] This news story may help to explain why the harassed Tostal Council suddenly changed its mind and decided that the play was unsuitable:

A letter was read at a meeting of the Dublin Council of Irish Unions last night on behalf of the Most Rev Dr McQuaid, Archbishop of Dublin, giving his reasons for withdrawing permission for any religious ceremony to inaugurate the Dublin Tostal this year.

The Council decided to send a strong protest to the Dublin Tostal Council against the production at the Tostal Drama Festival of plays of an objectionable nature.

Mr John Dunne, secretary of the Dublin C.I.U. Council, said that as a result of a discussion at the previous meeting of the Council, he had sent the following letter to Mr T. A. Boyle, secretary of the Dublin Tostal Council. This read:

'I am directed to write and ask if it is the intention of An Tostal Council to have staged, as part of the festival programme, plays of an objectionable nature, as reported in Irish and English newspapers.'

Mr Dunne said that he had received a reply from Mr Boyle which stated: 'I am directed to inform you that the Dublin Tostal Council will not produce plays the contents of which may be of an offensive nature. All matters concerning productions for the 1958 festival are under strict examination.'

He had also got in touch with Dr McQuaid, and had received the following letter:

'I am asked by his Grace the Archbishop to acknowledge the receipt of your letter of January 15th, and to state in answer to your query the following facts:

'The secretary of the Dublin Tostal Council requested permission for a Solemn Votive Mass to inaugurate the Tostal. His Grace gave permission to approach the Very Rev Administrator of the Pro-Cathedral to have celebrated a Low Mass, as on previous occasions. Then, having learned from the Dublin Tostal Council that it had sanctioned the production in Dublin of a dramatization of Joyce's "Ulysses" and a play by Sean O'Casey, his Grace withdrew permission for any religious ceremony, more especially for the celebration of the Holy Sacrifice of the Mass in connection with the Dublin Tostal of 1958.'

Mr F. Quinn said a strong protest should be sent to the Tostal Council against the production of immoral and objectionable plays. The Council and the unions should boycott the Tostal. Mr John O'Brien also favoured a boycott, unless the plays were withdrawn. Mr P. O'Keeffe said the Tostal gave employment, and they should not interfere with anything that did so. As representatives of working men, the Council should think of the workers.

Mr J. Lynam said that if the clergy took objection to the production of these plays, they would be quite safe in stepping behind the clergy. If they disregarded the advice of the clergy, they were lost.

When a delegate suggested that a copy of the protest should also be sent to the Minister for Justice, Mr Frank Robbins, chairman, said that there was no censorship of plays in this country, and no law to ban their production. If a play was obscene, the Minister for Justice could then step in.

The delegate—There is a moral law.

Mr Robbins—Yes, there is a moral censorship, and that is what we are acting on.

The chairman said that the matter could be met by a strong letter of protest.

Mr Quinn said that he was willing to withdraw his boycott suggestion.

While it is true, as the chairman pointed out, that there is no 'official' censorship of plays in Ireland (the Government Censorship Board can ban any form of printed literature, but it has no jurisdiction over the theatre), the Council of Irish Unions and the Archbishop, in his indirect way, were successfully illustrating the methods and the power of the 'unofficial' censorship. The Tostal Council could do no less than uphold what the Union Council had called the 'moral law' against 'the production of immoral and objectionable plays', even though these highly questionable charges were aimed at two plays which no one on the Union Council had read. It was enough that the Archbishop, who hadn't read the plays either, had announced his disapproval; for as one of the delegates had put it, 'they would be quite safe in stepping behind the clergy. If they disregarded the advice of the clergy, they were lost'.

On the following day, 13 February, there was a further comment in the press from O'Casey: 'Through his wife, he told an *Irish Times* reporter in London yesterday that the Council had not asked him to make alterations to his play, but had suggested that the alterations be made in Dublin . . . The Council definitely

wanted to make the alterations itself . . . nowhere in the correspondence between him and the Council was it stated what was objected to in his play. Mrs O'Casey described the play as "a harmless comedy", and "good-natured". When asked if it was more
harmless than *The Bishop's Bonfire*, she said, "Oh, yes—that was a
different kind of a play altogether".'

Three days later, on 15 February, the thoroughly terrorized
Tostal Council surrendered again and decided to drop the play of
Ulysses. In its statement to the Press the Council made a special
point of the fact that it was acting under the pressure of 'public
controversy', since it insisted that it had itself found nothing
'offensive' in the Joyce work, and nothing 'unsuitable' in the
O'Casey work. The *Irish Times* report added a significant comment on the combined role that the Church and the State had
played in the collapse of the Festival: 'It was learned that the suggestion to drop the play had come from Bord Failte [the Government Tourist Board] which subsidises the Festival. The board, it
is understood, felt that recent "adverse publicity" which had followed the expression of the Most Rev Dr McQuaid, Archbishop of
Dublin, made the production of *Bloomsday* inadvisable.' The
Archbishop's disapproval had initiated the 'adverse publicity' and
the De Valera Government, in charge of the purse strings, had expediently decided to pull the strings and end it all.

This report was accompanied by a number of statements from
the aggrieved parties. O'Casey explained that he had originally
been invited to offer his play to the Festival, although he had told
the director it would probably be better to put on plays by young
new dramatists. But when the director read the play he immediately accepted it. About his play, O'Casey said: 'It is just fun
from beginning to end. But it is my own play, and I can't think the
suggestion that it should be reconstructed in Dublin was made
seriously. I am sure it was made to give them the excuse not to put
it on . . . It is quite evident that the Archbishop's objections have
been accepted and acted upon by the Tostal Council. His objections were against the authors, not the plays.' Alan McClelland
said: 'No matter what play they do, there will be no end to it.
They have taken away all their authority and made it into a
parochial tea-party. One thing I am certain is that the Archbishop
has not read the script. I know that, because I had the play vetted
by an authority on moral dogma and I was advised on any blas-

phemous passages, which I naturally agreed to cut . . . my play is a merry play. It is a comedy of life filled with sparkling language, all Joyce's.' Several days later Samuel Beckett announced in Paris that he was withdrawing his plays from the Festival as a protest against the Council's decision to drop O'Casey and Joyce from the programme.

One of the more candid comments by a Dubliner was made by Hilton Edwards, the famous actor-producer of the Gate Theatre, who was to have directed *Bloomsday*: 'What this really means is that there is, as there always has been, a rigid censorship of plays and everything else. It is working in different ways, and putting pressure on things. All right—I am no rebel. If the people of this city think the play is not for them I'm not upset . . . I think it is a very exciting work for the theatre . . . the Festival will end up in the kind of silly joke for the rest of the world that most things have happened here [*sic*]. Everyone will feel very smug and very pure here, and they will be wrong as usual.'

'Final Curtain?' This question introduced the following remarks in an *Irish Times* editorial on 15 February: 'Last year's Theatre Festival, an innovation which brought An Tostal for the first time into international recognition, ended ignominiously with the effective suppression by the police of *The Rose Tattoo*, a play that enjoyed the Tostal Council's backing. For the forthcoming Festival, the two "highlights" were to have been presentations of a new play by Mr Sean O'Casey, the most distinguished of living Irish playwrights, and a dramatic adaptation from James Joyce's *Ulysses*. No evidence has been adduced that either of these productions contains a hint of obscenity or blasphemy; yet pressure has been brought to bear against both of them from high places, and the Council has kissed the rod.'

Before the curtain is drawn on this melancholy farce, which might well be called The Archbishop's Bonfire, or The Kissing of the Rod, something must be said about *The Rose Tattoo* Case, which could be considered the melodramatic sub-plot. Throughout the time that the O'Casey and Joyce works were being attacked as 'immoral and objectionable', the director of the Dublin Pike Theatre, Alan Simpson, who had produced Tennessee Williams' *The Rose Tattoo* at the Tostal of the previous year, was still in the courts defending himself against the charge that he had put on an 'indecent and profane' play.

Simpson was arrested on 23 May 1957 at the Pike, an old Georgian coach-house which had been converted into a small club theatre. Several days earlier he had received an unexpected warning from the police that he was breaking the law and would be liable to arrest if he did not drop the play; but since there had been no specification of what law was involved or why the performance was illegal, he refused to obey the vague order and kept the play on. After a night in the Bridewell gaol he was charged in the Dublin District Court with having 'produced for gain an indecent and profane performance'. This charge was made in spite of the fact that the play had been approved and subsidised by the Tostal Council as part of the government sponsored International Theatre Festival. The production had received high praise in all the newspapers, and the published play, which had not been banned by the Censorship Board, was on sale in all the Dublin bookshops. Nevertheless, the prosecution claimed that the production was in violation of the 'Common Law'. The defence counsel stated that a letter had been sent to the Police Commissioner before the arrest asking him to explain how the law had been infringed and what parts of the play were objectionable, but the Commissioner's reply was very laconic and merely indicated 'that the matter was being dealt with by the proper authorities'. [191] The prosecution then 'explained' that presiding Justice O'Flynn had been given a copy of the play which 'is generally, lewd, indecent, offensive, and tends to corrupt the mind and destroy the love of decency, morality, and good order'. Over the protests of the prosecution, Simpson was released on £100 bail.

It should be pointed out that since the founding of the Pike Theatre in 1953, Alan Simpson, with his wife and co-director, Carolyn Swift, had built an impressive reputation. Some of his successes included the Irish première of Samuel Beckett's *Waiting for Godot*; the world première of Brendan Behan's *The Quare Fellow*; the bi-annual *Pike Follies*, an intimate review written by Carolyn Swift; Tennessee Williams' *Summer and Smoke*; and now the European English language première of *The Rose Tattoo*. By 1957 the Pike had become an established and notable 'off-Broadway' theatre which made an important contribution to the cultural life of the city. The arrest of Simpson had therefore come as a shock. A group of Dublin actors immediately launched a defence fund, and a similar action was taken in England when the magazine *Encore* announced that it was setting up 'The Rose Tattoo Fighting Fund', sponsored by the following people: Sean O'Casey, Peter Hall, John Osborne, John Gielgud, Benn W. Levy, Wolf Mankowitz, George Devine, Harold Hobson.

As the court proceedings developed, it turned out that the police has based their case on the test for obscenity laid down by Chief Justice Cockburn in 1868. Justice Cockburn's ruling applied only to publications 'which tended to deprave and corrupt those whose minds were open to such immoral influences, and into whose hands the publications might fall'. [192] But the prosecution argued that this ruling 'still held good for a performance or exhibition such as this particular play was alleged to have been . . . that this play largely concerned itself with the portrayal of sex, that its words, theme and actions, and, generally, the over-all picture, was a portrayal of sex in a lustful, suggestive way. In that portrayal and performance, a breach of the law had been committed. . . .'

In his glowing review of the play in the *Sunday Times*, Harold Hobson made an allusion to a contraceptive that falls from the pocket of one of the actors—'(unless I am mistaken) something not mentionable in Ireland'. [193] It had therefore been expected that the prosecution would use this 'unmentionable' matter as part of its case—the actor had actually used a piece of white paper, thus avoiding the Irish law against contraceptives. However, the detectives who had watched the play incognito for three nights before making their arrest had somehow managed to miss the episode each night. Perhaps they were too busy making copious notes, or looking for something of a blatantly erotic nature. In their testimony they stated that they had read the play and knew the stage directions indicated the dropping of 'a white disc', but since they had not seen it, it did not become an issue, at least, not an overt issue.

During cross-examination when the defence counsel asked the detectives what their instructions had been, the witnesses claimed special police 'privilege' and refused to divulge any information. The defence was thus blocked in its attempt to discover if any persons or organizations were behind the case, who had prompted the police to act and under what instructions. To prove the legality of its position of silence, the prosecution asked the District Court

Justice to seek a ruling on the point of 'privilege' from the High
Court, and the request was granted.

In December 1957 the High Court upheld the prosecution's
stand on police 'privilege'. Simpson had lost a crucial point, and
at this stage he was faced with the prospect of defeat, imprisonment and certain bankruptcy. The possibility of such an outcome
must have occurred to many people in 'high places', and at this
time it must have been considered extremely dangerous for anyone
to plan the production of a play that might be interpreted, or mis-
interpreted, as 'indecent and profane'. It is not altogether unlikely
that some of the more nervous members of the Tostal Council,
realizing only too well that they had sanctioned and subsidized this
play which now had Alan Simpson in such serious trouble, had
reason to doubt their choice of plays for the new Theatre Festival.
Even in normal times, the works of O'Casey and Joyce were suspect in many influential quarters of Dublin. There were any number of militant defenders of decency and morality, lay as well as
clerical, in high and low places, who would have no doubts about
whether the government sponsored Tostal should honour the works
of those two 'controversial' exiles. The notorious *Rose Tattoo* case
had already been in the headlines for seven months, and now the
High Court had ruled against Simpson. Perhaps it was more than
a coincidence that the open attacks on O'Casey and Joyce began
a month later.

Thereafter the headlines were dominated by the new uproar
over the 1958 Theatre Festival, and the Simpson sub-plot dragged
on less spectacularly in the courts for six more months. Simpson
appealed the High Court's decision before the Supreme Court; the
Supreme Court refused to give a ruling and sent the case back to
the District Court, where it was finally settled on 9 June 1958.
Justice Cathal O'Flynn, accustomed to handling the traffic viola-
tions and minor offences that normally make up the business of a
District Court, rose to the occasion. He questioned the police
claim of 'privilege' in such a case; he found that the prosecution
had not introduced evidence sufficient for an indictment. He
praised the police for their great devotion to duty, but he felt that
they had over-reached their authority this time: 'I can only infer
that, by arresting the accused, the object would be achieved of
closing down the play. But surely if that was the object nothing
could be more devastating than through restraint of production

before even a hearing is held. It smacks to me of the frontier principle, "Shoot first and talk after".'[194] He therefore acquitted the defendant.

This was an important victory for Simpson himself and for the freedom of the theatre, and yet it came as something of an anticlimax. For thirteen months he had been the victim of 'the frontier principle'—he had been assumed guilty and had gone through the fight of his life in order to prove his innocence. His belated victory therefore had its pyrrhic aspects: there had been no award of costs and he found he had amassed legal debts of £2,600; furthermore, he found that he could not wipe out the stigma of 'obscenity' that had been associated with his theatre. The Pike was a Theatre Club which depended largely upon the support of its signed members: after *The Rose Tattoo* case the membership had fallen from 2,000 to 300. In the spring of 1959, Simpson announced that he intended to put the play on again to prove to the wary Dubliners that it was not obscene. He planned to produce it in a larger theatre than the Pike, in the hope of clearing up some of his legal debts, but he was refused every theatre in the city.

As a result of this case, the Pike Theatre was forced to close. It is obvious that Simpson had unknowingly offended some persons in 'high places' by producing *The Rose Tattoo*. But who? It is unlikely that the police would have acted on their own without some complaint or 'tip'; however, it has never been discovered who was behind the case.

Epilogue: the Banned Turn Banners. In July, a month after the case was thrown out of court, O'Casey issued a final pronouncement. He had decided to ban all performances of his plays in Ireland until further notice, on the stage and on Radio Eireann. Then Samuel Beckett placed a similar ban on all his plays. The writers were fighting the enemy with his own weapons. Perhaps the whole sordid business of the two ill-fated Theatre Festivals could be summed up with a comment by Sean O'Faolain—some of whose books have been banned by the Censorship Board—which he made in 1953 in discussing the pressures that conspire against the writer in Ireland: 'I think my reader will have begun to realize the difficulties of writing in a country where the policeman and the priest are in a perpetual glow of satisfaction.'[195]

O'Casey continued to reveal some of these difficulties in *The*

Drums of Father Ned, but on the whole he had written a play of good-natured satire and merriment. It is as he accurately described it, 'just fun from beginning to end'—a comedy which, coincidentally, deals with the preparations for a Tostal celebration in the Irish village of Doonavale. Again his main techniques are farce and fantasy, and his theme is freedom and joy. But there is nothing sinister in this play. The old scourger is still up to his favourite game of satirizing the ridiculous apes; however, there are no 'villains' this time, and all the buffoons are more humorous than dangerous.

The play opens ingeniously with a fantastic 'Prerumble', a flashback set in the 1920's during 'the trouble'. It is a rowdy prologue in which some Black and Tans tease two stubborn Irishmen, Binnington and McGilligan, who hate each other more than they hate the British. They grew up together, went to the same schools, and courted sisters, yet they do not speak to each other for they are now both die-hards, Binnington a Free Stater and McGilligan a Republican. The soldiers force them to speak and trot up and down together, firing shots over their heads whenever they refuse to obey orders. And when the two men get into inevitable arguments, speaking to each other indirectly through the soldiers, a strange Echo repeats and mocks their words. 'When the wind is right the high hills around the town give an echo', and it usually adds ironic emphasis to the speeches at the end of scenes.

The satiric high-jinks of the prerumble set the burlesque tone of the play, and after the final Echo, the scene shifts back to the present where the Tostaleers of Doonavale are in the midst of their feverish preparations for the festival. Binnington is the Mayor and owns the General Store, McGilligan is the Deputy Mayor and a building contractor; and although they make business deals together they haven't spoken since the Civil War. Their wives are bourgeois gorgons who snub each other and affect the grand manner, but their children, Michael Binnington and Nora McGilligan, are in love and represent the only hope for Doonavale— and Ireland. Michael and Nora and their young friends are rehearsing a costume melodrama about the Rising of 1789. Mr Murray, the temperamental organist, is rehearsing the choir in some rousing songs, which the perpetually alarmed Father Fillifogue thinks are not religious enough. Binnington and McGilligan and their wives are rehearsing elaborate bows and curtsies for the formal reception. And in the background Father Ned, who does not appear on stage, is often heard beating his symbolic drum as he goes about the countryside rehearsing for the procession which will touch off the Tostal on an exuberant note.

When the elder Binningtons and McGilligans, aided by Father Fillifogue, protest that the young people are displaying too much joy and revelry, the Echo mocks their words, or Father Ned's drums drown them out. The effervescent Mr Murray stamps his feet and calls for more spirit from his choir, and the rehearsing actors roar out their flamboyant lines as they clash swords in a harum-scarum duelling episode. The young lovers, Michael and Nora, the saucy maid Bernadette and the workman Tom, defy Fillifogue's breathless warnings of piety and restraint. The young people go on laughing and dancing in the full spirit of the spring festival. They speak of Angus the Young, the Celtic God of Love, with his harp and his four bright singing birds. Nora adds that the Blessed Lord would also have been pleased to see them celebrating: 'If He didn't dance Himself, He must have watched the people at it, and, maybe, clapped His hands when they did it well. He must have often listened to the people singin', and been caught up with the rhythm of the gentle harp and psalter, and His feet may have tapped the ground along with the gayer sthrokes of the tabor and the sound of the cymbals tinkling.' And Michael says of God—echoing Stephen Dedalus in *Ulysses*—'He may be but a shout in th' street.'

It is Father Ned, they all say, who has taught them these things, and the beat of his drums is a constant reminder of the love and joy of life. Father Ned does not perform comic miracles like the Cock, but there is something miraculous in his influence upon the young people of Doonavale. Under his guidance they go on to run the Tostal their own way and rout the old fools. At the end of the play Michael and Nora decide to stand for the offices of Mayor and Deputy Mayor and bring a new concept of life to Doonavale.

Could it have been this miraculous power of Father Ned's drums that frightened the Dublin Tostal Council and their superiors? O'Casey's play was clearly intended as a prophecy for Ireland, and it may have offended those who felt they had something to fear from a younger generation that knew what it wanted and was determined to get it. But it was only a play, a comic fantasy, the lightest and happiest play O'Casey had written. It was truly a festival play. Sean, hovering in the background in the guise of Father Ned, had struck a drum for the new Ireland, his first and only love.

◄◄·►►◄◄·►►◄◄·►►◄◄·►►◄◄·►►◄◄·►►◄◄·►►◄◄·►►◄◄·►►◄◄·►►◄◄·►►◄◄·►►

CHAPTER VI

The Playwright as Poet

◄◄·►►◄◄·►►◄◄·►►◄◄·►►◄◄·►►◄◄·►►◄◄·►►◄◄·►►◄◄·►►◄◄·►►◄◄·►►◄◄·►►

> On the stage one must have reality, and one must have
> joy; and that is why the intellectual modern drama
> has failed, and people have grown sick of the false joy
> of the musical comedy, that has been given them in
> place of the rich joy found only in what is superb and
> wild in reality.
>
> J. M. Synge

> ... when men lose their poetic feeling for ordinary life,
> and cannot write poetry of ordinary things, their
> exalted poetry is likely to lose its strength of exalta-
> tion, in the way men cease to build beautiful churches
> when they have lost happiness in building shops.
>
> J. M. Synge

I. RICH JOY AND SUPERB REALITY

IN TAKING a retrospective view of O'Casey's achievements as a
poetic playwright, it will be useful to begin by considering some
aspects of the relationship between drama and poetry. It is,
for example, one of the paradoxes of modern drama that the
most poetic plays have been written in prose. Although there have
been some notable but isolated achievements in verse drama—by
Yeats and Eliot—it would seem that the poetry of drama does not
necessarily depend upon versification. What then do we mean
by the poetry of drama, and how have modern playwrights created it in prose, particularly Irish playwrights like Synge and
O'Casey?

In his Preface to *The Playboy of the Western World*, Synge presented a theory of poetic drama which was based upon a synthesis
of the unique language and world that should be available to the
playwright. The poetic language of the drama was to be found in

the 'rich joy' of a spoken idiom and the 'superb reality' of an indigenous life. In the modern world, Synge believed, such a synthesis or 'collaboration' was most readily available in countries like Ireland; and yet the essence of his theory is sufficiently universal to be relevant to all countries and all playwrights. This is how he explained it in a well-known passage:

All art is a collaboration; and there is little doubt that in the happy ages of literature, striking and beautiful phrases were as ready to the story-teller's or the playwright's hand, as the rich cloaks and dresses of his time. It is probable that when the Elizabethan dramatist took his ink-horn and sat down to his work he used many phrases that he had just heard, as he sat at dinner, from his mother or his children. In Ireland, those of us who know the people have the same privilege. When I was writing *The Shadow of the Glen*, some years ago, I got more aid than any learning could have given me through a chink in the floor of the old Wicklow house where I was staying, that let me hear what was being said by the servant girls in the kitchen. This matter, I think, is of importance, for in countries where the imagination of the people, and the language they use, is rich and living, it is possible for a writer to be rich and copious in his words, and at the same time to give the reality, which is the root of all poetry, in a comprehensive and natural form. In the modern literature of towns, however, richness is found only in sonnets, or prose poems, or in one or two elaborate books that are far away from the profound and common interests of life. One has, on one side, Mallarmé and Huysmans producing this literature; and on the other, Ibsen and Zola dealing with the reality of life in joyless and pallid words. On the stage one must have reality and one must have joy; and that is why the intellectual modern drama has failed, and people have grown sick of the false joy of the musical comedy, that has been given them in place of the rich joy found only in what is superb and wild in reality.[196]

What Synge had in mind for the drama, then, was a poetic and living language which avoided the literary richness of Symbolism and the literal reality of Naturalism. The Symbolists wrote 'elaborate' books as part of a private cult, and the Naturalists used 'joyless and pallid' words as part of a public exposé. Synge may not have been entirely fair to writers like Mallarmé and Huysmans, Ibsen and Zola, but his generalizations were valid in so far as they pointed out some of the characteristic excesses of the two major movements in modern literature. His alternative was an attempt to draw upon the imagination and spoken language of people who remained in touch with what he called 'the profound and common interests of life'.

Yeats had begun with similar aims when he experimented with the folk idiom in his earliest plays, though he soon realized it was not his medium and left it to Synge and Lady Gregory. Lady Gregory went on to use the Kiltartan idiom of the West Country with fine success in her plays and stories. She had helped Yeats with the dialogue of plays like *Cathleen Ni Houlihan* and *The Pot of Broth*, but he did not believe he could capture the language himself and he explained his difficulties in a letter to her: '. . . I could not get down from that high window of dramatic verse, and in spite of all you had done for me, I had not the country speech. One has to live among the people, like you, of whom an old man said in my hearing, "She has been a serving maid among us", before one can think the thoughts of the people and speak their tongue.' [(197)] That 'high window' has frustrated many modern lyric poets who have tried their hand at verse drama. Lady Gregory did not have the genius of Yeats, but she was able to approach the drama through the low window of living speech, and in her minor yet significant achievements she illustrated the soundness of Synge's theory. And, incidentally, Yeats illustrated some aspects of this theory in the great poems of his later phase when he used a more colloquial language, and, as he put it, 'I cast off traditional metaphors and loosened my rhythm.'

The application of Synge's theory should not be limited to the language and life of peasants, as O'Casey later proved, instinctively, when he found a language of rich joy and superb reality among the proletarian Dubliners. Synge had not been convinced that the writer could find a rich and living language in the squalid life of the city, but O'Casey used the idiom and milieu of the tenements to achieve the poetic collaboration of richness and reality. Before he died, however, Synge himself was planning to write a play about the Dublin slums—he had made a close study of tenement life around Patrick Street, the slum neighbourhood of the Liberties that had aroused Swift's indignation and sympathy—so that he must have come to the realization that his theory had wider potentialities.

And surely these potentialities extend beyond rural and urban Ireland. The writer's search for a living language and a milieu of common experiences, his need to identify himself with an indigenous society, is a universal one, and many poets, playwrights, and novelists, before and since Synge, have directly or indirectly followed this path. One is reminded, for example, of Wordsworth's famous Preface to *Lyrical Ballads*, in which he set out 'to choose incidents and situations from common life, and to relate or describe them throughout, as far as was possible in a selection of language really used by men [Synge's reality], and, at the same time to throw over them a certain colouring of the imagination, whereby ordinary things should be presented to the mind in an unusual aspect. . . .' [Synge's richness]. In his poems Wordsworth did not succeed in capturing the spoken language of the rustics—he may have had some trouble with that 'high window' of Yeats's—but he nevertheless did much to liberate poetic diction from the artificial language of declining neo-classical poetry. His principles were sound, and many writers of poetry and prose have tried to follow them.

T. S. Eliot wrote verse drama with similar principles in mind. In his important little book, *Poetry and Drama*, he discusses his experiments with metrical language based on colloquial speech. He does not believe that prose is the best medium for drama: 'There are great prose dramatists—such as Ibsen and Chekhov—who have at times done things of which I would not otherwise have supposed prose to be capable, but who seem to me, in spite of their success, to have been hampered in expression by writing in prose.'[198] And yet, in his frank analysis of his own plays, he admits that he has himself been hampered in his attempts to write his plays in verse. It is apparent from what he says about *The Cocktail Party*, for example, that in trying to make his play more dramatic he may ironically have succeeded in making his verse sound more like prose: '. . . I laid down for myself the ascetic rule to avoid poetry which could not stand the test of strict dramatic utility: with such success, indeed, that it is perhaps an open question whether there is any poetry in the play at all.'[199] Does this mean that, for the modern verse dramatist, at any rate, there may be something incompatible between dramatic utility and verse? The possibility of such a conclusion becomes more apparent in Eliot's two last plays, *The Confidential Clerk* and

The Elder Statesman, where it is perhaps an open fact that his verse is often indistinguishable from prose, and the dramatic utility has not gained by this sacrifice. Eliot was one of the outstanding poets and critics of our time and he revealed his fine sensibility in everything he wrote, even when he fell short of his lofty aims in verse drama; however, one would be hard-pressed to find much genuine poetry or vital drama in these plays.

He tells us that after *Murder in the Cathedral*—a fully achieved verse drama in which he had been able to use the ceremonial language and milieu of church ritual and history—he began to write verse plays about contemporary life in a metrical language that maintained the rhythms of contemporary speech. Above all, he explained, with echoes from Wordsworth and Synge, he wanted to use modern colloquial speech and common experiences of modern life:

As I have said, people are prepared to put up with verse from the lips of personages dressed in the fashion of some distant age; they should be made to hear it from people dressed like ourselves, living in houses and apartments like ours, and using telephones and motor-cars and radio sets. Audiences are prepared to accept poetry recited by a chorus, for that is a kind of poetry recital, which it does them credit to enjoy. And audiences (those who go to a verse play because it is in verse) expect poetry to be in rhythms which have lost touch with colloquial speech. What we have to do is to bring poetry into the world in which the audience lives and to which it returns when it leaves the theatre; not to transport the audience into some imaginary world totally unlike its own, an unreal world in which poetry is tolerated. What I should hope might be achieved, by a generation of dramatists having the benefit of our experience, is that the audience should find, at the moment of awareness that it is hearing poetry, that it is saying to itself: '*I* could talk in poetry too!' Then we should not be transported into an artificial world; on the contrary, our own sordid, dreary daily world would be suddenly illuminated and transfigured.(200)

To regain touch with colloquial speech, to bring poetry into the world of ordinary experience and thus illuminate and transfigure that world—here is Eliot's method of finding richness and reality in the drama. His theory is excellent; but unfortunately his attempt to practise it can only serve as a warning to a generation of dramatists who might benefit from his experience. For one of the chief lessons to be learned from his experience would seem to be that the versification of colloquial speech does not in itself create dramatic poetry; in fact, it can produce a hybrid prose-verse that is somewhat deficient in poetic and dramatic values. A case in point is *The Elder Statesman*, which is about as poetic and dramatic as an effete parlour game.

Furthermore, and this may well be the heart of the matter, Eliot was hampered by his necessary choice of language and milieu—that of the urbane drawing-room—which apparently did not provide him with a particularly rich idiom for dramatic poetry. This language and milieu served him admirably in some of his poems, but there is a world of difference between a dramatic monologue and the dialogue of drama. Henry James used the language and milieu of the urbane drawing-room in his beautifully discursive and poetic novels, yet he was unable to succeed with the same material in his plays. Perhaps that success can only be achieved by a genius like Oscar Wilde, or the Restoration dramatists, who had the magnificent style and poetic wit to carry it off. And they wrote in prose.

Novelists as well as dramatists have illustrated that prose can achieve the rhythm and richness of poetry. Flaubert, for instance, one of the earliest of modern writers to prove this, once explained his intentions in the following manner: 'To desire to give verse-rhythm to prose, yet to leave it prose and very much prose, and to write about ordinary life as histories and epics are written, yet without falsifying the subject, is perhaps an absurd idea. Sometimes I almost think it is. But it may also be a great experiment and very original.' [201] And many of the major novelists and dramatists of the nineteenth and twentieth centuries have carried out Flaubert's great experiment with remarkable success. It should be clear that these poetic achievements in prose in no way belittle or compete with the great achievements in modern lyric poetry. One can only record the fact that when the modern lyric poet has tried to 'compete' (the term is Eliot's) with the playwright in the theatre, the prose play has emerged as a more poetic and dramatic work of art. Eliot's experiments with verse drama are worthy of attention, but they have led to some misconceptions about poetic drama which Francis Fergusson has accurately pointed out: 'To Eliot's experiments, and to his immense authority, we owe the notion that the problem of poetic drama in our time is simply that of finding a type of verse that will work on stage. And many young poets proceed as though drama could somehow be deduced from the lyric by further exploration of the properties of verse.'[202]

Fergusson also takes up a more basic misconception which arises from the assumption 'that the art of drama itself is not a form of poetry; it cannot be poetic without verse. As long as [Eliot] holds that view he will, I think, fall short of an adequate conception of poetic drama. He will not know what to do with Ibsen and Chekhov, or for that matter, the prose passages in Shakespeare'.[203]

It is possible that Eliot did not know what to do with Synge either. He called him a 'special case' because his plays 'are based upon the idiom of a rural people whose speech is naturally poetic, both in imagery and rhythm. I believe that he even incorporated phrases which he had heard from these country people of Ireland. The language of Synge is not available except for plays set among that same people'.[204] Now, it is obvious that the particular language that Synge would only be available for plays about Irish peasants. The important lesson to be learned from Synge's plays, and from O'Casey's plays as well, is not that the modern playwright should take up residence in Ireland, but that he should follow the example of these two playwrights in his own country, in the village or the city. When regional or parochial writers do this we call it local colour; but in the hands of major writers this indigenous material takes on the dimensions of significant art.

Any writer who lives among and understands a people who share a common idiom and common experiences has the opportunity of discovering the roots of a unique and potentially poetic language. If that makes him a special case, he will certainly be in the company of some worthy poets, novelists, and dramatists of many lands. Yeats appeared to have something like this in mind when, in the Preface he wrote to the first edition of *The Well of the Saints*, he made this comment about the universal aspect of Synge's living language:

If one has not fine construction, one has not drama, but if one has not beautiful or powerful and individual speech, one has not literature, or, at any rate, one has not great literature. Rabelais, Villon, Shakespeare, William Blake, would have known one another by their speech. Some of them knew how to construct a story, but all of them had abundant, resonant, beautiful, laughing, living speech. [205]

And one might approach this problem in another way by drawing up a representative but by no means complete list of writers and the people who provided them with a living language that was naturally poetic: the Londoners and provincials of Chaucer, Shakespeare, Fielding, Dickens, Hardy, Lawrence, and Shaw; the Scottish peasants of Burns; the Dubliners of Joyce and O'Casey; the Russian provincials and city-dwellers of Tolstoy, Dostoevsky, Chekhov, and Gorki; the Spanish peasants of Lorca; the Southerners of Twain and Faulkner; the Welsh country people of Dylan Thomas, especially in *Under Milk Wood*.

It should also be pointed out that most of these writers used a rhetorical as well as a colloquial language, usually developing the two styles in the same work in a contrapuntal manner. Eliot did this with outstanding success in *The Waste Land*, and probably the most famous example of it in modern literature is Joyce's *Ulysses*. Synge once made an important comment on the relationship between these two styles. He recognized the supremacy of what he called the exalted style, but he went on to say that 'when men lose their poetic feeling for ordinary life, and cannot write poetry of ordinary things, their exalted poetry is likely to lose its strength of exaltation, in the way men cease to build beautiful churches when they have lost happiness in building shops'. [206]

It is possible that the main answer to questions about poetic drama lies in a full commitment to this dual experience. Whether our playwrights try to write poetic prose, or our poets try to write dramatic verse, they should be inspired by that impetus which has led men to build shops as well as churches.

And playwrights like Synge and O'Casey actually went one step farther—they not only used both styles, the exalted and the colloquial, they created the poetry of exaltation out of the colloquial. They exalted the ordinary—the living language and the common life—and the art they made was rich and joyous, superb and wild.

2. THE O'CASEY POETRY

Synge and O'Casey, then, achieved the poetic collaboration of art and life by exalting a colloquial language. But while their achievements are similar, their styles are different in many ways for they used different methods and materials.

Synge's style is based upon the lilting rhythms and speech patterns of the peasant idiom; and yet it is constructed as a highly idealized and somewhat quaint language, the result of an artistic transfiguration which makes it distinct from the actual language spoken by the peasants. It is mainly the world of nature that he idealizes in his imagery and themes. His primitive characters are instinctively a part of nature and they worship its grandeur and mystery, for Synge is primarily concerned with the relationship between man and nature not man and god, although he often deifies the objects and landscapes of nature in pantheistic idylls. His satire is invariably aimed at those people who are unwilling or unable to accept the wonders and dangers of the world of nature.

Nature, however, could not play a significant role in the seething life of the Dublin slums, and so O'Casey had to develop his style out of the strident rhythms and speech patterns of an urban idiom that did not particularly lend itself to quaintness or idealization. The city itself with all its discordant harmonies became his poem—'dear dirty Dublin'—and all the people who fought to stay alive amid the dangers and wonders of its tenements and streets and pubs, and its War of Independence. His characters are primitives, too, but their uninhibited customs and expressions are largely a reaction against the poverty and uncertainty that constantly threaten their lives. Frustrated in their struggle for life's material necessities, they can only find a sense of liberation, even glory, in the voluble and extravagant language that O'Casey gives them. They are profligate with vivid words and phrases in a world in which they can be profligate with little else. Their unique language is for them a delight and a defence: a delight in the one luxury they possess, the joyous life of the imagination; a defence against the hard realities of slum life which could be spelled out only too painfully in grim monosyllables. Prodical's proliferous announcement in *The Bishop's Bonfire* about his inviolable soul is characteristic of this delight and defence: 'Me soul's me own particular compendium. Me soul's me own spiritual property, complete an' entire, verbatim in all its concernment.'

Whether they protest to each other, to the representatives of authority, or to the world at large, most of O'Casey's characters find rich and copious words to express their independent spirit. Even the absurd Uncle Peter in *The Plough and The Stars*, 'tormented and twarted' as he is by the sly Covey, takes his stand when he declares: 'As long as I'm a livin' man, responsible for me thoughts, words, an' deeds to th' Man above, I'll feel meself instituted to fight again' th' sliddherin' ways of a pair o' picaroons, whisperin', concurrin', concoctin', and conspirin' together to rendher me unconscious of th' life I'm thryin' to live!' On such terms, their own terms, O'Casey's characters are able to defend themselves against the varieties of 'chassis' that pervade their lives.

O'Casey's style is essentially a comic one, although it is often charged with tragic overtones. In this ironic mingling of the comic and tragic modes, the total effect of his style is often close to that of Synge. However, his language is not as carefully wrought as Synge's, and it does not have the delicately measured cadence of the 'Synge-song' style; yet it has a cumulative rhythm and intense music of its own. O'Casey did not idealize the colourful Dublin idiom, he magnified it, increased its tempo and rhetorical vigour. Like Synge, he incorporated many phrases he had heard, but his language is no more a literal recording of actual speech than Synge's was. Too much emphasis has been placed upon that notorious chink in the floor of a Wicklow farmhouse. Undoubtedly Synge would have agreed with O'Casey's view that 'no real character can be put in a play unless some of the reality is taken out of him through the heightening, widening, and deepening of the character by the dramatist who creates him'.

It is important to examine the nature of the language that O'Casey heard in Dublin, and some of the methods of 'heightening, widening, and deepening' that he used to reshape it and give it dramatic form. Most Irishmen, but particularly the proud and garrulous people of the Dublin slums, have an instinctive love of word-play. It has been one of their chief amusements in a generally impoverished and provincial city, and the uninhibited conversation of these people has remained a living and impromptu art. Their characteristically emphatic speech is coloured with archaisms, malapropisms, puns, invectives, polysyllables, circumlocutions, alliterations, repetitions, assonances and images. Such a word-hoard of colloquial rhetoric suggests that there may be a relationship between the spoken language of Elizabethan Londoners and the spoken language of modern Dubliners. This parallel derives from Irish history.

P. W. Joyce, the Celtic scholar, in a book he published at the time when O'Casey was thirty years old and only beginning to plan his career as a writer, traced the origins of this parallel to the time when the early English colonists settled in the eastern part of Ireland. He wrote:

When these Elizabethan colonists, who were nearly all English, settled down and made friends with the natives and intermarried with them, great numbers of them learned to use the Irish language; while the natives on their part learned English from the newcomers. There was give and take in every place where the two peoples and the two languages mixed. And so the native Irish people learned to speak Elizabethan English—the very language used by Shakespeare; and in a very considerable degree the old Gaelic people and those of English descent retain it to this day. For our people are very conservative in retaining old customs and forms of speech. Many words accordingly that are discarded as old-fashioned—or dead and gone—in England, are still flourishing—alive and well—in Ireland. They are now regarded as vulgarisms by the educated—which no doubt they are—but they are vulgarisms of respectable origin, representing as they do the classical English of Shakespeare's time.[207]

These vulgarisms may not have been very 'classical' after the Dubliners took them over, but they certainly retained their Elizabethan vitality and vividness. As one among many illustrations of this idiom, Joyce cited a typical remark he had heard from a Dublin nurse: 'The bloody throopers are coming to kill and quarther an' murther every mother's sowl o' ye.'[208] The semi-literate Dublin woman who sang out this hyperbolic sentence would have been as much at home in Elizabethan London as in twentieth century Dublin.

One still hears this kind of rhetoric spoken by the people of Dublin. Here are some examples of 'overheard' expressions. A dock foreman who found that he had to do a chore that one of the carters had either forgotten or slyly ignored came out with, 'Why am I afther keeping a dog and barking meself.' While listening to a campaign speech during an election a tradesman turned to his neighbour and said, 'I'll tell you free, gratis, and for nothin, that your eejut up there's absolutely, postively, and teetotally wrong.' On a rare cloudless day a charwoman greeted some of the people who passed by with the remark, 'That's an adjacent bit of weather we're having, very adjacent indeed.' Throughout a disorderly argument at a union meeting a member kept shouting, 'Hey yous, mind the mejenda, jaysus, mind the bloody mejenda!' An excited street debator once warned his listeners against 'Them that are offering insults to the sentiments that are entangled and entwithered in the sacred hearts of the holy people of Ireland'. [209]

In a lecture on Irish folk-poetry, Gerard Murphy, the Celtic scholar, discussed a typical expression he had heard from a Dublin workingman in order to illustrate the influence of the Gaelic language on the characteristically poetic idiom of the people. He believed that the everyday conversation in the city streets had 'the perfect order of speech and the beauty of incantation'—the phrase is Eliot's. Murphy had been standing with the man waiting for a bus, and although the man signalled to the bus to stop it was moving too fast and pulled up a short distance beyond them.

'Where are you running and racing to at all?' said the workingman to the conductor, as he boarded the bus some ten yards away from where he had hailed it.

'Where are you running and racing to at all?' is a typically Irish phrase. It is a phrase the equivalent of which, or many equivalents of which, would be in daily use in any society in which Irish was the habitual language of the people. In English, however, it is something strange, something which is bound to die with the progress of time, for the whole flow and tendency of the English language is in another direction. No one is taught in English-speaking schools to compose sentences in the mould of 'Where are you running and racing to at all?' English books and newspapers normally contain no examples of them.

'Where are you running and racing to at all?' must then be regarded as a foreign element in English conversation and English literature. In Irish conversation, on the contrary, such phrases are the rule.

What am I thinking of when I say that such phrases are the rule in Irish literature and the best Irish speech?

First, I am thinking of style. 'Where are you running and racing to at all?' is no ordinary sentence: it is a sentence of distinction, a sentence marked by a deliberate style.

With its rhythm and alliteration, and its use of the emphatic 'at all', it has obviously been composed by an artist anxious to give body and harmony to what he has to say, and to express by the added 'at all' a shade of emphasis, an attitude of mind, that can hardly be expressed in book English.

That feeling for style, that alliteration and peculiar emphasis, are typically Gaelic.[210]

These views of Gerard Murphy's complement P. W. Joyce's theory, for both influences, the Elizabethan and the Gaelic, can be found in Dublin speech, and they are both discernible in O'Casey's style. It must be remembered that as a young man O'Casey had become a fluent speaker and reader of Gaelic, and that he had taught the language in one of the branch schools of the Gaelic League. He would have known many of the Irish folk-poems and bardic poems in the original Gaelic, poems which were based upon alliteration, assonance, and middle rhymes—rhetorical devices which he often incorporated in his dialogue. He also knew and used many Gaelic constructions and expressions which had been carried over into the highly flavoured Dublin English—the distinctive idiom of alliterations and emphatic rhythms that Murphy had described as an imaginative, non-book English. Some of the direct echoes of Gaelic in O'Casey's language appear in his use of inversions like 'Bring in that fella a glass o' wather'; in the aorist use of 'after' in 'that's afther puttin' the heart across me'; in the literal translation of the preposition *ast* (out of) in phrases like 'I caught him hee-hee-in' out of him'; in the typically Gaelic use of the co-ordinating 'and' construction instead of a sub-ordinating clause in 'You plunged like a good one through hummin' bullets, an' they knocking fire out o' th' road'; in the use of the pronoun 'aself' as an intensive adverb (from the Gaelic *féin* meaning both 'self' and 'even') in 'And, if I get up aself, how am I going to get down agen?' He also incorporated a number of Gaelic words like 'mallavogin'' (*mealbhóg*, bag; metaphorically, a shrewish woman, hence, abuse); 'traneen' (*tráithnín*, a bit of straw); 'omadhaun' (*amadán*, a fool); 'gom' (*gamach*, a clown or simpleton); 'foostherin'' (*fustarach*, fussy); 'gostherin'' (*gastra*, a group of people, and by association, people conversing); 'blatther' (*bladar*, foolish talk or flattery).

He also incorporated or invented many slang expressions and pronunciations that illustrate the Dubliner's love of word-play:

'a glitherin' aroree boree allis'; 'the whole worl's in a state o'
chassis ; 'a second Christo For Columbus'; 'there's a terrible
tatheraraa' (loud noise); 'a weeshy, dawny bit of a man' (small and
sickly); 'affeydavey'; 'a gradle' (a great deal); 'a tither o' sense'
(a bit of sense); 'folly' (follow); 'borry' (borrow); 'barney' (conversation); 'banjax' (ruin); 'billickin"' (cheating); 'childer' and
'chiselurs' (children); 'leppin'' (leaping); 'upperosity' (snob-
bishness); 'thrue', 'murdher'. The pronunciation of these last two
words illustrates the typical carry-over from the Gaelic of the *th*
and *dh* sounds, which occur especially in words where the *t* and
d are followed by *r*. Although he used less of the Gaelic expressions
in his later plays, O'Casey retained the pronunciation and the
essential Dublinese in his dialogue. [211]

Another influence upon his style was his early Protestant background and his knowledge of the Bible. As a boy he often heard
biblical stories and phrases from his very devout mother, he
studied the Bible and the Prayer Book when he was learning to
read and write, and later he taught Sunday school at St Barnabas
Church. Some examples of this influence in his plays can be seen
in the speeches of Adolphus Grigson in *The Shadow of a Gunman*,
Bessie Burgess in *The Plough and the Stars*, Brennan o' the Moor
and the Rector in *Red Roses For Me ;* in the ironic paraphrases from
Ezekiel in *The Silver Tassie*, and the paraphrases from the Psalms
in *The Plough and the Stars* and *The Drums of Father Ned*. Bessie
Burgess is an ironic and heroic figure, and toward the end of *The
Plough* she has a chance to practice the evangelical christianity
that she turns loose on everyone. Here is an example of her
biblical rhetoric, which strikes ironic echoes from chapter 5 of the
1st Psalm: 'There's th' men marchin' out into th' dhread dim-
ness o' danger, while th' lice is crawlin' about feedin' on th' fatness
o' the land! But yous'll not escape from th' arrow that flieth be
night, or th' sickness that wasteth be day—an' ladyship an' all, as
some o' them may be, they'll be scattered abroad, like th' dust in
th' darkness!' The biblical passage reads: 'Thou shalt not be
afraid for the terror by night; nor for the arrow that flieth by day;
nor for the pestilence that walketh in darkness; nor for the destruction that wasteth at noonday.' When Nora in *The Drums of
Father Ned* says that the Lord might have clapped His hands in
approval when He heard the people singing and dancing to the
joyful music of the harp and psalter and cymbals, O'Casey is play-

ing variations on the theme and language of the 98th Psalm, which begins: 'O sing unto the Lord, a new song; for he hath done marvellous things . . . Make a joyful noise unto the Lord, all the earth make a loud noise, and rejoice, and sing praise. Sing unto the Lord with the harp; with the harp, and the voice of a psalm . . . Let the floods clap their hands; let the hills be joyful together.' This is the theme and spirit of all the later plays.

In one of the most powerful speeches in *Juno and the Paycock*, Mrs Tancred's lament for her dead son, which Juno Boyle repeats at the end of the play, O'Casey creates the language of elegaic incantation by combining the Dublin idiom with several key phrases from the Bible. Ezekiel 11: 19 reads: '. . . and I will take the stoney heart out of their flesh, and will give them an heart of flesh.' Here is Mrs Tancred's lament, a striking example of exalted colloquial speech:

Me home is gone now; he was me only child, an' to think that he was lyin' for a whole night stretched out on the side of a lonely counthry lane, with his head, his darlin' head, that I often kissed an' fondled, half hidden in the wather of a runnin' brook. An' I'm told he was the leadher of the ambush where me nex' door neighbour, Mrs Mannin', lost her Free State soldier son. An' now here's the two of us oul' women, standin' one on each side of a scales o' sorra, balanced be the bodies of our two dead darlin' sons . . . Mother o' God, Mother o' God, have pity on the pair of us!—O Blessed Virgin, where were you when me darlin' son was riddled with bullets, when me darlin' son was riddled with bullets!—Sacred Heart of the Crucified Jesus, take away our hearts o' stone—an' give us hearts o' flesh!—Take away this murdherin' hate—an' give us Thine own eternal love!

Then there are instances where O'Casey creates a mock-elegaic mood, as he does in this speech of Mrs Gogan's in *The Plough and the Stars*, in which she expresses her fear that Fluther's attempt to rescue Nora has failed:

God grant it; but last night I dreamt I seen gettin' carried into th' house a sthretcher with a figure lyin' on it, stiff an' still, dhressed in th' habit of Saint Francis. An', then, I heard th' murmurs of a crowd no one could see sayin' th' litany for th' dead; and then it got so dark that nothin' was seen but th' white face of th' corpse, gleamin' like a white wather-lily floatin' on th' top of a dark lake. Then a tiny whisper thrickled into me ear, sayin', 'Isn't the face very like th' face o' Fluther?' an' then, with a thremblin' flutther, th' dead lips opened, an', although I couldn't hear, I knew they were sayin', 'Poor oul' Fluther, afther havin' handed in his gun at last, his shakin' soul moored in th' place where th' wicked are at rest an' th' weary cease from throublin'.'

Speeches like these, with their stylized cadence, imagery, and selection of heightened details, are something quite different from a collection of colloquial phrases that might have been overheard in the street. There are many women like Mrs Tancred, Juno Boyle and Mrs Gogan in Dublin, in all cities, but it is not likely that they have such an ordered and sustained command of the popular idiom in 'real' life.

One of O'Casey's favourite methods of heightening his language, especially in comic or satiric scenes, is his development of incremental rhythms in his sentence patterns. With a rush of alliteration, assonance, concrete images, and ever-expanding phrases, he builds up a cumulative momentum and the speeches fairly burst with rhetorical energy. As an example of this incremental language, and how it is admirably suited to the temperament of his volatile characters and the emotional situations that provoke them, here is an episode from *The Plough and the Stars*. It is the beginning of the second act when Fluther and Peter, already intoxicated by the patriotic speeches at the street demonstration, enter the Pub. Rosie Redmond has just commented that all the men are in 'a holy mood . . . you'd think they were the glorious company of th' saints, an' th' noble army of martyrs thrampin' through th' sthreets of paradise'—and the two puffed-up patriots give their best impersonation of her description:

PETER. A meetin' like this always makes me feel as if I could dhrink Loch Erinn dhry!
FLUTHER. You couldn't feel any way else at a time like this when th' spirit of a man is pulsin' to be out fightin' for th' thruth with his feet thremblin' on th' way, maybe to th' gallows, an' his ears tinglin' with th' faint, far-away sound of burstin' rifle-shots that'll maybe whip th' last little shock o' life out of him that's left lingerin' in his body!
PETER. I felt a burnin' lump in me throat when I heard th' band playin 'The Soldiers' Song', rememberin' last hearin' it marchin' in

military formation, with th' people starin' on both sides at us, carryin' with us th' pride an' resolution o' Dublin to th' grave of Wolfe Tone.

FLUTHER. Get th' Dublin men goin' an' they'll go full force for anything that's thryin' to bar them away from what they're wantin', where th' slim thinkin' counthry boyo ud limp away from th' first faintest touch of compromisation!

PETER (*hurriedly to the Barman*). Two more, Tom! (*To Fluther.*) Th' memory of all th' things that was done, an' all th' things that was suffered be th' people, was boomin' in me brain—every nerve in me body was quiverin' to do something' desperate!

FLUTHER. Jammed as I was in th' crowd, I listened to th' speeches pattherin' on th' people's head, like rain fallin' on th' corn; every derogatory thought went out o' me mind, an I said to meself, 'You can die now, Fluther, for you've seen th' shadow-dhreams of th' past leppin' to life in th' bodies of livin' men that show, if we were without a titther o' courage for centuries, we're vice versa now!' Looka here. (*He stretches out his arm under Peter's face and rolls up his sleeve.*) The blood was BOILIN' in me veins!

This is an illustration of O'Casey's mock-heroic style, in which the mood is closer to ironic exhilaration than exaltation. It is the conception of the characters as well as the language that is magnified, in such a way that O'Casey allows the characters to expose and enjoy their sublime folly. He uses this kind of rhetoric for most of his comic characters when they are stimulated or provoked, which is most of the time. There are any number of examples of this style in the speeches of Seumas Shields, Tommy Owens, and Adolphus Grigson in *The Shadow of a Gunman*; Captain Boyle, Joxer Daly, and Masie Madigan in *Juno and the Paycock*; Mrs Gogan, Bessie Burgess, the Covey, and Rosie Redmond, as well as Fluther and Peter in *The Plough and the Stars;* Sylvester Heegan and Simon Norton in *The Silver Tassie*; the London cockneys in *Within the Gates*; Brennan o' the Moor, Roory O'Balacaun, and Mullcanny in *Red Roses For Me*; and most of the Irish villagers (they actually speak the Dublin idiom) in *Purple Dust, Cock-a-doodle Dandy, The Bishop's Bonfire*, and *The Drums of Father Ned*.

O'Casey also owes an indirect debt to the traditional humour of the Irish music halls, and to Boucicault's rendering of that tradition

in his plays. In the nineteenth century some of the Dublin pubs
served as the poor man's music hall, for they often presented
comic 'entertainments' for their customers. The singing comedians were among the most popular artistes. They carried on a
series of running gags and asides in the midst of their songs
(somewhat in the manner of the present-day Jimmy Durante's
song-and-patter routines), and many of them introduced comic
monologues between the verses of a ballad. As an example of the
dramatic humour of these performances, here is a typical song-and-
monologue:

BLACK TURF

A celebrated Irish Song
Sung by Mr Gallagher, the Ventriloquist,
in his popular Entertainment.
(Air—'Buy a Broom')

Through Dublin's sweet city, I ramble my hearty,
  With my kish of black turf for a cold wintry noon,
They're cut from the bog of one Felix M'Carthy,
Arrah, now buy a cushla from your own Jack Muldoon.
              Black turf, black turf, &c.

Spoken—Will you buy a Mock? I will give you twenty-four black
sods for one penny; devil the like of them ever was burnt before for
heat, or boiling your pot; just take one of them in your hand, troth I am
after selling four pinnerth to Mistress Toole, of Coal Alley, and her
decent husband, who is a knife grinder, declared to me that he can work
without the dispensation of a candle, since he began to burn my black
turf. Will you buy, Misther? do a-cushla, Will you, Mistress? do mam;
don't be foolish to be spendin' your good-lookin' money for coals; in
troth, there wasn't luck nor grace in this country since the invention
of coals, or any ill-lookin' chimmistical commodity like them—will you
buy a mosk? Orra buy of Jack Muldoon his flaming black turf.

When your feet is all snow, and your toes are frost-bitten,
  Arrah then you'll discover my turf is your friend,
There's such light from the blaze that a letter I've written,
  To my sweetheart Moll Grogan, for Christmas to spend.
              Black turf, black turf, &c.

Spoken—Come now, girls, I am just come out, and the first that hansels me will get a fine sod over, orra jewels if you war after seeing the big boat-load I got consigned to myself, by my father-in-law, Murty Grogan. O millia murther! this is the lucky turf, the quality of Dublin shud be fond of; for the very bog it was cut from, moved half-way to Dublin to see you, and only the *polis* overtook it, and wouldn't let it come any further than my father-in-law's it would be livin in Dublin now, and all the young bogs would be Dublin people—this is the reason, I tell yez, that all yez should lose no time to buy as much as you can. Will you buy, Misther? I can only give twelve sods for a penny of this turf, for you may well depind on it, the parents for them are well known; the devil fire the sod of this turf, but after it's burnt, will walk out of the grate and get themselves blackened over and over again, fit for use, and ready for to boil any kittle, saucepan, or any of the family, every bit as well as before, so that you see plainly you will never have the same 'otunity any more of buying such lucky turf. So yez won't buy —do you want any, my chap? Is that a pinny in your hand? Come and buy now, avic; O rista! crista! what bad times it is, they don't know the vartue of the turf from the moving bog.

Black turf, black turf, &c.

Orra gramachree avourneen, avourneen, avourneen,
Will you buy, avourneen, my moving black turf;
I am now nearly broke, to the dog I must hurry,
And to Jim Casey's berrin I'll be in time for to go,
Och, he died t'other day, and many he's left sorry,
For he was a good-hearted fellow (cries), *but now he's laid low.*
Black turf, black turf, &c.

Spoken—Och! och! och! what sundry times those are, the world, in troth, is nothing but a boat load of decit, and the honest people, from the great gunchability of sickness, are leaping up out of the world just like young trout of a summer's day. Orra Jim Casey, avic, you're gone without as much as bidding one of us good-bye (*cries*), Och! heaven be your bed, Darby Quinn, if you were alive, its yourself would cry millia murther after poor Jim. I would be on the vartue of my oath, if Moll Casey took my advice, Jim would be at work today, the dirty sutrecan, I tould her to give him a little buttered punch, which would be the means of conglomerating his bowels; but stid of that, she gives him a skillet full of mouldy colcannon—Will you buy, &c.[212]

Whether or not O'Casey actually knew this song-and-mono-
logue, it illustrates the type of music-hall entertainment and
Dublin idiom that he would have known and enjoyed. He did not
use the stage-Irish expressions in his plays—'Orra gramachree
avourneen'—but there is a strong O'Casey flavour in the language,
particularly in phrases like 'chimmistical commodity', 'the great
gunchability of sickness', and 'the means of conglomerating his
bowels'. And O'Casey would have been attracted by the vigourous
characterization of Jack Muldoon, the mingling of farce and
pathos, and the Jim Casey under-plot, the tragi-comic digression
which dominates the last verse and monologue.

There is also a Boucicaultian flavour in this characterization of
Jack Muldoon, for he has much of the flamboyant 'shaughraun'
in him. Boucicault's Conn the Shaughraun had that roguish spirit
of 'careless Irish humour' which relies upon an original turn of
phrase, a comic image, a play on words, and a general feeling of
verbal extravagance. Synge and O'Casey admired these qualities
in Boucicault and often imitated them, although they usually
exploited them in an ironic and anti-stage-Irish context. Here are
some characteristic scenes from *The Shaughraun* which illustrate
the Boucicaultian humour that undoubtedly impressed Synge and
O'Casey. First, an episode from the first act between Conn's
mother Mrs O'Kelly, his sweetheart Moya, and Conn, making his
initial entrance:

MRS O'KELLY. Is that yourself, Moya? I've come to see if that
vagabond of mine has been round this way.
MOYA. Why should he be here—hasn't he a home of his own?
MRS O'KELLY. The shebeen is his home when he's not in gaol. His
father died o' drink, and Conn will go the same way.
MOYA. I thought your husband was drowned at sea?
MRS O'KELLY. And, bless him, so he was.
MOYA (*aside*). Well, that's a quare way of dying o' drink.
MRS O'KELLY. The best of men he was, when he was sober—a betther
never dhrawed the breath o' life.
MOYA. But you say he never was sober.
MRS O'KELLY. Nivir! An' Conn takes afther him!
MOYA. Mother.
MRS O'KELLY. Well.
MOYA. I'm afeared I'll take afther Conn.

MRS O'KELLY. Heaven forbid, and purtect you again him. You are a good, dacent girl, an' desarve the best of husbands.

MOYA. Them's the only ones that gets the worst. More betoken yourself, Mrs O'Kelly.

MRS O'KELLY. Conn nivir did an honest day's work in his life—but dhrinkin', an' fishin', an' shootin', an' sportin', and love-makin'.

MOYA. Sure, that's how the quality pass their lives.

MRS O'KELLY. That's it. A poor man that spoorts the sowl of a gentleman is called a blackguard.

CONN (*entering*). There's somebody talking about me.

MOYA (*running to him*). Conn!

CONN. My darlin', was the mother makin' little of me? Don't believe a word that comes out o' her! She's jealous—a devil a haperth less. She's choking wid it this very minute, just bekase she sees my arms about ye. She's as proud of me as an ould hen that's got a duck for a chicken. Hould your whist now! Wipe your mouth, an' give me a kiss!

MRS O'KELLY (*embracing him*). Oh, Conn, what have you been afther? The polis were in my cabin today about ye. They say you stole Squire Foley's horse.

CONN. Stole his horse! Sure the baste is safe and sound in his paddock this minute.

MRS O'KELLY. But he says you stole it for the day to go huntin'.

CONN. Well, here's a purty thing, for a horse to run away with a man's character like this! Oh, wurra! may I never die in sin, but this was the way of it. I was standing by ould Foley's gate, when I heard the cry of the hounds comin' across the tail-end of the bog, and there they wor, my dear, spread out like the tail of a paycock, an' the finest dog fox you'd ever seen sailing ahead of them up the boreen, and right across the churchyard. It was enough to raise the inhabitants. Well, as I looked, who should come up and put his head over the gate beside me but the Squire's brown mare, small blame to her. Divil a thing I said to her, nor she to me, for the hounds had lost their scent, we knew by their yelp and whine as they hunted among the gravestones, when, whish! the fox went by us. I leapt on the gate, an' gave a shriek of a view halloo to the whip; in a minute the pack caught the scent again, an' the whole field came roarin' past. The mare lost her head, an' tore at the gate. 'Stop,' ses I, 'ye devil!' and I slipped the taste of a rope over her head an' into her mouth. Now mind the cunnin' of the baste, she was quiet in a minute. 'Come home now,' ses I, 'asy!' and I threw my leg across her. Be gabers! No sooner was I on her bare back than whoo! holy rocket! she was over the gate, an tearin' like mad afther the hounds. 'Yoicks!' ses I; 'come back the thief of the world, where are you takin' me to?' as she went through the huntin' field an' laid me besides the masther of the hounds, Squire Foley himself. He turned the colour of his leather breeches. 'Mother of Moses!' ses he, 'is that Conn the Shaughraun on my brown mare?' 'Bad luck to me!' ses I, 'It's no one else!' 'You sthole my horse,' says the Squire. 'That's a lie!' ses I, 'for it was your horse sthole me!'

MOYA. An' what did he say to that?

CONN. I couldn't sthop to hear, for just then we took a stone wall and a double ditch together, and he stopped behind to keep an engagement he had in the ditch.

With his beguiling blarney, Conn may be the typical stage Irishman but he is also the prototype of the 'playboy' and the 'paycock'. Here is a farcical episode from the second act between Conn and his mother; Conn has received a secret letter from his imprisoned Fenian friend, the rebel Ffolliott, but neither Conn nor his mother can read:

CONN (*entering with a paper in his hand*). There's writing upon it. Himself has sent me a letther. Well, this is the first I ever got, and well to be sure (*looks at it—turns it over*) I'd know more about it if there was nothing in it; but it's the writin' bothers me.

MRS O'KELLY. Is that yourself, Conn?

CONN (*aside*). I wish it was somebody else that had book larnin'.

MRS O'KELLY. What have you there?

CONN. It's a letther the masther is afther writin' to me.

MRS O'KELLY. What's in it?

CONN. Tuppence was in it for postage (*aside*). That's all I made out of it.

MRS O'KELLY. I mane what does he say in it?

CONN. Rade it!

MRS O'KELLY. You know I can't.

CONN. Oh, ye ignorant ould woman!

MRS O'KELLY. I know I am; but I took care to send you to school, Conn, though the sixpence a week it cost me was pinched out of my stomach and off my back.

CONN. The Lord be praised that ye had it to spare, anyway.

MRS O'KELLY. Go on, now—it's makin' fun of yer ould mother ye are. Tell me what the young masther says.

CONN. In the letther?

MRS O'KELLY. Yes!

CONN (*aside*). Murther, what'll I do? (*Aloud.*) Now, mind, it's a sacret. (*Reads.*) 'Collee costhum garanga caravat selibubu luckli rastuck pig.'

MRS O'KELLY. What's that—it's not English!

CONN. No; it's in writin'—now kape that to yourself.

And here is part of the mock-wake episode in the last act. Conn is stretched out as a corpse, a trick to fool the police and rescue Ffolliott, and a group of keening neighbours have come to comfort Mrs Kelly and drink away their sorrow:

CHORUS. Why did ye die?—why did ye die?
　　　　Laving us to sigh, och hone!
　　　　Why did ye die?—why did ye die?
　　　　Oolaghaun!—oh, Oolaghaun!

BIDDY. Oh, oh, oho! (*rocking herself*). Oh, oo, Olaghaun! The widdy had a son—an only son—wail for the widdy!

CHORUS. Why did ye die?—why did ye die?

BIDDY. I see her when she was a fair young girl—a fine girl, wid a child at her breast.

CHORUS. Laving us to sigh! Och, hone!

BIDDY. Then I see a proud woman wid a boy by her side. He was as bould as a bull-calf that runs beside of the cow.

CHORUS. Why did ye die?—why did ye die?

BIDDY. For the girl grew ould as the child grew big, and the woman grew wake as the boy grew strong (*rising, and flinging back her hair*). The boy grew strong, for she fed him wid her heart's blood. Ah, hogoola! Where is he now? Cowld in his bed! Why did ye die?

CHORUS. Laving us to sigh! Och, hone!

BIDDY. None was like him—none could compare, and—Good luck to ye, gi' me a dhrop of something to put the sperret in one, for the fire's getting low.

　　　　　　(*Sullivan hands her his jug of punch.*)

MRS O'KELLY. Oh, oh! it's mighty consolin' to hear this. Mrs Malone, you are not ating.

NANCY. No, ma'am, I'm drinkin'. I dhrink now and agin by way of variety. Biddy is not up to herself.

REILLY. Oh! wait till she'll rise on the top of a noggin.

BIDDY (*after drinking places the jug beside her, and rises on low stool*). He was brave! He was brave! He was open-handed; he had the heart of a lion, and the legs of a fox.

(*Conn takes the jug, empties it quietly, and, unobserved by all, replaces it on the stool.*)

BIDDY. His voice was softer than the cuckoo of an evening, and sweeter than the blackbird afther a summer shower. Ye colleens, ye will nivir hear the voice of Conn again.

(*Sits and blows her nose.*)

CONN (*aside*). It's a mighty pleasant thing to die like this, once in a way, and hear all the good things said about ye, afther you're dead and gone, when they can do you no good.

BIDDY. His name will be the pride of the O'Kellys for evermore.

CONN (*aside*). I was a big blackguard when I was alive.

BIDDY. Noble and beautiful!

CONN (*aside*). Ah, go on out o' that!

BIDDY (*taking up her jug*). Oh, he was sweet and sthrong—— Who the devil's been at my jug of punch?

MRS O'KELLY (*sobbing and rising*). Nobody is dhrinkin'—yez all despise the occasion—if yez lave behind ye liquor enough to swim a fly—oh, hoo! There's a hole in your mug, Mr Donovan, I'll be glad to see it in the bottle—oh, hoo!

And later when the 'corpse' jumps up in time to trap the villains and save the day, Conn's mourning mother embraces him:

MRS O'KELLY. Where is he—where is my vagabone? Conn, ye thief o' the world—my boy—my darlin'!

(*Falls on his neck.*)

CONN. Whisht, mother, don't cry. See this—I'll never be kilt again.

MOYA. Sure, if he hadn't have been murdhered, he couldn't have saved us.

MRS O'KELLY. And after letting me throw all the money away over the wake! [213]

There are countless instances of this comic spirit in O'Casey's plays. Many of them have already been quoted in previous chapters, but they can be illustrated here with some representative selections. In *The Plough and the Stars*, Mrs Gogan expresses one of her macabre pleasures: 'It always gives meself a kind o' thresspassin' joy to feel meself movin' along in a mournin' coach, an' me thinkin' that, maybe, th' next funeral'll be me own, an' glad, in a quiet way, that this is somebody else's.' Fluther announces his pledge of total abstinence: 'You could stan' where you're stannin' chantin', "Have a glass o' malt, Fluther; Fluther, have a glass o' malt", till th' bells would be ringin' th' ould year out an' th' New Year in, an' you'd have as much chance o' movin' Fluther as a tune on a tin whistle would move a deaf man an' he dead.' In *Purple Dust*, when the news is passed along that Avril has gone off 'naked and unashamed', one of the literal-minded Workmen reacts to the shock with: 'This'll denude the disthrict of all its self-denyin' decency.' In *Red Roses For Me*, Brennan o' the Moor urges his bashful Singer to perform: 'Now, Sam, me son o' gold, excavate the shyness out of your system an' sing as if you were performin' before a Royal Command.' In *Cock-a-doodle Dandy*, Shanaar warns two old men about tempta-tion: '. . . for th' circumnambulatory nature of a woman's form often has a detonatin' effect on a man's idle thoughts.' In *The Bishop's Bonfire*, Reiligan and the Codger play with words in typical music-hall fashion:

REILIGAN. From this out, there's to be no talkin'; and if anyone does talk, everybody is to listen to nobody. Anyone—no one—mind yous! (*The three men stand mute.*) Damn it, are yous listenin' to me?

CODGER. Damn it, you; weren't you afther sayin' no one was to listen to no one?

REILIGAN (*wildly*). Not to me; I'm not no one! Not to me. Yous are all to listen to me. Nobody's to listen to anyone, but everybody's to listen to me!

In the non-Irish plays, *The Silver Tassie* and *Within the Gates*, O'Casey found equivalents for this colloquial comedy in the cock-ney idiom of the soldiers and park orators. For the most part, he used this language for the sub-plots, particularly in *Within the Gates*. And in both plays, in which he had ambitiously set out to dramatize the allegorical themes of world war and world depression, he experimented with the stylized language of chant. The experiment proved to be most successful in the symbolic and colloquial languages. The ironic counterpoint of biblical incantation and cockney rhythms revealed all the compassion and terror of the soldiers in a scene of terrible beauty. But O'Casey did not always solve the problem so successfully. In some of the chanted passages in both plays, where he doesn't use biblical or cockney rhythms, he manufactured a heavy alliterative diction in which the mere catalogue of similar sounds is not enough to sustain the language. For example, here is part of a chorus that is chanted by the People in *Within the Gates*, in which the sounds and the sentiments lack freshness and originality:

Bellow good-bye to the buggerin' lot'n come out
To bow down the head 'n bend down the knee to the bee, the bird, 'n the
*   blossom,*
Bann'ring the breast of the earth with a wonderful beauty!

This type of stilted rhetoric, here in the form of a stylized chant, sometimes reappears in the dialogue of the later plays. We become too conscious of the contrived alliteration in *Red Roses For Me* when some of the characters use phrases like 'marjoram moments scentin' the serious hilarity' and 'a hood of gentle magenta over her handsome head'. This is artificial language not living speech. Sometimes Ayamonn drifts into 'literary' jargon in his romantic moods, as when he says: 'Soon enough to browse with wisdom when Time's grey finger puts a warning speck on the crimson rose of youth. Let no damned frosty prayer chill the sunny sighs that dread the joy of love.' The first sentence is rather trite, and the second one fuzzy in meaning. O'Casey's adjectival use of colours can sometimes be mechanical, as it is in the above passage; but in the epiphany scene on the banks of the Liffey when the whole city is suddenly transformed as the setting sun breaks through the clouds, it is an effective and organic part of the dramatic situation. The river, the domes of the buildings, the clothing of the people, once drab greys and blacks, are now miraculously changed into a colour symphony of greens, scarlets, purples, bronze, and silver in the Dublin sunset. For Ayamonn and the people, this pageant of colours is a sign that 'Our city's in the grip o' God'.
O'Casey's ear for living speech seldom betrays him when he

writes about older characters, the comic eccentrics or the keening women, but he has a tendency to sentimentalize young lovers. This is evident in some of the scenes between Davoren and Minnie in *The Shadow of a Gunman*, the Dreamer and Jannice in *Within the Gates*, Ayamonn and Sheila in *Red Roses For Me*, Manus and Foorawn in *The Bishop's Bonfire*. Like many writers who have struggled with the language of sighing young lovers, O'Casey is probably out of his metier here. He has great sympathy for lovers, especially the women, but the dialogue he gives the men sometimes makes them sound like emoting swains. In the drama these characters often turn out to be handsome bores, a fact which becomes even more apparent in the theatre when we see the parts performed by 'romantic juveniles'. But this is not an excuse for Casey's well-meaning awkwardness.

The most glaring example of strained rhetoric occurs in *The Star Turns Red*, for in this play O'Casey seemed to have laboured to construct a special language to suit his political allegory. The dialogue of the Old Man and Old Woman is an exception, for they speak in the vivid Dublin idiom; and furthermore, they are often chorus-like observers who refuse to take sides in the ruthless struggle. But the stilted dialogue of the Communists and Fascists is almost exclusively composed of stark, non-comic invective. This unrelieved invective is reinforced by a cumulative catalogue of savage imagery, but it seems to be a rather mechanical process of piling up figurative epithets. Moreover, since both sides hurl the same kind of insults at each other, the language could be interchangeable. Here are two representative lists of this imagery. The Communists call the Fascists: 'misbegotten worm', 'slippery scut', 'slug-soul'd renegade', 'envy-stippled titivated toad', 'golden-snouted snails', 'silky sulky slow-worm', 'barking mongrels', 'eel-policy'd', 'gang of daws', 'gobbling cormorants'. The Fascists call the Communists: 'melting snails', 'coffin-fac'd get', 'wolves', 'dogs', 'bats', 'owls', 'your hands are claws and your nose a snout', 'red rats', 'oozy scum'. Throughout this play one is aware that the playwright is manipulating the language and the characters.

Thus, it is usually on those occasions when O'Casey departs from the Dublin idiom that his language tends to become 'literary' and artificial. Probably the fact that he was living in exile had something to do with such failures; nevertheless, he had stored up a rich word-hoard during his forty-six years in Dublin and most of the time he was able to draw upon his fabulous memory and imagination. In 1951 he published three one-act 'Irish' farces, *The Hall of Healing*, *Bedtime Story*, and *Time To Go*, which, along with his full-length comedies, indicate how vividly he had retained the Dublin idiom after twenty-five years of exile. One of these satiric farces, *Hall of Healing*, [214] the best of the three, was based upon an incident he had witnessed in a Dublin hospital back in 1924 when he had to get some medicine for his eyes.

Finally, in a consideration of O'Casey's language, something should be said about his expansive stage directions. He probably picked up the habit from his early reading of Shaw's plays. One could argue that, in the strict sense, the kind of subjective comments both of these playwrights make on their characters in the stage directions properly belong to the novel rather than the drama. The playwright can only use dialogue to introduce the reflections and judgements that the novelist develops through indirect discourse. But apparently O'Casey was not one to be intimidated by such strict logic, and like Shaw he assumed that genius can make its own rules. He looked upon the script of a play as a work of literature as well as lines of dialogue that had to be spoken by actors in a theatre, although he clearly intended the stage directions to be an aid to the actors as well as the readers. This information is also intended for the director and the set designer, and it helps the reader to visualize the characters, the scene, and some of the significant stage business. While the audience in the theatre sees only the result of this information, the reader uses it to create a mental picture of characters moving about on a stage. Perhaps it could be said, then, that while extensive stage directions are not an organic part of a play, they can make an important contribution to the reader's enjoyment of dramatic literature, especially when they are handled artfully by playwrights like Shaw and O'Casey. Such a conclusion can be supported by some illustrations from a play like *Juno and the Paycock*, in which O'Casey uses the stage directions to describe his characters and tell us what he thinks about them:

The Captain comes slowly in. He is a man of about sixty; stout, grey-haired and stocky. His neck is short, and his head looks like a stone ball that one sometimes sees on top of a gate-post. His cheeks, reddish-purple, are puffed out, as if he were always repressing an almost irrepressible ejaculation. On his upper lip is a crisp, tightly cropped moustache; he carries himself with the upper part of his body slightly thrown back, and his stomach slightly thrust forward. His walk is a slow, consequential strut. His clothes are dingy, and he wears a faded seaman's cap with a glazed peak.

Joxer steps cautiously into the room. He may be younger than the Captain but he looks a lot older. His face is like a bundle of crinkled paper; his eyes have a cunning twinkle; he is spare and loosely built; he has a habit of constantly shrugging his shoulders with a peculiar twitching movement, meant to be ingratiating. His face is invariably ornamented with a grin.

Mrs Madigan is a strong, dapper little woman of about forty-five; her face is almost always a widespread smile of complacency. She is a woman who, in manner at least, can mourn with them that mourn and rejoice with them that do rejoice. When she is feeling comfortable, she is inclined to be reminiscent; when others say anything, or following a statement made by herself, she has a habit of putting her head a little to one side, and nodding it rapidly several times in succession, like a bird pecking at a hard berry. Indeed, she has a good deal of the bird in her, but the bird instinct is by no means a melodious one. She is ignorant, vulgar and forward, but her heart is generous withal. For instance, she would help a neighbour's sick child; she would probably kill the child, but her intention would be to cure it; she would be more at home helping a drayman to lift a fallen horse. She is dressed in a rather soiled grey dress and a vivid purple blouse; in her hair is a huge comb, ornamented with huge coloured beads. She enters with a gliding step, beaming smile and nodding head.

In the description of the Captain it seems as if O'Casey were actually inventing the image of Barry Fitzgerald. In all these portraits he has captured the distinctive mannerisms and 'humours' of his characters with a Dickensian sense of the comic spirit. A purist might point out that O'Casey is assuming the role of the novelist, but surely the result is more important than the technical transgression.

In the descriptions of his settings O'Casey establishes the distinctive milieu of his plays with an equally imaginative eye for concrete details, though this is properly the responsibility of the playwright. He creates the physical scene like a painter. This is evident in his graphic pictures of tenement Dublin during the Civil War in his early plays; in the surrealistic war scene in the second act of *The Silver Tassie*; in the stylized park world in *Within the Gates*; in the transformation scene on the banks of the Liffey in the third act of *Red Roses For Me*; in the spectacular conception of the Cock and all the supernatural stage business in *Cock-a-doodle Dandy*.

These settings are a vital part of the pageantry of the theatre. When O'Casey combines the pageantry of words and the pageant of spectacle, his plays are truly dramatic and theatrical poems.

CHAPTER VII

◄─►◄─►◄─►◄─►◄─►◄─►◄─►◄─►◄─►◄─►◄─►◄─►◄─►

On a Rock in Devon

◄─►◄─►◄─►◄─►◄─►◄─►◄─►◄─►◄─►◄─►◄─►◄─►◄─►

> When the Irish artist begins to write, he has to create
> his moral world from chaos by himself, for him-
> self.[215]
>
> Stanislaus Joyce

> The earth was [Shaw's] home, and he loved it. He
> was at home among the mortals. His epiphany was the
> showing forth of man to man. Man must be his own
> saviour; man must be his own god.
>
> Sean O'Casey

I. THE RAGE FOR LIFE

THE THEME of exile is in its very nature a tragic one, and this
theme is foreshadowed from the beginning of O'Casey's autobiography, a story of poverty, disease, and frustration which reveals
that he was an exile long before he left Dublin. But though the
alienating forces that shaped his early life pointed inevitably to a
tragic struggle, he always remained in fierce contention with those
forces. As he grew up and became a dramatist he won few material
rewards, he was beaten many times, but he was never defeated.
And when they came, his successes were of the imagination, his
victories were of the spirit.

His life was tragic but it was not a tragedy. For the self-portrait
that emerges from the autobiography is that of a proud rebel with
a mighty rage for life who in the midst of tragic surroundings made
himself a great comic artist. That portrait is presented with such
remarkable integrity and vitality that the man continually rises
above the tragic conditions of his life. Had he been a man of less
spiritual and physical courage, it is doubtful whether he would have
survived the poverty and sickness of his early years, or the alienation and frustration of his later years. Yet the figure who engages

255

in this struggle is seldom idealized, for O'Casey is too honest to gloss over the eccentricities and prejudices that humanize the portrait. For a man of his enormous sympathy and understanding of human frailty, he can sometimes be bitter and even vindictive, especially when he feels he has been wronged or abused, and in these matters he has a very thin skin and a long memory. He maintains his prejudices and his loyalties with equal intractability and faith.

His rage is therefore an inseparable part of his integrity. While Joyce was living out his years of self-exile in Trieste, he once wrote the following prayer: 'O, Vague Something behind everything . . . Give me for Christ's sake a pen and an ink-bottle and some peace of mind, and then, by the crucified Jaysus, if I don't sharpen that little pen and dip it into fermented ink and write tiny little sentences about the people who betrayed me, send me to hell.' [216] And while O'Casey was living out his years of self-exile in Devon, he once made the following declaration: 'God is my judge that I hate fighting. If I be damned for anything, I shall be damned for keeping the two-edged sword of thought tight in its scabbard when it should be searching the bowels of knaves and fools.' [217] Joyce and O'Casey are proud, lonely, and paradoxical figures, injured men who left their native country to go their own eccentric ways; but as artists they remain courageous Dubliners who see the life of their city in relation to the universal order of mankind. Dublin often enraged and disappointed them, yet in the final reckoning it served them as faithfully as they served it. The last word of *Ulysses* is 'Yes', and the last word of the autobiography is 'Hurrah!'

This affirmation of life runs through the six volumes of the autobiography, for above all it is the great heart and the humour of Johnny Casside, his faith in his own destiny and the destiny of man, that illuminates his life. Many battles are fought in this story, and in some of them O'Casey wields his two-edge sword against some minor or undeserving targets. But in the main struggle he rises above pettiness and revenge, turning his wrath and satire against folly, knavery, and injustice. And in many instances his sword is not his only or most effective weapon, for the autobiography is finally controlled by the compassion of the tragi-comic artist.

For the rendering of his life story, O'Casey chose a flexible form and style which allowed him to exploit a variety of techniques. The form is essentially that of the novel, for he uses a third-person narrative approach and a fictional *persona* to represent himself. This is an unusual method for an autobiography, but it has many artistic advantages. It gives the writer a chance to see himself from an aesthetic distance and to avoid the ubiquitous personal pronoun. It frees him from many of the stock methods of the memoir and makes greater demands upon his originality and imagination.

The central point of view is revealed through the sensibility of Johnny Casside—in the later volumes Sean—yet at the same time O'Casey is at liberty, as the omniscient author who sees and knows more than Johnny, to introduce his own observations, asides, jests, and judgements. Thus the narrative is actually told through a double-focus which is varied to suit the demands of the particular mood and incident. He also uses what might be called the multiple-focus of the drama for scenes which are almost entirely rendered through dialogue, and here he relies upon the projection of a series of dramatic voices. These voices are usually identified with specific characters, but occasionally he will use representative or imaginary Dublin street characters. He will often create a whole situation the way it would appear in a play, and the characterization of the people is so complete in their speeches that little or no comment is necessary.

The freedom and virtuosity with which he develops these narrative and dramatic techniques, mixing and even superimposing them in some episodes when he combines comedy and tragedy, fantasy and farce, allows him to use a variety of styles and moods. Within the general framework of indirect discourse, interior monologue, and straight dialogue, then, he develops what might be called a kaleidoscopic style. His language can be terse and concrete, discursive and digressive, poignant and lyrical, satiric and ironic, burlesque and profane, purple and hortatory, inflated and oracular, colloquial and exalted. Like the voluble characters in his plays, O'Casey can be profligate with words, playing with their sounds and meanings, indulging in the game of puns, malapropisms, and comic invective; and using a steady stream of poems, songs, and parodies throughout the work.

At one point in the last volume he says, 'Come, let's thump the world with talk.' And that is what he has done in these six volumes that make up over half a million words. In a work of such magnitude

it is to be expected that the words may sometimes sputter fret-
fully, especially in the later volumes when the narrative tends to
run down and he deviates into polemics, but on the whole they
make a mighty thump.

Since he uses a fictional form, he often ignores the kind of
straight facts one ordinarily expects to find in an autobiography—
vital statistics, dates, and time sequences. He does this because it is
his chief concern to create the imaginative reality of his world and
the impressionistic shaping of his mind through the general years
of childhood, adolescence, and maturity. And like Joyce, he can
make great demands upon his readers, expecting them to know the
geography of Dublin and the men and events of Irish history. The
average reader may therefore miss some of the allusions and fine
points, he may sometimes be confused about the chronology, but
he will not really need any special knowledge to understand and
appreciate the epic account of the awakening of Johnny Casside
who grew up to become a promethean dramatist. That these works
can have a wide and popular appeal, especially the early volumes,
has been illustrated by the highly successful dramatic 'readings'
which Paul Shyre has staged in New York.

Five of the volumes each cover about a decade of his life, and the
last volume covers two decades—some seventy years in all. Here is
an approximate outline of the chronology: *I Knock at the Door*
(1939), 1880–1890; *Pictures in the Hallway* (1942), 1891–1904;
Drums Under the Window (1946), 1905–1916; *Inishfallen Fare Thee
Well* (1949); 1916–1926; *Rose and Crown* (1952), 1926–1934;
Sunset and Evening Star (1954), 1934–1953.

The first two volumes on his childhood and adolescence contain
some of O'Casey's most penetrating and lyrical prose, for here all
the sights and sounds and places of Dublin, and its people, are
reflected through the eager and innocent impressions of young
Johnny. In spite of his ulcerated eyes, he does not miss much,
and what he does not actually sees he feels and imagines with
the sensitivity of a poet. There are many instances of brooding sadness and naïve humour, and often the two moods inter-
mingle and complement each other. There are many instances of
pain and rebellion when Johnny comes in contact with the adult
world, or when his eyes torture him: 'Suddenly there shot into his
eyes a pain like the piercing of many needles, flooding into an
agony that shocked his brain and flashed a glare of crimson light

before him that made him clench his teeth and press his lids tight together till a stream of scalding evil tears forced their way between them, and ran hotly down his cheeks.' There are many instances of tenderness and reverence, especially in the boy's relationship with his mother. She is a noble woman and clearly the most important person in his life. It is the omniscient author who recollects one of his earliest impressions of his mother, and she comes fully alive in an unforgettable character sketch that has the texture of a fine old etching:

Forty years of age the woman was when the boy was three, with hair still raven black, parted particularly down the middle of the head, gathered behind in a simple coil, and kept together by a couple of hairpins; a small nose spreading a little at the bottom; deeply set, softly gleaming brown eyes that sparkled when she laughed and hardened to a steady glow through any sorrow, deep and irremediable; eyes that, when steadily watched, seemed to hide in their deeps an intense glow of many dreams, veiled by the nearer vision of things that were husband and children and home. But it was the mouth that arrested attention most, for here was shown the chief characteristic of the woman: it quivered with fighting perseverance, firmness, human humour, and the gentle, lovable fullness of her nature. Small strong hands, hands that could slyly bathe a festering wound or scour a floor—wet cloth first, then the brush soap-foamed, tearing the dirt out, then wet cloth again and, finally, the dry cloth finishing the patch in back and forward strokes and twisting circles of rhythmic motions. A sturdy figure carried gracefully and with resolution; flexible, at peace in its simple gown of black serge, with its tiny white frill round the neck that was fair and unwrinkled still. A laugh that began in a ripple of humour, and ended in a musical torrent of full-toned mirth which shook those who listened into an irresistible companionship.[218]

When he was six years old his father died, and that was the first of many funerals Johnny was to experience. He had never really had a chance to know his father, and he was bewildered on the day of the funeral, excited by the unusual commotion—the crowd of people, the hearse and the cab drivers in front of the house—and frightened by the mystery of death. Not satisfied merely to record the pathos of Johnny's confused innocence, O'Casey skilfully highlights that pathos by allowing it to develop in contrast to a series of overlapping comic incidents. It is a superb example of O'Casey's characteristic mingling of the serious and humorous modes which occurs so often in the plays and the autobiography. This illustration is a section of the funeral scene:

Johnny stiffened with pride and stroked the band of crisp crêpe on his arm as he saw kids in the crowd watching him and Connor. Stretching out a hand timorously, he stroked the haunch of the nearest horse. The animal gave a shuddering start, and kicked viciously, making the hearse shake and Johnny jump away from him in fright.

—Gaaaa, you mischeevous little bastard, roared the driver wearing the yellow muffler, gaaaa, out o' that, an' leave th' animal alone, or I'll go over an' kick the little backside off you!

Johnny slunk away a little, and turned his back to Connor, so that his shamed and frightened face couldn't be seen.

—Fifteen pints between eight and eleven said the driver wearing the bowler hat, I wouldn't ask anything betther, even on the night of me first daughter's weddin'. We got home, he went on, we got home, but it took two hours to do it, where it should ha' taken only twenty minutes: two solid hours o' mighty sthrivin', but we done it in the end.

—They ought to have the old man warmly folded up be this, said the man wearing the yellow muffler, didderay didderee didderum.

—The both of us were rotto, went on the driver wearing the bowler hat, the two of us strugglin' together, him helpin' me an' me helpin' him, whenever help was needed. We sung The Heart Bowed Down all the way home, fall an' up again, fall an' up again; I'd call it a red-letther night, even afther a day of thinkin'.

—Last week was a rotten one with me, said the third driver; a few roll-an'-tea-for-lunch laddies, who are always lookin' for the return of their fare in the change.

Johnny felt Connor beside him again, and whispering at him over his shoulder.

—Mother says, he whispered, that in a week or so you won't be so cocky.

—You're not comin', anyway, answered Johnny, for I heard me mother saying that she hoped the Connors wouldn't thry to shove their noses in at the funeral.

—Yah, sneered Connor, you're shapin'. Just because your father's dead you think you're big in your black suit, but me mother says it isn't new at all, but only dyed.

Johnny turned slantwise, looked at Connor in the eye, and murmured, If it wasn't for me father bein' dead, I'd go round the lane with you, an' break your snot.

—On the way home, said the man wearing the bowler hat, we met two lovely big-diddied rides, and they were all for us going home with them, but neither of us could let go his hold on the other, and so we had to keep everything buttoned up.

—Wonder they didn' thry to lift yous, said the third driver.

—We were so dhrunk, went on the man wearing the bowler hat, that we didn't know our own religion, but we weren't dhrunk enough for that.

—I'd ha' done something, said the man with the yellow muffler, even if I hadda lie down to do it, didderay, didderee, didderum.

A woman came running to the door of the house, looking about her, saw Johnny, beckoned excitedly to him, and shouted, You're to come in, Johnny, an' give your poor father a last kiss before he's screwed down.

Johnny stood still, shivered, and gaped at the woman standing in the doorway. He retreated a little, and caught hold of Mrs Connor's skirt.

—I won't go, he said. I don't want to go in.

—Here, come in at once, sir, said the woman in the doorway, roughly, an' pay the last respects to your father, who's in heaven now, an' watchin' down on all your doin's, an' listenin' to all your bold sayin's.

—I'll not go in, he repeated plaintively. I'm afraid, an' I'll not go in.

—*I* wouldn't be afraid, Johnny heard Connor say, to kiss me father, if he was dead, would I, mother?

—Don't be afraid, son, said Mrs Connor, patting Johnny's head, your father wouldn't do you any harm, an' when you're grown up, you'd be sorry you hadn't given him a last kiss.

—Come in, you little rut, when you're told, shouted the woman at the door, an' don't be keepin' every one waitin'.

She ran towards him, but he dodged her, and made off down the street, running full-tilt into the man wearing the yellow muffler, trampling on his foot, and hitting his head into the man's belly.

—Jasus, me foot! yelled the man, you lightning-blooded little bastard, where the hell are you goin'!

—He's the dead man's little boy, said the woman, getting hold of Johnny's arm, an' he's wanted to give his dead father a last kiss before he's screwed down.

—An' he was makin' off, snarled the man, an' knockin' the puff out o' people. A nice way of showin' his love for his father.

—Let me go, let me go, screamed Johnny, kicking viciously at the woman's legs, as she dragged him towards the house. I won't go, I don't want to kiss him.

—Your mother'll have a handful in you when you grow up, me boy, she said, as she gathered him forcibly into the house in her arms.

She held him tightly in the midst of the crowd in the room waiting for the coffin to be screwed down. His mother turned round when he began to scream again, came over, and caught his hand in hers.

—Let him down, let him down, Mrs Saunders, she said to the woman. Then she bent down over him, putting her arm round his trembling body and kissing and kissing him, she murmured, There, there, hush, nothing is going to happen to you.

He circled her with his arms, pressed his face into her skirts, and she felt his fingers cleaving through her skirt to the flesh of her thighs.

—I couldn't, I couldn't, he sobbed. Don't ask me, mother, don't ask me to kiss him, I'm frightened to kiss a dead man.

He felt a gentle, sympathetic pressure of an arm around him, and softened his sobbing.

—No one'll ask you to do it, she said, I'll kiss him good-bye for you myself. Just touch the side of the coffin with the tip of your finger.

She gently drew out his arm, and he shuddered deeply when he felt the tip of his finger touching the shiny cold side of the coffin.

—That's the brave little son, she murmured; and now I'll give your father a last kiss from his little boy.

She bent down and kissed the thing in the coffin, and he heard her say in a steady whisper, Good-bye, my Michael; my love goes with you, down to the grave, and up with you to God.

She stepped back, and he felt her body shaking. He looked up and saw her lips quivering in a curious way, as she said quietly to the waiting hearsemen, You may put the lid on top of him now.[219]

He is not afraid when he is with his mother, when he is playing in the streets, or when he is alone in the child's world of imagination. The simplest experiences of everyday life can become little epiphanies for him. Here he stares out of the window at the lamplighter as night falls: 'Johnny watched the little lamplighter running, with his little beard wagging, carrying his pole, with a light like a sick little star at the top of it, hurrying from lamp to lamp, prodding each time a little yellow light into the darkness, till they formed a chain looking like a string of worn-out jewels that the darkness had slung round the neck of night.' [220] And here, as he stands in the doorway of his house watching a summer rainstorm and thinking about the Deluge, a rainbow suddenly arches over the city and he associates it with the biblical story: 'There was the very rainbow, now, sparklin' fine, one end restin' on the roof of Mrs Mullally's house, and the other end leanin' on the top of one of the Dublin Mountains, with the centre touchin' the edge of the firmament; an', if only our eyes were a little brighter, we'd see millions an' millions of burnished angels standin' on it from one end to the other, havin' a long gawk at all that was goin' on in the earth that God made in the beginnin', an' that had to make a fresh start the time that Noah an' his wife, an' his sons, an' his sons' wives came outa the ark with the elephants, the lions, the horses, and the cows that musta given Noah the milk he needed when he was shut off from everything, till the dove came back with the olive branch stuck in her gob.' [221]

And always his sharp ears picked up the talk of the people in the streets. One night when his mother took him for a tram ride to see the decorations and illuminations in the centre of the city in celebration of Queen Victoria's birthday, he overheard the tram conductor arguing with some of the people for turning out to honour Ireland's enemy. The tram conductor is one of O'Casey's favourite Dublin characters and his typical 'Flutherian' voice is heard in many of the volumes. Here are several examples of the speeches that Johnny overhears; they illustrate O'Casey's heightened version of the Dublin idiom, and they represent some of his best dialogue. The conductor speaks first:

—A man 'ud want St Pathrick's crozier to knock a little decency into yous, he said viciously as he tried to turn the pushing into an orderly parade. A nice way the whole of yous musta been reared, with your pushin' an' shovin', like a horde of uncivilized savages that has never seen anything beyond the rim o' their own land! I don't know th' hell why Parnell's wastin' his time thryin' to shape yous into something recognizable as men an' women. Honest to Jasus, I'm getting ashamed of me life to mention I'm Irish in front of anyone showin' the meanest sign or vestige of dickorum. And all of yous riskin' the breakage of your bodies to see a few twinklin' lights set over our heads to do honour to a famine queen rollin' about in a *vis-à-vis* at a time the Irish were gettin' shovelled, ten at a time, into deep an' desperate graves.

—You mind your own business be pullin' the bell for decent people to get on the thram, an' decent people to get off the thram, said a man, having a wide watery mouth with a moustache hanging over it like a weeping willow; an' don't be so sure that the personalities thravellin' are set on givin' a delicate or delirious show of loyalty to anyone thryin' to devastate the efforts of our brave Irish Party fightin' for us on the floor of the House of Commons!

Johnny turned and pulled his mother's sleeve.

That oul' fella, he whispered, is Georgie Middleton's da. Whenever he appears in the street, the boys shout afther him, Georgie Middleton's ma wears the pants of Middleton's da.

—Thrue for you, mister, said a fat woman with a big bustle on her big behind, puffing her way as well as she could on to the tram; for a man who starts fluttherin' idle thoughts in front o' people's faces, accusin' them of hidin' the harp behind a gaudy crown, is just takin' advantage of a special time; an' ought, if things were in a settled state, to be walkin' close to the danger of a sensible castigation.

—Speakin' for meself, only, said the man carrying the wide watery mouth with a drooping moustache hanging over it like a weeping willow, I've serious business to deal with in the heart of the town; an' if th' illuminations were brighter than even all the comets terrifyin' the sky, an' blazin' along at the same time, I'd sit with me face fast in front of me, seein' only the need for Home Rule, an' the green flag with the sunburst in the centre, wavin' everywhere the thram brings me.

—A prime lot of pathriots yous all are, to be sure, said the conductor sarcastically as he pulled the bell-strap for the tram to start; but I notice once yous get safe in, none of yous get out till the cruise is over. It's waitin' a long time I'll be to see yous busy bandagin' your eyes to keep at a distance the signs an' shows of revelry when the thram penethrates into the sthreets, alive with the flags of all nations, save our own.(222)

The second volume begins on the day of Parnell's death in 1891, and the name of Parnell dominates the first third of the book. Johnny is only eleven years old at the time and he is confused by the bitter arguments he hears about Ireland's dead 'King' by the people who praised and damned him, and he feels that the Pro-testants are no better than the Catholics: 'Parnell! What had this man done that all the people were so upset about him, one way or another? The mention of his name always gave rise to a boo or a cheer. The roman catholics, who wouldn't let a word be said against him a while ago, now couldn't pick out words villainous enough to describe him; while the protestants, who were always ashamed of him, now found grace and dignity in the man the roman catholics had put beyond the pale.'[223] (Much has been made of O'Casey's eccentric refusal to use capital letters for 'roman catholic', but it should be noted that he also writes 'protestant' in lower case throughout the autobiography. He is fair, or unfair, to both churches.) It was the Parnell controversy that first made Johnny aware of the hypocrisy of the adult world. He seldom received satisfactory answers when he asked his elders what Parnell had done. A short time after Parnell's death, Johnny's Uncle Tom took him on a trip to see Kilmainham Jail where Parnell had once been imprisoned by the British. His uncle had served in the Crimean War and had received a severe sabre wound which Florence Nightingale herself had bandaged. On the trip to Kilmainham, Johnny asked his uncle a lot of questions about Parnell and many other Irish heroes, and about his brothers Tom and Mick who at the time were in the British Army. Johnny's innocent questions and his uncle's embarrassed answers uncover many of the paradoxes of Irish history, and the episode is a brilliant example of O'Casey's comic irony, handled almost exclusively through dialogue. Here is the main part of it:

Johnny thrust his chest out, and walked swift beside the lanky figure of his uncle, glancing now and again at the soft, dark-brown eyes, the wide mouth sthretchin' nearly from ear to ear, and the snow-white hair tumbling over his ears and falling over his forehead.

Away in a tram from Nelson's Pillar they went for miles an' miles, having first managed Cork Hill where the two tram horses were helped by another, called a pulley-up, that waited there to link itself in front of any tram wanting to mount the Hill; along Thomas Street, Uncle Tom pointed out St Catherine's Church, where, he said, Robert Emmet had been hung, drawn, and quartered for rebellion against England.

—Is it a roman catholic church? asked Johnny.

—No, no, said Uncle Tom; it's a protestant one.

—You'd think they'd hang a roman catholic rebel outside a roman catholic church, said Johnny.

—But poor Emmet was a protestant, Johnny.

—Now, that's funny, said Johnny, for I remember the night of the illuminations, the conductor of the thram we were in, singing about someone called Wolfe Tone, an' me Ma told me he was a protestant too.

—Ay, was he, said Uncle Tom, an' Parnell an' Grattan an' Napper Tandy too.

—They all seemed to have been protestants, murmured Johnny, relapsing into thoughtful silence for some moments. What's dhrawn an' quarthered? he asked suddenly.

—Oh, said his uncle, when a man's hanged, they cut off his head and divide him up into four parts.

—An' was that what was done to poor Robert Emmet?

—It musta been when he was sentenced to it.

—Why was Robert Emmet a rebel, Uncle?

—Oh, I suppose he didn't like to have the English here.

—What English, Uncle? I've never seen any English knockin' about.

—The soldiers, Johnny, the English soldiers.

—What, is it Tom an' Mick you mean?

—No, no; not Tom or Mick; they're not English—they're Irish.

—But they're soldiers, aren't they?

—Yes, yes; I know they're soldiers.

—They're Irish soldiers, then, Uncle, that's what they are. Aren't they, Uncle? Same as you were when you fought in the Crimea.

—No, no, no; not Irish soldiers.

—Well, what sort of soldiers are they?

—English, English soldiers, really.

—Then Emmet musta wanted to get them outa the counthry, as well as the others, if they're English soldiers. But Mick an' Tom an' you are Irish, so how could you be English soldiers?

—We're Irish, but we join the army to fight for England, see?

—But, why fight for England, Uncle?

—Simply because England's our counthry, that's all.

—Me Ma says me Da said it isn't, but that Ireland's our counthry; an' he was a scholar, an' knew nearly, nearly everything, almost; so it isn't, you see.

Uncle Tom stroked his chin, glanced at Johnny with his big soft eyes, and looked puzzled.

—Isn't what, what isn't what? he asked.

—That England's not our counthry at all, and that everyone here's Irish.

—Well, so they are, said Uncle Tom.

—Well, went on Johnny, if Mick an' Tom are Irish, how can they be English soldiers?

—Because they fight for England; can't you understand?

—But why do they, an' why did you fight for England, Uncle?

—I had to, hadn't I?

—How had you?

—Because I was in the English Army, amn't I afther tellin' you! said his uncle, a little impatiently.

—Yes, but who made you, Uncle?

—Who made me what?

—Fight for England?

—Good God, boy, don't you know your Bible? And Uncle Tom took a fat-headed pipe from his pocket, and was about to stick it in his mouth when he remembered he couldn't smoke in a tram, so he put it back again. Johnny felt that his uncle was puzzled, and a little cross because he was puzzled. So he sat silent, and for a few moments looked out of the tram window, thinking how hard it was to get anything out of grown-ups unless they had a book in their hand. He wanted to know these things; he felt he must know. He glanced at his uncle's kind face. He had heard that long ago, and Tom a young man, that he had been a policeman, wearing comical clothes, sky-blue cut-away coat, top-hat, and white duck trousers; that he hated pulling anyone; that when he did, and they came near the station, his uncle would push the prisoner from him and say, For God's sake go home, and have a rest, and come out again when you've had a sound sleep; and that all the oul' fellas an' oul' ones called out after him when he passed, God bless you, God bless Mr. Hall who wouldn't harm anybody, so that, in the end, he had to leave the police.

—Where in the Bible does it say, Uncle, that the Irish must fight for the English?

—In the seventeenth verse o' the second chapter o' the first o' Pether, it says, Fear God, honour the king, so there you are, Johnny; we can't get out of it. My father before me learned it; I learned it; and you're learning it now.

—An' whoever doesn't is a very wicked person, and is bound to go to hell, isn't he?

—Very wicked and bound to go to hell, echoed Uncle Tom.

Johnny thought for a moment, watching the horses' heads nodding as they strained forward to pull the heavy tram along.

—Me Ma says me Da said that Parnell was anything but a wicked man, Uncle.

—Parnell a wicked man? 'course he wasn't. Who said he was?

—Why didn't he fight for England, Uncle, then?

The fat-headed pipe came again out of Uncle Tom's pocket, who looked at it longingly, then put it back again.

—What are you goin' to buy with the penny your mother gave you, when we get outa the thram? he asked Johnny.

—Oh, just jawsticker or a sponge-cake or something—why didn't he, Uncle?

—Why didn't he who?

—Why didn't Parnell fight for England an' not go again the Queen?

—I wouldn't say that Parnell went again her.

—Oh yes, he did, said Johnny deliberately, for me Ma heard me Da sayin' once that Parnell paid no regard to the Queen; and would sooner rot in jail than obey any law made be her, an' that he worked, night an' day, to circumvent them because, he said, English law was robbery. An Georgie Middleton told me he had a terrible row with his father because Georgie stuck up for Parnell, and his oul' fella was afraid of him, and slunk out to get dhrunk and came home cryin'.

—Georgie shouldn't go against his father be sticking up for Parnell.

—But why shouldn't he stick up for him, Uncle, when you say that Parnell wasn't a wicked man?

—Because Georgie Middleton's a protestant, that's the why, Johnny.

—Yes, but Parnell you said was a protestant too, so why shouldn't a protestant stick up for another protestant?

—Oh, you're too young yet to understand things, replied Uncle Tom with a little irritation. When you're older, you'll know what's right and what's wrong.

—Grown up, like you, Uncle?

—Grown up, like me, Johnny.

—When I'm like you, I'll understand everything, won't I?

—Yes, yes; then these things won't be a bother to you any more.(224)

But of course these things did bother Johnny when he grew up, and he went on asking embarrassing questions for the rest of his life. One cannot help feeling sympathy for his poor Uncle Tom— that fine old man with the big soft eyes who had been unsuccessful as a policeman because he didn't have the heart to make an arrest— fumbling over his answers, longing to escape with a smoke of his 'fat-headed pipe', and finally taking refuge in the Bible and the inscrutability of life. Johnny admired and loved his uncle, even though he enjoyed teasing him, but he was not always so charitable with his less admirable victims when he grew up. This passage illustrates, perhaps better than anything O'Casey wrote about himself, the shaping of his character and the aims he was to set for him self when he became a dramatist. It reveals his stubborn determination to get at the heart of the hypocrisies and deceits that most men accept or ignore; it reveals his shrewd ability to perceive the comic ironies that appear when people are encouraged to unmask themselves. And behind his pointed questions there is that impetus which drove him to educate himself so that he could enter the adult world well armed with the knowledge that would help him fight against those who tried to alter or suppress the truth.

In the third and fourth volumes, after Johnny learned the Gaelic language and became Sean, and then decided to become a dramatist, his underlying traits and aims are strengthened and more sharply defined. As he gradually loses his innocence and gains in confidence, the story is told through the maturing vision of a man who knows what he wants from life. In the main, the narrative is now presented as on a revolving stage with the ever-present Sean leaning against the proscenium arch, observing the rapidly changing tableaux of his life and times and offering his commentary, impassioned and defiant, merry and malicious, on the passing parade. It was a time of great agitation and excitement, for during those years leading up to 1916 many drums were heard in Dublin. And for a time Sean followed some of them.

His chief heroes in *Drums Under the Window* are Dr Michael O'Hickey, the 'lost leader' in the struggle for the language revival, and Jim Larkin, the 'promethean' leader of the labour movement. Sean waves his rhetorical sword in moving tributes to both men. Dr O'Hickey who was dismissed and broken by the bishops and then quickly forgotten by the inglorious 'Gaelahads' whose battle he had fought: 'Here is one who remembers you, O'Hickey. Here is one who, when you died, had but a flitter of a coat on his back, who walked on the uppers of his boots, who hadn't the penny to buy the paper telling of your death; here is one left to say you were a ray in Ireland's Sword of Light—a ray then, and a ray still, and no episcopal pall can hide its flaming.' [225] Larkin the mighty champion of labour who offered the oppressed masses of Dublin the promise of bread and poetry: 'Gifts of the Almighty, went on the voice, labour—a gift not a curse—poetry, dancing, and principles; and Sean could see that here was a man who would put a flower in a vase on a table as well as a loaf on a plate.'[228]

These are the things that are most important to Sean, and he is scornful of the men who forget them. He views with satiric scorn the leaders who beat their religious and political drums. He makes fun of Arthur Griffith's brand of narrow nationalism which denounced Synge and Yeats and had no use for militant labour. He calls Griffith 'Marthur Gruffith' and 'Arthur Up Griffith', the latter a pun on the Welsh patronymic prefix 'Ap' and the Irish cheer, as in 'Up the Rebels'. Most of the puns are turned against the nationalists and the clergy. A Gaelic Leaguer protests against the 'sulfurious infamity'[227] of Synge's *Playboy*, and the statue of St Patrick comes to life to object that Larkin's aims for the people are the equivalent of 'hitchin' your flagon to a bar'.[226]

Sean and/or O'Casey satirizes both Catholic and Protestant churchmen; the Catholics largely for their sins of commission, their political manœuvring and denunciations of Larkin; the Protestants largely for their sins of omission, their sanctimonious disregard of the needs of the people. He can indulge in long arguments about the blunders of the clergy, but he can also dramatize these issues in wild scenes of fantasy and farce that recall the mocking, surrealistic humour of Joyce's *Ulysses*. One such scene takes place during a riot in O'Connell Street in 1913 when the striking workers were locked out and the Catholic Hierarchy sided with the employers, urged the people to reject Larkin's 'satanic' leadership and break the strike. Suddenly, from the roof of the Pro-Cathedral, just off O'Connel Street, the statue of St Patrick shouts down at a distressed Bishop Eblananus, warning him that he must control his rebellious flock, make them obey the laws and send them back to work. And presently Nelson, looking down from the greater height of his Pillar in the centre of the street, gets into the act with some Anglo-Saxon advice, whereupon the bishop and the saint, intimidated by the common enemy, forget themselves and end up by defending the Irish strikers against the Englishman. Here is the last part of this devastating burlesque:

—Oh! I've thried, an' thried, an' thried, said the Bishop, petulantly, till I'm tired.

—Well, thry again! shouted the saint. Don't they know the law—that, in its blessed equality, it forbids the rich as well as the poor to resist

authority coming from God, to steal bread, to sleep in the open, or to
beg in the streets? Have you been teaching them anything at all, man?
They must be taught to be trim, correct, and orderly like the English—
d'ye hear us talkin', man?

—'Course I hear you—I'd want to be deaf if I didn't.

—Well, roared the saint, losing his temper for the first time in his life,
why don't you come here an' shout it down at them?

—Shout it yourself, if you're so eager, an' see what you'll make of it!
vehemently replied the patient bishop, now aroused for the second time
in his life.

—Oh, said Patrick in despair, clasping his hands, and turning up his
eyes to Heaven. Oh! *Hibernica salubrio, este pesta quaesta essentia terrifica
tornadocum!*

—Yah! leered the figure of Nelson, leaning precariously over his
pedestal, and shoving his cocked hat farther over his blind eye with
his remaining hand, to get a better view; now yous know a little of
what we have to contend against to keep yous in the bonds of law'n
order!

—Yah, yourself! shouted Patrick, now beside himself at being jeered
at be an intherloper, drummin' the platform with the butt-end of his
staff; if all had their rights, me bucko, it's not you'd be stuck up there in
a state of honour, but me, or that other dacent man standin' there, Eddy
Eblananus, born an' reared only a stone's-throw from Lam Doyle's an'
th' Three-Rock Mountain. An' who but the foolish Irish lifted you to
where y'are?

—Ay, said Eblananus, now on his feet, and standing well out to fix
his eyes on Nelson, with a fighting swing of his frock, an' let him be
aware he'd be wantin' th' epaulettes on his shouldhers an' th' gold lace
on his cocked hat, if it wasn't for the Finucanes, the Finnegans, Fogar-
ties, and the Flaherties at Trafalgar's Bay, and among the slimy rushes
at the open mouth of th' Nile!

—Moreover, me gentleman, went on Patrick, it's not to th' English
we'll look for lessons in spiritual or corporal deportment, I can tell you
that!

—Let him get down here on the platform, shouted Eblananus, an',
ould an' disabled as I am with a touchy heart, I'll show him a few
military manœuvres that'll stagger him!

—Control yourselves, gentlemen, murmured the stony voice of
Nelson; try to control yourselves.

—Control yourself! shouted Patrick up at him. If you could, you

wouldn't send your murdherous polis out to maim an' desthroy poor
men lookin' for no more than a decent livin'. Gah! If me crozier could
only reach up to you, I'd knock your other eye out! [229]

Such scenes of fantasy and farce continue to appear in *Inishfallen Fare Thee Well*, but this volume which brings Sean through
the most crucial decade of his life is mainly written in tragic and
ironic moods. It covers a series of tragedies, triumphs, and anti-
climaxes, beginning with the death of his mother and ending with
his journey into exile. The description of his mother's death and
her pauper's funeral in the chapter 'Mrs Casside Takes a Holiday'
contains some of his finest elegiac and ironic prose. Thereafter,
heartbroken and alone, he goes on to give a tragi-comic account of
the turbulent Irish war—the guerrilla warfare against the Black
and Tans and the outbreak of Civil War over the Free State
treaty—as seen through the eyes of a tenement-dweller; he describes his failures and finally his successes as an Abbey playwright, his impressions of Lady Gregory and Yeats, and his bitter
disillusionment over the *Plough* riots; he turns his wrath against
the Catholic Hierarchy for their suppression of Dr Walter Mc-
Donald; he mocks the post-war Irish Government as a petty-
bourgeois alliance of politicians and priests; he is shocked into revealing his snobbery when he sneers at Yeats and AE because they
read detective and western stories; he satirizes the literary saloons
where he is looked upon as a 'gutter-snipe' dramatist from the
slums; he decides in his lonely anger that he must leave Ireland
if he is to maintain his integrity as a man and a writer. 'He would
be no more of an exile in another land than he was in his own. He
was a voluntary exile from every creed, from every party, and
from every literary clique. . . .' [230]

But it is not only his own feeling of isolation that releases his
wrath. He can never forget the inferno of the Dublin slums, and
he cannot forgive those who keep the people trapped in their
miserable hovels. His compassionate rage against the inhumanity
of the rotting tenements is noble. Nevertheless, when he turns
from the stark realism of life in Catholic Ireland to the rosy idealism of life in Communist Russia, he can sound somewhat naïve as
he launches into flights of impressionistic rhetoric. Toward the
end of the chapter 'A Terrible Beauty Is Borneo', as he wanders
through the slum streets, he writes:

Frequently he wandered, hurt with anger, through these cancerous streets that were incensed into resigned woe by the rotting houses, a desperate and dying humanity, garbage and shit in the roadway; where all the worst diseases were the only nobility present; where the ruddy pictures of the Sacred Heart faded into a dead dullness by the slimy damp of the walls oozing through them; the few little holy images they had, worn, faded, and desperate as the people were themselves; as if the images shared the poverty and the pain of them who did them reverence. Many times, as he wandered there, the tears of rage would flow into his eyes, and thoughts of bitter astonishment made him wonder why the poor worm-eaten souls there couldn't rise in furious activity, and tear the guts out of those who kept them as they were.[231]

How right, how magnificent this rage. But then, as if to avoid going mad from his fierce grief, he thinks hopefully about the life in Russia that he has never seen and his visionary imagination takes over:

The Red Star is a bright star. No pope, no politician, no cleric, no prince, no press-lord can frighten it down now, or screen its ray from our eyes. It is the evening star, and it is the bright and shining star. It is the star shining over the flock in the field, over the mother crooning her little one to rest, over the girl arraying herself for the bridal, over the old couple musing by the fireside, over the youngster playing in the street, over the artist achieving a new vision in colour, over the poet singing his song, over the sculptor carving out a fair thing that he alone can see hidden in a stone, over the hammer building the city, over the sickle cutting the corn, over the sailor sailing the seven seas, over the dreaming scientist discovering better and more magical ways of life, over the lover and his lass in ecstasy on the yellow sands, coming through the rye, or sauntering through the indifferent business of some city street, over the miner bending in the deep tomb where the sun-embalmed coal lies low, over the soldier guarding his country's life, over doctor and nurse, forgetting themselves that they may coax back health into all sick persons and young children.

Morning star, hope of the people, shine on us!

Star of power, may thy rays soon destroy the things that err, things that are foolish, and the power of man to use his brother for profit so as to lay up treasure for himself where moth and rust doth corrupt, and where thieves break through and steal.

Red Mirror of Wisdom turning the labour in factory, field and
workshop into the dignity of a fine song;

Red Health of the sick, Red Refuge of the afflicted, shine on us all.

Red Cause of our joy, Red Star extending till thy five rays, covering
the world, give a great light to those who sit in the darkness of
poverty's persecution.

Herald of a new life, of true endeavour, of common sense, of a
world's peace, of man's ascent, of things to do bettering all things
done;

The sign of Labour's shield, the symbol on the people's banner;

Red Star, shine on us all![232]

How beautiful, how ideal this vision. But is it Russian Communism? One might substitute for O'Casey's Red Star, the Star
of Bethlehem or the symbol of almost any religion based upon the
brotherhood of man, and this glowing incantation of semi-
biblical dithyrambs would lose none of its significance and power.
This is a characteristic example of what O'Casey means when he
says he is a Red—and he is like Ruskin who in his visionary
'Letters to the Workmen and Labourers of Great Britain' described his Communism as the 'reddest of the red . . . the ver-
milion, or Tyrian-red sect of us'.[233] There is indeed much point
in O'Casey's claim that he was a Communist before he had heard
of Karl Marx. He says at one point: 'Communism isn't an invention of Marx; it is a social growth, developing through the
ages, since man banded together to fight fear of the unknown, and
destroy the danger from mammoth and tiger of the sabre-tooth.'[234]
His Red Star is therefore an ethical not a political symbol; it is a
universal symbol of his humanistic creed. It has its mythic
analogues in Blake's vision of Jerusalem, in Shelley's unbound
Prometheus, in Ruskin's Fors Clavigera, in Whitman's Song
En-Masse, in Shaw's Communistic Christianity.

Although O'Casey associates his myth with an idyllic Russian
society, a dialectical Marxist would probably find little room in his
system for this type of eclectic and poetic humanism. And a devout Irishman would probably dismiss it as a pagan's vision of
Tir na nOg, the Land of Heart's Desire. The vision itself and the
motives that inspired it are no less noble for that, but the context
in which O'Casey contrasts an Irish inferno with a Russian paradise—the one all-too-real, the other all-too-imaginary—betrays

his political *naïveté*. Obviously the Russians were taking important steps toward the elimination of poverty, but presumably there were and still are many reasons for discontent in Russia—ethical as well as economic—and yet O'Casey overlooks the fact that if he wrote about Russian life in the critical way that he wrote about Irish life, the commissars would probably treat him more roughly than the clerics did. Furthermore, since his hymn to the shining Red Star is above all a celebration of freedom, it is difficult to see how he could be any more receptive to the authoritarian discipline of Russian Communism than he has been to the authoritarian discipline of Irish clericalism. Unquestioning obedience is one of the main dogmas of both systems, and O'Casey, a proud man of conscience, has spent all his life damning 'braces' and blessing 'relaxes'.

There is plenty of high-spirited damning and blessing in the last two volumes, and through the lonely and often heart-breaking years of exile he remains so loyal to his humanistic creed that the overwhelming passion of the man transcends the prejudices. Nevertheless, his prejudices leave their mark on him, for exile can be a curse as well as a release. He can never forget Dublin, its glories and mostly its miseries, and he remembers old wounds, settles old scores, and pursues a treadmill of arguments against Catholic apologists.

He is not, he insists, against the faith of the Church but the pontifical and reactionary churchman whose blunders he is always quick to point out. That proverb that Shaw loved to quote seems to be his guiding principle: 'The nearer the Church, the farther from God.'[235] When his friend Barry Fitzgerald, the actor, writes to tell him sadly that he fears religious prejudice is still strong in Dublin, which 'is very catholic now',[236] Sean replies, 'Less catholic, Barry, more clerical'. He is more convinced than ever that the over-zealous Irish clergy have distorted Christianity into a joyless faith, puritanical and negative. But he does not limit himself to Irish Catholics in this respect, for he mocks the churchmen and writers of all persuasions who reduce the glorious mystery of life to a wail of sin and self-mortification when he roars: 'Original sin has got us all by the short hairs!'[237]

He is determined to thump the world with what is on his mind. For a time after he arrived in England he was invited to some of the big houses of London, but as he describes these episodes in *Rose and Crown* he often emerges as a rambunctious Fluther Good turned loose in high society, and he was not long for that world. He was still faced with the struggle of trying to support his wife and children, especially after 1934 when his new plays were seldom performed. But he found some peace when he finally settled in a quiet little Devonshire village in 1939, and the modest earnings from the successive volumes of the autobiography, especially the American sales, gradually eased though they never eliminated his financial burdens.

In spite of those burdens he continued to live and write on his own terms. When someone challenged those terms he could defend himself with a verbal broadside that devastated his opponent. But he could also be vindictive in his retaliation, and in *Sunset and Evening Star* he wrote a nasty attack on George Orwell, whom he repaid in kind for having written a nasty review of *Drums Under the Window*. His writing suffers most when he lingers in one of his contentious moods, and then even his attempts at satire become fretful and forced. Take for example this laboured passage in which he attempts to play with some Joycean puns:

All Ireland's temporal activities had been placed under saintly protection—Textiles under St Clotherius, Building under Saints Bricin and Cementino, Brewing and Distilling under St Scinful, Agriculture under St Spudadoremus, Metal Work under St Ironicomus, Pottery under St Teepotolo, Fishing under St Codoleus, Book-making under St Banaway, the whole of them presided over by the Prayerman, St Preservius, a most holy man of great spiritual preprotensity, who was a young man in the reign of Brian Boru, and who passed to his rest through a purelytic seizure the day he tried to read the first few lines of Joyce's damnable *Ulysses*. [238]

And yet the man who could write such a laboured passage could also write, several pages farther along in the same chapter, 'Under an Irish Window', a sparkling passage of sustained satirical brilliance like the ingenious jeep-invasion of Ireland episode. He later expanded this episode for *The Bishop's Bonfire*, and even in its original form it proved that he had not lost his touch. He could also write that memorable chapter, 'Black Oxen Passing By', on his reconciliation with Yeats, in which he pays a gallant and moving tribute to the great poet; he could recapture all the excitement of his Whitmanesque discovery of America in the account of his journey to that country in 1934, which covers the last third of *Rose and Crown*. And in the final volume he could write vividly and shrewdly about his visit to Cambridge University, where he had fun with the students and fought with the dons, and gave a lecture called 'The Holy Ghost Leaves England'; he could write with infinite compassion about the poor children of London who were evacuated to Devon during the war; he could write amusingly and passionately about his friendship with the Shaws in a chapter that concludes with a lyrical testament to Shaw.

When one considers the total image of the man that is revealed in the autobiography—his faith and his courage, his frustrations and his frailties—one cannot help feeling that O'Casey might have been describing himself when he said of Shaw:

The earth was his home, and he loved it. He was at home among the mortals. His epiphany was the showing forth of man to man. Man must be his own saviour; man must be his own god. Man must learn, not by prayer, but by experience. Advice from God was within ourselves, and nowhere else. Social sense and social development was the fulfilment of the law and the prophets. A happy people made happy by themselves. There is no other name given among men by which we can be saved, but by the mighty name of Man. [239]

2. A PORTRAIT OF THE ARTIST AS A GREEN CROW

Two years after he finished his autobiography, O'Casey drew a portrait of himself as a Green Crow, in his book of that name. It is a very significant portrait because it highlights the two essential impulses that have motivated him throughout his life—the mock-heroic and the heroic, the satiric laughter and the visionary faith.

The Green Crow is a complex old bird, the most uncommon of common birds. He can be gay and gregarious, proud and lonely. He is capable of profound hope and faith, but he has seldom shown charity toward his enemies. He loves a jest for its own sake, yet he also sees laughter as a weapon against evil. He can mock all aspects of life that displease him, but behind the anti-heroic laughter of the crow there is the heroic faith of an artist who envisions a better world. He says at one point:

A laugh's a great natural stimulator, a pushful entry into life; and once we can laugh, we can live. It is the hilarious declaration made by man that life is worth living. Man is always hopeful of, always pushing towards, better things; and to bring this about, a change must be made in the actual way of life; so laughter is brought in to mock at things as they are so that they may topple down, and make room for better things to come.(240)

But when those better things come too slowly, or not at all, he can turn from laughter to rage. He is seldom cautious or diplomatic in his struggles to uphold his own integrity or what he considers the dignity and needs of his fellow men. Unlike Joyce's birdman, Dedalus, the Green Crow chose exile and cunning but not silence:

Some Latin writer once said: 'If a crow would feed in quiet, it would have more meat.' A thing this Green Crow could never do: it has always and has still to speak and speak while it seeks and finds its food, and so has had less meat than it might have had if only it had kept its big beak shut.(241)

There is a double moral in this beast-fable, and it is also revealed in his career as a dramatist, for we see in his plays that in order to live, he must laugh and he must take a stand. The crow and the artist are motivated by these two essential impulses. The first, the mock-heroic, could be called his aesthetic impulse to create a tragi-comic image of the world as he saw it; the second, the heroic, could be called his ethical impulse to create a prophetic image of the world as it might be.

He is at the height of his power when he fully exploits the first impulse. in an early tragi-comedy like *The Plough and the Stars*, and when he successfully combines both impulses in a later comic-fantasy like *Cock-a-Doodle Dandy*. It was with *The Silver Tassie* that he first began to combine these aesthetic and ethical impulses in a bold and original way, and the symbolic second act of that play remains one of the outstanding achievements in modern drama. Nevertheless, he was thereafter to be confronted with the danger that his moral passion might over-ride his tragi-comic genius, and that is what happened in plays like *The Star Turns Red* and *Oak Leaves and Lavender*. As for the rest of the later plays, that danger was always present, yet he overcame it brilliantly more often than he succumbed to it, in moralities like *Within the Gates* and *Red Roses For Me*, in comedies like *Purple Dust* and *The Bishop's Bonfire*. He took great risks, and in spite of some partial failures, his notable achievements were invariably gained as a result of his inspired treatment of the theatrical and dramatic arts. He chose ingenious theatrical techniques and superb comic characters for the dramatization of his ethical themes.

It is easy to say, as many people have, that O'Casey should not have taken such risks; that he should have rejected his ethical impulse and trusted his aesthetic impulse; that, in short, he should have saved himself and left to others the quixotic job of trying to save the world. But the trouble with such advice is that it entirely overlooks the artistic temperament of the man and the tragedy of exile which shaped his life. First of all, where his art was concerned he was absolutely incapable of compromise. He could not bargain for a cheap or easy success; he would not go on rewriting his early plays to satisfy his critics. There is perhaps no better way to stress this point than to apply to O'Casey what Stanislaus Joyce wrote about his brother James, in comparing him to those writers who make their compromises: 'What he condemned was their vacillating, compromising attitude toward literature and the host of issues it raised, their willingness to come to terms with the rabblement for the sake of a little peace and success, their literary simony. Falsity of purpose was the literary sin against the Holy Ghost, and he was vigilant to detect it.'[242] Joyce and O'Casey were inspired by different daemons—Dedalus the cunning artificer and Prometheus the rebellious light-bringer—but they were alike in their incorruptible dedication to their art. And they both chose the bitter freedom of exile in order to pursue their art on their own terms.

For O'Casey exile has meant heart-break not only because he was cut off from Ireland but because he saw his country turn into a joyless island dominated by crawthumping priests and politicians. Determined to be heard on this issue, he wrote a series of comic-fantasies in which he combined his aesthetic and ethical impulses. He spoke out against the repressive measures of Church and State in the only way he knew, with his mock-heroic satire and his promethean joy of life.

Many years earlier Shaw had anticipated the Church and State

issue in *John Bull's Other Island* (1907). The unfrocked Father
Keegan, perhaps the real hero of the play, bitterly proclaims that
Ireland is hell, and he goes on to present his mad dream of heaven,
which is his prophecy for the redemption of his country. 'Every
dream is a prophecy', he says, and then he states his dream:

In my dreams it is a country where the State is the Church and the
Church the people: three in one and one in three. It is a commonwealth
in which work is play and play is life: three in one and one in three. It
is a temple in which the priest is the worshipper and the worshipper is
worshipped: three in one and one in three. It is a godhead in which all
life is human and all humanity divine: three in one and one in three. It
is, in short, the dream of a madman.[243]

The play begins with Larry Doyle's outcry against 'the torturing, heart-scalding, never satisfying, dreaming, dreaming, dreaming, dreaming!' and it ends with Keegan's prophecy, the dream of
a frustrated madman. But Shaw himself added a prophetic dream
of his own in the more hopeful Preface, where he forecast that the
third force in Keegan's trinity, the people—or Democracy—
would be the means of realizing the dream, after Ireland won her
political freedom from England. According to Shaw, the end of
British tyranny would bring about the end of the 'sacerdotal
tyranny' of the Roman Catholic Church in Ireland:

In a word, the Roman Catholic Church, against which Dublin Castle
is powerless, would meet the one force on earth that can cope with it
victoriously. That force is Democracy, a thing far more Catholic than
itself. Until that force is let loose against it, the Protestant garrison can
do nothing to the priesthood except consolidate it and drive the people
to rally round it in defence of their altars against the foreigner and the
heretic. When it is let loose, the Catholic laity will make short work of
sacerdotal tyranny in Ireland as it has done in France and Italy. And in
doing so it will be forced to face the old problem of the relations of
Church and State. A Roman Catholic party must submit to Rome; an
anti-clerical Catholic party must of necessity become an Irish Catholic
party.[244]

Alas, Shaw was as mad as Keegan. And maybe O'Casey is as
mad as both of them—but noble madmen all—if he thinks his

satires on 'sacerdotal tyranny' and his dreams of the joy of life can change the relationship between Church and State in present-day Ireland; two in one and one in two. As for the people—Ireland is officially a democracy, but unofficially it is a clerical state, and there is no indication that the people, ninety-five per cent of whom are Roman Catholic, and more mindful of the strictures of their clergy than the people of any other country, would desire or be in a position to desire a change. The Irish Catholic hierarchy has no official voice in the government and it does not need it, because it has done such a thorough job of conditioning and controlling what Irishmen think and do—faith and morals cover practically every aspect of Irish life—that it is justifiably confident that no Irish parliament will pass legislation which is in any way critical of or inimical to the vested interests of the Church.

Some people, even some of the more liberal priests, may grumble privately about the Archbishop's prohibitions and pronouncements, but not many individuals who expect to go on living and working in Ireland take the risk of making their views public. As we have seen, one word from the Archbishop was enough to condemn O'Casey's *The Drums of Father Ned* and the dramatization of Joyce's *Ulysses*. The Irish Catholic Church does not encourage a free and open discussion of ideas, and anti-clericalism is invariably interpreted as anti-Catholicism. If, in Shaw's paradox, Democracy is more Catholic than Catholicism itself, modern Ireland is something less than Catholic, something less than a Democracy.

There are a few exceptional men in Ireland today who have spoken out courageously against the rigid authority of the Church, which is indirectly implemented by the censorship law of the State, and they are usually the writers who see the danger of this dual control most clearly and suffer most from it. One such writer, Sean O'Faolain, has underscored the gravity of the problem in the following manner:

In Ireland, today, priests and laity rest at ease—with one qualification. Only one group is held at arm's length, the writers or intellectuals. They . . . see that the intellectual struggle is upon Ireland's doorstep. They want questions to be raised, and answered. The Church relies on the weapon of rigid authority. It could do that as long as it was concerned with an Ireland protected and sheltered from the world. The writers

see clearly that this isolation is now a dream. Walls of censorship have
been erected to keep out books and films that raise awkward questions.
Practically every Irish writer of note has at one time or another been
thrown to the lambs, i.e. in the interests of the most unsophisticated
banned in his own country, some over and over again.[245]

There is also a notable exception among the Irish press, and
that is the *Irish Times*, which has consistently opposed the official
censorship of the State and the unofficial censorship of the Church.
But it must be remembered that this politically independent and
religiously uncommitted newspaper—an Irish anomaly—is read
by less than ten per cent of the population of Dublin, and has a
negligible circulation in the rest of the country. In recent years the
State has been broadening its censorship activities by allowing its
Customs authorities to seize any books which they consider to be
indecent or undesirable, before the Censorship Board has had a
chance to judge them. In the Spring of 1959 an *Irish Times*
editorial sharply condemned this new method of enlarging the
already overcrowded 'literary concentration camp'.[246] It stated
that 'the methods of direct or indirect censorship, as applied to this
country, have set a premium on pietistic illiteracy—or, alternatively, illiterate pietism'. The occasion was the unexplained
decision of the Customs authorities to seize all copies of Joyce
Cary's posthumous novel, *The Captive and the Free* (an ironic
title!), and the editorial concluded on a note of outrage:

Who makes these decisions? How are they qualified? On what grounds
are they justified in setting their own minds before the minds of thousands of other people? Living in a democracy, one is entitled to ask these
and related questions. If no satisfactory answer is given, then one can
assume that one does not live in a democracy.[217]

But such questions are not readily answered in Ireland. The
State and the Church apparently do not consider them to be of
primary importance. And the people? The overwhelming majority
of them are in no position to be disturbed by the fact that they live
in a country where their reading and thinking are rigidly controlled. If such repression had been imposed while the British
were ruling Ireland it would in all probability have been condemned as tyranny over the mind of man.

Three of O'Casey's books have been banned officially, and although two of these have been unbanned, a purged writer cannot easily escape the stigma of the original ban. *Windfalls* was banned when it appeared in 1934 and is still banned today, even though the short stories in that work, some of which deal with sex and apparently caused the book to be banned, have been reprinted in *The Green Crow*, which is unaccountably not banned. *I Knock at the Door* was banned in 1939, *Pictures in the Hallway* in 1942, presumably because Johnny Casside, like many normal boys, had some adolescent experiences with sex, but both books were unbanned in 1947.

Sex is one of the chief taboos in Ireland, chastity one of the chief virtues. Without necessarily defending unchastity, one can question the tendency of the censors, who apparently take their cue from the Church, to judge the morality of a work of literature by its treatment of sex. One cannot help wondering how this aspect of Irish Catholicism would measure up to the following views on Christian morality, as expressed by an orthodox writer like C. S. Lewis: 'If anyone thinks that Christians regard unchastity as *the* great vice, he is quite wrong. The sins of the flesh are bad, but they are the least bad of all sins. All the worst pleasures are purely spiritual: the pleasure of putting other people in the wrong, of bossing and patronizing and spoiling sport, and backbiting; the pleasures of power, of hatred.'[248]

The Irish Catholic version of Christianity is a hard one. It is not surprising that O'Casey has satirized it so vigorously and exalted the joy of life. It is not surprising that one of the characters in *Cock-a-doodle Dandy*—which incidentally has never been performed in Ireland—says about the country: 'A whisper of love in this place bites away some of th' soul.'

And yet, that bitter line occurs in a play which is as comic as it is tragic, for the very forces of repression understandably inspire an opposing zest for life in the creative Irishman. He must laugh in order to go on living. Although he sees his country as a hell—nor is he out of it even when he is in exile—he goes on writing about this bedevilment with such wild humour and poetic vitality that his art saves him from damnation. Perhaps this is the magnificent curse of the alienated Celt: his exile gives him a mock-heroic vision of his unholy martyrdom which makes him approach his alienation and his country with titanic humour; it gives him what is essentially a tragi-comic view of life, for what he has to say in his art is too tragic to be said tragically.

History has a way of repeating itself, and in Ireland ironic echoes from the past often linger to mock the present. During the same year that Shaw published *John Bull's Other Island*, Synge and Joyce were reacting to some of the frustrations that troubled Larry Doyle and Father Keegan, and which continued to trouble O'Casey throughout his years of exile. The returned exile Synge was beginning to long for Paris again when he wrote this bitter comment on *The Playboy* riots in a letter to a friend: 'I sometimes wish I had never left my garret in the Rue d'Assas—it seems funny to write the words again—the scurrility and ignorance of some of the attacks upon me have rather disgusted me with the middle-class Irish Catholic.'[249] The exiled Joyce found it impossible to choose between tyrannies when he said in a lecture in Trieste: 'I confess that I do not see what good it does to fulminate against the English tyranny while the Roman tyranny occupies the palace of the soul.'[250]

For a writer like O'Casey, too, 'the palace of the soul' was inviolable. He was the kind of man who always insisted upon gaining his own soul even if it meant losing the material world. This is the personal price he had to pay for the high-principled way he lived, but he remained his own man and maybe the world was well lost. This was also the condition upon which he wrote his tragi-comic and visionary plays. He remained his own dramatist, and for this the world must ultimately return to him.

CHAPTER VIII

◄◄◄►►►◄◄◄►►►◄◄◄►►►◄◄◄►►►◄◄◄►►►◄◄◄►►►◄◄◄►►►◄◄◄►►►

A Final Knock at O'Casey's Door

◄◄◄►►►◄◄◄►►►◄◄◄►►►◄◄◄►►►◄◄◄►►►◄◄◄►►►◄◄◄►►►◄◄◄►►►

Read what Christ said in the Bible: 'Ask, and it shall be given you; seek and you shall find; knock, and it shall be opened unto you.' The world needs more of them— Askers and Seekers and Knockers. Now take that word Knock, that's a fine word—Knock, Knock, Knock. There are many doors in the world that need a powerful Knock.

Sean O'Casey

Mr. O'Casey is a master of knockabout in this very serious and honourable sense—that he discerns the principle of disintegration in even the most complacent solids, and activates it to their explosion. This is the energy of his theatre, the triumph of the principle of knockabout in situation, in all its elements, and on all its planes, from the furniture to the higher centres.

Samuel Beckett

1. SEAN O'CASEY, 1880–1964: THE MAN REMEMBERED

'TELL THEM I'm only talking to God now,' Sean said, prophetically as it turned out, for that was barely thirteen days before he died. I had answered the phone and called to him to say it was a reporter from London asking for permission to come down to Torquay to interview him, and he had sung out his reply in mock-solemnity, to the world and all its reporters: he was too busy talking to God. He hadn't sounded like a man who was dying, yet if he himself had sensed that the end was near he had chosen to hide his secret in a characteristic jest about a serious thing, his shriving time. We will never know the nature of that holy and probably merry dialogue between God and O'Casey, but there can be little doubt that when it was

285

over, Sean was cleared and ready to pass on to the heaven in which he often said he did not believe. 'I'm an atheist, thank God,' he liked to say, taking pleasure and comfort in this paradoxical phrase of Shaw's. Heretical humanist though he was, in his beginning and in his ending O'Casey was God's man and he was his own man. Since he believed that 'the best way to fit oneself for the next world was to fit oneself for this world,' he must have died as he had lived, in a state of grace.

Few men had made themselves more fit for life in this world. Perhaps that was what he was talking about with God, life not death. 'I will show you hope in a handful of life,' he once said to me when we were discussing T.S. Eliot's 'The Waste Land.' He was too full of life to brood about fear and dust. For his wife and children, for his friends, there was no thought of his dying last year, or indeed at any time. He had survived so many pains and ordeals throughout his eighty-four years, earning his grace in the traditional way, through suffering, that we who loved him seemed to sense some intimations of eternal life in him, and we were somehow unable to conceive of the world without Sean in it. It was only after he had suffered his fatal heart attack on September 18 that we sought to temper our sorrow with amazement: 'The wonder is, he hath endur'd so long.'

He still seemed far from the end of his endurance when I met him for the last time on a bright week-end early in September. I had already seen him twice before for several weeks during the summer, in June and July, and now I had stopped at Torquay again on my way back from Dublin for the usual farewell visit before setting out on my homeward journey. He moved about more carefully now than he had earlier in the summer, for he was still recovering from an attack of his recurring bronchitis and other respiratory complications that had affected his heart, an illness which had laid him low in August and sent him, over his protests, to a nearby nursing home for several days. Apparently this attack had been more serious than anyone realized, but at the time we did not think it was cause for alarm, for he had come through greater dangers in the past. The worst was in 1956 when he had fought his way back from two major operations, kidney and prostate, only to have his heart broken at the end of the year when his twenty-one-year-old son Niall died suddenly of leukemia. He was a long time recovering from that shock.

Sean had minimized his August illness, refusing to behave like an invalid. In fact, shortly after we met in September and had settled ourselves comfortably in his room, as if to convince me and himself that he was not about to perform his swan song, he leaped nimbly out of his chair and enacted an energetic mime-dance, pacing around the room in an exaggerated strut, raising himself on tip-toe with each swinging stride and flapping his arms so that he looked like a comical old bird trying to fly and not quite making it. 'It keeps me from forgetting that human beings are gay and funny fellas,' he said with a broad grin as he sat down, rearranging the brightly colored beanie on the back of his head. 'And besides, it's good for the circulation.' I had begun by asking about his recent illness and he had demonstrated his reply, which was good for our mutual circulation. No, I thought then, that dancing Sean was not a dying man.

But there was another kind of shadow over his life now, in his mind more terrible than death, and that was the increasing threat of total blindness. He had lived with this danger all his life, for his eyes had troubled him since childhood when he developed an ulcerated cornea in his left eye, which thereafter remained dim and filmy, and this placed a heavy strain on his already weakened 'good' eye, which periodically became ulcerated. Every day of his life he had to sponge his eyes with water as hot as he could bear it in order to wash away the suppurating fluid that burned his eye-sockets and temporarily blotted out his vision. Over the many years that I had visited him, since 1954, I can hardly remember a day when he did not have to pause several times, in the afternoon and evening, remove his thick-lens glasses, press his thumb and forefinger over his closed and burning eyes, and then go to the sink in his room for the ritualistic eyewashing.

As if this affliction were not enough, some of the hairs on his lower eyelids grew irregularly, pointing inward so that they jabbed at his eyeballs like needles, and this meant that often his wife or one of the children had to pull them out with a pair of tweezers. Sometimes the hairs were difficult to see, let alone pull, and meanwhile he would have to endure the pin-pricking pain, which grew worse with each flick of his eyelid. I was initiated into this ritual myself during my July visit, for when his wife Eileen, who said she had plucked thousands of such hairs from his eyelids throughout their marriage, had trouble locating a seemingly invisible hair that was torturing him, I was urged to have a go at it. As I held his magnificent bony head up to the light and probed with the tweezers, I trembled lest I should tear away some of his skin with the stubborn hair. Fortunately I was able to nip the hair and pull it out cleanly. It couldn't have been more than a thirty-second of an inch in length, and he thanked me for delivering him from 'that bloody whoreson of a hair.'

He had been relieved of his pain by a stabbing thirty-second of an inch, but nothing, neither science nor God, could save his fading eyesight, which was apparently suspended now by little more than a hair's breadth. 'There is no pain he would not more willingly endure than blindness,' his wife had said to me in the kitchen. He did not talk much about it, but it was obviously troubling him and was especially apparent in the way he strained and squinted at any written material, with the page of a letter or book held so close to his right eye that it pressed against his nose. So I discussed the matter with Eileen when we were alone after I first arrived in June. Sean rested in bed for several hours every afternoon from around 2.30 to 4.30, a habit he had developed more to relieve his eyes than to sleep. He would slip a knotted handkerchief over his eyes and doze, or just lie there thinking; maybe he rehearsed some lines for a new play, or did what he called talking with God. While he rested, Eileen and I went for a stroll and had our talk. We walked from the crest of St Marychurch, the hilly suburb of Torquay where they lived, down the winding streets to the red cliffs of Babbacombe, overlooking a vast panorama of azure sea and sky. It was a familiar walk which Sean had taken with us in previous and better years, he with a cloth-cap tipped low over his forehead to protect his eyes from the dazzling light and high wind, an ashplant swinging in one hand, the other linked snugly in Eileen's. Although he was about twenty-five years older than she, anyone who saw them would have known immediately that they were deeply in love with each other.

Eileen O'Casey is a strikingly handsome woman of auburn beauty and fine proportions, an open-faced woman with a gentle manner and a quick smile; and as if nature had not been generous enough to her, she also had the great good fortune to have lived with Sean O'Casey for thirty-seven years. Like her husband she was born and raised in Ireland, but later went to England to pursue a career in the theatre. She became an actress in London, met Sean when she played the role of Nora Clitheroe in his *Plough and the Stars*, and soon afterward married him, in 1927. Since she was a Roman Catholic, they were married in church by a priest and their three children were properly baptized. But she no longer practices her faith, she practices Sean's faith.

We had moved away from the windy tor and settled under a tree on a grassy slope that led down to the sea-front. Then she began to talk about Sean's eyes. 'All the doctors say that in medical terms he should be blind now, and yet he can still see, just barely, because he *wants* to see, he *needs* to see in order to go on with his life and work. He couldn't bear to become a burden to us. So he sees through an act of will, an act of faith, and that's the way he has done everything all his life.' He could never be indifferent about anything, she said, no matter how minor it might be. He couldn't stand carelessness or untidiness, and always took great pains to be neat and clean in his personal habits. It worried him that he might one day become weak and helpless. He always had time for laughter and merriment, she said, but he had to keep his life and his mind in order.

They had gone up to London for several days early in the year to see a specialist when his already dim sight had suddenly begun to deteriorate at an alarming rate. After extensive examinations and x-rays, the specialist and his consultants had concluded that his left eye was stone blind, and there was little more than a faint flicker remaining in his right eye, so that while he might make out some vague shapes, he couldn't really see any more. His eyes were simply worn out. 'It was a terrible shock,' Eileen said. 'And yet, when we returned home he went back to his regular routine, writing letters every day, working on his new book of essays, and making plans for a new play. He couldn't read and I helped him with that, as I had in the past, though he did manage somehow to make out an odd word here and there. The doctors said he was blind, but he went on scribbling notes and touch-typing day after day. And on top of that came the bad news that we might have to move, and the mere thought of it terrified me. He would never survive that.'

Their landlord had died and there was a strong chance that the house would be sold, which meant they would probably have to vacate their flat. They rented six rooms on the second floor of an old villa that had been divided into three separate dwellings, located on the highest spot in St Marychurch, with green rolling valleys below them spreading out to the sea, which was visible on clear days. In good weather Sean sat in the sun on their small stone porch, wearing his broad-brimmed felt hat, or he went down to wander among the flowers and birds in their garden—'fifteen steps and then six steps, mind them carefully,' as he often cautioned me. They were stony and steep.

'He knows the exact distances of everything in the house,' Eileen said, 'and when people see him moving about so freely and confidently they don't realize that like a blind person he does it all by memory and instinct. If we have to move to a new place he'll become confused and go crashing into furniture and walls and break an arm or leg, and he'll probably be demoralized or dead in a week. He'll be all right if we can stay here.' That was in June. The threat of having to move hung over them all summer. But in the end, in September, it was not his eyes but his heart that failed him. As his good friend Brooks Atkinson wrote in a moving tribute, 'In eighty-four years of unselfish living it was the first time that his heart had failed him.'

There was no sign of failure in him when we met early in September. He was tired from the boredom of his convalescence, but his mind was fully alert and his humour was characteristically sly.

'What does God say when you talk to Him?' I asked after we had dispensed with the London reporter.

'He tells me the world is full of fools but He loves them anyway.'

'And what about you, do you love them, anyway?'

'I only have trouble loving them when their folly grows out of stupidity instead of honest ignorance. Then I'm more inclined to hate them, or to hate the things that make them stupid. I love everyone and everything that's alive. I'm only indifferent to the dead. And now, for the love o' God, don't be asking so many foolish questions and let's get on with our work.'

'Our work' was the problem of trying to clear up countless questions and references in his letters, which I was collecting and editing. He had exchanged letters with some of the major literary figures of his time, but he also corresponded with hundreds of unknown people from many countries, people who praised or criticised his works, asked him to explain or justify something he had written, carried on extended discussions about literature and life, politics and religion, told him their troubles, asked his advice, and even named their children after him. Throughout all the years that his plays were not being produced, these people became his intimate audience, and so the daily ceremony of writing and receiving letters kept him in constant touch with the world of ordinary people who apparently read and reacted to everything he wrote. He had written thousands of letters over the past fifty years, many of which I had been able to locate during a three-year search, and there were situations and controversies to straighten out, people and places to identify, and an involved network of events in his life to correlate. I had worked out a good deal of it, but a number of mysteries remained. Some of these matters taxed his memory, which was understandable, especially exact dates and time sequences, yet on many of them he seemed to possess an uncanny total recall. Often the point in question had happened forty or fifty years ago and, since I had been able to put together some of the pieces during my investigations in Dublin, I usually had enough details to know that his version was in all probability accurate, rounded out with shrewd and comic observations on why some people had spoken or acted as they did. He invariably told his stories in dialogue, giving what the others had said and what he had said, acting out all the parts in a well-flavored style, and he was an excellent mimic. Listening to him one would have guessed that Sean himself was the original of the 'fluthered' Irishmen that Barry Fitzgerald created in his plays. He spoke in a rasping tenor voice, drawing out the syllables of words with a consequential Dublin brogue that still retained the lilting cadences heard on the northside of the Liffey. He could smile like a Dublin charwoman and swear like a Dublin docker.

But there was much more in him than the randy comedian. There was a glint of steel in his bony face, power in his transfixed eyes, courage in the bite of his jaw. There was a craggy grandeur in his aquiline profile which sometimes invested him with the magisterial dignity of a Renaissance Cardinal painted by El Greco, especially when he complemented his perennial red beanie by wearing his blood-red robe on chilly days. His small eyes burned fiercely behind his thick glasses and he could lower his voice to a mighty whisper of rage when he reacted to some injustice in the world.

But there was much more in him than the courageous patriarch. By nature a shy and gentle man, he was uncommonly tender and solicitous with people he trusted, a gallant charmer with women and children, a sweet companion with friends. There was a gesture of ceremonial fun in the assortment of gaily designed and coloured beanies or skull-caps he always wore, some of them made by his daughter, others sent to him from friends all over the world. He smoked a pipe continuously, and he might drink an occasional glass of wine with guests, but he was a whiskey teetotaler, for he remembered too well his early life in Ireland when the labourers were paid in the pubs and often drank up their wages before they could bring them home to their wives and children. He loved all kinds of music. During his younger days in Dublin he had worn a saffron kilt and played the bagpipes, and he fancied himself something of a singer. At any moment he might burst into song with a lively ballad—perhaps one of his own, for he had written songs for all his plays—and whatever it may have lost in his croaking voice it gained in his delicate feeling. He was a man of deep impulses, and he could be moved so profoundly by the misfortune of a friend, or even a stranger, that he became ill with grief. For a man of his achievements, he had a tendency to doubt the merit of his work: 'Tell me what you thought was bad in it, not what was good,' he said to me on a number of occasions after I had praised something he had written.

His moods were often mixed, and he could be an outraged comedian, a gentle genius, an insecure rebel. Perhaps he had lived too long in self-imposed exile from his native land, for his extended quarrel with Ireland was a lover's quarrel: he was impatient with his country's frailties but would leap to the defense if an outsider attacked them. He was capable of unwarranted extremes and could make rash judgements from reasonable assumptions; he could see slights where none were intended; he could be quick to anger and slow to forgive. Sometimes he rolled out his heavy weapons for minor skirmishes, and he could hurl rhetorical thunderbolts when he felt he had been unjustly used or abused.

When I mentioned some of these extremes to him, he shook his head sadly, then rubbed his beanie so vigorously that wisps of silvery hair flared wildly around its edges. 'Put it down to my tactlessness,' he said, 'my inability to keep my big mouth shut, much to my sorrow and the sorrow of others. But what was the alternative?' He rubbed his beanie with another flourish and straightened his back. 'Tact? Polite submission, that's what tact really is, and it's something I never learned. Children are naturally tactless, but it's knocked out of them in school where they learn to be polite and submissive. I never had any formal education and maybe that's why I became the way I am.'

'Are you saying that formal education is a dangerous thing because it isn't dangerous enough?' I asked.

'I'm saying there should be a way of teaching young people without breaking their spirit and making them so damned submissive. When they learn right from wrong they shouldn't be afraid to say so if they see it around them, and they shouldn't be so refined that they're unable to do anything about it. The first thing a fella has to do if he wants to accomplish anything of value is to be tactless. The world is full of powerful people who want everyone else to bow down before them and be tactful, and if they're not running the schools they're running the churches. But formal religion is worse than formal education when it comes to filling people full of fear and submission. Did you ever see anyone as tactful as a Bishop?

'But Christ wasn't very tactful, was He? Let's face up to it, He was a great public nuisance, always stirring things up, always telling people what they should and shouldn't do, and so few of them ever listening to Him that He had to shout it out again and again. Was He polite and submissive? Was He afraid to speak out? All for one and one for all, that's what He preached, and He was a great communist.'

'Christ, a communist?' I asked.

'Of course He was. Read Shaw's great Preface to *Androcles and the Lion*. I wonder do they teach that in the schools, or in the churches? Christianity was communist from the beginning, it had to be if all men were to hold all things in common and be their brothers' keepers. But you'd never know it from the way the clergy talk and act today, for they're all tactful capitalists now. Read what Christ said in the Bible: "Ask, and it shall be given you; seek and you shall find; knock, and it shall be opened unto you." The world needs more of them—Askers and Seekers and Knockers. Now take that word Knock, that's a fine word—Knock, Knock, Knock. There are many doors in the world that need a powerful Knock.

'Read what Shaw said about what Christ said and did. "*Gentle Jesus meek and mild* is a sniveling modern invention, with no warrant in the gospels", that's what Shaw said. We can't get around it, you see, Christ was a tactless communist, God help Him, so don't be so damned skeptical about it.'

'It's just this, Sean,' I said, 'every time I hear you talk about Christianity and communism, the Star of Bethlehem and the Red Star seem to become interchangeable, as they do in *The Star Turns Red*. And I have a strong feeling that the Russians, to say nothing of the Christians, would be even more skeptical than I am.'

'Ah, what is the stars?' he said with a mischievous smile. 'They're all in the one blue sky that shelters every mother's son, Christian and communist, beggar and thief.'

That was a typical response. Whenever he got around to telling me what communism was and why he was a communist, he often began as if he were determined to drive the moneychangers out of the temple and ended by becoming gentle and dreamy. It wasn't that he was trying to be evasive, for he was wholly dedicated and even visionary on this subject. He was essentially a yea-sayer and loved to introduce hallelujah quotations from the Psalms in his conversation. How often I have heard him emphasize a point with such a quotation: 'Make a joyful noise unto God. . . . Blow up the trumpet in the new moon. . . . O let the nations be glad and sing for joy. . . . O sing unto the Lord a new song. . . .' He was tired of the old songs and pietistic slogans. He felt that the political jargon and cold-war clichés of the West and the East had obscured the basic goals of mankind, and he could set forth those goals in a disarming if over-simplified manner. 'Every man who puts his best effort into his life and work, be he a doctor or a bricklayer, is a communist whether he knows it or not, for he's helping to improve the common good and making the world a better place for himself and his family and his country, and all the countries of the world.' Thus, communism was his touchstone for the ideal society, and the fact that it was a scare-word to many people only increased his impulse to use it, tactlessly, as he would have said. It was his way of knocking on doors.

He seldom mentioned Marx or Lenin when he spoke about communism; he was more likely to quote from Christ and Shaw, Shelley and Keats, Blake and Burns, Emerson and Whitman, Ruskin and Morris. On one occasion he called my attention to a little-known passage in Keats's poem 'Isabella' in order to show me 'what communism was all about.' He asked me to take the book from his shelf and read the stanzas aloud to him, and he joined me from memory on the third stanza so that we must have sounded like a Greek chorus:

> With her two brothers this fair lady dwelt,
>   Enriched from ancestral merchandize,
> And for them many a weary hand did swelt
>   In torched mines and noisy factories
> And many once proud-quiver'd loins did melt
>   In blood from stinging whip;—with hollow eyes
> Many all day in dazzling river stood,
> To take the rich-ored driftings of the flood.

For them the Ceylon diver held his breath,
And went all naked to the hungry shark;
For them his ears gush'd blood; for them in death
The seal on the cold ice with piteous bark
Lay full of darts; for them alone did seethe
A thousand men in troubles wide and dark;
Half-ignorant, they turn'd an easy wheel,
That set sharp racks at work, to pinch and peel.

Why were they proud? Because their marble founts
Gush'd with more pride than do a wretch's tears?—
Why were they proud? Because fair orange-mounts
Were of more soft ascent than lazar stairs?—
Why were they proud? Because red-lin'd accounts
Were richer than the songs of Grecian years?—
Why were they proud? again we ask aloud,
Why in the name of Glory were they proud?

He took great delight in repeating the questions in the final stanza, and many times thereafter, when we happened to be talking about the oppressors and the oppressed of the world, he would roar out the last two lines in a lusty chant:

Why were they proud? again we ask aloud,
Why in the name of Glory were they proud?

So he would usually turn to literature or the Bible when he wanted to underscore the nature of his communism, which was more deeply rooted in ethical values than in a political system. And it is not surprising that these values should have developed out of the doctrines of Christianity, for what little formal education he had received as a boy was obtained in the Church of Ireland. He had to leave the church school, St Mary's, at an early age because of his weak eyes, which were covered with ointments and bandages for several hours of every day. He recorded some of this information in his autobiography, but since he was vague about specific details I always tried to locate documented evidence during my visits to Dublin. On one occasion I found a copy of his Confirmation Papers, which indicated that he had been confirmed at Clontarf Church in 1898, at the age of eighteen, that he had received his First Communion on Easter Day of that same year at St Barnabas Church,

and that he had been baptized in 1880 at St Mary's. For a long
time he had been uncertain about the day and year of his birth, and
a search through the files of the Registry Office, under his baptized
name of John Casey, revealed the date as 30 March 1880.

Two summers ago I brought back from Dublin a copy of another
forgotten document out of his past to show him, this time the record
of a prize he had won in Sunday School at the age of seven. It read:
'Church of Ireland, United Dioceses of Dublin, Glendalough and
Kildare. At a Diocesan Examination in Connexion with the Board
held at St Mary's Schoolhouse on the [the day is blank] of 1887,
II Class was awarded to John Casey of St Mary's Parish, for Proficiency in Holy Scripture and Church Formularies. Signed,
Plunkett—Dublin [the Archbishop].'

'Are you sure it was only a second class prize?' he asked when I
read it to him.

'No doubt about it, it says second class.'

'Ah, well,' he said with a grin, 'that's not so bad for a half-blind
little chiseler.'

'Then you do remember your childhood proficiency in Holy
Scripture?'

'I remember it as through a glass lightly. It must have been the
year after my father died. He was a great reader of books, and that
was unusual then, for he was the only person in the neighbourhood
who actually had bookcases filled with them. I wasn't able to read
at the age of seven, because of my eyes, but like all children I could
repeat anything if I heard it several times. The Bible was the important book in our house, and full of fine stories and mysterious
words for a curious kid to imitate. I liked the sound of the words
long before I knew what they meant, and it gave me a feeling of
power to spout them in the house and in front of the other kids.
And don't forget, my sister Isabella was a teacher at St Mary's, so
she stuffed me full of the right things to say to make certain I didn't
disgrace her and the family name. Then there was my dear mother,
who never missed a Sunday at church, and later there was the Reverend Edward Griffin of St Barnabas. I was a stubborn kid with a
mind of my own, but I wouldn't have done anything to let them
down.'

Only last summer I had located one of the Reverend Griffin's
daughters. She had gone to England with her clergyman husband,
but now they were living in retirement in Ireland. She gave me

some of her recollections of Sean—'John, not Sean; he was John Casey when we knew him'—as a young man of twenty-four at St Barnabas, the details of which I corroborated with him during my July visit. Sean, or John, and her father, the Rector, were as close as father and son in those days. At the particular time that she remembered, around 1904, prayer-meetings were often held on week-day evenings in the Church schoolhouse, and at the conclusion of the service the Rector would ask for a volunteer to lead the final prayer. 'It was then,' she said, 'after an awkward pause while father waited for the volunteer, that my sister and I—we were girls of eight and ten—would nudge each other and whisper, "It'll be John again, he'll jump up again, and oh, he'll go on and on as he always does." He sat behind us and we were afraid to turn around and look, but soon we heard his voice ringing out loud and clear, in that drawling, lilting way he had of speaking. He didn't read from the prayer-book as the others did, he just made up his prayer as he went along, using some biblical passages but mostly his own words about the glory of God. As I said, at the time my sister and I joked about how he would go on and on with it, but we were silly little girls then, and when I think of it all now it comes back to me as something very moving and beautiful. He would have made a great preacher.'

Maybe he did become something of a lyrical preacher, especially in his later plays, where he wrote humourously and heroically about the joy of life, in the fantasy of an enchanted Cock or in the ecstasy of a miracle on the banks of the Liffey. In *Red Roses For Me*, when his autobiographical hero, Ayamonn Breydon, who attends a church called St Burnupus and is a close friend of the Rector, joins the people of Dublin in a transformation dance and exhorts them to seek a new life, he might well have been making up another of his lilting prayers: 'Friend, we would that you should live a greater life; we will that all of us shall live a greater life. Our sthrike is yours. A step ahead for us today; another one for you tomorrow. We who have known, and know, the emptiness of life shall know its fullness. All men and women quick with life are fain to venture forward. The apple grows for you to eat. The violet grows for you to wear. Young maiden, another world is in your womb. . . . Our city's in th' grip o' God.'

The Rector's daughter also remembered that John was interested in other things besides prayer in those days, which explained why he soon changed his name to Sean. 'He was full of the Gaelic language and told us proudly that no Irishman was a true Irishman unless he could speak Irish. You see, on Sundays after church he often accompanied my sister and me on the long walk from St Barnabas to the Rectory, which was on Charles Street off Mountjoy Square. First we would walk his mother home, around the corner on Abercorn Road. We always called her Granny Casey. She was a neat little woman, she wore a pretty bonnet, and she gave us sweets. When we set out on our walk John was swinging a hurley stick, which he hid outside the Church. It was an ancient Irish game, he told us, and Irishmen should be proud to play it. After he left us at the Rectory, he went on to Jones's Road to play with his friends. Well, on those walks he would tell us stories about the Irish heroes, and sing songs in Irish. Once he taught us the chorus of "Cruiskeen Lawn", the part that's in Irish, and do you know, I still remember those lines:

> *Gramachree, mavourneen, slanta gal avourneen,*
> *Gramachree ma Cruiskeen Lawn, Lawn, Lawn.*

He sang the song and we joined in on the chorus. We must have been a strange sight as we marched along singing merrily, two little girls in our Sunday dresses and John waving out the rhythm with his hurley stick.'

'Like the pied piper of Dublin,' I said to him. 'You kept your faith in the Irish language through the years, but when did you lose faith in the Church?'

'I never lost my faith, I found it. I found it when Jim Larkin came to Dublin a few years later and organized the unskilled laborers. I found it in Jim's great socialist motto: "An injury to one is the concern of all".'

'Socialist and Christian?'

'Socialist and Christian. They've both the one thing—communism—if only the people knew it. Jim knew it as well as he knew his penny-catechism, but the clergy condemned him for it during the 1913 strike, saying hell wasn't hot enough nor eternity long enough for the likes of him. Yet he was the saviour of Dublin. He put his faith in the people and their need to live a better and fuller life. And that's where I put my faith.'

We must take him at his word and deed, for that is the faith to which he devoted his life as man and artist. He expressed it in his plays in comedy and tragedy, farce and fantasy. He expressed it in his autobiography and books of essays in narrative, argument, and satire. He was a visionary humanist, a man of this-worldly spirit. As an artist, the form as well as the substance of his plays is of such a magnitude that even in death he remains ahead of his time, for there is still no theatre able or daring enough to do justice to his pioneering achievements in dramatic technique, beginning with *The Silver Tassie*. He spent the last thirty-six years of his life exploring new forms, rejecting all the orthodoxies and conventions of the theatre, even his own.

He was writing about that form and faith right to the end. When I saw him a fortnight before he died, he was finishing a satiric essay called 'The Bold Primaqueera'. (The joke in the title is aimed at the theatre of the absurd and alludes to Ionesco's play 'The Bald Prima Donna', known in America as 'The Bald Soprano'.) Sean said he was fed up with what he called 'absurd plays by absurd playwrights who sing the same dreary song on the one weary note and then have the gall to make a bloody mystery out of it.' He had in mind Ionesco and Pinter and their imitators. 'Not Beckett and Brecht,' he insisted. 'They have the leap of the life force in them, even when they're pessimistic, because they're poets as well as playwrights, and I like what they do with words. Ionesco and Pinter belong in the cinema, where pictures and pauses are more important than words. And speaking of words, exciting words in the theatre, look at the plays of John Arden, the best of the young playwrights today. I have an aggressive admiration for his *Sergeant Musgrave's Dance*. But those absurd fellas, they'd put years on you. It's obvious they were never touched by the Holy Ghost.'

He was also fed up with what he called the 'primaqueera' element that he associated with the absurdities in the theatre—'the bona fide homosexuals and pseudo-intellectuals who infest the theatre.' By coincidence, while we were checking through some letters, I came across several that he had written twenty years earlier to a friend in the London theatre. At that time he had expressed similar views, and when the friend protested that Sean was prejudiced, he had replied: 'I shouldn't call dislike of "conceited amateurs, arrogant homosexuals, & impertinent dilettantes" a prejudice. I hate them— except when they're comic, like most of our Irish ones. We don't hate enough in England. The English don't know how. They think it a virtue. It isn't. It shows a lack of life force.' To which he added 'amen' twenty years later.

But at eighty-four and approaching blindness he was not yet
ready to say 'amen' to life. Somehow he managed to press on with
his work, a new book of essays. Every day he sketched out some
ideas or wrote letters, working laboriously with a pen or tapping
away at the typewriter, and his wife knew things were going well
if she heard him humming tunes to himself. Since his failing sight
prevented him from re-reading what he had written, he had to have
his wife or a friend read it back to him so that he could think about
where he had been and where he was going, make various changes,
and move on again. The genial gardener came by once a week and
he helped out with the reading and writing, also doing some of the
re-typing. It was a slow and frustrating process, one that would
have defeated anyone except a man like Sean, who was as patient
as he was stubborn. So he went on with his words, asking and seeking and knocking. He was disturbed because his eyes were so bad
that he could no longer read books. He regretted that he couldn't
re-read Joyce, Shaw, Yeats, and George Moore, though he still retained a remarkable memory of their works. Joyce he loved the most.
'He tells us everything in *Finnegans Wake*, that beautiful dream book
of reality. I don't know what a lot of it means, but he created such
magical patterns of words that I feel them long before I understand
them; and often I simply feel them without understanding them.
Only a true poet can do that to us.'

When we were together in June, talking about religion, he suddenly pointed his palms under his chin and chanted, 'In the name
of Annah the Allmaziful, the Everliving, the Bringer of Plurabili-
ties, haloed be her eve, her singtime sung, her rill be run, unhemmed
as it is uneven.' He and his wife often talked about *Ulysses* and *Dubliners*, especially their favorite story, 'The Dead'. Eileen read to him
every day, and he listened to talks and plays on the radio, and to the
recordings of classics sent down by the Society for the Blind.

I read to him on our final evening together. We had taken a short
walk before tea, up to the wall of St Mary's Church—in previous
times we had regularly gone the whole distance around the wall and
come back through the peaceful churchyard—and later we settled
comfortably in his room. 'Don't call it my study,' he corrected me.
'It's where I work.' There were signs of his work everywhere in
the room. Crowded bookcases lined the walls and overflowed on
the floor; piles of books and magazines were scattered over the large
round table, at one end of which was an old Underwood with a

half-typed sheet of paper in it; beside the machine a green eye-shade was hung over a goose-neck lamp; on the window ledge were two boxes stuffed with incoming and outgoing letters; a red moroccan folder on the bed was full of sheets of paper on which he had scrawled notes and random phrases. The electric fire glowed brightly, and there was a pungent smell of tobacco in the air. Sean sat on the bed puffing at his pipe, his legs stretched out and crossed at the ankles, a red-and-white Tashkent beanie on the back of his head.

'Are ye there, truepenny?' he called.

'I see you have the new editions of poetry by Austin Clarke and Patrick Kavanagh.' I had been browsing through some of the books on the table.

'Eileen was reading them to me. Clarke's a better poet than any of us knew, a fine poet. Poor fella, he was overshadowed by Yeats. But Yeats's shadow fell over everyone.'

I read some of Clarke's poems aloud. Eileen had read 'Forget Me Not' to him, so I began with the title poem of *Flight to Africa*, which drew some hearty laughter from him. Then I read from the *Later Poems*—'Inscription for a Headstone,' 'Three Poems About Children,' 'The Blackbird of Derrycairn,' and 'Night and Morning'.

'Read the Headstone one again,' he asked. 'The one about Larkin.'

> *What Larkin bawled to hungry crowds*
> *Is murmured now in dining-hall*
> *And study. Faith bestirs itself*
> *Lest infidels in their impatience*
> *Leave it behind. Who could have guessed*
> *Batons were blessings in disguise;*
> *When every ambulance was filled*
> *With half-killed men and Sunday trampled*
> *Upon unrest? Such fear can harden*
> *Or soften heart, knowing too clearly*
> *His name endures on our holiest page,*
> *Scrawled in a rage by Dublin's poor.*

He was deeply moved by this ironic poem, for he had lived through the 'Bloody Sunday' that it celebrated; he had served under Larkin at the time as Secretary of the Irish Citizen Army; and he saw himself as one of the 'infidels' of 1913. His voice thickened with a Dubliner's rage at the mention of those times and Jim Larkin, the man he had called the Irish Prometheus. Then we talked about Jim Plunkett, who had written a play about Larkin, and was now writing a novel about the events leading up to the 1913 strike. 'Are there any people over there besides Jim Plunkett who still care about Larkin's Dublin?' he asked. 'Really care in their Christian hearts?' He relit his pipe angrily and sent great clouds of smoke billowing through the room.

He was silent for a while, and I began to read some of Kavanagh's poems, of which he seemed to like 'Kerr's Ass' and passages from 'The Great Hunger' the best. When I finished reading the last lines of 'The Great Hunger':

> *The hungry fiend*
> *Screams the apocalypse of clay*
> *In every corner of this land*

it was clear that he was still brooding about Larkin. 'There it is again, the hungry fiend, in Mucker or in Dublin, and it takes the rage of a poet to put it right. Larkin was the poet of the people. Why, even Yeats, aristocrat though he was—in his own mind, not in his class—spoke out for Larkin and the workers.'

So we came at last to Yeats, and the poems of Yeats. Contrary to what many people thought, Sean insisted, he did not feel bitter towards Yeats because of the Abbey Theatre's rejection of *The Silver Tassie*. 'I was bloody mad at him, not bitter. That was in 1928 when I had a wife and a kid on the way, so the rejection meant hard times for the O'Caseys. But it wasn't only that, I was ripping mad because he was wrong about my play. And I still think he was wrong. Maybe one day there'll be a real production of that play— it's still one of my favorites, and I can see the whole thing, in my mind, glowing on a stage—then we'll find out who was right about it. After the rejection there were people in Dublin who did feel bitter towards Yeats—they always had, mainly because they were jealous and afraid of him—and they tried to get me to join them and go against him. Well, I told them what they could do with their dirty game, they could stuff it where the monkey put the nut. Yeats was wrong about my play, but he made the Abbey a great theatre, he and Lady Gregory. And after he died it went down hill. There was no one left to fight for it and protect it from the political and clerical yahoos who torment the artist in Ireland. They're the fellas I feel bitter about.'

Then he began to praise Yeats as a poet. He didn't think much of him as a playwright. 'His poems are more dramatic than his plays, and his plays are really poems.' I began to read Yeats's poems to him, some of the *Last Poems*, which he especially wanted to hear. I read 'The Circus Animals' Desertion', 'Parnell', and 'The Spur.' Then I mentioned that Liam Miller had set some of the poems to traditional Irish airs and had them sung by a group of young ballad singers in one of Dublin's pocket-theatres during the previous summer. This interested him and I read several of them, including 'The Three Bushes' and 'The Ghost of Roger Casement.' He enjoyed them and said they had a word-music of their own which revealed another side of Yeats, his close touch with the people, from whom he usually remained aloof. 'That was part of his greatness', Sean said, 'he hated the Irish crowd but he loved the Irish people.'

We closed out the evening with 'Under Ben Bulben', and Sean quoted the well-known fifth section from memory:

> *Irish poets, learn your trade,*
> *Sing whatever is well made,*
> *Scorn the sort now growing up*
> *All out of shape from toe to top,*
> *Their unremembering hearts and heads*
> *Base-born products of base beds.*
> *Sing the peasantry, and then*
> *Hard-riding country gentlemen,*
> *The holiness of monks, and after*
> *Porter-drinkers' randy laughter;*
> *Sing the lords and ladies gay*
> *That were beaten into the clay*
> *Through seven heroic centuries;*
> *Cast your mind on other days*
> *That we in coming days may be*
> *Still the indomitable Irishry.*

'Good poetry', he said, 'but bad advice for Irish poets. Is it the Ireland of aristocratic parasites and enslaved peasants he's asking us to go back to? The Ireland of plaster saints and hedge scholars? The Ireland of the Big House and the little people? The Ireland of purple dust? Not bloody likely we'll go back to those corpses. But

it's still a damn fine poem. And so like Yeats, to make good poetry
out of bad opinions. I wonder why he wasn't up to saying the same
thing about *The Tassie*, that I might be able to write a good play
out of what he thought were bad opinions? Ah, that's a head without
a tail.'

Yeats had tried to make some amends for his rejection of *The
Silver Tassie* when, in 1935, he finally had the play performed at
the Abbey Theatre, in spite of virulent opposition. Thus, one of
Yeats's last of many famous fights at the Abbey was for O'Casey;
and when the two men met in Dublin for what turned out to be a
final reunion in September of 1935—it was O'Casey's last visit to
Ireland, and Yeats died four years later—they settled their differences as men, though they remained in different worlds as artists,
but both of them symbolic of 'the indomitable Irishry' in their
different ways.

Eileen had come in with a pot of tea for the road, for it was late
and soon I would be leaving for America. When I finally stood up
to go, Sean said, 'My favorite lines of Yeats are not from the last
poems but from his first play, *The Countess Cathleen*. Do you remember what Oona says at the end, after the Countess has given
up her soul to save Ireland?' And he intoned softly:

> Tell them who walk upon the floor of peace
> That I would die and go to her I love;
> The years like great black oxen tread the world,
> And God the herdsman goads them on behind,
> And I am broken by their passing feet.

We walked out to the porch and he embraced me in a tender
bear-hug.

'We've heard the chimes at midnight', he said.

'Bless you, Sean.'

'And you, too. Give my love to America.'

'See you next summer.'

He smiled. 'Right-o, next summer, and all the summers that
warm the green world.'

It was a clear night and the sky over St Marychurch was ablaze
with stars. What is the stars? I didn't know, but I knew they were
all up there, 'all of them in the one blue sky that shelters every
mother's son'. As I reached the end of the garden, I turned for one
last look and caught a glimpse of him through the trees, standing

at the top of the steps. He was still there in the gentle night, gazing at the stars.

I feel now as I felt then, that he would always be there, as long as the summers warmed the green world.

2. MASTER OF KNOCKABOUT: THE WORK REVISITED

Although there are no doubt many ways to reassess the genius of O'Casey, I believe he remains above all a master of knockabout or antic comedy, in his tragi-comedies, his symbolic moralities, his comic fantasies, his one-act farces, his extravagant autobiography. If he often releases his knock of comic aggression in a world of tragic suffering, the provocation of broad laughter is calculated to mitigate the ache of the tragedy, in precisely the way that gallows humor mocks the indignity of suffering and death. Eric Bentley, perhaps our wisest critic of drama, has stated that

Gallows humor is an accommodation to the gallows, to a world that is full of gallows. . . . The expression 'grin and bear it' says all. It is the grinning that enables us to bear it. Gallows humor again: such humor is not an outlet for aggression to no purpose. The purpose is survival: the easing of the burden of existence to the point that it may be borne.[251]

Bentley here is commenting on the nature of aggressive humour in modern tragi-comedy, particularly in the plays of Samuel Beckett, but it should be apparent that his remarks also illustrate the compensatory function of knockabout comedy in the works of O'Casey, and indeed in Irish comedy in general, whether in the fiction of William Carleton and James Joyce, the poetry of Brian Merriman and the *Vision of MacConglinne*, or the drama of J. M. Synge and Brendan Behan.

The comic aggression of O'Casey's knockabout, then, is an ironic accommodation to what Captain Jack Boyle calls a 'world of chassis'. The antic characters confront the chaos with an hilarious alternative to despair, a series of comic explosions, visual and verbal, that mock the process of disintegration which threatens to annihilate their world. This comic counter-attack is in fact the chief source of the 'energy of his theatre', as Beckett described it in a little-known review of an early O'Casey work, *Windfalls*.[252] It is this same source of knockabout energy and resilience which accounts for the comic survival of the Blooms in Joyce's *Ulysses*, and Christy Mahon, the

Douls, the tramps and tinkers in Synge's plays. And in this context it might be appropriate to modify Yeats's tragic vision in the following manner: 'The centre cannot hold; mere *comic* anarchy is loosed upon the world'; which is an ironic modification that Yeats himself saw fit to dramatise as his comic vision in his mock-heroic *Player Queen*.

Beckett, in his approach to what he accurately described as 'the principle of disintegration' in O'Casey's early works, concentrates on *Juno and the Paycock* and two one-act farces, *A Pound on Demand* and *The End of the Beginning*; but O'Casey was to go on extending his mastery of knockabout throughout his career, even into his eightieth year when he was writing such playful works of mere comic anarchy as *The Drums of Father Ned, Behind the Green Curtains, Figuro in the Night*, and *The Moon Shines on Kylenamoe*. Meanwhile Beckett, in defining 'the principle of disintegration' in O'Casey's works in 1934, was also anticipating the future path of his own career as a dramatist, since he was to create a somewhat similar world of comic disorder twenty years later, in *Waiting For Godot, Endgame, Krapp's Last Tape*, and *Happy Days*. The prophetic parallels between the methods of comic disintegration in the works of O'Casey and Beckett are magnified when we discover the knock of recognition in these comments by Beckett:

Mr. O'Casey is a master of knockabout in this very serious and honourable sense—that he discerns the principle of disintegration in even the most complacent solidities, and activates it to their explosion. This is the energy of his theatre, the triumph of the principle of knockabout in situation, in all its elements and on all its planes, from the furniture to the higher centres. If 'Juno and the Paycock,' as seems likely, is his best work so far, it is because it communicates most fully this dramatic dehiscence, mind and world come asunder in irreparable dissociation— 'chassis' (the credit of having readapted Aguecheek and Belch in Joxer and the Captain being incidental to the larger credit of having dramatised the slump in the human solid). This impulse of material to escape and be consummate in its own knockabout is admirably expressed in the two 'sketches' that conclude this volume, and especially in 'The End of the Beginning,' where the entire set comes to pieces and the chief character, in a final spasm of dislocation, leaves the scene by the chimney.[253]

O'Casey, like Beckett after him, relies upon these comic spasms of disintegration—dissociations and dislocations in which 'mind and world come asunder'—in order to expose the disruptive forces in society, 'even in the most complacent solidities'. It is a most ingenious method of fighting folly with folly: tragic chaos is exploded by comic chaos, and 'the slump in the human solid' is consummated in its own knockabout. This is the cathartic function of farce or antic comedy in the plays of O'Casey and Beckett: the disorder of society creates its hilarious antidote in comic disorder, and as a result profane laughter shakes the sacred foundations, 'from the furniture to the higher centres', until Cathleen Ni Houlihan becomes as illusory and discredited as Mister Godot.

This method of achieving a catharsis through profanation, or a psychic release from repression, may well be indigenous to low comedy, for as Wylie Sypher has shrewdly observed, 'The comic rites are necessarily impious, for comedy is sacrilege as well as release'.[254] Commenting on the specific nature of this comic release or catharsis in relation to comic irreverence, Sypher adds further evidence in support of Beckett's principle of disintegration in these illuminating remarks on tragedy and comedy:

Tragedy has been called 'mithridatic' because the tragic action, inoculating us with large doses of pity and fear, inures the self to the perils we all face. Comedy is no less mithridatic in its effects on the self, and has its own catharsis. Freud said that nonsense is a toxic agent acting like some 'poison' now and again required by the economy of the soul. Under the spell of this intoxication we reclaim for an instant our 'old liberties', and after discharging our inhibited impulses in folly we regain the sanity that is worn away by the everyday gestures. We have a compulsion to be moral and decent, but we also resent the obligation we have accepted. The irreverence of the carnival disburdens us of our resentment and purges our ambivalence so that we can return to our duties as honest men. Like tragedy, comedy is homeopathic. It cures folly by folly.[255]

The mithridatic cure may be more psychic than actual, the return to duty and honesty may be less credible or desirable, when the laughter has subsided, but in their varieties of risible subversion O'Casey and Beckett dramatise this irreverent carnival of disorder and catharsis. While they are both masters of knockabout, the reverberations set off by their farcical explosions operate on different wave lengths and call for somewhat different responses. O'Casey's comedy is more insurrectionary and therefore more aggressive in its sweeping disorder; Beckett's comedy is more nihilistic and therefore more portentous in its teasing irresolution. O'Casey's comic syntax is loose or open, more voluble and self-indulgent in its rhetoric; Beckett's comic syntax is taut or hard, more stoical and astringent in its rhetoric. Words are more often weapons of assault for O'Casey's characters, whose comic garrulity eases the burden of existence by animating a state of outrage in the game of survival; words are more often scrupulously measured rituals of restraint for Beckett's characters, whose comic incantations ease the burden of existence by animating a state of paralysis in the game of survival. O'Casey's plays become progressively more urgent and joyful in their freewheeling attacks on the hardening orthodoxies of society; and some of the later works, *Purple Dust* and *Cock-a-doodle Dandy*, *The Bishop's Bonfire* and *The Drums of Father Ned*, call for a comic apocalypse. Beckett's plays become progressively more fatalistic as their ever-shrinking orbits of graveyard knockabout undermine the metaphysical structures of the universe itself; and if they call for anything at all it might only be an oblique form of comic subversion that may ultimately dissolve the whole system along with its comic scapegoats, which is implicit in the ominous tone of *Waiting For Godot* and *Endgame*, and explicit in *Krapp's Last Tape* and *Happy Days*.

Nevertheless, for all these differences in the language and tone of their comic subversion, O'Casey and Beckett have structured the action of their plays along similar patterns of plot reversal. Their plays actually invert the traditional order of main-plot and sub-plot, so that in this new ironic structure the sub-plot and its comic supernumeraries become the central focus, while the normally heroic main-plot action is now consigned to a secondary position and often occurs off-stage. And since the main action of *Gunman* and *Juno* and *Plough*, *Godot* and *Endgame* and *Krapp*, is dominated by antic comedians, the patriotic and cosmic figures and forces of potentially tragic proportions, now hidden in the wings, at the barricades, in the heavens, or in the tapes, are mocked structurally as well as thematically. James Agate must have been aware of these ironic implications when, in his review of the London premiere of O'Casey's second play, he wrote:

Juno and the Paycock is as much a tragedy as *Macbeth*, but it is a tragedy taking place in the porter's family. Mr O'Casey's extraordinary knowledge of English taste—that he wrote his play for the Abbey Theatre, Dublin, is not going to be allowed to disturb my argument—is shown by the fact that the tragic element in it occupies at the most some twenty minutes, and that for the remaining two hours and a half the piece is given up to gorgeous and incredible fooling.[256]

Agate's shrewd estimate of the disproportionate time allotted to the comedy in contrast to the tragedy is characteristic of the plays of O'Casey and Beckett and reveals the structural strategy of their tragi-comedies.

Furthermore, Agate is certainly accurate in his argument that the gratifyingly impure taste of English and Irish audiences demands an excess of 'gorgeous and incredible fooling' in the theatre, even in the midst of tragedy. It is a phenomenon that once more reminds us of man's psychic necessity to grin in order to bear the pain of existence. In a related argument, William Empson has commented on the stubborn survival of the tragi-comic double plot in English drama:

The old quarrel about tragi-comedy, which deals with part of the question, shows that the drama in England has always at its best had a certain looseness of structure; one might almost say that the English drama did not outlive the double plot.[257]

Empson also describes this loose double plot structure as part of the ' "tragic king—comic people" convention', so characteristically illustrated in Shakespeare's plays, notably *I Henry IV*. Modern Irish drama certainly did not outlive the loose structure of the double plot; in fact, in the plays of O'Casey and Beckett and Behan, for example, it sustained the double plot by inverting it, by relocating the 'comic people' in the main-plot and the 'tragic king' or his surrogates in the sub-plot. Harold Pinter accomplished precisely this relocation in many of his plays, particularly *The Dumb Waiter* and *The Birthday Party*; and Tom Stoppard did it brilliantly with his tragi-comic reversal of the *Hamlet* structure in *Rosencrantz and Guildenstern Are Dead*. There are of course further examples of this structural inversion in the plays of Genet and Ionesco.

In his remarks on the tentative nature of the setting and the characters in *Waiting For Godot*, Hugh Kenner seems to be raising a similar point about structural inversion when he tells us that Gogo and Didi appear to be supernumeraries filling in time while we wait for the main action to begin:

The tree is plainly a sham, and the two tramps are simply filling up time until a proper dramatic entertainment can get under way. They are helping the management fulfill, in a minimal way, its contract with the ticket holders. The resources of vaudeville are at their somewhat incompetent disposal: bashed hats, dropped pants, tight boots, the kick, the pratfall, the improper story. It will suffice if they can stave off a mass exodus until Godot comes, in whom we are all so interested.[258]

This ironic denial of our expectations goes to the heart of the structural joke: the tramps have displaced Godot and all his profundities, just as Boyle and Joxer have displaced Cathleen Ni Houlihan and her off-stage patriots. And Kenner's reference to 'the resources of vaudeville' should remind us that O'Casey and Beckett share an unqualified affinity for the profane delights of the music-hall tradition, the consummate theatre of knockabout, with its decrepit comedians and anarchic routines, its slapstick disintegration of the furniture and all the respectable foundations of society. Sometimes the guardians of society recognize the function of music-hall comedy as a safety valve for repression, as Empson's anecdote illustrates: 'I believe the Soviet Government in its early days paid two clowns, Bim and Bom, to say as jokes the things everybody else would have been shot for saying.'[259] But in the unintimidated world of art, comic subversion is not for sale. The dramatist must be free to create his own Bims and Boms, Boyles and Joxers, Gogos and Didis, even at the risk of liquidation or exile.

Captain Boyle and Joxer Daly owe as much to Gallagher and Sheen, Laurel and Hardy, as they do to Mak and Gill, Sir Toby Belch and Andrew Aguecheek, Falstaff and Bardolph, Pistol and Nym; and with reasonable modifications the same lineage applies to Gogo and Didi. This line of comic descent, from medieval drama to Shakespeare to O'Casey, has been reinforced by J.L. Styan. Writing about Empson's notion of the loose structure that traditionally accompanies the double plot, Styan believes that this looseness 're-produces the sensations of life with its complexities and contradictions':

We get the feeling that, in Empson's words, 'the play deals with life as a whole.' From the spontaneous eruption of tomfoolery within the sacred framework of the medieval mystery plays to the contrivances of O'Casey to show his subject from opposed points of view in, say, *The Plough and the Stars*, we are reminded again that the point of reference is life; but if this is true, the looseness is merely apparent and not real.

After the magnificent Shakespearian rhetoric of Henry's 'Once more unto the breach . . . ,' which ends, we remember, with an injunction to 'follow your spirit,' what better way of having us keep our wits and hear a ring of truth than by dragging on Nym, Bardolph and Pistol immediately?

BARDOLPH. On, on, on, on, on, to the breach, to the breach.

NYM. Pray thee Corporal stay, the knocks are too hot.[260]

The terrible knocks of life and possible death are indeed too hot. And therefore these clowns must counter with some profane and heated knocks of their own which celebrate their comic survival. This process occurs in most of the O'Casey plays with the counter-knocks of Seumas Shields, Boyle and Joxer, Fluther Good, Bessie Burgess, Ginnie Gogan, The Covey, Peter Flynn, Rosie Redmond; and in the later plays with all the shrewd Irish peasants in *Purple Dust*, *Red Roses For Me*, *Cock-a-doodle Dandy*, *The Bishop's Bonfire*, *The Drums of Father Ned*, and all the one-act plays.

This counter-knock of comedy can also be explained as a psychological strategy of defense, if we consider some of R. D. Laing's studies of schizophrenia from a comic point of view. Laing reports 'that *without exception* the experience and behavior that gets labeled schizophrenic is *a special strategy that a person invents in order to live in an unlivable situation*'.[261] Comedy, then, can be an alternative to madness. The mask of the clown becomes his special strategy which the terrors of life have forced him to invent in order to go on living in an unlivable world. When the knocks become too hot, he creates his knockabout.

Consider some affirmative aspects of this survival strategy in O'Casey and Beckett. At the end of *Juno and the Paycock*, when the drunk and bewildered Boyle and Joxer stagger into an empty room to find their world in 'a state o' chassis', they could well be rehearsing for or anticipating the appearance of Gogo and Didi, or even Hamm and Clov, Nagg and Nell. 'The blinds is down, Joxer, the blinds is down!' It is the end of a slapstick survival game that never ends. Knockabout comedians never die, they only play games, they wait or fall down, suffering and laughing for all of us. In *Wait-*

ing For Godot Didi pleads, 'Come on, Gogo, return the ball', and in his incompetent way Gogo always does. In *Endgame* Clov asks, 'What's to keep me here?' 'The dialogue', Hamm replies, returning the ball. In *Juno* Boyle says, 'I ofen looked up at the sky an' assed meself the question—what is the stars, what is the stars?' And Joxer returns the ball: 'Ah, that's the question—what is the stars?' They all grin and bear it because, as Didi says, 'We're inexhaustible'. In the midst of an argument Clov says, 'There's one thing I'll never understand. Why I always obey you. Can you explain that to me?' and Hamm replies, 'Perhaps it's compassion. A kind of great compassion.' After an argument Boyle says, 'Now an' agen we have our differ, but we're there together all the time.' And Joxer returns the refrain: 'Me for you, an' you for me, like the two Musketeers.' Thanks to their comic duels and duets, they're all there in the chaos together; they're all inexhaustible; they're all bound together by the great compassion of low comedy. They can't affirm the world, but they can affirm each other.

A knock of affirmation emerges clearly from O'Casey's later plays, but even in the tragi-comic dislocation of his earlier works he never doubts the saving grace of mundane humanity in his grotesque clowns, and continually celebrates their comic vitality. Only insofar as the sheer energy of low comedy is itself a form of stubborn survival is there anything that resembles an open affirmation or celebration in the plays of Beckett. But the inexhaustible art of knockabout comedy may itself be an affirmation for Beckett. On this fine point, however, it is again necessary to invoke the wisdom of Eric Bentley, who rightly insists that 'artistic activity is itself a transcendence of despair, and for unusually despairing artists that is no doubt chiefly what art is: a therapy, a faith'.[262] And Beckett, he would have us believe, 'got rid of the despair, if only for the time being, by expressing it'.[263]

O'Casey's comedy is his therapy, his faith. He was in full control of his artistic power whenever he relied upon his abundant resources of knockabout comedy to transcend a despair that grew out of man's failure to eliminate or control the chaos of modern life His work is more likely to be uneven or excessively hortatory, didactic, when he departs from his comic or tragi-comic muse, for his non-comic characters often if not always fail to achieve a life of their own, an authentic life apart from O'Casey's own voice. Philosophy and comedy can be strange bedfellows in the theatre, and even Shaw

had his difficulties in trying to yoke them. But it is in the nature of
Beckett's stoical genius that he can be philosophic and comic at the
same time; it is in the nature of O'Casey's effusive genius that he
can be least comic when he is most philosophic. At his best, however, like Synge, O'Casey is a comic and tragi-comic poet in the
theatre.

The poetry of laughter is the antidote to despair. If the sources
of Beckett's despair are cosmic in origin, associated with the ca-
pricious and inaccessible mind of Godot, the sources of O'Casey's
despair are social in origin, associated with the tyrannizing hier-
archies of society; it involves the difference between a comic quarrel
with God and a comic quarrel with the household gods. Although
O'Casey liked to call himself an atheist, he really had no quarrel
with God—'He may be but a shout in th' street', he echoed Joyce.
His quarrel was with man, with God's self-appointed guardians of
church and state and their self-sanctified institutions of repression.
In his appropriately titled essay, 'The Power of Laughter: Weapon
Against Evil', he identified some of those household gods who were
among the chief targets of his profane and liberating knockabout:

Laughter tends to mock the pompous and the pretentious; all man's
boastful gadding about, all his pretty pomps, his hoary customs, his
wornout creeds, changing the glitter of them into the dullest hue of lead.
The bigger the subject, the sharper the laugh. No one can escape it: not
the grave judge in his robe and threatening wig; the parson and his saw;
the general full of his sword and his medals; the palled prelate, tripping
about, a blessing in one hand, a curse in the other; the politician carrying his magic wand of Wendy windy words; they all fear laughter, for
the quiet laugh or the loud one upends them, strips them of pretense,
and leaves them naked to enemy and friend.[254]

Of course O'Casey preferred the loud upending laugh for these
impostors or *alazons*, but the overall strategy of his knockabout
technique is not fully apparent until we see how he exploited the
clowns who were responsible for the pratfalls, his rascally *eirons*.
Henri Bergson's theory of comedy, limited to a brilliant study of
the *alazons* or humour-characters, whose rigidity or automatism
exposes their folly, does not take into account the role of the *eirons*
or laughing characters, whose flexibility or instinctive wit unmasks
the *alazons*. We must therefore reach beyond Bergson and turn to
that illuminating work, Francis Macdonald Cornford's *Origin of*

Attic Comedy, where the traditional game of comedy is described as a duel between those incomparable adversaries, the *eirons* and *alazons*, the ironical or cunning self-deprecators and the inflated impostors or pretenders. But even more important, Cornford insists that the *eirons* often assail the *alazons* "with a mixture of "Irony" and "Buffoonery",' and it is precisely this mixture of wisdom and folly which defines the double nature of O'Casey's knockabout comedians. It is a dual function that allows us to laugh with as well as at these ridiculous and resilient characters. Borrowing from Aristotle, Cornford accounts for this comic mixture in the following manner:

Aristotle seems to have classified the characters in Comedy under three heads: the Buffoon (*bomolochos*), the Ironical type (*eiron*), and the Impostor (*alazon*). . . . The Buffoon and the Ironical type are more closely allied in Aristotle's view than a modern reader might expect. They stand together in opposition to the Impostor in all his forms. It will be remembered that in the *Ethics* the Ironical man and the Impostor or swaggerer confront one another in the two vicious extremes which flank the virtuous mean of Truthfulness. While the Impostor claims to possess higher qualities than he has, the Ironical man is given to making himself out worse than he is. This is a generalised description, meant to cover all types of self-depreciation, many forms of which are not comic. In Comedy the special kind of Irony practised by the Impostor's opponent is feigned stupidity. The word *eiron* itself in the fifth century appears to mean 'cunning' or (more exactly), 'sly.' Especially it meant the man who masks his batteries of deceit behind a show of ordinary good nature; or indulges a secret pride and conceit of wisdom, while he affects ignorance and self-depreciation, but lets you see all the while that he could enlighten you if he chose, and so makes a mock of you. It was for putting on these airs that Socrates was accused of 'irony' by his enemies. The *eiron* who victimises the Impostors masks his cleverness under a show of clownish dullness. He is a fox in the sheep's clothing of a buffoon.[265]

The archetypal comic character in O'Casey's plays, then, is invariably something of a fox masquerading in the sheep's clothing of a buffoon. His comic weapons are therefore that mixture of irony and buffoonery that Cornford describes because he must pretend to be a greater fool than he is in order to disarm his more pretentious and dangerous opponents. His disguise of 'feigned stupidity' may be conscious or unconscious—more instinctive in Captain Boyle, more calculated in Joxer Daly—but he is a buffoon with the cunning of an *eiron* 'who masks his batteries of conceit' behind a stratagem of 'ignorance and self-depreciation'. In the context of the Roman comedy of Plautus, this would be the equivalent of saying that O'Casey's clowns combine the folly and cunning of the braggart warrior *and* the clever slave, which is a parallel to Cornford's way of describing the comic complexity of wise fools: the irony and buffoonery of Sir Toby and Falstaff, Seumas Shields in *The Shadow of a Gunman* and Fluther Good in *The Plough and the Stars*, as well as Boyle and Joxer. At various times O'Casey's *eirons* succumb to what might be called the Gadshill-folly, for they are all comically discredited for their cowardice and mendacity; and yet they are also capable of a complementary attitude that could be called the Shrewsbury-wisdom, for they all know that a corpse on the battlefield, or in the war-torn slums of Dublin, is a poor excuse for honour. They are comically and ironically damned and saved; and in their knockabout salvation they profane whatever is excessively rigid or sacred in society. And holy Ireland is a country of many sacred nets, outside of which lies comic freedom.

Knockabout comedy can therefore be a game of salvation as well as a carnival of pratfalls. In her standard study of the Fool, Enid Welsford recognizes the general wisdom in the clown's masquerade of folly, but she tends to deny him his essential irony; she dilutes his power and treats him as an innocuous entertainer when she writes: 'The Fool does not lead a revolt against the Law, he lures us into a region of the spirit where, as Lamb would put it, the writ does not run. . . . There is nothing essentially immoral or blasphemous or rebellious about clownage.' [266] It might equally be argued that there is nothing essentially moral or pious or respectable about clownage. House-broken or amenable clowns may be found in Ruritania but not in Ireland; not in the England of Falstaff or Tony Lumpkin, either, or the America of Huck Finn or Buster Keaton. So the whimsical sentiments of Miss Welsford with her quaint appeal to Lamb's airy-fairy-land cannot help us here. For the ultimate wisdom of disguised folly, for the flexible *eiron's* comic revolt against the world of rigid *alazons*, we must turn to Cornford not Welsford.

Cornford can also guide us to a confrontation with the non-comic or ethical side of O'Casey's works. In his references to Aristotle and Socrates, Cornford identifies another kind of ironic wisdom, the serious wisdom of the ethical man who occupies the middle ground or golden mean between the Ironical clown and the pretentious Impostor—'the virtuous mean of Truthfulness'. In some of his later plays O'Casey creates a non-comic or truthful hero who defends that 'virtuous mean'—it may even be a 'virtuous extreme' if the middle ground has become an excuse for the status quo—a character who suffers or dies for an ideal value. This attitude would apply to his two outstanding martyrs, Harry Heegan in *The Silver Tassie* and Ayamonn Breydon in *Red Roses For Me*, the most obvious examples of his serious or ethical *eirons*. It would be unfair to insist that O'Casey had to continue writing in his best tragi-comic or comic manner, for it is clear that he felt the artistic and emotional need to experiment with serious themes and symbolic techniques. Nevertheless, it would be inaccurate to insist that he did not pay a price for these ambitious risks. The portentous rhetoric of Heegan and Breydon is often too 'literary' and contrived, and as characters they suffer from an excess of romantic idealism or Truthfulness. Their symbolic voices are too prophetic, too pure, too didactic. Perhaps they are too noble in their sacrificial conception, which unfortunately means that they are immune from the saving graces of irony and buffoonery. Vivian Mercier properly raised this issue when he wrote:

O'Casey's decline as a comic dramatist dates from the period when he ceases to have a divided mind about most of his characters. Compare, for instance, two *personae* of O'Casey himself: the poltroon poet Donal Davoren in *The Shadow of a Gunman* and the All-Irish boy Ayamonn in *Red Roses For Me*, a much later play.[267]

But in light of his curious illustrations, Mercier's otherwise sound judgement must be qualified and corrected. He is right in claiming that O'Casey was at the height of his comic power when he approached his characters with 'a divided mind', a very perceptive description of the double-view that accounts for the resilience and richness of his comic *eirons*. He is less than accurate, however, in his comparison of characters. Breydon is undoubtedly an autobiographical figure, an ethical hero who, admirable as he may be, is so close to O'Casey himself that he lacks aesthetic objectivity as well as irony. But it is highly questionable whether Davoren is in any

sense intended to be a self-portrait of the playwright, since he is
damned for his dangerous illusions and detachment, his shadow-
self which deceives the people around him, especially the innocent
Minnie Powell, and precipitates the tragic denouement. If anyone in
the play speaks for O'Casey it must be the peddler Seumas Shields,
who does it indirectly through the *persona* of a wise clown, an ironist *and* braggart, a buffoon *and* coward. He is full of comic complexities. In revealing his own frailties he also exposes the greater
folly of patriotic fanaticism and poetic illusions. Therefore, in his
characteristic manner, O'Casey has 'a divided mind' about Shields,
his comic mock-hero, not Davoren, his straight-man. And if one is
to draw comparisons between some of the characters in these two
plays—granting that Breydon is over-burdened with the idealistic
image of the 'All-Irish boy'—why not make a connection between
Shields and Brennan o' the Moor, Brennan the miserly *and* mag-
nanimous clown, the bigot *and* balladeer, about whom the audience
as well as O'Casey must have the 'divided' feelings of folly and wisdom, the double-view that distinguishes all the comic *eirons*?

It is also questionable whether O'Casey 'declined' as a comic
dramatist in his later plays, since so many of them are mock-pastoral
comedies with a profusion of knockabout clowns and music-hall
antics, even though some pastoral straight-men occasionally try to
dominate the scene—such rampant comedies as *Purple Dust, Cock-
a-doodle Dandy, The Bishop's Bonfire, The Drums of Father Ned,
Figuro in the Night, The Moon Shines on Kylenamoe*. And even in
those darker plays in which he shifted the main focus from comedy
to prophecy—*The Silver Tassie, Within the Gates, Red Roses For
Me, The Star Turns Red, Oak Leaves and Lavender*—he subordi-
nated but did not abandon those comic characters who continue
to inspire 'divided' feelings and persist in stealing any scene in
which they appear; jesters like Sylvester Heegan and Simon Norton,
Roory O'Balacaun and Mullcanny, Feelim O'Morrigun and Mrs.
Watchit, to name a half-dozen among many. Nor should we overlook the fact that there are notable successes as well as failures in
these plays, particularly such spectacular innovations of total theatre—symbolic stagecraft, ritualistic action, stylized imagery—as the
surrealistic second-act war configuration in *Tassie*, the cinematic
and cyclical versions of pastoral in *Gates*, and the miraculous third-
act transformation in *Red Roses*. These are monumental achievements, especially when one considers that they are the dramatic

metaphors of a half-blind exiled playwright working in the theatre of his mind. Perhaps Gordon Rogoff raised the ultimate issue when he commented that these plays, and all the later works, are beyond us until we find the right director and theatre group to do them justice:

Published and frozen before reaching the stage the most intriguing of them—*Red Roses For Me*, *Purple Dust*, *Time To Go*, and most of all *Cock-a-Doodle Dandy*—never found *their* director.... What may well be missing is some gloriously dotty Irish Berlin Ensemble led by an equally improbable Bertolt Littlewood.[268]

In further pursuit of the comic O'Casey, it might also be enlightening to concentrate briefly on the language of some of the minor but memorable clowns in the too often neglected one-act plays. These characters all indulge themselves in O'Casey's favorite game of comic survival in a world of knockabout disintegration, the mock-battle of the flyting, a game which they share with all the Boyles, Fluthers, and Prodicals. The tradition of the flyting, a contest of raillery and ridicule, goes back to the Greek satyr plays, the medieval Celtic bards, Chaucer and Shakespeare, the renaissance Scottish poets, and in our own time comes forward to the parallel game of 'the Dozens' played by American blacks.[269] It is a mock-battle of poetic invective in which words become the weapons of otherwise disarmed combatants, and the trading of comic insults is inflated to a rude and merry art of psychic liberation. It is a survival game that can also be explained by Freud's theory of the function of jokes as a safety valve for repression, what he calls the circumventing process of jokes: 'They make possible the satisfaction of an instinct (whether lustful or hostile) in the face of an obstacle that stands in the way. They circumvent this obstacle and in that way draw pleasure from a source which the obstacle had made inaccessible.'[270] The obstacle in the flyting is another character, another clown or *alazon*, though one has the distinct feeling that in the plays of O'Casey it is the repressive and disintegrating world itself, with its sacred institutions of restraint, that is the ultimate *alazon*.

Consider these illustrations of pure or impure flytings in three of the one-act plays. In *Time To Go* a Young Man, who has just been cheated by the 'two most meritorious rogues in th' disthrict', strikes back with this riposte:

High hangin' to ye on a windy night, yeh bunch of incandescent thieves!

And the Widda Machree, who feels guilty because she may have cheated someone in the sale of a cow, confronted by the same two rogues, circumvents them with this blast:

Looka, you; if sins were written on people's foreheads, th' two of yous would pull your caps well down over your eyes!

In *The Hall of Healing* Alleluia, the 'expostulating' caretaker of the dispensary, whom no one can control or silence, turns on his tormentors:

Are yous goin' to have me expostulatin' all th' day! Close your gobs, an' cease from shattherin' me explanations to this man!

And Jentree, the wine porter who has been sampling so much of his work that the doctor orders him to drink half a gallon of water a day to dilute the wine, shoots back with his own expostulations to another patient, to Alleluia, to the world:

I'd have you remember, ma'am, that I'm th' custodian of me own ailments, an' am fully endorsed on their concern and their keepin'! Gulp it down! I wondher would you relish gulpin' cold wather down till your heart was stunned into stoppin' its beatin'? Would you gulp cold wather down you till every vital organ in your poor body was frightened of what was floodin' into them? Negify the effects o' wine! An' if I go on, what'll I take to negify th' effects of wather?

In *The Moon Shines on Kylenamoe*—O'Casey's last play, written when he was in his eighties—Mick Mulehawn, the Railway Guard, in one of his confrontations with Sean Tomasheen, the 'Pro-Tem Stationmaster', aims this barb at the enemy:

All th' pharmaceutical chemists of th' world couldn't mix a man into a bigger bastard than you, Tomasheen!

And Corny Conroy, the old railway laborer who has been aroused from his sleep by the comedy of errors and arguments on the platform, circumvents it all with this retort:

Eh, you're not goin' to dislocate me in th' tangle of your disputes. No, sir. I seen nothin' nor I heard nothin' either.

These illustrations can be reinforced with infinite variations of the flyting in all the plays. From the beginning, however, some of O'Casey's critics have been reluctant to recognize that his genius is deeply rooted in the comic tradition. Irish critics like Andrew E. Malone and Daniel Corkery were embarrassed or angered by the low comedy in the early plays, which they felt should have been serious tragedies. More recently a number of academic critics have ignored the possibility that the plays might be tragic *and* comic, arguing that they are imperfect tragedies because they break the 'rules' of Aristotle. T.R. Henn had trouble trying to make O'Casey's tragi-comedy fit into a strictly classical mold and therefore concluded:

It fails to become great or moving tragedy because it possesses no inner core, because it seeks to achieve depth by mere counterpointing of emotions, and because the speech cannot encompass the emotions which it needs to express. There is a deliberate forcing of O'Casey's characters into a language which is admirable for low comedy, provided the actors can achieve its peculiar intonations, but which has no flexibility to cope with pity and fear.[271]

Why should plays that are so 'admirable for low comedy' be forced to measure up to Aristotle's catharsis of high tragedy? Robert Bechtold Heilman grants the 'excellent' use of comic ironies in *Juno*, but then he too reverts to Aristotle and laments the fact that they are not the ironies of tragedy:

It is a melodrama of disaster that gains a special character from a large infusion of Falstaffian and satiric comedy. . . . The joining of diverse elements is O'Casey's great talent. But the irony is not that of tragedy.[272]

Why should it follow the irony of classical tragedy if O'Casey's 'great talent' went in the different direction of yoking the 'diverse elements' of tragedy and comedy?

Then there are critics like William Irwin Thompson and Robert Brustein who insist that *Plough* is a failure because Nora Clitheroe is not a tragic heroine, though she was never intended to be one. Thompson argues:

O'Casey is trying to lift Nora's laments into the realm of tragedy, but Nora is incapable of understanding her situation, and therefore she is incapable, as a dramatic figure, of generalizing her situation into anything resembling a tragic predicament. . . . Medea, Clytemnestra, Lady Macbeth: these are tragic heroines, but poor Nora is only an object of pity.[273]

Why shouldn't she be 'an object of pity', since she is one of the innocent victims in the play and therefore in no way comparable to a Medea or Clytemnestra? Not satisfied with this peaches-should-be-pears logic, Thompson also becomes curiously syllogistic by claiming that *Plough* had to be a failure because O'Casey was a Marxist and 'tragedy is not a Marxist genre'.[274] Aside from the specious assumption that O'Casey was a Marxist playwright when he wrote *Plough*, or any of his plays, there must be an easier way to prove that he was not trying to write a classical tragedy than to argue: tragedy is not a Marxist genre; O'Casey was a Marxist; therefore, O'Casey's play is not a tragedy! Robert Brustein also reverts to the critical method of condemning peaches for not being pears when he objects that Nora is not like Brecht's Mother Courage:

The responses evoked by Brecht's heroine are a good deal more complicated than those evoked, say, by the pathetic Nora Clitheroe, the heroine of another antiwar play, O'Casey's *Plough and the Stars*: Courage is not just a passive sufferer, playing on the sentiments of the audience, but also an active source of suffering.[275]

Of course Nora is no more like Courage than she is like Medea. And if Brustein is looking for a more complicated character in the play, why ignore the formidable Bessie Burgess, who might more accurately be called O'Casey's tragi-comic heroine, a woman of many dimensions and complexities who is neither pathetic nor passive and can indeed be compared favorably with Courage?

Some influential critics have actually begun to change their minds about O'Casey, notably Raymond Williams. In his first response to the plays in 1952, Williams commented acidly, in a brief Note at the end of a chapter on Synge, that O'Casey's excesses of language and misplaced comedy add up to 'Naturalistic caricature . . . a particularly degenerate art'.[276] Many years later, however, in 1968, Williams had second thoughts, devoted a chapter to O'Casey, and conceded that he had misunderstood the rhetorical and comical excesses:

I remember reacting very bitterly against them, and against the repeated tricks of colour—the naming of colours—which O'Casey carried to the point of parody. But the real point is more complex. Through all the early plays, it is the fact of evasion, and the verbal inflation that covers it, that O'Casey at once creates and criticizes: Boyle and Joxer, or again Fluther, are in the same movement engaging and despicable; talking to hold the attention from the fact that they have nothing to say.[277]

Actually, the real point is even more complex than this because they do have something ironic to say; but perhaps one should be satisfied that after sixteen years Williams is beginning to make sense about O'Casey.

It is when we explore comments on the later plays that we find a maximum of disagreement and a minimum of good critical sense. Irish critics consistently attack the pastoral plays, particularly *Cock-a-doodle Dandy* and *The Bishop's Bonfire*, as too anti-Irish and anti-clerical. One extremely enlightened Irishman, however, Tim Pat Coogan, documents and justifies O'Casey's lifelong quarrel with his countrymen, noting that his Irish critics consistently assume a pious attitude of outraged nationalism: 'an attitude of "How dare you hit me now with Cathleen ni Houlihan in my arms".'[278] Another exception is John Jordan, whose essay on 'Illusion and Actuality in the Later O'Casey'[299] provides a fresh and open-minded approach to the moralities and comic fantasies. And it was not a drama critic but a professor of economics, Dr. Patrick Lynch of U.C.D., who substantiated the main premise of these plays, O'Casey's comic desecration of the forces of repression in Irish life, when he wrote about Ireland of the 1930s, forties and fifties:

In the decades immediately following the treaty in a mood of disillusion and frustration, it was to be expected, perhaps, that the emphasis should be on the more inward-looking aspects of our culture. In a heady spate of puritanism a riot of censorship banned novels by some of the greatest of contemporary Irish writers as well as the works of foreign artists of international repute. This, indeed, was a shameful fruit of political freedom.[280]

Some influential drama critics in America have been the chief defenders of O'Casey's early and later plays, men like George Jean Nathan, Brooks Atkinson, John Gassner, and Eric Bentley; and among the younger university critics Robert Hogan and Ronald Ayling have made the most significant contributions. Ayling's Introduction to the volume of collected essays on O'Casey's work is an extremely wise and thorough assessment of the critical field; and he is right in drawing our attention to a parallel challenge for critics of the work of Dickens and O'Casey:

It has taken a long time for critics to come to terms with Charles Dickens as an artist because of similar extremes of vulgarity and fine sensibility in his work. And as with Dickens, it will be found, I think, that O'Casey had to fail badly occasionally in order to succeed audaciously at other times.[281]

This comparison is especially appropriate, and I am convinced that the successes of Dickens and O'Casey depend upon their commitment to the comic tradition. Ayling is also very sharp in his evaluation of the biographical as well as critical errors and inadequacies in the books by Saros Cowasjee and Gabriel Fallon.

Robert Hogan's contributions are constantly enriched by his ability to combine dramatic theory with a practical knowledge of theatrical techniques—he co-directed and played the role of Binnington in the world premiere of *The Drums of Father Ned*. In his essay 'In Sean O'Casey's Golden Days',[282] he made an important breakthrough by examining the later plays in relation to the conventions of pastoral drama. The canon of O'Casey criticism is gradually opening up now, with the number of outstanding essays in Ayling's *Sean O'Casey*, by William A. Armstrong, John Jordan, Robert Hogan, G. Wilson Knight, Katharine Worth, and Jack Lindsay. For the first time a major literary magazine (the *James Joyce Quarterly*, Fall 1970) has devoted a full issue to O'Casey criticism. Robert G. Lowery is on the verge of founding an O'Casey journal. Thomas Kilroy is editing a collection of essays on O'Casey's work for the Twentieth Century Views Series, soon to be published. E.H. Mikhail recently published his pioneering *Sean O'Casey: A Bibliography of Criticism* (Seattle, University of Washington Press, 1972); and Ronald Ayling and Michael Durkan are finishing a bibliography of all O'Casey's writings, to be published in 1975.

Since the fate of O'Casey's reputation must depend upon the insight of future critics, I might conclude with some specific references to a strikingly original contribution made by several of my students in a seminar on Irish drama conducted at Brown University in 1973. Jacqueline Doyle, in 'Religious Structure and Imagery in *The Silver Tassie*', an unpublished paper written for that course, believes that

the entire play participates loosely in the structure of the Mass. . . . The first act is the 'Mass of the Catechumens,' the portion of the Mass open to the uninitiated—O'Casey's 'faithful'. . . . The second act corresponds to the Offertory of the Mass—offering the soldiers as the sacrificial victims of the 'faithful'. . . . The third act traces the Consecration, and the reluctant bathing of Simon and Sylvester represents a sort of mock-purification, and certainly the breaking of the Host (Christ's body) is tragically present in Harry Heegan's crippled body. And this leads to the failed Communion of the fourth act.

As an extension of Miss Doyle's illuminating approach to the four-act structure as 'Public Mass—Offertory—Consecration—Euchar-ist', another student in the class, Michael Cervas, suggested that the four acts also correspond to the last four days of Christ:

Thus Act I includes the Last Supper and Holy Thursday (Gethsemane and the vision of the chalice), Act II is Holy Friday and the Crucifixion (and certainly the crucifix plays a prominent part in the act), Act III is Holy Saturday (with the body interred in the hospital rather than the tomb), and Act IV is Easter Sunday.

Miss Doyle includes these remarks in her paper, which brings a new dimension to the play, and she adds this final irony:

Both Acts III and IV contain denials of miracle; the women came to Christ's tomb but Jessie refuses, and, of course, the Resurrection in Act IV is a failed one.

O'Casey's profanations are ironic but therapeutic in that their denials are meant to bring us back to the source of our failed values. Herbert Howarth has claimed that the Irish writers, under the messianic impulse of the martyred Parnell, were obsessed with 'The Irish passion for a sacred book'.[283] One might also insist that these writers—Joyce and Yeats, Synge and O'Casey—under the mythic impulse of the last of the Celtic heroes, the tragi-comic Oisín, were obsessed with the Irish passion for a profane book. O'Casey, like the others, was determined to knock what was superficially sacred in Ireland in the belief that ironic or comic profanation might ultimately redeem the sacred values.

In the mock-heroic tradition of Irish comedy, that which is sacred must be ridiculed, not because it is false but precisely because it was once true. This is the compliment that the profane pays to the sacred; it is a liberating impulse that knocks in order to save.

NOTES

All the quotations from O'Casey's plays used in the text are taken from the *Collected Plays* Vols. I, II (London, Macmillan, 1949), Vols. III, IV (1951); *The Silver Tassie* (London, Macmillan, 1928); *Within the Gates* (London, Macmillan, 1933); *The Bishop's Bonfire* (London, Macmillan, 1955); and a manuscript copy of the unpublished *The Drums of Father Ned*, which Mr O'Casey kindly allowed me to read.

CHAPTER I: PROMETHEUS OF DUBLIN

1 There has been some confusion about the actual date of his birth (it has often been listed as 1881 and 1884), but his birth certificate recorded at the Irish Register Office, Dublin, conclusively indicates that the date was 30 March 1880.

2 *The Medical Press*, A Weekly Journal of Medicine and Medical Affairs, 7 January 1880, Dublin, Vol. LXXX, p. 12.

3 'The mortality-rate of Dublin'—Ibid., 17 January 1900, Vol. CXX, p. 40.

4 *Dublin Housing Inquiry:* Report of the Departmental Committee appointed by the Local Government Board for Ireland to Inquire into the Housing Conditions of the Working Classes in the City of Dublin, in *Parliamentary Papers*, Cd. 7273, Vol. XIX, p. 5. All the statistical information on pp. 7–9 is from this Housing Inquiry Report.

5 *The Green Crow* (New York, Braziller, 1956), p. 239.

6 *Freeman's Journal*, 6 October 1913. Larkin made these remarks as part of his testimony before the Board of Trade Inquiry, conducted by Sir George Askwith, Chief Industrial Commissioner. The Inquiry had been established to investigate 'the causes and circumstances of the existing industrial deadlock in Dublin', i.e. the 1913 General Strike and Lock-Out. Representatives of business and labour testified at the five-day hearings, and Larkin appeared as

counsel and spokesman for the Irish Transport and General Workers' Union, of which he was the General Secretary.

7 Arnold Wright, *Disturbed Dublin:* The Story of the Great Strike of 1913–14 (London, Longmans Green, 1914), p. 29. Desmond Ryan states that 'Arnold Wright was paid £500 by the Federated Employers of Dublin for writing Disturbed Dublin', in *The Workers' Republic:* A Selection of the Writings of James Connolly, edited by Desmond Ryan (Dublin, At the Sign of the Three Candles, 1951), p. 174.

8 *Freeman's Journal,* 6 October 1913. 'An injury to one is the concern of all' was the slogan of Larkin's union.

9 *New Statesman and Nation,* 24 December 1938.

10 *Irish Catholic,* 27 September 1913.

11 'From beginning to end'—Ibid.

12 *Labour, Nationality and Religion* (1910), reprinted in *The Workers' Republic:* A Selection from the Writings of James Connolly, edited by Desmond Ryan (Dublin, At the Sign of the Three Candles, 1951), pp. 249–50, 263–4.

13 *Freeman's Journal,* 20 February 1912.

14 *Sligo Independent,* 30 March 1912.

15 *Irish Worker,* 20 September 1913.

16 *Irish Independent,* 21 October 1913.

17 'that taking the children away'—Ibid., 28 October 1913.

18 W. P. Ryan, *The Irish Labour Movement* (Dublin, Talbot Press, 1919), pp. 230–31. See also AE's famous 'Open Letter to the Masters of Dublin', *Irish Times,* 7 October 1913.

19 *Disturbed Dublin,* pp. 223–4. Mr Wright was apparently playing upon the sympathies of his Catholic readers in this passage, and he does this often in the book. Although he had written a strong attack on Larkin and the labour movement, in his final chapter, 'A Study of Larkinism', he tried to make a fair assessment of the man, and some of his comments are worth noting, especially his interview with Larkin.

'The extraordinary personality of the leader of the movement, the amazing audacity of his plans, and the strangely powerful influence he exercised over the working population of Dublin and over many outside that class, all gave to the recent labour struggle in Dublin an interest peculiarly its own. Though outwardly invested with the attributes of an industrial conflict, the movement stands quite outside the ordinary category of labour disturbances. It was in essence a revolutionary rising, one in which the ultimate aims of its promoters involved the destruction of Society quite as much as the betterment of the wage conditions of the workers. Red Republicanism, Anarchism, Syndicalism, and all the extremest forms of modern revolutionary thought found expression in the literature and oratory of the movement. Even anti-clericalism of a kind was not wanting to complete the syllabus of advanced ideas to which the rising gave such blatant expression. And this is Dublin, the centre and citadel of the most disciplined force of Roman Catholicism in Europe, and the home of perhaps the sincerest conservatism—using that phrase in its broadest sense—in the Empire! Many strange things have happened by the banks of the Liffey, but none probably stranger than that open flouting of authority—ecclesiastical quite as much as civil—which marked the progress of Larkinism. . . .

'Appropriately enough, the interview took place in Croydon Park, the recreation ground belonging to the Irish Transport Workers' Union. At the period of my call Mr Larkin, with two assistants, was engaged in erecting a platform for a meeting to be held later in the week in the park. Standing in his shirt sleeves with his pipe in his mouth, he was directing with practised skill the joining of the planks which were the main support of the structure. A tall, loose-limbed man, with a slight stoop in the shoulders, he gave at the moment little impression of the popular idol; but we had not been speaking long before I discovered that the man was no ordinary type of agitator. His brain was full of ideas, crude and impracticable for the most part, but suggesting originality of thought and a wider outlook than that commonly attributed to him.

'With the aid of some notes I made of the conversation at the time I may, perhaps, profitably reproduce here the views he expressed, as they throw an interesting light upon the psychology of the man. In reply to a statement of his that his movement was more advanced than most labour agitations, I hazarded the remark that

it was on continental lines. He answered that it was and it was not.
It was being conducted on the old Guild principle, on lines which
were admirably laid down in a series of articles in the *New Age*,
written by Mr Orage (since published in book form under the title
*National Guilds : An Inquiry into the Wage Question and the Way
Out*), which he recommended for my persusal. I told him that as a
writer on municipal questions I had studied the history of guilds
very closely, and had accumulated a mass of material with the
intention of some day writing a book on the subject. He seemed
interested, and we discussed for some time the peculiar feature of
the ancient Guild system. . . .

'He then went on to talk of general affairs. The priest and the
politician, he stated, were the curses of Ireland. "Between the
Pope and King Billy the people come to the ground." He spoke in
scathing language of the Ancient Order of Hibernians. He called
them Catholic Orangemen, and said they were worse than the
Protestant Orangemen. The latter, he said, were misguided but
sincere, and something might be made of them with proper treatment. The "Catholic Orangemen", on the other hand, were "un-
scrupulous ruffians"—they stuck at nothing. . . .

'He said that there was great unrest everywhere. New ideas were
penetrating the brain of the labouring classes. Long ago a priest
told him that they would build a high wall around Ireland to keep
out the evil influences of the outside world. Where was that wall
today? People were thinking for themselves, and were moving,
slowly perhaps, but they were certainly moving, and no one could
stop the movement. But they were terribly handicapped by the
educational system. The priests controlled the schools and taught
people only just what they pleased, with the result that young men
were turned out into the world with very inferior equipment as
compared with the young men in England and Scotland. He knew
of youths of seventeen or eighteen who had been through the Irish
schools who could hardly write their own names. Education should
be under popular control. It was useless if it was not. . . .'

The hierarchy of the Church and the majority of the priests were
bitterly opposed to Larkin, yet there were some exceptions. Sir
William Orpen, the then famous Irish painter who was a friend of
Larkin's and often visited him at the union headquarters, once
described Larkin's experiences with two contrasting types of
clergymen:

'I used to go down to the dirt and filth of Liberty Hall and sit in [Larkin's] office in the afternoon just for the interest of watching the man. He was always sincere, always modest, always thinking of others, during those terrible strike times when he was out against "graft", drink, and starvation in the city. The poverty in Dublin during that time of riots and strikes was terrible, and the basements of Liberty Hall were used as soup kitchens. I remember a few little things that may show some reason for my admiration of this man. On a certain Saturday afternoon I was with him. A letter had come in saying that the Roman Catholic Archbishop was going to speak against him from the pulpit on Sunday morning. About 4.30 up came a man and said a priest from some village near Dundalk insisted on seeing him. "Show him up," said Jim. In came a very excited priest. "Well," said Jim, "what is it all about?" "About!" he shouted. "I hear they are going to speak against you from the pulpit tomorrow, and that your people are going to have a procession through the city. I want you to let me lead them. You are the Saviour of Dublin." Jim rang his bell. A man came in. He muttered something to him and the man departed. Jim lit a cigar slowly and said, "I thank you from my heart for your goodwill, and what you wish to do for me, but I cannot allow you to do it. Now, you will really trust me and do what I tell you?" "Surely," said the priest. "Then," said Jim, "you are to go back to your village at once and carry on your duties there, and forget that you ever came to Liberty Hall." Then turning to one of the clerks he said, "Show His Reverence downstairs. There is a cab waiting at the door. Take him to Amiens Street Station and see him off in the train to Dundalk." Then turning to the priest he said, "Good-bye, Father. This is the best thing you can do for me and for yourself. Pray for me." And out went the poor priest in tears, with his head bowed. One of the next visitors that afternoon was a high prelate of the Church. He thundered at him. Did he not realize that on the morrow, he was going to be spoken against from the pulpit; that "the Church" had ordered him not to hold his meeting on that Sunday afternoon in the Phoenix Park; that if he did he was defying the Church? So he railed on at him for a long time, his arms flying about, and occasionally thrusting his forefinger close to Jim's face. All this time Jim was sitting back in his chair puffing his cigar, with his clear eyes fixed on the prelate. Not a move did he make. When the prelate's outburst ceased from want of breath, Jim got slowly out of his chair and said very gently, "Pray God, Holy Father, that when you rise tomorrow morning you will be able to say your prayers to your God with the same peace of mind that I will say mine." And turning to one of his men he said, "Show the Holy Father the way out." And he departed amid great silence. And Jim continued his work and his cigar."

Sir William Orpen, R.A., *Stories of Old Ireland and Myself* (London, Williams and Norgate, 1924), pp. 82–4.

20 *The Workers' Republic*, p. 128. The word *seoinin* is a Gaelic slang expression meaning a flunkey of the British.

21 W. P. Ryan, *The Labour Revolt and Larkinism* (London, *Daily Herald* Office, 1913), p. 3.

22 'Going to Dublin'—Ibid., p. 4.

23 W. P. Ryan, *The Pope's Green Island* (London, James Nisbet, 1912), p. 273.

24 'The clerical opposition'—Ibid., pp. 274–9.

25 'Sound the Loud Trumpet', by An Gall Fada (The Tall Foreigner or Protestant; one of O'Casey's early pseudonyms), *The Peasant and Irish Ireland*, 25 May 1907.

26 'Prometheus Hibernica'—see *Drums Under the Window* (London, Macmillan, 1945), pp. 219–41.

27 *Irish Nation*, 30 January 1909.

28 *The Irish Bishops and An Irish University*, by An Irish Priest (Dublin, Sealy, Bryers and Walker, 1909). Although this six-page pamphlet was published anonymously, it was an open secret in the city that Dr O'Hickey was the author. His name had appeared on the first pamphlet, *An Irish University, or else*—— (Dublin, Waterford, Gill and Son, 1909), which contained eight letters and a lecture, most of which material he had previously read at public meetings.

For details on the O'Hickey Case see W. P. Ryan, *The Pope's Green Island*, Ch. XI 'People vs Bishops', and Ch. XII 'Maynooth as a Storm-Centre'; Dr Walter McDonald, *Reminiscences of a*

Maynooth Professor, edited by Denis Gwynn (London, Jonathan Cape, 1925), Ch. 17 'The O'Hickey Case (a) In Ireland', Ch. 18 'The O'Hickey Case (b) In Rome', Ch. 24 'The O'Hickey Case Again. The Last Concursus', Ch. 25 'Death of Dr O'Hickey'; *Drums Under the Window*, pp. 31–2, and 'Lost Leader', pp. 151–65. Aside from these sources, there is very little material available on Dr O'Hickey; no book has yet been written on his life and unpublished papers.

O'Casey dedicated *Drums Under the Window* 'To Dr Michael O'Hickey: A Gael of Gaels, one-time Professor of Irish in Maynooth College. In a fight for Irish, he collided with arrogant Irish bishops, and was summarily dismissed without a chance of defending himself; taking the case to Rome, he was defeated there by the subtlety of the bishops, helped by a sly Roman Rota, ending his last proud years in poverty and loneliness.

'Forgotten, unhonoured, unsung in Eire, here's a Gael left who continues to say Honour and Peace to your brave soul, Michael O'Hickey, till a braver Ireland comes to lay a garland on your lonely grave.'

29   *Reminiscences of a Maynooth Professor*, p. 357.

30   'It was imprudent'—Ibid., p. 357.

31   'To many, if not most'—Ibid., p. 167.

32   'I do not know whether'—Ibid., 232.

33   Stephen Gwynn, *Saints and Scholars* (London, Butterworth, 1929), p. 212.

34   'I satisfy myself'—Ibid., pp. 212–13.
     See *Inishfallen Fare Thee Well* (London, Macmillan, 1949), the chapter called 'Silence', pp. 248–86, in which O'Casey defends and pays tribute to Dr McDonald. He also dedicated this book 'To Walter McDonald, D.D. Professor of Theology in St Patrick's Roman Catholic College, Maynooth, for forty years; a great man gone, and almost forgotten; but not quite forgotten'.

35   'The Grand Oul' Dame Britannia'—Lady Gregory printed this song, which was written in 1917, in her *Kiltartan History Book* (London, Fisher Unwin, 1926), p. 142. But she did not identify O'Casey as the author.

36 'His soft sweet voice'—'An Ruathar Ud Agus A nDeachaigh Leis' (That Raid and What Went With It), by Michael O Maolain, in *Feasta*, Bealtaine, 1955. This article was translated for me by Mr Padraig O'Neill.

The late Mr O Maolain was the 'original' for Seumas Shields in *The Shadow of a Gunman*, and in this article he gave his version of what happened in their tenement in Mountjoy Square on the night the Black and Tans raided the house. O'Casey had used this incident in his play.

37 *The Sacrifice of Thomas Ashe* (Dublin, Fergus O'Connor, 1918), p. 14.

38 *The Story of the Irish Citizen Army* (Dublin and London, Maunsel, 1919), p. 67. Something must be said about Larkin and Connolly after 1914, and O'Casey's prediction that 'Labour will probably have to fight Sinn Fein'—the nationalists.

In the autumn of 1914, when the strike was over, Larkin went to America to raise funds to continue the fight of organized labour in Dublin, but due to the World War he was unable to return to Ireland. He tried unsuccessfully to get back, but as an 'agitator' he was a marked man and neither the British nor the American authorities wanted him to return to an uneasy Ireland that might have been on the verge of a revolt in the midst of a World War. He had left Connolly in charge of the Irish Transport and General Workers' Union, and the Citizen Army. During the period leading up to the 1916 Rising, Connolly probably had little choice but to merge his small Citizen Army forces with the larger Irish Volunteers, in spite of the antagonism that existed between the two groups, one representing labour, the other nationalism. When the Rising was crushed, Connolly and the nationalist leaders were executed by the British.

W. P. Ryan made the following comment on Connolly's death: 'Connolly, the Marxian Socialist, the convinced industrial unionist, the devoted labour leader, said to his daughter Nora on the eve of his execution: "The Socialists will never understand why I am here. They all forget that I am an Irishman".' (*The Irish Labour Movement*, p. 248.) It would be accurate to add that too many Irishmen failed to understand and soon forgot that he was a Socialist labour leader, for they made him the martyr of Irish nationalism, free from any taint of 'Satanic' Socialism.

Meanwhile, the volatile Larkin, unable to return to Ireland, had

become active in the Socialist Party and the Industrial Workers of
the World in America, making speeches all over the country. He
worked with radical leaders like Big Bill Haywood, John Reed, and
Benjamin Gitlow. In 1919 when America was swept by an hysterical
reaction against radicalism and anarchism, Larkin was arrested for
'criminal anarchy' and convicted in what appears to have been a
'star chamber' trial. He spent nearly three years of a five-to-ten-
year sentence in Sing Sing prison before he was pardoned by New
York's Governor Al Smith in 1923. See R. M. Fox's account of
'The Larkin Trial' in his book, *Jim Larkin: The Rise of the Under-
man* (London, Lawrence & Wishart, 1957), pp. 136–48.

Before his imprisonment, Larkin had written to Thomas Foran,
then General President of the Irish Transport and General
Workers' Union, protesting that Connolly's daughter Nora, and
Mrs Hanna Sheehy-Skeffington (whose husband, a pacifist and a
socialist who, though he took no part in the Rising, had been shot
by the British) were waving the flag of Irish nationalism in America.
While on lecture tours across America, the two women had spread
the gospel of Sinn Fein, entirely ignoring the role that labour had
played in the struggle for Irish freedom. Here are two excerpts
from these letters:

'I hope that O'Brien [William O'Brien, who was soon to become
General Treasurer and eventually General Secretary of the Union,
as well as Larkin's chief enemy] and the others are not to be led
astray by the propaganda of fellow-Irishmen of the Sinn Fein
movement. Mrs S. [Skeffington] is coming home. She travelled
here under the control of the *best people*—Moryah! Made some
money and a reputation as a safe and sane person. Was received
by the President. Oh, my! yes. I was received by the proletariat,
thank God for them . . . What are O'Brien and the rest doing in
allowing the Griffith gang to monopolize all the credit for the
effort? They call it the Sinn Fein R. here. I wish O'Brien and the
others would declare themselves. Are they all turned Sinn Fein?
Why cannot they state officially their position? Ask them to write
explaining what line of procedure they are adopting. The work of
the Irish Labour and Socialist movement is deliberately ignored by
the Sinn Fein envoy and his group.' (Undated, received in Dublin,
April, 1918.)

'I must again call attention to the fact that Mrs S—— is just an
apologist for the Sinn Fein crowd. She never speaks of the labour

movement nor of the Socialist Party. She leaves the impression that
Skeffy and herself were members of the Sinn Fein movement at
home. Nora C. [Connolly] follows the same lines . . . the gang here
are more fearful of our movement getting ahead in Eire than if
Johnny Bull played the same game as in '98 . . . They make out
Arthur G. [Griffith, the founder of Sinn Fein] as a God-given saint
and statesman; nobody in Ireland done anything but Sinn Fein.
Connolly and the other boys all recanted Socialism and Labour,
and were good Sinn Feiners. My God, it is sickening.' (Undated.)

Doubtless these two women, one who had lost a socialist father,
the other a socialist husband, were merely echoing the respectable
sentiments of the majority of patriotic Irishmen, in America and
Ireland. But Larkin felt this was all the more reason why his union
should act to put the case of labour and socialism more accurately
and more forcefully before the Irish people and the world. O'Casey
could not have known Larkin's views at this time, yet he had foreseen the problem in his book on the Citizen Army.

The above letters, along with many others, appear in the Appendices of *The Attempt to Smash the Irish Transport and General
Workers' Union* (Dublin, 1924). When Larkin returned to Ireland
in 1923, he provoked a legal battle for control of the union; he lost
in the courts and was forced to acquiesce to the formation of a new
union, The Workers' Union of Ireland. This book was issued by
the executives of his former union in an attempt to indict him in
the court of public opinion, in which effort they apparently failed.
Until his death in 1947, Larkin remained the most popular and
important labour leader in Ireland. Nevertheless, his old enemies,
Irish nationalism and clericalism, had become so firmly entrenched
that there was little chance of his country becoming the Workers'
Republic for which he had fought.

Interest in Larkin has been revived in recent years, mainly
through the efforts of one of Ireland's most significant and gifted
younger writers, James Plunkett. Mr Plunkett was a Branch Secretary of the Workers' Union of Ireland, and was closely associated
with Larkin for several years. He has written two plays about
Larkin and the 1913 period, one a radio play, *Big Jim*, produced by Radio Eireann in 1954; the other a three-act play, *The
Risen People*, produced by the Abbey Theatre in 1958.

39 *The Story of the Irish Citizen Army*, p. 2.

40 'Suddenly the window'—Ibid., pp. 2–3.

41 *Lady Gregory's Journals*, 1916–30, edited by Lennox Robinson (New York, Macmillan, 1947), p. 72.

42 'I believe there is something'—Ibid., p. 73.

43 'Casey was bad'—Ibid., p. 75.

44 Mr O'Casey made these remarks in a letter to me.

45 *Lady Gregory's Journals*, p. 75.

46 Lennox Robinson, *Ireland's Abbey Theatre*, A History, 1899–1951 (London, Sidgwick and Jackson, 1951), p. 121.

47 Some months after these pages were written, the following news item appeared in the Dublin *Sunday Review*, 15 March 1959:

'"CENSORS" BAN U.C.C. PLAYS. University College, Cork, was not represented at the Universities' Drama Festival held in Dublin during the week. Students there are upset because their choice of play was turned down by the college authorities.

The play was *Exiles* by James Joyce. Anouilh's *Antigone*, a second choice, was also banned.

Yesterday Dr H. St John Atkins, President of U.C.C., told SUNDAY REVIEW:

"The plays weren't suitable. Cork is a small provincial town—city—and we cannot afford to offend the susceptibilities of the people here. There were also internal domestic complications."

There was a small group of students, he said, who wanted to put on these plays, but the majority were not in favour of them.

"I didn't go into them at all," said Dr Atkins, "I took advice from a censoring committee who disapproved of the plays and acted on it."'

It might be added that Cork is the second largest city in the Republic of Ireland. At the time of the last Census Report in 1956, Dublin had a population of 539,476, Cork 80,011. These figures do not include suburban areas: 45,007 in the suburbs of Dublin; 34,417 in the suburbs of Cork. Thus what might be called 'greater Cork' has a population of 114,428.

48 Peter Kavanagh, *The Story of the Abbey Theatre* (New York, Devin-Adair, 1950), p. 13.

49 *Irish Times* and *Irish Independent*, 12 February 1926.

50 *Inishfallen Fare Thee Well* (London, Macmillan, 1949), p. 186.

51 Mrs Hanna Sheehy-Skeffington.—Her letter appeared in the *Irish Independent*, 15 February 1926.

52 It was actually James Montgomery, the Government Film Censor —fortunately he had no jurisdiction over the theatre—who made this remark to Holloway. Here is the entry for 10 February 1926 in the unpublished Holloway *Diary*, in the National Library, Dublin, in which he records the reactions of Montgomery [Monty], Kevin O'Higgins, the Minister for Justice, the writer Oliver St John Gogarty, and the actor F. J. McCormick [Peter Judge]:
'Monty didn't like "The Plough and the Stars" at all. O'Casey read Eugene O'Neill and Synge without digesting them properly. Synge once said to Monty, a man could write a great play out of his ignorance and perhaps out of supreme knowledge, but never when experimenting between. O'Casey is evidently in the between stage now. Out of his ignorance was born "Juno and the Paycock". His latest is just simply a crude disagreeable play. The last act of "Hamlet" or "The Duchess of Malfi" are [*sic*] not in it with the last act [of "The Plough"] for horrors—a dead consumptive in a coffin, a maniac with her dead baby, men shot dead outside, and a woman shot dead in the room, and a companion bringing news of the maniac's dead husband with revolting details of his mutilated state. The second act is sheer ugliness. There was a theatre full of highbrows afraid to speak out their mind on the matter till they get the opinion of the United Arts Club. Lord Chief Justice Kennedy frankly declared he thought it abominable. Kevin O'Higgins was silent until Monty thanked God he was off duty, and added "that is a likely lovely Irish export". Then O'Higgins owned up he didn't like it. Meeting Dr O. Gogarty, Monty said, "I hope you are not going to say you liked it?" "I do," owned up Gogarty (whose reputation for filthy limericks is very widespread), "it will give the smug-minded something to think about." "Dirt for dirt's sake", Monty calls such-like sordid, nasty pictures. The prostitute plying her trade in a low pub should never be allowed on the stage. He thinks more of Peter Judge [the actor F. J. McCormick] than ever on hearing he refused to let his wife appear as Rosie Redmond. Judge could make nothing out of his part [Jack Clitheroe]. Most of

the characters refused to "live". Their talk was involved and long-winded and rarely came from the lips of characters as real speech. Shaw and other dramatists repeat their dialogue aloud to see does it become speech or remain only book talk.'

Mr Holloway also noted that *Dublin Opinion*, the 'national humour magazine', filled many of its columns with the typical O'Casey jokes that were heard about the city. Here are some examples from the March 1926 issue:

'Even the Government couldn't find a plot in Sean O'Casey's new play.'

'2,000 doctors are looking for work in the Irish Free State. And yet the Abbey Directors decided not to put on the "Plough and the Stars" for that second week.'

'Sean O'Casey has been painted by P. J. Tuohy, R.H.A., and whitewashed by Senator W. B. Yeats.'

'Mr O'Casey, it is said, wrote the "Plough and the Stars" in three weeks.'

'What delayed him?'

'Needle machinery now in use can punch eyes at the rate of 7,000 an hour.

'Mr Barry Fitzgerald is stated to have felt like that on Thursday, 11th February.'

'Foul Play—"The Plough and the Stars".'

'If the "Plough and the Stars" is a first-class drama, there are third-class people in it travelling on the wrong ticket.'

'An enthusiastic correspondent writes that part of the name of Mr O'Casey's sensational play is exceptionally apt. The duty of a plough, our correspondent claims, is to turn up the dirt.'

'In her reply to Mr S. O'Casey, Mrs Sheehy-Skeffington says that (*pace* Mr Yeats) the police do not confer immortality. But they do, if they hit hard enough.'

'When O'Casey put his hand to the "Plough and the Stars" he began to look back.'

The 'Talk of the Town' columnist was not in a humorous mood when he remarked: 'We always write with restraint, and, therefore, we shall say that we found Mr O'Casey's "Plough and the Stars" the reverse of the Curate's egg—that is to say, rather decayed in spots. Mr O'Casey in his apologia claims the drama as "his place of expression". Would he express himself before a mixed audience in a drawing-room in some of the terms which he employed in the play under notice? Why, then, did he so express himself before our wives and mothers and sisters in the mixed audience of the Abbey Theatre?...'

'A fragrant little thing, "She Stoops to Conquer" has succeeded "The Plough and the Stars" at the Abbey Theatre. Mr Yeats of the apotheosis, are they both for immortality—Goldsmith and O'Casey?'

On the night of the riot at the Abbey, Lyle Donaghy, an Irish poet, encountered Mr Holloway, and Lady Gregory has given an account of their conversation:

'Donaghy had met Holloway in the hall, in a state of fury— "An abominable play".

D.: "I see nothing abominable in it."

H.: "Then you have a dirty mind."

D.: "No. I haven't."

H.: "Well, you have a filthy mind. There are no streetwalkers in Dublin."

D.: "I was accosted by one only last night."

H.: "There were none in Dublin till the Tommies brought them over."' (*Lady Gregory's Journals*, p. 99.)

53 Andrew E. Malone—*Dublin Magazine*, March 1926; see also his *The Irish Drama* (London, Constable, 1929), Ch. XII 'Melodrama and Farce'—Liam O'Flaherty—*Irish Statesman*, February 26 1926 —F. R. Higgins—*Irish Statesman*, 6 March 1926.

54 *Evening Herald*—12 February 1926—*Catholic Bulletin*—March 1926. See also Yeats's 'A Defence of the Abbey Theatre', *Dublin Magazine*, April–June 1926; and a defence of the O'Casey play by Dr Walter Starkie, *Irish Statesman*, 13 February 1926.

55 'Under Ben Bulben'—*Collected Poems* (London, Macmillan, 1952); p. 397. One might add that if Yeats had referred to Synge's study of conditions in the West of Ireland, 'In the Congested Districts', he would have found that the impoverished Irish peasantry were more full of misery than 'randy laughter'.

And perhaps Robert Burns also came closer to reality, for Irish as well as Scots peasants, when he wrote in 'Man was Made to Mourn':

> See yonder poor, o'erlaboured wight,
> So abject, mean and vile,

Who begs a brother of the earth
To give him leave to toil,
And see his lordly fellow worm,
The poor petition spurn,
Unmindful, tho' a weeping wife
And helpless offspring mourn.

56 'Gas From a Burner'—Flushing, September 1912. There is a photostat of this broadside in the National Library, Dublin. Also reprinted in *The Critical Writings of James Joyce*, edited by Ellsworth Mason and Richard Ellmann (London, Faber, 1959). Joyce was provoked to write this 98-line poem when the Dublin publisher Maunsel destroyed the first printing of *Dubliners*.

57 'Ireland After Yeats', in *The Bell*, Summer, 1953, Dublin. All of Sean O'Faolain's comments are from this article.

CHAPTER II: THE TRAGI-COMIC MUSE

58 'Some Account of the Life &c. of Mr William Shakespear'; Rowe's Introduction to his 1709 edition of Shakespeare's plays, in *Eighteenth Century Essays* edited by D. Nichol Smith (Glasgow, Maclehose, 1903), p. 10.

59 'Four Elizabethan Dramatists', in *Selected Essays* (London, Faber, 1932), p. 114.

60 'The Tragic Theatre', 1910, in *Cutting of an Agate* (London, Macmillan, 1919), pp. 28–9.

61 'Four Elizabethan Dramatists', in *Selected Essays*, pp. 111, 113.

62 See Ch. III, 'The Playwright's Not For Burning'.

63 *The Journals of André Gide*, translated by Justin O'Brien (London, Secker & Warburg, 1949), vol. III, p. 139. Eric Bentley has drawn attention to the similar reactions of Gide and O'Casey to 'westernized' Noh drama—*In Search of Theatre* (New York, Knopf, 1933), pp. 259–60.
    Here is Gide on Copeau's use of Noh drama:
    'He frightens me when he declares that he was never closer to achieving his aim than in the Japanese *No* drama he was putting on, which an accident prevented him from presenting to the public,

and of which I saw the last rehearsals. . . . . A play without any relation to our traditions, our customs, our beliefs; in which, artificially, he achieved without much difficulty an arbitrary "stylization", the exactitude of which was absolutely unverifiable, totally factitious, made up of slowness, pauses, something indefinably strained toward the supernatural in the tone of voice, gestures, and expressions of the actors.' *The Journals*, III, p. 139.

Here is O'Casey on Yeats's use of Noh drama:

'He remembered once when he went to the house of Yeats, in Merrion Square, to see *The Hawk's Well* played in the drawing-room . . . Yeats had read in a big book all about the Noh Plays, had spoken about them to others, and had seized on the idea that he could do in an hour what had taken a thousand years to create. And so with the folding and unfolding of a cloth, music from a zither and flute, and taps from a drum, Yeats's idea of a Noh Play blossomed for a brief moment, then the artificial petals faded and dropped lonely to the floor, because a Japanese spirit had failed to climb into the soul of a Kelt . . . No; charming and amiable as it all was, it wasn't a Noh Play. Poet and all as he was, Yeats wasn't able to grasp a convention, grown through a thousand years, and give it an Irish birth in an hour. Zither and flute and drum, with Dulac's masks, too full of detail for such an eyeless play, couldn't pour the imagination into the minds of those who listened and saw.' *Inishfallen Fare Thee Well*, pp. 289–90.

64 *The Poetry of W. B. Yeats* (London, Oxford University Press, 1941). See Ch. IX, 'Dramatist and Prose-Writer'.

See also Valentin Iremonger's 'Yeats as a Playwright', *Irish Writing*, Special Number: W. B. Yeats (Dublin, 1955). Mr Iremonger makes some important observations on the 'impurity' of drama: 'To begin with, was Yeats ever interested in the theatre as we understand it today in its development over the last four hundred years? The theatre, as we know it, is a place of public entertainment which creative writers use to express their reflections and interpretations of the behaviour of people under the stress of idea or emotion. By its nature, it vulgarizes: however pure or finely imagined an idea or an emotion in the mind of an author, he cannot allow that idea or emotion full play or give it all his attention since he is and must be conscious that he himself cannot transmit the idea or emotion unalloyed to each member of the audience.'

He then examines some of Yeats's theories of drama and remarks: 'All this impels one to ask whether Yeats ever had any interest whatsoever at any time in the theatre as we know it. I think the answer must be that he hadn't . . . He had therefore no dramatic gift that would ensure him success as a playwright in the contemporary theatre; but inside the limited terms of reference which he set himself in the theatre, his success as a dramatist is considerable.'

For a penetrating analysis of Yeats's limited 'success' as a dramatist see Eric Bentley's 'Yeats's Plays' in *In Search of Theatre*.

65 *Shakespeare and the Popular Dramatic Tradition*, With an Introduction by T. S. Eliot (London, Staples Press, 1944), p. 29. Mr Bethell presents an extremely valuable concept of drama as 'a mixture of conventionalism and naturalism'—the drama of 'Multi-Consciousness'.

66 'Wilkie Collins and Dickens', in *Selected Essays*, p. 431.

67 *Poetry and Drama* (London, Faber, 1951), pp. 34–5.

68 See Bernard Shaw's 'Tolstoy: Tragedian or Comedian?' 1921, in *Pen Portraits and Reviews* (London, Constable, 1932), Standard Edition, pp. 260–66. Note particularly these remarks of Shaw's:

'Was Tolstoy tragedian or comedian? The popular definition of tragedy is heavy drama in which everyone is killed in the last act, comedy being light drama in which everyone is married in the last act. The classical definition is, of tragedy, drama that purges the soul by pity and terror, and, of comedy, drama that chastens morals by ridicule. These classical definitions, illustrated by Eschylus-Sophocles-Euripides *versus* Aristophanes in the ancient Greek theatre, and Corneille-Racine *versus* Molière in the French theatre, are still much the best the critic can work with. But the British school has always scandalized classic scholarship and French taste by defying them: nothing will prevent the English playwright from mixing comedy, and even tomfoolery, with tragedy. Lear may pass for pure tragedy; for even the fool in Lear is tragic; but Shakespeare could not keep the porter out of Macbeth nor the clown out of Antony and Cleopatra. We are incorrigible in this respect, and may as well make a merit of it.'

He goes on to trace the development of tragi-comedy in Fielding, Dickens, and Tolstoy, and he concludes that 'Ibsen was the dramatic poet who firmly established tragi-comedy as a much deeper and grimmer entertainment than tragedy.'

69 Preface to *Thérèse Raquin*—See Barrett H. Clark's *European Theories of Drama* (New York, Crown, 1947), pp. 400–402.

70 *The Symposium*, translated by W. Hamilton (Penguin Classics, 1951), p. 113.

71 'Preface to Shakespeare', 1765, in *Johnson on Shakespeare*, edited by Walter Raleigh (Oxford University Press, 1908), p. 15.

72 'Shakespeare's plays are not in the rigorous'—Ibid., pp. 15–16.

73 *The Playwright as Thinker* (New York, Reynals & Hitchcock, 1946), p. 161.

74 'Detailed study of particular works'—Ibid., p. 190.

75 'A Letter to a Young Man', in *The Works of J. M. Synge*, vol. I, *Plays* (London, Allen & Unwin, 1932), Revised Collected Edition, p. vii.

76 'Four Elizabethan Dramatists', in *Selected Essays*, p. 109.

77 *Inishfallen Fare Thee Well*, p. 290.

78 'The Psychology of Farce'—Introduction to *Let's Get a Divorce!* and other plays (New York, Mermaid Dramabook, 1958).

79 *The Academy and Literature*, 11 June 1904.

80 Lennox Robinson, *Ireland's Abbey Theatre* (London, Sidgwick and Jackson, 1951), p. 36.

81 *Irish Independent*, 9 October 1903.

82 *United Irishman*, 17 October 1903. The performance at Molesworth Hall had been a triple-bill of Yeats's *The King's Threshold*, Synge's *In the Shadow of the Glen*, and Yeats's *Cathleen Ni Houlihan*. Griffith began his editorial by objecting to Yeats's choice of plays for a National Theatre. He didn't like *The King's Threshold* because his sympathies were all with the King and against the 'selfish' poet who insisted on sitting at the King's table as a recognition of the artist's position in society. Incidentally, Yeats was to act out the symbolism of this conflict in his own life. But the main burden of Griffith's attack was aimed at Synge's play.

'The Irish National Theatre Society was ill-advised when it decided to give its imprimatur to such a play as "In a Wicklow Glen" [*In the Shadow of the Glen*.] The play has an Irish name, but it is no more Irish than the Decameron. It is a staging of a corrupt version of that world-wide libel on womankind—the "Widow of Ephesus", which was made current in Ireland by the hedge-schoolmaster . . . Mr Synge's play purports to attack "our Irish institution, the loveless marriage" [J. B. Yeats, the poet's father, had used this phrase to describe the play in a previous issue of *The United Irishman*]—a reprehensible institution but not one peculiar to Ireland. We believe the loveless marriage is something of an institution in France and Germany and even in the superior country across the way, and, if we recollect our books, it was something of an institution in that nursery of the arts—ancient Greece . . . Man and woman in rural Ireland, according to Mr Synge, marry lacking love, and, as a consequence, the woman proves unfaithful. Mr Synge never found that in Irish life.'

In the following issue of *The United Irishman*, 24 October 1903, Yeats replied to Griffith and all the 'obscurantists' who had attacked Synge. His article was called 'An Irish National Theatre and Three Sorts of Ignorance'; and he identified them as the obscurantism of the 'Gaelic propagandist', the obscurantism of 'the more ignorant sort of priest', and the obscurantism of 'the politician'. (For a further discussion of this matter, see Chapter III, part 4. Popular and Vulgar Devils.) Yeats went on to defend and verify Synge's characterization of an unfaithful Irish wife—'a Cleopatra in the villages. Everyone knows who knows the country-places intimately, that Irish country-women do sometimes grow weary of their husbands and take a lover. I heard one very touching tale only this summer'. To which Griffith replied: 'Had Mr Yeats heard a score of such stories, it could not alter the fact which all of us know—that Irishwomen are the most virtuous women in the world. A play which leads those who witness it to form a contrary conclusion can only be a lie and nothing more.'

And in that same issue, none other than Maud Gonne MacBride added a further rebuke to Yeats, in an article on the controversy: 'Mr Yeats asks for freedom for the Theatre, freedom even from patriotic captivity. I would ask for freedom for it from one thing more deadly than all else—freedom from the insidious and destructive tyranny of foreign influence.' There was also an attack on

Yeats by someone who signed himself James Connolly; but this was not Connolly the labour leader and martyr of 1916, as many people have assumed. Connolly had left for America in September 1903, and the writer of the article was actually a Seumas Connolly, a friend of Griffith. Cathal O'Shannon cleared up this confusion in an article in the Irish *Evening Press*, 5 June 1959.

83 Lennox Robinson, *Ireland's Abbey Theatre*, pp. 28–9.

84 W. G. Fay and Catherine Carswell, *The Fays of the Abbey Theatre* (London, Rich and Cowan, 1935), p. 212. Willie Fay tended to look upon the drama as an exercise in crowd psychology, and he was deeply concerned about the 'psychological rules' which the playwright had to follow. During rehearsals he tried to anticipate how the audience would react to a play, and if he suspected that it might be offended by some of the characterizations or lines, he tried to convince the playwright to change the script accordingly. This is not an altogether unsound approach, but the trouble was that Fay's favourite 'rule' for appeasing audiences was to change any potentially 'offensive' characters into 'decent', 'lovable', 'good-natured', 'easy-going' people. Here is Fay explaining some of the troubles he had with Yeats and Synge on the matter of 'psychological rules', and illustrating how he would have rewritten and probably ruined Synge's *The Well of the Saints*.

'It is only after years of experience with all kinds of plays and all kinds of audiences that one acquires the working knowledge of crowd psychology that enables one to tell, while a play is in rehearsal, whether it is likely to offend or not. That is the most one can do. There is no way of foretelling success. The most experienced producers and actors can be deceived, and are so every day. But one can at least discern any factor that will militate against success and try to eliminate it before the public sees the play. Here I believe the author has to be consulted, and authors are notoriously obstinate. I never could get either Yeats or Synge to understand that if you write plays to be acted, not read by the fireside, there are certain rules that you cannot break without destroying the sympathy between the stage and auditorium. The rules I refer to are not technical but psychological. For example, as *The Well of the Saints* took shape, I realized that every character in the play from the Saint to Timmy the Smith was bad-tempered right through the play, hence, as I pointed out to Synge, all this bad temper would inevitably infect the audience and make them bad-tempered too. I suggested that the Saint anyway might be made into a good-natured easy-going man, or that Molly Byrne might be made a lovable young girl, but Synge would not budge. He said he wanted to write "like a monochrome painting, all in shades of one colour"' (pp. 167–8).

85 Peter Kavanagh, *The Story of the Abbey Theatre* (New York, Devin-Adair, 1950), pp. 56–7.

86 George Moore, *Hail and Farewell*, vol. III, *Vale* (London, Heinemann, 1914) pp. 191–2. Moore also makes some interesting comments on Synge, Ireland, and the Abbey:
'Irishmen have written well before Synge, but they had written well by casting off Ireland; but here was a man inspired by Ireland, a country that had not inspired any art since the tenth or twelfth century, a country to which it was fatal to return. Was Synge the exception, and was he going to find his fortune in Ireland? His literary fortune, for *The Well of the Saints* had very nearly emptied the Abbey Theatre. The audiences in the stalls had always been scanty—fifty or sixty spectators—but after the performance of *The Well of the Saints* we were but twenty, the patrons being the Yeats family, Sarah Purser, William Bailey, John Eglinton, AE, Longworth, myself, and dear Edward, who supported the Abbey, believing himself in duty bound to do so. He was averse from peasant plays, and *The Well of the Saints* annoyed him very much, but he held on and the *Playboy* was produced' (p. 191).
Perhaps the fact that *The Well of the Saints* 'nearly emptied the Abbey' supports Willie Fay's 'rules' of crowd psychology. But when one considers that the alternative was to let Fay rewrite the play as an inoffensive crowd-pleaser, it may have been better for the Abbey to be nearly empty but artistically honest. This at any rate was what Yeats settled for. When Willie Fay demanded more control over the theatre—full powers of Manager and Producer, Yeats and Lady Gregory refused to give in, and both Fay brothers resigned from the Abbey in January 1908.

87 W. B. Yeats, *The Autobiography* (New York, Macmillan, 1953), p. 311.

88 Bernard Shaw, *John Bull's Other Island* (London, Constable, 1931), pp. 84–5.

89 Andrew E. Malone in *The Dublin Magazine*, March 1925.

90 Andrew E. Malone, *The Irish Drama*, p. 263.

91 'The audience could be induced'—Ibid., p. 263.

92 W. B. Yeats, *Plays and Controversies*, p. 206.

93 *The Nation*, 21 December 1927.

94 Joseph Wood Krutch, *Modernism in Modern Drama* (Cornell University Press, 1953), p. 99.

95 Raymond Williams, *Drama From Ibsen to Eliot* (London, Chatto and Windus, 1952), p. 170.

96 Introduction to *Five Great Modern Irish Plays* (New York, Modern Library, 1950), pp. xi–xii.

97 Ronald Peacock, *The Poet in the Theatre* (New York, Harcourt, Brace, 1946), pp. 8–9.
    For a similar judgement of the modern world see Joseph Wood Krutch's *The Modern Temper* (New York, Harcourt, Brace, 1929).

98 Eric Bentley, *The Playwright As Thinker* (New York, Reynal and Hitchcock, 1946), p. 366.

99 David Magarshack, *Chekhov the Dramatist* (London, John Lehmann, 1952), pp. 13–14.

100 William Empson, *Some Versions of Pastoral* (London, Chatto and Windus, 1950). See pp. 27–9.

CHAPTER III: THE PLAYWRIGHT'S NOT FOR BURNING

101 Lady Gregory, *Our Irish Theatre* (London, Putnam, 1914), pp. 8–9.

102 W. B. Yeats, *Plays and Controversies* (London, Macmillan, 1923), p. 32.

103 W. B. Yeats, *Ideas of Good and Evil* (London, Bullen, 1903), p. 259.

104 W. B. Yeats, 'Certain Noble Plays of Japan', (1916) in *The Cutting of An Agate* (London, Macmillan, 1919), p. 2.

105 'I hope to have attained'—Ibid., pp. 1–2.

106 *Plays and Controversies*, p. 416.

107 *Six Plays of Strindberg*, translated by Elizabeth Sprigge (New York, Doubleday Anchor, 1955), p. 193.

108 *Our Irish Theatre*, p. 91.

109 *Irish Statesman*, 9 June 1928.

110 'He's groping after'—Ibid. See also Walter Starkie's essay, 'Sean O'Casey', in *The Irish Theatre*, edited by Lennox Robinson (London, Macmillan, 1939).

111 *Irish Statesman*, 9 June 1928.

112 'YEATS. Your play was sent'—Ibid. I do not believe that the O'Casey letter has been reproduced anywhere; the Yeats letter has been reprinted in the Alan Wade edition of *Yeats's Letters* (London, Hart-Davis, 1954). Here are the remaining passages from both letters which were not included in the 'dialogue'.
'My Dear Casey,—I read the first act with admiration; I thought it was the best first act you had written, and told a friend that you had surpassed yourself. The next night I read the second and third acts, and tonight I have read the fourth. I am sad and discouraged . . . This is a hateful letter to write, or rather, to dictate—I am dictating to my wife—and all the more so because I cannot advise you to amend the play. It is too abstract, after the first act; but the second act is an interesting technical experiment, but it is too long for the material; and after that there is nothing. I can imagine how you have toiled over this play. A good scenario writes itself; it puts words into the mouths of all the characters while we sleep, but a bad scenario exacts the most miserable toil . . . Put the dogmatism of this letter down to splenetic age and forgive it. W. B. Yeats, 82 Merrion Square, Dublin, April 20, 1928.'
'Dear Mr Yeats,—And we'll send into exile for the present the "dogmatism and splenetic age", and have a look at the brood of opinions these have left behind them . . . You say—and this is the motif throughout the intonation of your whole song—that "I am not interested in the Great War" . . . I am afraid your statement (as far as I am concerned) is not only an ignorant one, but it is a

silly statement too . . . You say "you never stood on its battlefields". . . . And does war consist only of battlefields? But I have
walked some of the hospital wards. I have talked and walked and
smoked and sung with the blue-suited wounded men fresh from
the front. I've been with the armless, the legless, the blind, the
gassed and the shell-shocked; one with a head bored by shrapnel
who had to tack east and tack west before he could reach the point
he wished to get to; with one whose head rocked like a frantic
moving pendulum. Did you know "Pantosser", and did you ever
speak to him? Or watch his funny, terrible, antics, or listen to the
gurgle of his foolish thoughts? No? Ah, it's a pity you never saw
or never spoke to "Pantosser". Or did you know Barney Fay,
who got field punishment No. 1 for stealin' poulthry (an Estaminay
cock, maybe) behind the trenches, in the rest camps, out in
France? And does war consist only of hospital wards and battlefields? . . . You say: "You illustrate these opinions by a series of
almost unrelated scenes as you might in a leading article." . . .
And do you know what you are thinking about when you talk of
leading articles, or do you know what you are talking about when
you think of leading articles? Surely to God, Mr Yeats, you don't
read leading articles! . . . I'm afraid I can't make my mind mix
with the sense of importance you give to "a dominating character". God forgive me, but it does sound as if you peeked and
pined for a hero in the play. . . . You say that "my power in the
past has been the creation of a unique character that dominated
all round him, and was a main impulse in some action that filled
the play from beginning to end". In "The Silver Tassie" you
have a unique work that dominates all the characters in the play
. . . in my opinion, "The Silver Tassie" because of, or in spite of,
the lack of a dominating character, is a greater work than "The
Plough and the Stars". . . . You say that after the first and second
acts of "The Silver Tassie" there is—nothing. Really nothing?
Nothing, nothing at all? Well, where there is nothing, where there
is nothing—there is God. Turning to your advice that I should
ask for the play back; that I should tell the Press that I want to
revise it, and so slip aside from the admonition of the Abbey
Directorate, I refer you to what I have written already to Mr
Robinson. I shall be glad for the return of the script of the play,
and a formal note of its rejection—Best personal wishes, S.
O'Casey, 19 Woronzo Road, St John's Wood (London, no date).'

113 Joseph Hone, *W. B. Yeats* 1865–1939 (London, Macmillan, 1942), p. 106.

114 'We were biased'—Ibid., p. 389. Mr Hone made the following comment on the rejection of the play: 'The Directors thought *The Silver Tassie* was a bad play, and one that would mar the fame and popularity of the author, but as the Abbey had latterly produced many poor plays, the public felt that, with a man of O'Casey's stature, it was entitled to form a judgement' (p. 388).

115 Introduction to *The Oxford Book of Modern Verse* (Oxford, 1936), p. xxxv.

116 *Rose and Crown* (London, Macmillan, 1952), p. 128.

117 *The Liberal Imagination* (New York, Doubleday Anchor, 1953), pp. 268–9, 270, 279.

118 'A Prayer For My Daughter'—*Collected Poems*, p. 213.

119 *World Drama* (London, Harrap, 1949), p. 795.

120 For some examples of the changes O'Casey made in these chanted passages, compare the first version of the play (London, Macmillan, 1928), pp. 64–5, with the 'Stage Version' in *Collected Plays*, vol. II, pp. 52–3.

121 *Plays and Controversies*, p. 206.

122 Herbert Gorman, *James Joyce* (London, John Lane, 1941), p. 73.

123 'The Irish Literary Theatre'—Ibid., p. 72.

124 *United Irishman*, 24 October 1903.

125 '1st. There is the hatred'—Ibid.

126 'The Curse'—*The Complete Works of John M. Synge* (New York, Random House, 1935), p. 297.

127 *W. B. Yeats* 1865–1939, p. 386.

128 'the happiness of finding idleness'—Ibid., p. 404.

129 *Lady Gregory's Journals*, pp. 123–4.

130 'But my mind goes back'—Ibid., p. 124.

131 *Rose and Crown*, p. 42–3. For the similar letter which Shaw wrote to Lady Gregory, see *Lady Gregory's Journals*, pp. 110–11.

132 *Lady Gregory's Journals*, p. 87.

133 'to prevent the outbreak'—Ibid., p. 91.

134 *The Story of the Abbey Theatre*, pp. 148–9.

In 1944 when some of the Abbey's leading actors resigned, the *Irish Times* ran a series of articles by a staff reporter on the 'Abbey Theatre Crisis'. Some comments from these articles are worth noting.

'Investigating the reasons for the departure of some of the Abbey Theatre's best players I spoke yesterday to directors, actors, playwrights and theatre-goers. There can be no doubt that financial considerations have had something to do with the migration to the commercial stage. I learnt that the highest paid Abbey actor receives £7. 3s. per week during the period of his actual appearance on the stage. His salary is half that sum during rehearsals. Some of the actors appear in less than half the year's productions, which means that for six months they are on half-time salary, though they must spend their afternoons at rehearsals. It must be pointed out that only the top-ranking players receive the £7. 3s. The figure averages £3 to £4 for the others. . . .

'£1,000 subsidy looms too largely over the directors' choice of plays. The fact that what was acknowledged to be one of the most provocative and popular recent plays, "Remembered For Ever" [by Bernard McGinn], was never revived, is cited as an example. Though receiving very wide public support, "Remembered For Ever" was withdrawn shortly after a Government Minister attacked it two years ago.' (29 July 1944.)

'"The principal complaint now," one disillusioned playwright said, "was against [the Abbey's] stagnancy and lack of adventure, whereas in the past the outcries from a certain section of the public were against its then buoyant spirit of adventure. It thrives on those outcries."' (31 July 1944.)

As far as the Abbey Directors were concerned, the *Irish Times* reporter stated, this 'crisis' went unnoticed. There would be no change in the theatre's policies, since the protests were merely 'criticism of a national institution through an unnational newspaper'. (2 August, 1944.)

The newspaper then asked three leading Irish playwrights to comment on the 'Abbey's Decline'.

Bernard Shaw simply remarked that 'mediocrity must be the staple of all daily enterprises'.

Sean O'Casey said that whether a playwright writes in Gaelic or English 'he must write nothing to displease the powers or the nominees who place the power there. There is the crux—for Eire. She will be, is now in fact, in the condition of control of thought so often attributed to the Socialism of the U.S.S.R.'

Paul Vincent Carroll stated: 'Dublin's censorious, provincial and pietistic attitude is chiefly responsible for the Abbey debacle. The introduction of foreign puritanism has proved inimical to native art. Ireland has shed immortality and clothed herself in the rags of a bogus, bombastic freedom. Here lies the ruins of the glorious Anglo-Irish European tradition.' (11 August 1944.)

Writing in *The Bell*, Summer 1953, Sean O'Faolain traced the trouble back to the early days of the Irish Government and the subsidy: 'It is to be remembered that the new Irish Government decided to subsidize the Abbey Theatre; which, at the time, seemed to us all a splendid gesture—disillusion was to come slowly with the gradual realization that when governments give money they receive influence in exchange . . . Unless we imagine that literature exists in a vacuum we must see what sort of official influences played on the Theatre at this period. I will give two examples. In 1932 when the Abbey Theatre visited the United States the usual hyper-patriotic societies protested against some of the plays, including O'Casey's, and at home deputies were prompted to ask awkward questions in the Dail. In reply to one questioner, the Prime Minister, De Valera, said (26 April 1933) that the government had made indirect representations to the Abbey Theatre, and that it was hoped that if the Company visited America again plays of the kind objected to by the American-Irish would not be produced. In 1934 a similar angry question received a similar reply, De Valera then saying that such plays damage the good name of Ireland. Yeats stood his ground, and was attacked bitterly by the popular press.'

More recently Seamus Kelly, resident columnist and theatre critic of the *Irish Times*, summed up the situation in the following manner: 'There is a strong school of thought in Dublin today which holds that it is quite hopeless to submit a play of ideas to the National Theatre, or alternatively, that if such a play is by any chance accepted, it is likely to be produced and cast in a manner that will horrify its author—usually played as the broadest comedy, irrespective of the dramatist's intentions.

'Challenged on these lines, the Abbey directorate will probably reply that they are governed by economics. They have a small government subsidy—about enough per year to clothe a ballerina for one new production at Covent Garden. To balance their budget, they claim, they must cater for "the new Abbey audience", and this audience likes comedy, either farmhouse kitchen or Dublin middle-class.

'The Abbey Directors are right, up to a point. Customers today *do* swarm in for meretricious comedies, and no doubt this helps balance the budget. They evade the issue that in Yeats's day budgets had to be balanced too, but that this essential never disbarred worth-while non-commercial plays from presentation.

'There have been multitudes of complaints, some of them from the auditorium of the Abbey itself, about the misdirection of the Theatre in recent years . . . Those who protest find that they are beating their heads against a stone wall of indifference. The dictator of the Abbey for more than ten years has been its Managing Director, Mr Ernest Blythe, who was for a time a Cabinet Minister in the first government of the Irish Free State. Mr Blythe has proved himself a convinced believer in the divine rights of Managing Directors. He has a predilection for the Irish language; and although this is shared by many of his countrymen, including the present writer, a number of them feel that too many Abbey plays are cast on the grounds of the players' proficiency in Gaelic, rather than in acting. He is also as impervious to criticism, constructive or destructive, as a granite pre-Celtic dolmen is to weather; in a radio documentary on the Third Programme some years ago, "I'm a politician," said Mr Blythe, the successor of W. B. Yeats. "I'm a politician, and I have a thick skin, so I don't give a damn what they say about me—not one damn!"' *Spectator*, Irish Number, 20 April 1956.

135 *Rose and Crown*, p. 46.

136 *Irish Independent*, 28 August 1935. A week later Mr J. Costeloe, Honorary Secretary of the National Council of the Federation of the Catholic Young Men's Society of Ireland, wrote a letter to the

354   NOTES

Irish Press, 3 September 1935, stating that his Council had passed a resolution against the Abbey Theatre's production of *The Silver Tassie*: 'The action of the Galway Branch had the wholehearted support of the National Council of the C.Y.M.S.'

137   *Irish Catholic*, 7 September 1935.

138   'If *The Silver Tassie* withstands'—Ibid.

139   *The Standard*, 30 August 1935. Two weeks earlier, in its 16 August issue, this paper had stated in a lead editorial entitled 'An Outrage On Our Faith':

'Through the faith we possess we should under God be the advance guard of the army of Christ—an example to an unbelieving world of the purity and strength, the nobility and glory to which Catholicism leads. But the devil envies our happy state, so he stirs up international strife and religious war, intensifies political passion—and fills the Abbey Theatre to overflowing. This is not lightly stated. The forces behind the scenes of the Abbey are directed against Christianity. The "tomorrow" they hope for in Ireland is its dechristianization . . . "The Silver Tassie" with its vulgarity, its scarcely veiled blasphemy, its mockery of what Catholics hold sacred is, with its successor [*Within the Gates*], an attack upon the Christian faith and an attempt to hold it up to the ridicule of mankind.'

In the adjoining column there was an editorial attacking the Dance Halls in Ireland, which suggested that O'Casey, Yeats, and the Abbey Theatre were not the only allies of the devil in the country: 'The dance hall has done more than any other single agency to demoralize the countryside. It has proved a source of evil of the first magnitude.'

140   *Irish Independent*, 21 August 1935.

141   *Irish Independent*, 29 August 1935.

In the 24 August 1935 issue of the *Catholic Herald*, an English weekly, the paper's Irish Correspondent called *The Silver Tassie* 'blasphemous' and full of 'evil language': 'And the reactions of the audience? Not a single protest: they laughed uproariously at the coarse farce, and were thrilled into hushed silence by the stark irreverences. Only a few—very few—hissed almost inaudibly at the final curtain. They were drowned in unstinted applause.' But a week later, in the paper's 30 August issue, Robert W. Speaight, the Catholic actor and writer, wrote a reply called 'In Defence of Sean O'Casey'. Mr Speaight, who said he was speaking for many English Catholics 'who have been disgusted by the acrimony of the press', made the following remarks:

'It has been impossible to open the majority of the papers without being deafened by the puritanical howls. The soul of the bourgeoisie has betrayed itself. And this, surely, is the essence of the bourgeois mind that it cannot look tragedy in the face. For O'Casey has seen into the heart of the horror of war and wrenched out its dreadful secret; that the co-heirs with Christ destroy one another in the sight of the Son of Man . . .

'Mr O'Casey is a very honest writer. He does not suppose that every man from Catholic Ireland, who came back maimed and torn from the trenches, filled the hospital wards with the peace of Christian resignation.

'He knows more about his own humanity. He knows that the words of these men would have been as bitter and as savage as their thoughts. He knows what it would mean, even to a Catholic footballer, to be struck down in the prime and flush of life. He knows, in short, what the saints have known: that man struggles against his fate and seldom wins peace until he finds that the combat is unequal.

'I do not wish to exaggerate. *The Silver Tassie* is a statement not a solution of suffering. It is the outcry of a passionate, embittered mind. But it is much nearer to Christianity, because it is nearer to life, than the complacent criticisms levelled against it. And it is worth recording the last words of the crippled footballer, in the fourth act, when he has seen his girl go to another and contemplates the wreck of his body—— "The Lord has given, but man has taken away".

'It is difficult to foretell the future of Sean O'Casey. I am not in agreement with those who would confine his genius to the tenement and the alley. I believe he is destined to play an important part in the restoration of language and symbolism to the stage. He has a command of pathos, passion, rhetoric and humour unrivalled in our generation. He is feeling his way towards the lyric, although his approach is a trifle tentative. His verse cannot, at present, soar.

'And he goes astray when he writes outside his experience. His genius is emotional, and he is not capable of consistent thought.

But he is a seeker after truth, even if he lacks the means to find it. And above all he prefers to risk commercial failure and critical censure rather than repeat his successes.

'His faults are blatant—his occasional sentimentality, his facile pity, his carelessness of form; but all great writers boldly display their errors. O'Casey's are redeemed by his shining sincerity and his refusal to rest upon his laurels.'

142　'Parnell's Funeral'—*Collected Poems*, p. 319.

CHAPTER IV: THE PLAYWRIGHT AS PROPHET

143　Edmund Wilson, 'The Historical Interpretation of Literature', in *The Triple Thinkers* (London John Lehmann, 1952), pp. 254–5.

144　'The Second Coming'—*Collected Poems* p. 210.

145　'Rouze up, O Young Men'—*Blake's Poems and Prophecies* (London, Everyman's Library, 1927), pp. 109–10.

O'Casey is not a mystic, but he certainly shares the great compassion and prophetic aims that Blake expressed in poems like 'Milton', 'Jerusalem', 'Europe', and 'America'. Few modern writers have dedicated themselves as completely as O'Casey has to the fight against the tyranny Blake described in 'Europe' (ll. 132–7):

'*Every house a den, every man bound, the shadows are fill'd*
With spectres, and the windows wove over with curses of iron;
Over the doors " Thou shalt not", & over the chimneys " Fear" is
*   written;*
With bands of iron round their necks, fasten'd into the walls
The citizens; in leaden gyves the inhabitants of suburbs
Walk heavy; soft and bent are the bones of villagers'

and the freedom that he had envisioned in 'America' (ll. 42–51):

'*Let the slave grinding at the mill run out into the field,*
Let him look up into the heavens & laugh in the bright air:
Let the inchained soul, shut up in darkness and in sighing,
Whose face has never seen a smile in thirty weary years,
Rise and look out; his chains are loose, his dungeon doors are open,
And let his wife and children return from the oppressor's scourge.
They look behind at every step & believe it is a dream,

Singing: "The Sun has left his blackness, & has found a fresher morning,
And the fair Moon rejoices in the clear & cloudless night;
For Empire is no more, and now the Lion & Wolf shall cease."'

146 *The Intelligent Woman's Guide to Socialism and Capitalism* (London, Constable, 1928), p. 469.

147 Niall in 1936—Niall O'Casey died suddenly of leukemia in 1956.

148 James Agate, *First Nights* (London, Nicholson and Watson 1934), p. 60.

149 'There is a nest of wasps'—Ibid., p. 181.

150 'But first we must'—Ibid., p. 182.

151 '"Within the Gates" is obviously'—Ibid. p., 272.

152 London *Times*, 8 February 1934.

153 Title page of *The Flying Wasp* (London. Macmillan, 1937).

154 'Pictures that are not'—Ibid., pp. 42-3.

155 'Mr Agate fails to see'—Ibid., pp. 22-3.

156 'I do not know what'—Ibid., pp. 45-6.

157 'We do not want merely'—Ibid., p. 123.

158 'Nietzsche has said that'—Ibid., pp. 4-5.

159 'A good acting play'—Ibid., p. 94.

160 'The truth seems to be'—Ibid., pp. 193-4.

161 'The principal persons'—Ibid., p. 152.

162 The word 'codology' is a Dublin slang expression meaning pretentious nonsense, from the word 'cod', to hoax or fool.

163 *Rose and Crown*, p. 153.

164 'Art is the Tree'—*Blake's Poems and Prophecies*, pp. 289-90.

165 *Within the Gates* (London, Macmillan, 1933,) p. 45.

166 'These quiet, Christian maenads'—Ibid., p. 11.

167 *Unto This Last* (London, George Allen, 1900), p. 14. This book was first published in 1860.

168 *Sunday Times*, 17 March 1940. Here are some passages from Mr Agate's enthusiastic review:

'Mr O'Casey's play is a masterpiece. "Aljaybra," says a character, "has nothing to do with hanging festoons at a right angle!" The passion, pathos, humour, and, above all, poetry with which this great play is hung, are there for all the world to see and hear, and I shall leave it to the Y.C.L. [Young Communist League] to decide whether the festoons are at the correct left angle or not. The angle, as another Irish playwright would have said, is immaterial. Further to be advanced on this play's behalf are its drive, its variety—the four acts constitute a globe of four continents—its perfect setting in the Ireland of "today or tomorrow". I find the piece to be a *magnum opus* of compassion *and* a revolutionary work. I see in it a flame of propaganda tempered to the condition of dramatic art, as an Elizabethan understood that art. To one such a proud prelate was a prelate whose pride was whole and absolute, and free of those erosions and nibblings insisted on by an age which realizes that nothing is whole and absolute. That is why the Red Priest in this play is more than a whole-hogger for things as they are; he is a medieval whole-hogger. It is a pity and must confuse many that this Priest should be called Red when his politics are what is known as anti-Red; the fact remains that he is as much of an out-and-outer as the Red Queen in "Alice".

'Opposite, as the films have it, to the Red Priest is the people's leader, Red Jim, who is as much a model of Communist virtue as, let us say, Shakespeare's Henry V was a model of manly excellence. And, of course, Priest and Leader go to it hammer-and-tongs, like those English and French armies. Remember how single-mindedly Shakespeare drew the two camps the night before the battle, one busy at prayer, the other given over to idle chatter. Did Shakespeare worry whether there were serious-minded exceptions in the French lot, or wanton fellows in the English? No! Mr O'Casey's play is Elizabethan. One side says "Ding", and the other "Dong". And that is all there is to it, excepting, possibly, the Brown Priest who, as the spirit of compromise, tries to bring ding and dong together by saying, "Dell!" Let me insist again upon this play's Elizabethan quality. No Shavian nonsense here, whereby the protagonists, in this case meaning antagonists, put their knees under the mahogany and obligingly put each other's cases!'

169 Mrs Deeda Tutting—This Deeda Tutting scene was apparently based upon a personal experience of O'Casey's. See the Creda Stern episode in the chapter, 'The Dree Dames', in *Sunset and Evening Star* (London, Macmillan, 1954), pp. 103–23. It is an instance of O'Casey in one of his intractable and vindictive moods.

170 'The Gaelic Sword of light'—This phrase which Roory mentions a number of times is the symbol of the Gaelic language revival movement. In Irish mythology, lightning was regarded as a flashing sword, wielded by the Celtic heroes. 'In folk tales the lightning-sword has survived as "the sword of light" (an cloid-heamh solais) possessed by a giant and won from him by a hero.' T. F. O'Rahilly, *Early Irish History and Mythology* (Dublin Institute For Advanced Studies, 1946), p. 68. O'Casey also used the symbolism of the 'Sword o' Light' in *Purple Dust, Collected Plays*, vol. III, p. 69.

171 'AYAMONN. There's th' great dome'—*Collected Plays*, vol. III, pp. 200–201. For the parallel 'epiphany' that Johnny Casside experienced on the banks of the Liffey, see *Pictures in the Hallway* (London, Macmillan, 1942), pp. 310–19.

CHAPTER V: THE COMEDIES: A CATHARSIS AND A CARNIVAL

172 Prologue to *Every Man Out of His Humour*.

173 'On the Essence of Laughter' (1855), in *The Mirror of Art* (London, Phaidon Press, 1955), p. 141.

174 *Laughter* (1900), in *Comedy*, Introduction and Appendix by Wylie Sypher (New York, Doubleday Anchor, 1956), p. 187. See also Mr Sypher's excellent essay, 'The Meanings of Comedy', in the Appendix.

175 *Collected Poems*, p. 112.

176 See the chapter, 'A Terrible Beauty Is Borneo', in *Inishfallen Fare Thee Well*, pp. 155–72.

177 'he couldn't see De Valera'—Ibid., p. 3.

178 'the Coney Island of misery'—Ibid., p. 297.

179 *New York Times*, 9 November 1958.

180 *The Standard*, 18 February 1955.

181 *The Standard*, 25 February 1955.

182 *Irish Times*, 2 March 1955.

183 *The Observer*, 6 March 1955.

184 Dublin *Evening Press*, 1 March 1955.

185 *The Standard*, 4 March 1955. See O'Casey's account of the play's reception in 'Bonfire Under a Black Sun', in *The Green Crow*, pp. 130–59.

186 *Christian Science Monitor*, 12 March 1955.

The reviewer of the Dublin *Evening Herald*, 1 March 1955, after denouncing the play, stated: 'In fairness to himself as a creative writer, Sean O'Casey should return to Ireland without delay. At present he is completely out of touch with modern Irish life and thought.' Only four months earlier, in the November 1954 issue of *The Bell*, there appeared an article in the form of a letter on Emigration by a John Kavanagh. Mr Kavanagh's account of life in an Irish village might have provided the scenario for a play like *The Bishop's Bonfire*, or *Cock-a-doodle Dandy*, and since it shows the extent to which O'Casey was in touch with Irish life and thought, it is of sufficient importance to be quoted in full:

'Emigration: A Letter

Dear Sir,

Thank you for answering my letter on the cause of emigration. I will try to give it to you to the best of my ability (not much) from my own experience (some).

During 1929 to '32 there were at least twice as many boys and girls between the ages of 19 to 25 years in this village as there are today. There was less employment and less money but we had plenty of enjoyment that cost us very little. Though there was no Pioneer Association branch in the parish 98 per cent. of the young people were T.A.

We had a choice of four or five kitchen dances every Sunday-night within a two-mile radius of home. One in every four was able to play some instrument, one in ten was able to sing—at least we thought we were. The rest were able to dance, some of them good step dancers. We had great fun and ourselves making it.

If anybody had a big barn we cleared it out and organised a "Hay Dance" a few times each year. It cost 2/6 for Ladies, 3/- for Gentlemen. The profit was small, but all there was usually went to the owner of the barn, to compensate him for having a wild gang tearing round his house. Shouting, laughing, eating bread and jam and doing their best to break down his barn floor. The crowd was gathered by sending invitation cards to popular boys and girls and the organiser's chief concern was not to make money but give an enjoyable night's entertainment. The good name of the village depended on the way their dances were run, and everybody helped. If a Civic Guard attended he paid at the door and was made respectfully welcome. If he came in uniform it was regarded as a challenge. He was not charged at the door, all the noise died down and the boys and girls left the vicinity where he stood or sat. If he got a girl to dance with him they had the floor to themselves and Fred Astaire couldn't dance to the music they got. He usually came in plain clothes the next time.

It was no crime for a girl to sit on a boy's knee. In fact the girl who had to sit on the bare seat was considered a wallflower. It was no crime for a boy to take a girl out to a car or even to a cock of hay during the night. It was the normal thing to do. If girls were scarce he would be asked not to keep her out for long. If he was a musician she would be asked not to keep him out for long and if he happened to be a stranger he'd be directed to the cock of hay. On the other hand if any girl went out with more than one boy she was under suspicion and there was very effective means for stopping that kind of courting. Every boy treated his girl as he expected his pal to treat his own sister.

There were no old people at the dance. If married couples attended, they soon found that nobody wanted them; left early and didn't come to the next one. The older people of the house went to bed early not to sleep but to be out of the way. If we went outside the parish to a Hay Dance we went in fours or more. We shouted and sang all the way. It was the normal thing to do. If we went quietly everybody would think we were up to some devilment.

In summer time when boy met girl it was at the cross-roads. He cycled four to ten miles on a Sunday evening to meet her and though there might be 20 to 60 other young people at the cross she left the crowd and went with him to the nearest wood. She often got her stockings torn and laddered with briars and her face bitten and stung by midges but she thought 'twas worth it. Of course there were plenty of "Had to get marrieds", but all the couples I've known have had very happy lives and have brought up their children in most cases better than the "made matches".

We thought a lot more of the fellow that got caught and married the girl than we did of the fellow who had all arranged before he married. In the odd case where the fellow let the girl down and refused to marry her, no matter how popular he was beforehand he soon found that he wasn't wanted in any company and he was the odd one that emigrated.

In 1931 we got a new P.P. He condemned dancing in every form, even the kitchen dances were sinful and against the wishes of our Church. Boys and girls should not be on the road after dark. The C.C. was sent out to patrol the roads and anybody found or seen on the roads had to give their names. The people who allowed boys and girls into their home to dance were committing a grave mortal sin. The people who had a dance after a "Station" were putting God out of their homes and bringing in the devil. Where there was dancing there could be no grace. Dancing was the devil's work. And so was company keeping. Woe to that father or that mother who allowed their daughter to go out at night. Woe to that boy and that girl who met and went to that lonely wood or that lonely place. They were damning their souls. Perhaps the change seemed more sudden in our parish as our old parish priest, may he rest in peace, had never interfered with the amusement of young people, but I know that we had a far greater respect for him than young people today have for any representative of our Church. He was a man apart and above everything else, who said very little and wanted very little, taught us our Catechism, explained what was good and bad and then left the rest to our own conscience.

The change came in every parish and before very long the odd fellow that could get a girl to meet him had to go deeper into the wood. Anybody who didn't agree that dancing and company keeping had to be sinful were dubbed Communists and were hinted at as getting money from Russia.

One day I went to confession. The priest asked me if I kept

company with a girl? Yes, Father. Do you kiss her? Yes. How often? Fifty times, two nights a week. How long has this been going on? About two years. Did you ever tell it in confession before? No, Father. Why? I didn't think it was a sin. Will you promise me now not to meet that girl alone again? I won't, Father. Why? Because I'd break my promise tomorrow night. Get out of this box: you're damned. I got up and went out but he called me back. Do you intend to marry this girl? I don't know. Why don't you know? I'm not in a position to get married. Then when will you be in a position to get married? I don't know. Will you promise me to stay on the public road with this girl in future? Yes, Father.

I kept my promise but she had other ideas and soon found somebody who was willing to go so far into the wood with her that they could come out the other side and left me chewing the bushes on the roadside.

The crowd left the cross-roads, pitch and toss schools started outside the pubs and before very long, being a man meant to be able to take a few pints and use dirty language. The girls were allowed to attend morning Mass, evening (daylight) devotions, then the family rosary and so to bed. If they were seen on the road even in daylight with a boy there were hints in a sermon on the following Sunday. In less than a year at least nine local girls had joined religious orders, 15 others left for England.

The boys went to visit in the local. There was plenty of work but no play. Some of the girls found jobs for the boys they knew, and in some cases paid their way to England. It started very slowly as most of them hated England. The few that went at the start wrote home to their pals telling them of the money they could earn, the dances, pictures and parties they could attend and the freedom they could enjoy so it soon became the custom.

A few years later dancing became legalised and commercialised. Huge dance halls were built giving every convenience to the dancers. The law of the Church had taken a complete turn-about in a few years.

In the meantime I was married and took little interest in dancing. Perhaps I was a bit prejudiced. I didn't like the new dances as I could see that the harm was done and though I often had to drive parties to so-called dances, I either went to the pictures or read a book for the two or three hours the dance lasted.

One night in 1947 I drove a party to and attended a dance in Caighwell in St Michael's Hall. Just imagine calling a dance hall after a saint. On the right just inside the door was a Civic Guard in uniform. On the left was the C.C. Along the wall on the left side was a row of girls sitting up straight with their hands crossed on their knees. There wasn't even a genuine smile on any of them. On the right was a row of men some sitting and the ones who weren't were well back off the beautiful maple well-polished floor. On the walls both sides were large official-looking notices: Don't Throw Cigarette Ends or Lighted Matches on the Floor. Don't Leave Hats, Caps, etc., on Seats. Don't Stand on the Seats. Respectable Girls Don't Sit on Gentlemen's Knees, etc.

At the end opposite the entrance-door was a stage. The band was up there. A pianist, a piano-accordionist, a violinist and a set of drums. On the left of the stage having a good view of everything that went on was the P.P.

"The next dance will be a modern waltz." There was no mad rush for partners. The boys moved across the floor and it didn't seem to matter what girl happened to be opposite; they began to walk around the floor. It was like looking at a dance in the silent picture days. There wasn't a sound except the band and when it stopped everybody dutifully clapped. When the modern waltz was over the girls went to their side of the hall and the boys to theirs. There was an interval of 10 to 15 minutes. There were a few boys standing on the edge of the floor and to break the monotony they started to push each other. The floor was so slippery that with a small push they could send each other sliding 10 to 12 feet. They were enjoying this and started to laugh but the P.P. came along and told them to stay quiet or he'd put them outside the door.

After watching a few quick steps, tangos, etc., I noticed that the steps were practically the same as we used for fox trots, one steps and slow waltzes, so I took a chance and picked what I thought was a fairly lively partner. As far as dancing went we got on all right, but I couldn't even get her to smile. I might as well be dancing with the broom. Most of the dancers went round the hall one way and that meant that she was facing the P.P. going one way and facing the C.C. going the other, so I tried going across in the middle. It actually worked. When she found that she couldn't be seen from the stage or the door she began to laugh and chat just as if she was at a real dance. I heard afterwards that if a girl appeared to enjoy herself at any of these dances she could be accused of having taken drink. On the way home some of my passengers asked me if I had enjoyed the dance. I don't remember all I said, but I told them we had more fun and freedom at the Corpus Christi Procession in Esker.

Another change is very noticeable. The boys and girls don't seem to trust each other. If I had two loads for one dance, the girls went together and so did the boys. They don't want to mix. Girls seem to think it's a sin to be a girl or to act like a girl, and boys seem to think it's sissyish to want to be with girls. It's more manly to get drunk and if possible get the girls drunk also. All responsibility is taken out of young people's hands. They are bossed and controlled till they have no sense of responsibility. It's amusing to hear "Come to the Ceili". The words of this song may apply to Ireland in 1594, but I could give you some words that would fit it for 1954.

If they sang on the way, they would find themselves up next court day and have their names published in the paper, but if they were caught in a pub after hours their names wouldn't be published. If they throw snowballs they are summoned to court and bound to the peace.

If they want the "latest" songs and music on the radio they are told they're ignorant or anti-Irish. If they read the daily paper it's mostly taken up with Church dignitaries and their goings and comings. There is very little in it of interest to young people except Little Panda or Rip Kirby. They are told all about the men that got us our "Dearly Bought Freedom", but deep down behind our backs they are beginning to think that the slavery was better.

You may think that I'm anti-Catholic or anti-religious, but after four years as an invalid I've had plenty of time to think and pray. Where young people are concerned it's overdone in this country. You can't put an old head on young shoulders, and as a wise priest told me: "Religion is no use to a man if you have to shove it down his neck."

My excuse for writing to you is simply my genuine interest in our young people. Yours faithfully, John Kavanagh.'

According to the 1956 Government Census Report, an average of 40,000 people emigrated from Ireland each year during the five-year period of 1951–5. For a detailed study of this alarming emigration rate and some of its chief causes, see *The Vanishing Irish*, edited by John A. O'Brien (London, W. H. Allen, 1954).

187 *The Green Crow*, p. 226.

188 See the version of this episode in *Sunset and Evening Star*, (London, Macmillan, 1954), pp. 280–86.

189 *Irish Times*, 10 January 1958. The article also stated: 'It was learned during the past three days that some members of the Dublin Tostal Council had applied to the archbishop for permission to have a Solemn Votive Mass celebrated to mark the opening of the 1958 Tostal. (Votive Masses are celebrated on such occasions as the opening of the Oireachtas [the Parliament] and Law Terms.) Within the past ten days, it is understood, a member of the council was given leave to understand that no such Mass would be celebrated for the Tostal. It was learned last night that no Mass—either a Votive Mass, or, as in previous years, an ordinary Low Mass—will inaugurate the Tostal on May 11th.'

190 'Unions to Protest'—It should be pointed out that the Dublin Council of Irish Unions was at this time dominated by the bitterly anti-Larkinite Irish Transport and General Workers' Union, Jim Larkin's old union.

The officials of this union had no more love for O'Casey than they had for Larkin. When the union celebrated its Golden Jubilee in 1959 with a special commemoration issue of its magazine *Liberty*, it made only a few indirect references to Larkin, although it featured the 1913 strike and lock-out, and no mention at all of O'Casey. One article was devoted to the founding of the Irish Citizen Army, but at no point did its author, Frank Robbins, refer to the original Secretary of the organization.

191 *Irish Times*, 25 May 1957.

192 *Irish Times*, 5 July 1957.

193 *Sunday Times*, 19 May 1957.

194 *Irish Times*, 10 July 1958.

195 *The Bell*, Summer 1953.

CHAPTER VI: THE PLAYWRIGHT AS POET

196 *Complete Works of J. M. Synge*, pp. 3–4.

197 Lady Gregory, *Our Irish Theatre*, p. 82.

198 *Poetry and Drama*, p. 43.

199 'I laid down for myself'—Ibid., p. 32.

200 'As I have said'—Ibid., pp. 26–7.

201 Edmund Wilson 'Is Verse a Dying Technique', in *The Triple Thinkers*, pp. 29–30. In this essay Mr Wilson makes some significant comments on the experience of 'poetry' in works of prose. He mentions the symptoms which A. E. Housman felt when he remembered a line of poetry while shaving: '. . . my skin bristles so that the razor ceases to act. This particular symptom is accompanied by a shiver down the spine; there is another which consists in a constriction of the throat and a precipitation of water to the eyes; and there is a third which I can only describe by borrowing a phrase from one of Keat's last letters, where he says, speaking of Fanny Brawne, "everything that reminds me of her goes through me like a spear". The seat of this sensation is the pit of the stomach.'

   Then Mr Wilson remarks: 'One recognizes these symptoms; but there are other things, too, which produce these peculiar sensations: scenes from prose plays, for example (the final curtain of *The Playboy of the Western World* could make one's hair stand on end when it was first done by the Abbey Theatre), passages from prose novels (Stephen Daedalus' broodings over his mother's death in the opening episode of *Ulysses* and the end of Mrs Bloom's soliloquy), even scenes from certain historians, such as Mirabeau's arrival in Aix at the end of Michelet's *Louis XVI*, even passages in a philosophical dialogue: the conclusion of Plato's *Symposium*. Though Housman does praise a few long English poems, he has the effect, like those other critics, of creating the impression that "poetry" means primarily lyric verse, and this only at its most poignant or most musical moments. . . .

   'Is it not time to discard the word "poetry" or to define it in such a way as to take account of the fact that the most intense, the most profound, the most beautifully composed and the most comprehensive of the great works of literary art (which for these reasons are also the most thrilling and give us most prickly sensations while shaving) have been written sometimes in verse technique, sometimes in prose technique, depending partly on the taste of the author, partly on the current fashion. It is only when we argue these matters that we become involved in absurdities. When we are reading, we appraise correctly . . .

'If, in writing about "poetry", one limits oneself to poets who compose in verse, one excludes too much of modern literature, and with it too much of life' (pp. 26–8, 31).

202   *The Human Image in Dramatic Literature* (New York, Doubleday Anchor, 1957), p. 91.

203   'that the art of drama'—Ibid., p. 104.

204   *Poetry and Drama*, p. 19.

205   *The Cutting of an Agate*, p. 115.

206   *Complete Works of J. M. Synge*, p. 271.

207   *English As We Speak It In Ireland* (Dublin, M. H. Gill, 1910), pp. 6–7.

208   'The bloody throopers'—Ibid., p. 120.

209   I heard several of these expressions myself, and I am grateful to Mr Alf MacLochlainn of the National Library, Dublin, and Mr James Plunkett, for having recorded the others for me.

210   *Glimpses of Gaelic Ireland* (Dublin, C. J. Fallon, 1948), pp. 7–8.

211   I must thank Mr Alf MacLochlainn for helping me with these Gaelic expressions, and with the examples of Dublin slang.

212   'Black Turf'—*The Dublin Comic Songster* (Dublin, James Duffy, 1845), pp. 15–17.

213   'MRS O'KELLY. Is that yourself'—*The Shaughraun*, Dicks' Standard Plays (London, John Dicks, n.d.), 'First Performed at Wallack's Theatre, New York, 1875'.

214   *Hall of Healing*—Lady Gregory mentions the incident around which this play was later written. See *Lady Gregory's Journals*, p. 320.

CHAPTER VII: ON A ROCK IN DEVON

215 *My Brother's Keeper* (London, Faber, 1958), p. 187.

216 'O, Vague Something'—Herbert Gorman, *James Joyce*, p. 144.

217 *Rose and Crown*, p. 133.

218 *I Knock at the Door*, pp. 4–5.

219 'Johnny stiffened with pride'—Ibid, pp. 54–8.

220 'Johnny watched the little'—Ibid., p. 81.

221 'There was the very rainbow'—Ibid., p. 106.

222 'A man 'ud want St Pathrick's'—Ibid., pp. 245–6.

223 *Pictures In the Hallway*, pp. 4–8.

224 'Johnny thrust his chest out'—Ibid., pp. 32–7.

225 *Drums Under the Window*, p. 165.

226 'Gifts of the Almighty'—Ibid., p. 221.

227 'sulfurious infamity'—Ibid., p. 143.

228 'hitchin' your flagon'—Ibid., p. 238.

229 'Oh! I've thried'—Ibid., pp. 239–41.

230 *Inishfallen Fare Thee Well*, p. 287.

231 'Frequently he wandered'—Ibid., pp. 169–70.

232 'The Red Star is a bright'—Ibid., pp. 171–2.

233 Letter VII (1871), *Fors Clavigera* (London, George Allen, 1896), vol. I, pp. 135–6.

234 *Rose and Crown*, p. 143.

235 Preface to *Androcles and the Lion* (London, Constable, 1916), p. xxxviii.

236 *Rose and Crown*, p. 151.

237 *Sunset and Evening Star*, p. 248

238 'All Ireland's temporal'—Ibid., pp. 272–3.

239 'The earth was his home'—Ibid., p. 250.

240 *The Green Crow*, p. 226.

241 'Some Latin writer once'—Ibid., p. xiv.

242 *My Brother's Keeper*, p. 121.

243 *John Bull's Other Island*, pp. 176–7.

244 'In a word, the Roman'—Ibid., 35.

245 *The Irish* (Harmondsworth, Pelican Books, 1947), p. 126.

246 *Irish Times*, 16 March 1959.

247 'Who makes these decisions?'—Ibid.

248 *Christian Behaviour* (London, Geoffrey Bles, 1943), pp. 29–30.
    In an interesting article, 'Priests and People in Ireland', in the March 1958 issue of *The Furrow*, a clerical magazine published at Maynooth College, Kevin Smyth, s.j., Professor of Fundamental Theology at Milltown Park, Dublin, made the following observations:
    'Do we over-emphasize the sixth commandment? Maybe, but both Voltaire and Newman saw in chastity a hall-mark of the Catholic Church. Maybe we frighten some girls so much off company-keeping that they miss the chance of courtship and marriage. I hope that is rare. The marriage rate of non-Catholics is still later and lower! Maybe we deprive the people of the joys of life as Sean O'Casey says. But the fact is that the country where sex is most uninhibited, where children in the primary schools are instructed in contraception—Sweden—has the highest suicide rate in the world. And from the point of view of the reverence of the people for the priest, we have done a good job, because the celibacy of the clergy, though not of the essence, is of the well-being of the Church. And priestly purity would not last if the people were not chaste: we depend more perhaps than we realize on the goodness of our people, and we are right in keeping them so good. But the whole criticism is weird: I should not have mentioned it if it were not so popular; and it is found even in Catholic writings (ORIENTIERUNG, Zurich, 30/9/56: "only one sin is recognized in Ireland: against the sixth".).'

249 David H. Greene and Edward M. Stephens, *J. M. Synge* (New York, Macmillan, 1959), p. 264.

In a review of this book, the Irish poet W. R. Rodgers remarked: 'A writer's first duty to his country is disloyalty, and
Synge did his duty by Ireland in presenting her as he found her
and not as she wished to be found. Ireland could do with such
artists today.' (*Sunday Times*, 7 June 1959.)

250   *Critical Writings of James Joyce*, p. 173.

CHAPTER VIII: A FINAL KNOCK AT O'CASEY'S DOOR

251   Eric Bentley, *The Life of the Drama* (New York, Atheneum, 1967),
pp. 346–7.

252   Samuel Beckett, 'The Essential and the Incidental', *Bookman*,
December 1934. This is a review of O'Casey's *Windfalls* (London,
Macmillan, 1934), a collection of stories, poems, and one-act plays.
For a further discussion of some comic connections between
O'Casey, Beckett, and the tradition of Irish comedy, see David
Krause's 'The Principle of Comic Disintegration', *James Joyce
Quarterly*, Fall 1970.

253   Beckett, 'The Essential and the Incidental'.

254   Wylie Sypher, 'The Meanings of Comedy', in *Comedy: An Essay
on Comedy* by George Meredith, *Laughter* by Henri Bergson (New
York, Doubleday Anchor, 1956), p. 223.

255   Sypher, 'The Meanings of Comedy', p. 222. And for another related
approach to the catharsis of low comedy, see Eric Bentley's chapter
on Farce in *The Life of the Drama*, pp. 219–56.

256   James Agate, *Sunday Times*, 16 November 1925; reprinted in *Sean
O'Casey*, ed. Ronald Ayling (London, Macmillan, 1969), p. 76.

257   William Empson, *Some Versions of Pastoral* (London, Chatto and
Windus, 1950), p. 27. Empson also traces the source of the double
plot to medieval drama and the *Second Shepherds' Play*, where the
serious theme of the Nativity is parodied by low comic characters,
Mak and his wife Gill, whose stolen sheep is identified with the
Paschal Lamb. For a modern approach to such profanations of

sacred myth, which is related to the irreverent masquerades in the plays of O'Casey and Beckett, see also Jerzy Grotowski's *Towards a Poor Theatre* (New York, Clarion Books, 1968), pp. 21–3: 'The theatre, with its full-fleshed perceptivity, has always seemed to me a place of provocation. It is capable of challenging itself and its audience by violating accepted stereotypes of vision, feeling, and judgment. . . . This defiance of taboo, this transgression, provides the shock that rips off the mask, enabling us to give ourselves nakedly to something which is impossible to define but which contains Eros and Caritas. . . . The theatre, when it was still part of religion, was already theatre: it liberated the spiritual energy of the congregation or tribe by incorporating myth and profaning or rather transcending it. . . . It was not by chance that the Middle Ages produced the idea of "sacral parody".' Unfortunately, Grotowski lacks a comic spirit, a sense of ironic humour; but if one could apply the broad techniques of knockabout comedy to his theatre of transgression and profanation, a more complete concept of 'sacral parody' in modern drama would emerge. For an attempt to explore this concept, see David Krause's 'The Barbarous Sympathies of Antic Irish Comedy', *Malahat Review*, April 1972.

258 Hugh Kenner, *Samuel Beckett, A Critical Study* (New York, Grove Press, 1961), pp. 134–5. And Jan Kott, in *Shakespeare Our Contemporary* (New York, Doubleday Anchor, 1966), p. 275, makes a similar observation about grotesque characters: 'In Shakespeare's world prose is spoken only by grotesque and episodic characters; by those who are not a part of the drama proper.' The point is that in the plays of O'Casey and Beckett the grotesque and episodic characters themselves become the drama proper, while their poetic betters are discredited or off in the wings.

259 *Some Versions of Pastoral*, p. 30.

260 J. L. Styan, *The Dark Comedy: The Development of Modern Comic Tragedy* (Cambridge, Cambridge University Press, 1968), p. 284.

261 R. D. Laing, *The Politics of Experience* (New York, Ballantine Books, 1967), pp. 114–15.

262 *The Life of the Drama*, p. 350.

263   Ibid., p. 350.

264   Sean O'Casey, *The Green Crow* (New York, George Braziller, 2956), p. 227.

265   Francis Macdonald Cornford, *The Origin of Attic Comedy* (originally published in 1914; new edition edited with a Foreword and Additional Notes by Theodor H. Gaster; New York, Doubleday Anchor, 1961), pp. 119–20. See also David Krause's 'The Barbarous Sympathies of Antic Irish Comedy', for a related discussion that deals with the mask of 'Comic Ketman', a game of deceptions played by Polish and Irish comic characters who assume the disguise of a jester in order to expose the impostors.

266   Enid Welsford, *The Fool* (originally published in 1935; new edition, New York, Doubleday Anchor, 1961), p. 321. For some significant correctives, see the works of Jan Kott and Leszek Kolakowski, in which the clown is presented as an ironic fool or jester who profanes what is sacred in his society. For example, Jan Kott, '*King Lear* or *Endgame*', *Shakespeare Our Contemporary* (New York, Doubleday Anchor, 1966): 'The profession of a jester, like that of an intellectual, consists in providing entertainment. His philosophy demands of him that he tell the truth and abolish myths'. Leszek Kolakowski, 'The Priest and the Jester', *The Modern Polish Mind*, ed. Maria Kuncewicz (Boston, Little, Brown, 1962): 'The philosophy of clowns is the philosophy that in every epoch shows up as doubtful what has been regarded as most certain; it reveals contradictions inherent in what seems to have been proven by visual experience; it holds up to ridicule what seems obvious common sense, and discerns truth in the absurd'.

267   Vivian Mercier, *The Irish Comic Tradition* (London, Oxford University Press, 1962), p. 240. The main limitation of this pioneering study of Irish comedy lies in its omission of any adequate treatment of Irish drama, which Mercier admits in his Preface: 'Also, in the absence of a chapter on stage comedy, I have said less than I should have liked to about Synge and O'Casey'. See also Mercier's 'The Riddle of Sean O'Casey: Decline of a Playwright', *Commonweal*, 13 July 1956, where he attributes O'Casey's decline to the pseudo-Freudian explanation that the playwright was supposedly carrying

a terrible burden of guilt because of his failure to take part in the 1916 Easter Rising. By a wild leap of critical psychoanalysis, then, O'Casey is equated with the ineffectual Davoren in *The Shadow of a Gunman*: ergo, the playwright must be a hidden coward because his mock-hero is a hidden coward! Furthermore, this specious argument entirely overlooks the fact that O'Casey had become disenchanted with the patriotic Republican movement at least five years before 1916, and he had taken an active part in the prior struggle of the socialist labor movement during the 1913 General Strike and Lock-out in Dublin. He made his lifelong commitment to labour, not nationalism.

268   Gordon Rogoff, 'Sean O'Casey's Legacy', *Commonweal*, 23 October 1964.

269   For a discussion of the sources of the flyting, see Robert C. Elliott, *The Power of Satire* (Princeton, Princeton University Press, 1960), pp. 73–5, 135–40. For some connections between the flyting and the Negro game of 'the Dozens', see John Dollard, 'The Dozens: Dialectic of Insult', *The American Imago*, I (Boston, 1939).

270   Sigmund Freud, *Jokes and Their Relation to the Unconscious*, originally published in 1905; translated and edited by John Strachey (New York, Norton Library, 1963), p. 101. And for a full-scale discussion of the ways that the restraining obstacles of society create the need for comic discontent, see Freud's *Civilization and Its Discontents*, originally published in 1930; translated and edited by John Strachey (New York, Norton Library, 1962).

271   T. R. Henn, *The Harvest of Tragedy* (London, Methuen, 1956), p. 214.

272   Robert Bechtold Heilman, *The Iceman, The Arsonist, and The Troubled Agent: Tragedy and Melodrama on the Modern Stage* (Seattle, University of Washington Press, 1973), pp. 258–9.

273   William Irwin Thompson, *The Imagination of an Insurrection: Dublin, Easter 1916* (New York, Oxford University Press, 1967), pp. 219–20.

274   Ibid., p. 224.

275 Robert Brustein, *The Theatre of Revolt* (Boston, Little, Brown, 1964), p. 271. Brustein is disinclined to see the drama, let alone the comedy, in any of O'Casey's plays; but there must be some hidden comedy in a book that deals with the theatre of revolt and excludes a dramatic rebel of O'Casey's credentials. Brustein doesn't criticise O'Casey, if criticism means some form of study and analysis; he apparently has a constitutional dislike for O'Casey's works and ignores them.

276 Raymond Williams, *Drama From Ibsen to Eliot* (London, Chatto and Windus, 1952), p. 170.

277 Raymond Williams, *Drama From Ibsen to Brecht* (London, Chatto and Windus, 1968), scc pp. 147–53.

278 Tim Pat Coogan, 'The Exile', *The World of Sean O'Casey*, ed. Sean McCann (London, Four Square, 1966), p. 114.

279 See *Sean O'Casey*, ed. Ronald Ayling (London, Macmillan, 1969), pp. 143–61. For a full-scale assessment of the O'Casey criticism, see David Krause's chapter on O'Casey in *Anglo-Irish Literature: A Review of Research*, ed. Richard J. Finneran, to be published in the Modern Language Association Series in 1975.

280 Patrick Lynch, 'Ireland Since the Treaty', *The Course of Irish History*, eds. T.W. Moody and F.X. Martin (Cork, Mercier Press, 1967), p. 339.

281 Ronald Ayling, Introduction, *Sean O'Casey*, ed. Ronald Ayling, p. 40. See also Ayling's fine Preface to O'Casey's *Blasts and Benedictions*, selected and introduced by Ronald Ayling (London, Macmillan, 1967).

282 Robert Hogan, 'In Sean O'Casey's Golden Days', *Dublin Magazine*, Autumn–Winter 1966; revised and reprinted in *Sean O'Casey*, ed. Ronald Ayling.

283 Herbert Howarth, 'Writers as Forerunners—The Sacred Book', *The Irish Writers: Literature and Nationalism, 1880–1940* (New York, Hill and Wang, 1958), pp. 16–20.

INDEX

◄◄•►►◄◄•►►◄◄•►►◄◄•►►◄◄•►►◄◄•►►◄◄•►►◄◄•►►◄◄•►►◄◄•►►◄◄•►►

(Works by O'Casey are preceded by an asterisk)